THE
MISSION
STATEMENT
BOOK

"Mission statement work is the single most important work because the decisions made there affect all other decisions. In addition to giving over 301 real company examples, this book contains many excellent suggestions on the characteristics and processes of producing outstanding mission statements."

—DR. STEPHEN R. COVEY, author of
The 7 Habits of Highly Effective People

THE
MISSION
STATEMENT
BOOK

301
Corporate Mission
Statements from
America's Top Companies

Jeffrey Abrahams

Ten Speed Press

The inclusion of these mission statements is not intended to convey business information to be relied upon in generating business statements or in making business decisions. Ten Speed Press does not explicitly or implicitly offer any representation or warranty that these mission statements will be of use in forming a business conclusion. People read these at their own risk.

Distributed in Australia by Simon & Schuster Australia; in Canada by Publisher's Group West; in South Africa by Real Books; in Southeast Asia by Berkeley Books; and in the United Kingom and Europe by Airlift Books.

A Kirsty Melville Book

Cover design by Ross Carron
Text design by Margery Cantor

Library of Congress Cataloging-in Publication Data

Abrahams, Jeffrey.
    The mission statement book : 301 corporate mission statements from America's top companies / Jeffrey Abrahams.
        p.   cm.
    ISBN 0-89815-680-7
    1. Mission statements—Authorship.   2. Mission statements—United States.
I. Title
HD 30.285.A27   1995
658.4'012—dc20

94-45138
C I P

Printed in Canada

4   5   —   02   01   00   99   98

To my mother

Betty Jane Abrahams

and my father

Harris Sanders Abrahams,

great communicators

And in memory of Sophie Spungen

CONTENTS

Acknowledgments 19

Introduction 21

PART I

The Mission of this Book 27

How to Use this Resource 28

In the Beginning...There Was the Mission Statement 32

So What Exactly *Is* a Mission Statement? 37

Inside a Mission Statement 45

How to Write a Mission Statement (Or Mission *Not* Impossible) 56

PART II

The Companies and Their Statements 69

Ace Hardware Corporation

Adia Personnel Services

Advest, Inc

Airborne Express

Alliant Techsystems Inc.

Allied Signal Inc.

American Protective Services, Inc.

American United Life Insurance Company

Ameritas Life Insurance Corp.

Ameritech

AMETEK, Inc.

AMP Incorporated

AMR Corporation (American Airlines)

Anheuser-Busch Companies, Inc.

❖ Aztech Controls Corporation

Anthony Industries, Inc.

Applied Materials, Inc.

Aristech Chemical Corporation

Armstrong World Industries, Inc.

AT&T Corp.

Atlanta Gas Light Company

Autodesk, Inc.

Avon Products, Inc.

Baldor Electric Company

Ball Corporation

Banta Corporation

Bard (C.R. Bard, Inc.)

Barnett Banks, Inc.

Bausch & Lomb, Incorporated

❖ Byers & Happel Iowa Realty

Baxter Healthcare Corporation

Bay View Capital Corporation

Becton Dickinson and Company

Ben & Jerry's Homemade, Inc.

Best Products Co., Inc.

Betz Laboratories, Inc.

Blockbuster Entertainment Group

Boise Cascade Corporation

Borg-Warner Security Corporation

Bruno's, Inc.

Burlington Northern Inc.

Burnett (Leo Burnett Company, Inc.)

Butler Manufacturing Company

Cabot Corporation

Carpenter Technology Corporation

❖ Business Psychology Associates

Caterpillar Inc.

CBI Industries, Inc.

Cenex, Inc.

Centerbank

Centura Banks, Inc.

Chase Manhattan Corporation

Chemfab Corporation

Chemical Banking Corporation

Chevron Corporation

Chicago and North Western Transportation Co.

Chrysler Corporation

Ciba-Geigy Corporation

Citicorp

❖ Cerner®

Clark Equipment Company

Clorox (The Clorox Company)

CMS Energy

CNA Insurance Companies

Coachmen Industries, Inc.

Columbia/HCA Healthcare Corp.

Comerica Incorporated

Commercial Federal Corporation

Comptek Research, Inc.

Computer Sciences Corporation

Computervision Corporation

Conner Peripherals, Inc.

Consolidated Freightways, Inc.

Continental Airlines

Continental Medical Systems, Inc.

Cooper Tire & Rubber Company

Copperweld Corporation

❖ CETAC Technologies Inc.

Corning Incorporated

Corporate Child Care Management Services

❖ Comprehensive Technologies International Incorporated

Cray Research, Inc.

CSX Corporation

CUNA Mutual Insurance Group

Dana Corporation

Delta Air Lines, Inc.

Deluxe Corporation

Deposit Guaranty Corp.

Diamond Shamrock, Inc.

Digi International Inc.

Donnelly Corporation

❖ Computer Media Technology

Dow Chemical Company, The

Dreyer's Grand Ice Cream, Inc.

Duke Power Company

Duriron (The Duriron Company, Inc.)

Eastern Enterprises

Eaton Corporation

Ecolab Inc.

Edwards (A.G. Edwards & Sons, Inc.)

Energen Corporation

Entergy Corporation

Ethyl Corporation

Federal Express Corporation

❖ Eriez Magnetics

Federal-Mogul Corporation

Federated Department Stores, Inc.

Ferro Corporation

First American Corporation

First Bank System

First Financial Corporation

First Financial Management Corporation

First Interstate Bancorp

First of America Bank Corporation

First Tennessee National Corporation

First Virginia Banks, Inc.

Firstar Corporation

Flagstar Companies, Inc.

Fleming Companies, Inc.

Forest Oil Corporation

FPL Group, Inc.

❖ Flying Colors Painting, Inc.

Fuller (H.B. Fuller Company)

Gannett Company, Inc.

Gates Rubber Company

GenCorp

General American Life Insurance Company

General Electric Company

General Mills, Inc.

General Motors Acceptance Corporation (GMAC)

General Motors Corporation

General Public Utilities Corporation

❖ Globe Metallurgical Inc.

Georgia Gulf

Geraghty & Miller, Inc.

Gibson Greetings, Inc.

Gillette (The Gillette Company)

Goodyear Tire & Rubber Company

Grace (W.R. Grace & Co.)

Haemonetics Corporation

Hanna (M.A. Hanna Company)

Harsco Corporation

Hershey Foods Corporation

Hewlett-Packard Company

❖ L. Norman Howe & Associates

Hibernia Corporation

Hoechst Celanese Corporation

HON Industries Inc.

Hormel Foods Corporation

Household International, Inc.

Houston Industries Incorporated

Huntington Bancshares Incorporated

IBM (International Business Machines Corporation)

ICN Pharmaceuticals, Inc.

Illinois Power Company

Inland Container Corporation

Inland Steel Industries

❖ Insight Direct, Inc.

International Dairy Queen, Inc.

International Game Technology

Johnson Controls, Inc.

Johnson Wax (S.C. Johnson & Sons, Inc.)

Jostens, Inc.

Kansas City Life Insurance Company

Kansas City Power & Light Company

Kaufman and Broad Home Corporation

Kaydon Corporation

Kellogg's (Kellogg Company)

❖ Ketchum Communications

Kellwood Company

Kemper Corporation

Kent Electronics

Keyport Life Insurance Company

Knight-Ridder, Inc.

Kroger (The Kroger Co.)

Lafarge Corporation

Landstar Systems, Inc.

Levi Strauss & Co.

Lincoln National Corporation

Loew's Companies, Inc.

LSI Logic Corporation

Lyondell Petrochemical Company

  ❧ Lens Express Inc.

Maritz Inc.

Marriott International, Inc.

Martin Marietta Corporation

Mary Kay Cosmetics, Inc.

Maxus Energy Corporation

MBIA Inc.

MBNA Corporation

MCI Communications Corporation

Medtronic, Inc.

Merck & Co., Inc

Meridian Bancorp, Inc.

Meyer (Fred Meyer, Inc.)

  ❧ Mastersoft, Inc.

Microsoft Corporation

Mid-American Dairymen, Inc.

Miller (Herman Miller Inc.)

Minnesota Mining and Manufacturing Company (3M)

  ❧ Mechanics Bank, The

Mobil Corporation

Montana Power Company

Nalco Chemical Company

National City Corporation

National Semiconductor

New England Mutual Life Insurance Company (The New England)

Niagara Mohawk Power Corp.

Nike, Inc.

Norfolk Southern Corporation

Northeastern Utilities

Northern States Power Company

Northwestern Mutual Life

Oklahoma Natural Gas Company

Old Kent Financial Corporation

Olin Corporation

Oneida Ltd.

Oryx Energy Corporation

Owens & Minor

PacifiCorp

Penney (J.C. Penney Company, Inc.)

Pennsylvania Power & Light Company

    ❖ Melaleuca, Inc.

PepsiCo

Perini Corporation

Pet Incorporated

Pillsbury (The Pillsbury Company)

Pioneer Hi-Bred International, Inc.

Ply Gem Industries, Inc.

Premark International, Inc.

Principal Financial Group

Promus Companies Incorporated, The

Protective Life Corporation

PSICOR, Inc.

Public Service Enterprise Group Incorporated

Rainbow Technologies

Raytheon Aircraft Company

Research Industries Corporation

Reynolds Metals Company

Rhône-Poulenc Rorer Inc.

    ❖ Monterey Homes

Rich Products Corporation

Roadway Services, Inc.

Rockwell International Corporation

Rollins Inc.

   ❖ National Register, Inc.

Rubbermaid Incorporated

Ryder System, Inc.

Rykoff-Sexton

Safety-Kleen Corporation

San Francisco Federal Savings (SFFed Corp.)

Sanwa Bank

SAS Institute Inc.

Savannah Foods & Industries, Inc.

Schwab (The Charles Schwab Corporation)

Scripps (The E.W. Scripps Company)

Sensormatic

Shaklee U.S., Inc.

Shell Chemical Company

SkyWest Airlines, Inc.

Sonoco Products Company

   ❖ Nypro Inc.

Southern California Edison Company

Southern Company

Southern Pacific Rail Corporation

SouthTrust Corporation

Southwest Airlines Co.

Spacelabs Medical, Inc.

SPX Corporation

St. Paul Bancorp, Inc.

Sta-Rite Industries

Standard Register Company, The

State Auto Insurance Companies

Stride Rite Corporation, The

❖ Shepard Poorman

Stroh Brewery Company, The

Sun Company, Inc.

Sundstrand Corporation

Sysco Corporation

TCF Financial Corporation

Texas Industries, Inc.

Times Mirror Company

Tootsie Roll Industries, Inc.

Total System Services, Inc.

Tribune Company

TRINOVA Corporation

TRW Inc.

❖ Skynet Worldwide Courier

Tultex Corporation

Turner (The Turner Corporation)

Union Carbide

Union Electric

Unisys Corporation

United Dominion Industries

United Parcel Service

United States Fidelity and Guaranty Corporation

United States Shoe Corporation, The

Universal Foods Corporation

Unocal Corporation

❖ Softub, Inc.

UNUM Corporation

UTILX Corporation

Valassis Communications, Inc.

Varlen Corporation

VF Corporation

Vons (The Vons Companies, Inc.)

Vulcan Materials Company

Wackenhut Corporation, The

Warner-Lambert Company

Washington Gas

Washington Mutual Savings Bank

Weirton Steel Corporation

Wellman, Inc.

Wendy's International, Inc.

❖ Travelpro®

Westin Hotels & Resorts

Weyerhauser

Whirlpool Corporation

WICOR, Inc

Winnebago Industries, Inc

Wisconsin Dairies Cooperative

Wisconsin Energy Corporation

Wisconsin Public Service Corporation

WMX Technologies, Inc

❖ United Vision Group

York International Corporation

A Taxing Mission: The Mission of the Internal Revenue Service
A Final Word

PART III

Index 1   Companies Arranged by Industry Category   612

Index 2   Companies Arranged by Number of Employees   621

Index 3   Companies Arranged by State   629

Index 4   Companies with Statements One Sentence in Length   638

ACKNOWLEDGMENTS

THIS BOOK COULD not have been written without the help of at least four hundred people.

Behind each of the more than 300 companies represented in these pages, there is at least one patient soul who responded to my letters, phone calls, and faxes over a period of three years. At some companies, I spoke or corresponded with as many as four and five different representatives in order to receive a copy of the latest mission statement and corporate data and to secure a legal release form. Listing all of these people would trivialize their importance to this project. But as you read through this book, you should know that while my name is on the cover, hundreds of other people have passed the information along to your hands.

I also had enormous help from friends and associates close to home—and computer.

First, my thanks to Phil Wood and Kirsty Melville at Ten Speed Press for embracing this project and welcoming me to their world. I'm enormously grateful to my editor Lorena Jones, who ushered me through the process of turning an unwieldy manuscript into a book. And thanks to my agent Michael Katz for making the connection with Ten Speed Press.

For helping me with the mountain of details required to gather and assemble all the information presented here, I am grateful to Chris Ackerman, Karen Zukor, Robin Wirthlin, Cecile Lozano, Cheryl and Jillian and Eric Olsen, Kim Pipkin, Kate Peterson, and Marc Greenberg.

Without the computer skills, generosity, and steady hand on the mouse provided by Richard Ackley, I simply could not have tackled the enormous task of assembling and massaging the database that gave birth to this manuscript.

For providing crucial support throughout the years of research and writing, I'm grateful to Bill McCoy, Elizabeth Peek, Mary

Cooper, Peter Anastos and Claudia Falconer, Susan Page, Tana and Michael Powell, Denise Powell, and Susan Fassberg. Thanks also to my colleagues at Ketchum Advertising, especially Christopher Jones, Leonard Pardoe, and Patrick Feely.

Research for this book was made possible with the help of the staff of the Alameda County Business Library, the Rockridge Branch of the Oakland Public Library, and the library at the Mechanics' Institute of San Francisco.

Finally, my thanks to all those people at companies all over the country, for doing the hard work of writing the following missions, visions, goals, objectives, creeds, philosophies, and other statements. I hope this book will make the task a lot easier the next time around.

INTRODUCTION

"YOU KNOW, I get five or six people in here every week asking me for a book on that, and there's nothing written on the subject."

That's the response I got from the head librarian of the Alameda County Business Library in Oakland, California, in the summer of 1991 when I asked if he had any books on the topic of corporate mission statements. I was astonished by his reply and inspired—there and then—to write the very first book on the topic. I figured if the librarian was getting so many requests for information, there *must* be an audience.

Why was I doing this research in the first place? In May of 1991, I changed jobs. I left Ogilvy & Mather Advertising in San Francisco, where I was a senior copywriter, to accept a position with a competitor down the street, Ketchum Advertising.

On my first day of work, I noticed a copy of the company's mission statement posted in the lobby. I was intrigued by Ketchum's corporate mission statement because it seemed so dramatically different from Ogilvy & Mather's, even though both companies are in the same business: both are large communications companies with advertising and public relations divisions at offices across the country and around the world.

I started asking friends to send me copies of the mission statements for their companies. Some had them, some didn't. The more examples I saw, the more intrigued I became. So, I went to my local business library to conduct some research—and had the fateful conversation with the librarian.

Just to be sure the topic hadn't been covered in another medium, the librarian and I checked all the library's resources, including the *Guide to Periodic Literature*, microfilm, and computer files. We discovered there had been no articles written on mission statements, either. No "how-to-write-one" pieces. Nothing in the business magazines. Or business newspapers. Nothing at all.

So I set out with even greater fervor to complete this book.

With more than fifteen years of experience in advertising, including eight years in direct marketing as well as five years in newspaper journalism, marketing, and promotion, I knew how to put together a direct mail campaign to obtain the information I wanted. I wrote to 2,600 companies requesting a copy of their mission statement along with an annual report and anything else that would help me provide some background information on each company I profiled.

Of the 1,300 companies I queried first—comprised of the *Fortune* 1000, the *Forbes* 200, the companies listed in *The 100 Best Companies to Work for in America**—I heard from about 875. Of those, 374 actually had mission statements. From General Motors to Ben and Jerry's, you'll find the mission statements from the top companies in America in the pages that follow.

I also wrote to 1,000 companies of the second tier of the *Fortune* 2000 to add more well-known and largely publicly held companies to the collection. Companies like Wendy's International, Stride-Rite Corporation, and Blockbuster Entertainment Group.

After assembling more than 301 mission statements from large companies, I decided to include, for balance, a selected group of small, privately held companies. So, I queried 300 companies listed among the *Inc.* 500 (*Inc.* magazine). From that pool, 25 are represented here. They range from a residential housepainting service in Connecticut that teaches college students how to run a small business to a luxury homebuilding company in Arizona. From a real estate firm in Iowa to a spa company in (where else?) California. Plus, a Virginia software company, an Idaho health care company, and a manufacturer of specialty magnet devices in Pennsylvania.

The purpose of including these small companies is to illustrate that companies of every size should have, and do have, a mission statement.

---

* Levering, Robert, Milton Moscowitz, Michael Katz. *The 100 Best Companies to Work for in America.* New York, NY: Plume, 1985.

In the course of writing this book, I had an opportunity to speak and exchange letters with hundreds of people from a wide variety of companies. Through these conversations and interviews, I learned firsthand about their struggles with the writing and rewriting of mission statements. It can be a grueling, lengthy process—or an inspiring, motivational experience. The results can yield words that truly distinguish the company and ring true for more than a hundred years.

It is my intention for you to benefit from their experience. And mine.

PART I

THE MISSION OF THIS BOOK

TO HELP BUSINESS people, executives, managers, employees, investors, students, and consumers achieve a greater understanding of corporate mission statements.

To achieve this mission, this book endeavors to explain:

- What is a mission statement;
- What a mission statement is used for;
- Why it is important for every company and organization to make a statement about its mission, vision, goal, or purpose;
- Which elements comprise a mission statement;
- How mission statements differ from one another;
- How to write a mission statement;
- And how 301 of America's biggest companies define their own mission statements, visions, values, principles, objectives, goals, strategies, aspirations, ethics, pledges, promises, and creeds.

If this book succeeds in educating, guiding, inspiring, and motivating the reader, it will have achieved its mission.

HOW TO USE THIS RESOURCE

THIS BOOK HAS been designed to help you understand the nature, structure, style, and language of mission statements. It is also intended to provide a how-to guide to help you write or rewrite your organization's statement, whether you work for a large corporation, small company, non-profit organization, government agency, municipality, or university. Moreover, I've structured the book so it is easy to use and refer to.

Part I is an introduction to the world of mission statements. In the next three chapters you'll find short, substantive sections that address the following topics:

- ❖ The history of the mission statement
- ❖ Its purpose
- ❖ Definition of terms
- ❖ Ways that companies compose, present, and distribute their mission statements
- ❖ Target audience, length, tone, and format
- ❖ Titles, key words, and phrases
- ❖ Presentation
- ❖ How a mission can evolve and change with the company

The last chapter in Part I, entitled "How to Write a Mission Statement (Or Mission *Not* Impossible)," may prove to be a very valuable chapter for you. I wrote it to be brief and instructive, rather than pedantic, respecting both your unique organizational structure and application. So while it may seem broad, it is by no means simplistic.

As you know, writing can be hard work. And when something as important and visible as a mission statement is being created, there may be many editors who have a hand at shaping the final words. Therefore, the guidelines I have provided are intended to help *facilitate* the process, not automatically formulate the results.

Part II is a compendium of more than 300 mission statements from among America's largest companies, selected from the *Fortune* 2000, *Forbes* 200, and other sources. I've also interspersed the statements of 25 small companies that are worthy of your attention. You'll recognize them by the ❖ symbol that accompanies each one.

Each mission statement is accompanied by a profile of the company. The profile is comprised of the company's address, a corporate description (usually in the company's own words as found in its annual report), industry category, and data such as annual revenues and number of employees. This data was compiled in order to create Part III.

Part III is a collection of indexes that list and arrange the companies by industry, number of employees, and state. There's even an index listing the companies that have a mission, vision, or other statement of one sentence in length. The indexes will help you target companies that are similar to yours (industry, size, geographic region) so you can see how they've handled the challenge of creating their mission statement.

GUIDELINES

Here are some extra guidelines for using this book:

1 If you're trying to write a mission statement from scratch:
   ❖ Read the chapters in Part I.
   ❖ Scan the collection of mission statements in Part II.
   ❖ Refer to the indexes in Part III for companies similar to yours. Make a list of those companies. Look them up one by one in Part II and study each company's approach, use of language and tone, and overall message.

❧ Look closely at the key words list on pages 49 and 50, "Inside a Mission Statement." Make a note of the words that would be applicable to your company's statement.

❧ Reread the chapter titled, "How to Write a Mission Statement," with step-by-step instructions on how to write a mission statement, so you can stay focused, especially if you're working with a committee. Many of the steps can be delegated.

2 If you're trying to update or rewrite your organization's statement:

❧ Do all of the above with your current mission by your side. You may be surprised how many parts of the old mission are worth retaining. Plus, integrating some of the old mission with the new will provide some continuity. This can go a long way to comforting employees/members/stockholders who may have questions about changes in the way they are being asked to perceive your organization.

Finally, this resource can help you initiate dialogue, conversation, and debate among your colleagues to determine exactly what kind of statement is appropriate for your group—or if more than one statement should be drafted. That's when you can truly put together the words and phrases that make a statement as distinctive as your organization.

A FEW WORDS ABOUT MISSION STATEMENTS AND NON-PROFIT ORGANIZATIONS

Every organization, whether it is a company in business to make a profit or a charitable organization with non-profit status, needs a mission statement.

In fact, many non-profit groups, social agencies, and service organizations *do* have mission statements. These statements serve the purpose of heralding the purpose of the group to the public and providing direction for its employees, members, and volunteers.

Creating a mission statement will also aid a non-profit group in their application for grants and other forms of financial aid. In some cases, a grant proposal isn't complete unless it includes a mission statement.

While this book is devoted primarily to the nation's largest corporations, members of non-profit organizations setting out to write a mission statement will find the information, how-to instructions, and examples from other companies quite valuable.

IN THE BEGINNING... THERE WAS THE MISSION STATEMENT

MISSION STATEMENTS HAVE been a part of working life and human history since the beginning of time. Perhaps the *very first* mission statement is recorded in Genesis, with the command, "Be fruitful, and multiply..."

More recently, Shakespeare wrote a mission statement for Marc Anthony, which he proclaims when he begins to eulogize Julius Caesar,

> Friends, Romans, countrymen, lend me your ears;
> I come to bury Caesar, not to praise him.

The Preamble to the Constitution of the United States is a kind of mission statement, establishing the reason for creation of the historical document:

> We the People of the United States, in Order to form a more perfect Union, establish Justice, insure domestic Tranquillity, provide for the common defense, promote the general Welfare, and secure the Blessings of Liberty to ourselves and our Posterity, do ordain and establish this Constitution for the United States of America.

One of contemporary culture's best-known mission statements is far ahead of its time:

> Space, the Final Frontier...These are the voyages of the Starship *Enterprise*. Its five-year mission: To explore strange new worlds, to seek out new life and new civilizations, to boldly go where no man has gone before.

When Gene Roddenberry wrote *Star Trek*, he also authored a mission statement that would become familiar to millions.

Ultimately, whenever and wherever men and women have endeavored to achieve something purposefully, a statement of mission or purpose is pronounced. It precedes the first step in a long march. And it is etched in stone over the entrances of great buildings.

People, by their very nature, seem to ennoble a task by endowing it with a stated mission.

COMPANIES ARE LIKE PEOPLE. THEY NEED A MISSION.

Corporations as entities and people as individuals share certain characteristics. Over time, they develop personalities that shape their philosophies and motivate their actions. And without a purpose or a mission, both a person and a company will flounder.

Shaping the identity of a corporation really begins with defining its mission. Its reason for being. Its purpose, focus, goal.

Every company, no matter how big or small, needs a mission statement as a source of direction, a kind of compass, that lets its employees, its customers, and even its stockholders know what it stands for and where it's headed.

A mission engenders a company with a sense of purposefulness, that there is a reason for working—aside from compensation.

A mission also serves to unify people in a company, especially when it is comprised of many different kinds of people, in different parts of the country and the world, with varying job titles as well as different levels of training and education.

As a unifying touchstone, a mission likewise provides the company and its employees with a sense of identity.

And finally, a mission, simply by its very existence, *provides a foundation* on which the company can build its future.

BRIDGING BORDERS

The unifying aspect of a mission statement cannot be overemphasized, especially for companies that are international in scope.

Johnson Wax (the most familiar brand name from the S. C. Johnson Company), publishes an eye-opening brochure, "This We Believe." In its introduction, the company states the important role a mission statement can play in unifying a worldwide company and bridging borders:

> ...our statement of corporate philosophy has been translated and communicated around the world—not only within the worldwide company, but also to key external audiences. It has served us well by providing all employees with a common statement of the basic principles which guide the company in all the different cultures where we operate. It has also provided people outside the company with an understanding of our fundamental beliefs. It communicates the kind of company we are.

A BLUEPRINT FOR SUCCESS

There's another way of perceiving what a mission is all about. Consider a mission as part of the *set of fundamental principles* by which a business operates. The rest of the set could include a vision, goal, slate of objectives, ethics statement, an environmental policy, operating policies, and a basic business philosophy—among many other statements.

Thinking of a mission statement as part of a company's overall blueprint for success—and communicating that to employees, customers and the public—gives a company a head start on *achieving* that success.

GUIDING PRINCIPLES

National Semiconductor Corporation designs, manufactures and markets semiconductors for the computer and electronics industry. Kevin Wheeler, the director of National Semiconductor University (described in its own publication as "an international network of employee development professionals chartered to enhance human capability"), explains the importance of a set of guiding principles to his company:

> We have spent a great deal of time over the past three years developing a corporate vision, a set of guiding principles and beliefs, and a mission statement that will help us achieve that vision.

> We believe that a set of guiding principles must be firmly in place if a company is to prosper. Indeed, all companies have guiding principles whether or not they are explicit. However, implicit principles can be counterproductive if they are in conflict with the vision.

> Many companies go through transition without examining these foundation principles by which all work gets done. To do so is dangerous—much like sailing a ship through a narrow channel without benefit of charts or pilot. Better to make them explicit—challenge them or reaffirm or change them openly for all to see and understand.

> And, of course, all of these beliefs have to be translated into behavior—into clear understandings of what each employee must do and not do. The process to achieve this must be interactive and must involve the very bottom of the organization as well as the very top. A set of descriptive terms will not suffice.

> We are in the midst of that process today. I believe that it takes five to ten years to achieve a complete shift from one set of beliefs to another, and I also believe that it is one of the most difficult things for a company to do successfully.

THIS VISION IS ALSO SHAPING THE FUTURE...

The impact of a company's own vision can be dramatic. Microsoft Corporation's Vision statement is a single sentence: "A computer on every desk and in every home."

Microsoft's 1993 Annual Report includes an explanation of their vision:

> We are single-minded in our commitment to this vision. And we have maintained that singular focus ever since our company was founded in 1975.

> This vision has created a revolution that's changed how people around the world do business...

> This vision is also shaping the future...

SO WHAT EXACTLY *IS* A MISSION STATEMENT?

AND HOW DOES it vary from a vision statement, business philosophy, objectives, values, strategies, pledge, tactics, purpose, promise, beliefs, standards, code of ethics, idea, call to action, guidelines, direction, focus, commitment, policy, discipline, covenant, standards of performance or credo? Or are all these titles just variations on the same theme?

Anyone who has ever been asked to write a company's mission statement sooner or later comes to these questions.

Fortunately, others have already tread this uphill path. Collectively, they've produced an astonishingly rich, varied, and colorful palette of definitions.

The following companies have embraced the challenge of defining a mission statement (and other related statements) prior to composing one. While they vary individually in premise and tone, dovetailed together they comprise a solid frame for housing this mission statement compendium.

Please note: I have used the term "mission statement" to include a broad range of approaches and titles by a wide variety of companies. Some companies put their vision and values before their mission, if they have one. Simply by shaping a "statement," these companies are stating or implying their corporate mission.

EXAMPLE #1 | TRINOVA Corporation

TRINOVA Corporation is a manufacturer of engineered components, headquartered in Maumee, Ohio. It produces a booklet that
not only states its corporate mission statement, statement of purpose and goals, and core values but also includes a section that asks
and answers the following questions for the benefit of employees:

- What is a mission statement?
- What is "Our Mission"?
- Does this replace other TRINOVA mission statements?
- What do we do with the mission?
- Who developed our mission?
- Do other corporations have mission statements?
- How is our mission different?
- What are the components of our mission?

Here is a sample of the text of the questions and answers.

What is a mission statement?

A mission statement is an enduring statement of purpose for
an organization that identifies the scope of its operations in
product and market terms, and reflects its values and priorities.

A mission statement will help a company to make consistent
decisions, to motivate, to build an organizational unity, to
integrate short-term objectives with longer-term goals, and
to enhance communication.

What is "our mission"?

(See TRINOVA's mission statement in Part II.)

Our mission is stated quite simply. It defines our key goals and
defines our values. It is also forward-looking. Our mission is
uniquely the property and the heritage of TRINOVA employees. And, it is the foundation upon which we can all build a
strong and successful future for TRINOVA and for ourselves.

What do we do with the mission?

It is the responsibility of each of us to make the mission a guide to our decision making and action. To accomplish this, we must each become proponents of the mission and exemplify it in our words and actions. Make its goals our goals, and make the six core values the very essence of how we act and how we expect others in TRINOVA to act.

Who developed our mission?

The Corporate Management Committee wrote our mission with considerable input from other managers throughout TRINOVA.

Do other corporations have mission statements?

Yes. Many corporations have adopted mission statements. Some have been successful while others have not. We take our mission seriously and we intend to live by it now and in the future.

How is our mission different?

Our mission captures our values; it does not invent new ones! It is not intended to radically alter TRINOVA. Rather, it is intended to make sure that we capitalize on our strengths and that we all move in the same direction. Our mission will be enduring and will become a natural part of our work.

If we can—over time—internalize our values and meet our goals, we will have the distinction of being a truly excellent company.

EXAMPLE #2 | Pennsylvania Power & Light Company

Pennsylvania Power & Light Company is an electric utility serving twenty-nine counties in Central Eastern Pennsylvania. The entry for PP&L in Part II of this book includes the current vision, values, and principles plus the earlier versions of the company's vision, values, mission, and philosophy developed in the 1980s (with the expressed written permission of the company).

One reason for including the previous version is to present portions of PP&L's extraordinary nine-page brochure produced in the 1980s that not only articulated the company's vision, values, mission and business philosophy, but defined the terms as well.

These definitions of vision, values, mission, and business philosophy read as follows:

Vision

The vision of an organization is a concise word picture of the organization at some future time, which sets the overall direction of the organization. It is what the organization strives to be. A vision is something to be pursued, while a mission (defined later) is something to be accomplished.

Values

Values are the collective principles and ideals which guide the thoughts and actions of an individual, or a group of individuals. Values define the character of an organization—they describe what the organization stands for.

Mission

A mission is a statement that specifies an organization's purpose or "reason for being." It is the primary objective toward which the organization's plans and programs should be aimed. A mission is something to be accomplished, while a vision (defined earlier) is something to be pursued.

Business philosophy

The business philosophy establishes the "rule of conduct" for operating the organization. It translates the values of the organization into more concrete descriptions of how the values will be applied to run the business.

In the chapter entitled "How to write a mission statement," you'll find an interview with PP&L's Director of Corporate Communications, James Marsh, in which he explains how the company revised its vision, values, mission, and philosophy statements.

EXAMPLE #3 | San Francisco Federal Savings

San Francisco Federal Savings has prepared a policy statement booklet for their employees, which includes a section entitled, "A Unique Factor: Our Mission Statement." This section asserts the reason for having a mission statement and how the mission is to be considered, and it defines a mission statement in a very simple, succinct manner that would be accessible to employees of just about any company.

The text reads:

> The key to success for businesses whose products and services are similar, is to be *different* from the others. To create that distinguishing characteristic, that unique factor that makes the statement, "We are a step ahead. We are leaders in our industry."

> While products, services, pricing and promotion are all important elements, our future success depends on identifying and living up to the unique promises our Mission Statement outlines. ... [Mission statement follows. See Part II for full text.]

> We believe that strict adherence to the spirit contained in this statement will set us apart from our competition.

> This Mission Statement tells people who we are and what we stand for. It creates a unique place for San Francisco Federal in the minds of the public.

OTHER EXAMPLES

Weyerhaeuser President Jack Creighton defines what a vision statement means in the introduction to his company's statements "Our Vision" and "Our Values":

A vision describes the desired future state of an organization. To be valid, a vision statement must endure and not change with every business cycle.

The vision statement for Herman Miller Inc., the furniture manufacturer, not only lists the company's values, expectations, goals, and strategies but describes what those terms mean:

Our Values: Who We Are

Our Expectations: The Way We Work Together

Our Goals: What We Are Working Toward

Our Strategies: How We Intend To Achieve Our Goals

Meridian Bancorp explains "Our Vision" as "Meridian's statement of core values that defines the company's culture and the Meridian way of working."

Levi Strauss' "Business Vision" begins with "The Company developed its Business Vision to identify its goals and provide direction for prioritizing all its initiatives and strategies."

Bausch & Lomb devotes a lengthy portion of text explaining the definition, importance, and role of "Values" in the introduction of its company publication, "The Values We Share at Bausch & Lomb." See Part II and the Bausch & Lomb entry for the entire text.

Wisconsin Public Service Company is an electric and gas utility company. In their statement, "Our Vision," the company says, "A vision is a mental image of the company we want to be. It's intended to give all employees, as well as everyone else the company works with and serves, a consistent picture of the company we are creating." The company also defines the words behind their mission statement: "A mission describes the aim of our current business practices. It offers us direction."

CMS Energy of Jackson, Michigan, is the nation's fourth largest combination electric and gas utility. Their comprehensive publication "Our Strategic Plan" includes the company's Vision, Goals, Strategies, and Creed. They explain each term, as follows:

❖ Our Vision declares how we as a company will operate in philosophical terms—in decision making, serving customers and measuring success.

❖ Our Goals describe what we will do to cement positive relationships with our stakeholders.

❖ Our Strategies explain how we will reach our goals.

❖ Finally, the company Creed is our pledge of performance. Good service and value to our customers is a must.

Anheuser-Busch begins its mission statement with the following explanation:

This mission statement clarifies the direction and general goals of Anheuser-Busch Companies, enabling employees at all levels to better understand their company and the role they play in its success. Additionally, by looking beyond any one product or operating company, this statement provides a reference point from which specific business strategies can be assessed and progress can be measured.

Clearly, defining terms and explaining the purpose of a mission, vision, principle, or strategy helps to communicate the statement more effectively and with greater impact.

INSIDE A MISSION STATEMENT

IF, IDEALLY, A company's mission statement should be as unique as the company itself, it stands to reason that no two mission statements are exactly alike.

As Part II will illustrate, there is great variety in the ways that companies compose, present, and distribute their missions. The differences become apparent when you examine the four basic elements that comprise and distinguish a mission statement: *target audience, length, tone,* and *format.*

TARGET AUDIENCE: THIS MISSION'S FOR YOU

Who is the mission statement intended for? The employees of a company? The general public? Stockholders? Some companies compose a mission that's intended for all audiences. Others purposefully create a mission for employees' eyes only. Still others post their missions in annual reports where they'll be seen only by stockholders or prospective investors.

AMP, in its brochure describing the company's mission, values, and vision, begins with a letter from the Chairman and CEO, H. A. McInnes, which begins, "To Our Customers..."

Other CEOs precede their company's mission with the salutation, "Dear (Company) Employee..."

Deluxe Corporation covers all conceivable target audiences in the statement entitled "Our Commitment" by addressing:

To Customers

To Employees

To Shareholders

To The Community

Similarly, the Knight-Ridder Promise, which accompanies the Knight-Ridder statement of values, is directed:

To Our Customers

To Our Employees

To Our Shareholders

To Our Communities

To Our Society

In the same vein, Warner-Lambert states "Our Creed" and addresses each of the target audiences to which the company commits itself:

To Our Customers

To Our Colleagues

To Our Shareholders

To Our Business Partners

To Society

Notice the similarities and the differences among the three examples. Perhaps most notably, each one begins by addressing customers, employees, and shareholders.

The target audience has a significant impact on the length, tone, and visibility of the mission statement.

LENGTH | HOW LONG IS LONG ENOUGH?

According to a popular folk legend, when Abraham Lincoln was president, he was asked by a reporter, "How long should a man's legs be?" Lincoln is said to have responded, "Long enough to reach the ground." The same philosophy applies to a mission statement.

For some companies, a single sentence is sufficient. Others have produced great, lengthy documents that begin with a mission and include vision statements, values, philosophies, objectives, plans, and strategies in supporting roles. And still others are somewhere in between, longer than one line, but contained within one page. *All that's necessary is that the mission be long enough to reach the target audience.*

For insights on the art of brevity, see Index #4 in Part III for a list of statements that are comprised of a single sentence.

COMPANIES WITH MORE THAN ONE MISSION

A company *can* have more than one mission statement. That is, it may be appropriate for *each division* of a corporation to have its own mission, vision, values, and objectives—especially if that corporation is heavily diversified.

Premark is comprised of eight separate divisions, each producing its own line of consumer goods. Familiar brandnames of these divisions include Tupperware and West Bend. Each division has a mission statement of its own. And each is as unique as the division it speaks for.

Consolidated Freightways provides a mission for each of its three divisions. Ben & Jerry's has a product mission, a social mission and an economic mission.

TONE | AVOIDING FLAT NOTES

The tone of a mission statement is a crucial part of its makeup. It takes a certain tone to resonate with the target audience.

Should a statement be conversational? Formal? Originate from the office of the chief executive officer? The president? The head of human resources? The corporate communications manager? It all depends on the company and, again, the target audience.

If the language is too lofty, haughty, or ponderous, it won't be taken very seriously. And, more significantly, it will defeat its very purpose.

So what kind of language should one employ? That is best answered by examining the individual parts that comprise a mission statement. These include the title, key words, and phrases.

TITLE

Establishing the right tone requires the deliberate choice of specific words that give a statement its own character. The *title* itself can set the tone. It's certainly sufficient to entitle a mission statement with the prominent headline, "Mission Statement." (And hundreds of companies presented in these pages do exactly that.) But a significant number of companies apply their own stamp to the genre.

Northwestern Mutual Life's mission is entitled "The Northwestern Mutual Way."

Johnson Wax provides a booklet with its mission, entitled "This We Believe."

Bausch & Lomb orients employees with a publication, "The Values We Share at Bausch & Lomb."

The brochure published by AMP is entitled "The Journey." The trek referred to here is the company's "Journey to Excellence" which is supported by its mission, values, and vision.

Gannett Company, Inc. presents its "Strategic Vision" and "Operating Principles" as part of "Gannett's Basic Game Plan."

A title can also establish a tone as visionary and forward-thinking.

Niagara Mohawk, a New York utility company, has a booklet outlining its Corporate Strategic Plan 1993–95. Jostens' mission statement and goals statements are part of its strategic plan for 1994–96.

KEY WORDS

Key words and phrases also set the tone for a statement. A list of key words are included below along with the number of times that word appears in each of the mission statements in Part II. (Note bold-faced listings for the most often-cited words.)

- Ability—23
- Accomplished—8
- Accountability—22
- Asset—40
- **Best**—102
- Change—42
- **Commitment**—88
- Communicate—10
- **Communities**—93
- Conscience—2
- Corporate citizen—40
- **Customers**—211
- Dedicated—35
- Dedication—17
- Dignity—29
- Direct—37
- Diversity—26
- **Employees**—157
- Empower—34
- Enthusiasm—7
- **Environment**—117
- Ethics—26
- Excellence—78
- Exciting—3
- Fair—67
- Fun—43
- Future—40

- Goal—76
- Goodwill—3
- **Growth**—118
- Harmony—4
- Individual—79
- Initiative—22
- Innovation—69
- Joy—2
- **Leader**—104
- Leadership—63
- Life—49
- Long-term—72
- **Mission**—221
- Mutual—34
- Passion—6
- Performance—82
- Potential—28
- Pride—18
- Principles—40
- Productivity—26
- Profit—114
- **Quality**—194
- Relationships—43
- Reliable—19
- **Respect**—98
- Responsibility—55
- Return on equity—19

- ❖ Risk—38
- ❖ Security—17
- ❖ Serve—84
- ❖ **Service**—230
- ❖ **Shareholders**—114
- ❖ Solution—21
- ❖ Strategy—24
- ❖ Strength—60
- ❖ **Success**—105
- ❖ Support—74
- ❖ **Team**—91
- ❖ Teamwork—61
- ❖ Tomorrow—5
- ❖ Trust—51
- ❖ Unique—6
- ❖ Value—183
- ❖ **Values**—73
- ❖ Vision—95

PHRASES

As you read through the various mission statements in Part II, you'll encounter certain phrases that stand out in tone and spirit.

For instance, National Semiconductor urges its employees to "Be curious, imaginative, and courageous in challenging our current thinking."

Both Nike, the shoe company, and Comerica, a banking corporation, have mission statements that refer to "enriching people's lives." Imagine, two companies devoted to completely different businesses, but with nearly identical phrasing in their mission statements.

Vons urges employees in its vision statement to have a "give a darn" attitude.

Sundstrand Corporation states that one of its "Beliefs" is "Developing and maintaining relationships rather than just executing transactions."

Pet Incorporated cites one of its "Pet Values" as "Fulfillment of our commitment—what we say we do, we *do* do."

General Electric has a series of "GE Values" statements, which explains that GE leaders "have a passion for excellence, hating bureaucracy and all the nonsense that comes with it."

First Bank System of Minneapolis declares that one of its official values is "Diversity." And while dozens of companies endorse the merits of diversity, FBS states, "We value individual differences and work to leverage their inherent creative potential."

Ecolab Inc. declares its "Quest For Excellence" with a mission, philosophy, and standards of performance. The section about "Our Customers" begins "The company that fails its customers, fails!"

Corning Incorporated stands behind its list of company Values, including integrity, by saying, "Integrity is the foundation of Corning's reputation."

Comerica's "Core Values and Beliefs" end with "...we are proud to be members of the team and enjoy coming to work."

Coachmen Industries' "Principles" statement begins "How we accomplish our mission is as important as the mission itself." Later in this same section, the subject of customers is addressed: "Our deep-seated philosophy is that 'Business goes where it is invited and stays where it is well cared for.'"

There are hundreds of other fascinating phrases, lines, and statements in the samples of mission statements that follow in Part II.

FORMATS | **WHAT SHOULD A MISSION STATEMENT LOOK LIKE?**

How a company regards its mission statement is often reflected in the manner in which it's presented to customers, employees, stockholders, and the public at large.

In other words...looks do mean everything.

Some statements are printed principally in the company's annual report (many of these are featured on the cover). Others appear in the annual report and in other formats and venues so they can be distributed, promoted, and championed as representative of the company's profile.

SUITABLE FOR FRAMING

Some companies print their mission statement on high-quality, 8½ by 11-inch paper so it is suitable for framing.

The oldest mission for an American company cited in this book is from Northwestern Mutual Life, which composed its statement in 1888. (See Part II.) To dignify this legacy, the company publishes its mission statement on card stock, in the 8½ by 11-inch format, with a calligraphic, hand-lettered style.

And where should a framed mission or other statements be displayed? In the lobby? In each employee's office? In the lunchroom or cafeteria? It all depends on the company's particular culture.

How many companies go to the trouble and minor expense of presenting their mission statement in a formal, "dressed up" format? Here is a partial list of companies profiled in Part II that feature their mission statements in "presentation mode":

3M
Airborne Express
Allied Signal Inc.
Airborne Express
American Protective Services, Inc.
Anheuser-Busch Companies, Inc.
Aristech Chemical Corporation
Chevron Corporation
CUNA Mutual Insurance Group
Edwards (A. G. Edwards & Sons, Inc.)
Ethyl Corporation
First Bank System
Hormel Foods Corporation
Nalco Chemical Company
Rhône-Poulenc Rorer Inc.
Safety-Kleen Corporation
Sanwa Bank
Southern Company

Southwest Airlines Co.
SpaceLabs Medical, Inc.
Sundstrand Corporation
TRW Inc.

Levi-Strauss uses a beautiful paperstock with a blue denim tone.

Westin Hotels presents its vision statement with a beautifully scripted text in a 8½ by 6-inch horizontal format.

HAVE MISSION, WILL TRAVEL

Many companies produce their mission, vision, values, goals, and objectives in both the large card-stock format and again in a small format that's appropriate for each employee to carry in a wallet.

Total System Services, Inc. is a company devoted to credit card processing. So, its mission statement appears on…guess what? A plastic credit card. This medium has been adopted by other companies as well.

And while not all companies produce their statements on a card the size and weight of a credit card, many do print their statements in miniature form. These include: Ace Hardware Corporation; AMETEK; Atlanta Gas Light Company; Diamond Shamrock, Inc.; Federal-Mogul Corporation; Gates Rubber Company; General Public Utilities Corporation; Goodyear; Mary Kay Cosmetics, Inc.; Southern California Edison; Tultex Corporation; Vons; and Warner-Lambert Company.

Butler Manufacturing Company and Rollins Inc. both have their mission statements printed on the back of employees' business cards.

Inland Container Corporation's mission, values, vision, and objectives are printed on a 3⅓ by 5½-inch laminated card, so it is especially durable as well as portable. Pillsbury distributes its mission statement on a laminated card as well.

BROCHURES, BOOKLETS, AND HANDBOOKS

To give greater visibility and credibility to their statements, many companies publish brochures, booklets, and handbooks in various sizes and formats that are separate from the annual report.

Like the suitable-for-framing sheets on heavy stock, these formats have great impact and are custom-made for easy distribution to a variety of target audiences.

So, it's not surprising that they appear in a wide variety of sizes, too. Some include:

- 8½ by 11-inches
- 7½ by 11-inches
- 7 by 4⅜-inches
- 5½ by 8½-inches
- 4½ by 9½-inches
- 3⅞ by 9-inches
- 3⅝ by 8½-inches
- 3½ by 5½-inches

Companies with separate booklets for their statements include Borg-Warner Security Corporation; Centerbank; Centura Banks, Inc.; Ciba-Geigy Corporation; CMS Energy; Comerica; Corning Incorporated; Delta Air Lines, Inc.; First Interstate Bancorp; Fleming Companies; Gillette; Kansas City Power & Light; Lafarge Corporation; Martin Marietta Corporation; Pet Incorporated; Rubbermaid Incorporated; San Francisco Federal Savings; and Weyerhaeuser.

MULTIPLE FORMATS

Weyerhaeuser, like many companies, publishes its vision and values statements in a couple of different formats. They publish both an 8½ by 3¾-inch brochure and a miniaturized version on a wallet-sized card. This allows the statements to be distributed in a number of ways.

COPYRIGHTS

Remember that all the statements a company publishes, whether in the form of a mission, values, vision, principles, creed, etc. are the properties of that company. All of the statements reprinted here are done so with the expressed written permission of each company.

Hormel Foods Corporation, Borg-Warner Security Corporation, Chemical Banking Corporation, and Gibson Greetings, Inc. are just some of the companies that have a copyright symbol (©) accompanying their mission statement. (The symbols ™, SM, ® also appear in some of the companies' statements and related materials. These symbols signify that the company is officially recognized as the owner of a specific brand or trade name.) But you should consider a copyright implicit with all company statements.

Please respect the copyrights of the mission statements included in Part II. And be sure to copyright your own mission statement. How? Simply insert the symbol © at the bottom of the final page of your statement. Remember, your statement must be original for the copyright to apply. For more information about copyright law and registration, consult your local library's reference section.

HOW TO WRITE A MISSION STATEMENT (OR MISSION *NOT* IMPOSSIBLE)

IN THE COURSE of conducting research for this book and talking with people from all walks of business, I encountered a lot of enthusiasm for this project. I also heard a lot of stories about companies that started the process of creating a mission statement but never quite finished.

People kept asking me, "Is this going to be a 'How to Write a Mission Statement' book? And when will it be available?"

So many people seem to get stopped in their tracks by a kind of mission-statement-writing-process quagmire. This dilemma was confirmed by firsthand accounts. But, happily, the following examples demonstrate how companies can set out to complete the task.

EXAMPLE #1 | **The Case of Pennsylvania Power & Light Company (PP&L)**

Pennsylvania Power & Light Company updated their vision & values statements in 1994. James Marsh, director of corporate communications, explains why and how the company went about drafting and finalizing the new statements, in an interview conducted in September, 1994. (Both the older and updated vision and values statements are included in the PP&L entry in Part II.)

Q: What lead up to the decision to update and change your vision and values statements?
JM: The Energy Act of 1992 provides for the eventual deregulation of the electric utility industry and it is driving us toward a more

competitive environment. We're moving from regulated rates to rates for electricity driven by the marketplace. Our Statements needed to change to reflect the changes in our industry and how we're changing to deal with the new, competitive environment.

Q: Who determined the process?

JM: Our Corporate Management Committee, which is five senior officers, got together at the beginning of the year and worked with a facilitator, an outside consultant. We looked at what a vision statement should be and do, and we kept pounding away at it at meetings over several months. We came up with a new draft, sent it out for comments among the staff, and then out for focus group testing among employees, which gave us even more input. The responsibility for developing this material rests with senior management, but it was developed with the input of a wide section of employees. PP&L has 7,600 employees.

Q: In 1992, PP&L had a vision, values, mission, and philosophy statement. Now the company has created new vision and values statements. Will there be mission and philosophy statements, eventually, too?

JM: We haven't by design dropped them, we just started with the vision and values. They superseded the philosophy statement. It doesn't mean we won't work on it. The principles are about the same as those developed for our Continuous Performance Improvement Process, PP&L's "quality" program. We have put together a union/labor partnership that has developed CPIP. Our corporate principles are close to this.

As I mentioned, since publication of our vision, values, mission, and philosophy in the '80s, the Energy Act of 1992 is changing our industry. We have just in the last eight to nine months gone through a revision of the vision statement to reflect this changing industry.

So, we've got an updated vision and values statement. Now, we're working on a financial strategy. We may be going back and looking at a philosophy. This is a living thing and as it becomes appropriate we may make changes and improvements. As for the other statements…our business philosophy is kind of rolled into the values statement.

Q: How did you end up finding a facilitator to help your company create the new statements?

JM: We went out and sent a proposal to a number of outside business consultants and facilitators. They came in with a "process." They did just what is implied. They "facilitated" the thought process and rationale, rather than doing the actual writing. The back and forth revisions and drafts was with our top management people.

Q: What was the best part of going through this process?

JM: As director of corporate communications it was my responsibility to be actively involved. It's really exciting, just looking at what a vision statement is supposed to do. It is supposed to be a few words that are energizing to an organization. I was very excited with what we came up with.

Q: What else did your company do differently than last time to get new statements drafted?

JM: This time, management went out a number of times and sought input and feedback directly from employees. It did change the content, to some extent, because of that feedback.

Q: Have there been positive employee comments?

JM: Very definitely positive. They saw the process in the context of a lot of things we're trying to do to change the culture around here to emphasize teamwork and partnership. As you may know, the electric utility industry is a conservative culture. In order to be successful, we're going to have to be able to get more of a buy-in from employees and make them feel that they're truly part of the process.

The statements are different, but the commitment is not different. As times change, we feel the need to change with them, and have a more up-to-date Vision that's reflective of this company and what's in it for everyone.

EXAMPLE #2 | **The Case of Southern Pacific Lines**

Southern Pacific Lines is part of Southern Pacific Rail Corporation, the country's leading rail carrier of containerized freight. The story behind Southern Pacific Lines' mission statement is provided by Michael C. Brown, managing director of corporate communications:

> When Southern Pacific Lines began to craft a corporate Mission Statement in late 1990, it was not to satisfy an organizational need for solidarity with American industry's latest fad. Southern Pacific needed a plan, clearly stated objectives and a slogan that all employees could voice and support as they worked toward their common goals.

> In his kickoff meeting at the time, Chairman Philip F. Anschutz said, "This meeting...is about how we move this railroad from where it is today to where it needs to be tomorrow to be a vital competitor in a complex 21st Century global economy. Therefore, it is really about change."

> With that guiding tenet in hand, SP's Vice President–Quality, Kent Sterett set about writing a brief, straightforward statement that would embody the chairman's vision and would also serve as the catalyst for the many disparate tasks which, when completed, would take SP into its new environment.

> First Sterett interviewed other senior executives and showed them mission statements from other companies, some in the transportation industry and some not. He got his colleagues'

views on what "key points" SP's message should contain and what they liked or disliked about other companies' statements. With that information, Sterett drafted what he called four "railroadized" statements and went back to his fellow executives for comment and boiled the four statements down to a final choice of two. That process resulted in SP's official Mission Statement: "Southern Pacific Lines' mission is to anticipate and satisfy the requirements of its customers for highly responsive and cost effective transportation and distribution services."

In the rollout of the mission statement to all SP employees, nine "strategies" were identified, all of which tied back to the statement and, in turn, served as the basic means of achieving a series of "key performance indicators" which every group within SP would need to adhere to in its five-year plan. The mission statement was cascaded throughout the railroad, from chairman down to maintenance of way track workers, both in formal meetings, printed materials and on E-mail terminal screens, posters, coffee cup coasters and stickers.

Today, four years into the company's five-year plan, Sterett credits the mission statement with having helped set the standard that has led to Southern Pacific's turnaround. "One measure of that success is reducing our operating ratio (expenses as a percentage of revenues) from 104 to 89 percent," he said. "By using a mission statement to provide a common point of reference, we have found that an overwhelming majority of our employees understand the corporate mission, subscribe to its intent and believe we are on track to accomplish our objectives."

EXAMPLE #3: THE CASE OF CORPORATE CHILD CARE MANAGEMENT SERVICES

Corporate Child Care Management Services is a Nashville, Tennessee-based *Fortune* 2000 company that develops and manages child care centers for employers that are tailored to meet the unique needs of the workplace.

Company President and Chief Executive Officer Marguerite W. Sallee describes what her company's Corporate Mission Statement means, how it was crafted and how it is used, displayed, and integrated into the company's communications:

> I believe that the process of developing and refining a mission statement is as important as the statement itself. Our Mission Statement was crafted six years ago shortly after the company was founded. My entire management team helped to develop it, and as a team we review it at least annually. It is a living document, a work still in progress. We strive to make certain that the statement clearly and precisely articulates what our company is about. This process also helps us to stay focused on our purpose.

> I also believe that everyone at all levels of a company must be personally familiar with the mission statement. In order for any fast growing company like Corporate Child Care to be successful, everyone in the organization must believe in what they do and where they are going. At Corporate Child Care, our simple Mission Statement calls everyone in our company to embrace the importance of our work with vitality and passion. Our statement is prominently displayed in our home office and at every location. It is included in communications to all employees. We have also incorporated our company values in our mission statement, so that every employee knows and understands both our purpose and our values.

EXAMPLE #4 | **The Case of *Architectural Record***

Architectural Record, headquartered in New York, is a professional magazine for architects. In the September, 1993 issue, the Publisher's column, "Notes from Behind the Scenes," gave an account of the process by which that magazine attempted to produce a mission statement. While this magazine is not included among the 301 companies profiled in Part II, the candid account of how the magazine's management set out to create a mission statement is noteworthy.

Former publisher Roscoe C. Smith III writes:

Starting in early May and proceeding through August, a series of meetings was held for the purpose of writing a definitive plan for the future of this magazine involving every aspect of what we produce. We're looking at how the magazine can be improved, expanded in its usefulness, even transformed into other useful products—print or electronic, all based on the needs expressed by our "customers"—you, our readers, and you, our advertisers. Above all, it was agreed that it must be a plan that management and staff can unanimously endorse and execute.

Attending our meetings were people from editorial, marketing, circulation, advertising sales, production and accounting. Twelve in all…but our titles were left outside the meeting-room door. One person, one vote. Total agreement was our goal. The first order of business was to draft a precise and clear Mission Statement. To start the process, each attendee was asked to submit his or her thoughts on the matter in writing. We all assumed it would then be an easy task to combine our ideas and reconcile the differences. And, with that out of the way, go on to the planning stages.

We were mistaken. It wasn't that easy.

However, weeks later—with the 4th of July looming in the horizon and having more than once recalled a group that also met through a long hot summer (in Philadelphia)—it was agreed by all concerned to adopt the following Statement. Every word having been weighed, every thought examined, and every resource considered…over and over again, I want to share it with you:

The mission of *Architectural Record* is to provide original, reliable, and useful information to the architectural marketplace worldwide, in timely and easy-to-use formats which:

❖ Create an industry-wide forum.

❖ Set the standards for excellence in architectural design.

❖ Present insights and practical solutions for current challenges in design, building construction, and business practice.

❖ Build success for our readers, our advertisers, our associates and investors, and ourselves.

❖ Establish the authoritative record of architecture.

With this commitment in hand, we are in the process of rethinking every part of what we do.

These examples point out how much work goes into the creation of a mission statement. But the rewards provide a great return on the investment in time and effort.

A STEP-BY-STEP GUIDE TO WRITING A MISSION STATEMENT

Writing any document can be a daunting and arduous task. Just because someone is a good engineer, chemist, shop foreman, salesperson, or loan officer doesn't mean he or she is very comfortable with putting words down on paper.

Even the Founding Fathers became exasperated with trying to write the *Declaration of Independence* by committee and finally left things in the hands of Thomas Jefferson. Their problem was they had no recipe, formula, or blueprint for creating a new form of government.

But history is on your side. Others have blazed a trail before you and left an easy step-by-step method for writing a mission statement.

STEP 1 | Decide who is going to write the mission statement

Is this a solo task or a group effort? Take a lesson from the real-life examples of other companies and consider the advantages of creating a committee with representatives from every department in your company. That way, everyone will have a chance to feel like they had a voice in the statement's creation and will be more likely to embrace its content and spirit.

STEP 2 | Agree on when the statement is going to be written

During business hours or in evening sessions? In a single weekend? At the office or off-site where there will be fewer distractions? And how much time will you allow?

A single afternoon or evening? A weekend? A month? Six months? A year? Impose a deadline and stick to it.

STEP 3 | Determine the target audience(s)

Employees of your company? Customers? Suppliers? Stockholders? The general public? You have to figure out *who* you're talking to before you can figure out *what* to say.

STEP 4 | Decide what kind of language is appropriate

Start with a list of key words and phrases that apply to your business. Bring a group of people together, invite a free flow of ideas, and write down words and phrases that come to mind. Refer to the list of key words provided earlier on pages 49–50.

This may lead to a discussion about what kind of statement you're writing in the first place and what its title should be. You may wish to create a mission statement that describes your company's purpose or goal. But you may also want to include a vision statement that addresses the issues of people, service, and the future of the company—that is, how your company is going to achieve its goal. That's only the beginning. Remember, there are also value statements, statements of principles, philosophies, ethics, environmental policies, and more.

It's ultimately up to you to decide the nature, length, and tone of the document.

STEP 5 | Adopt a format

Will the mission statement be presented to the target audience in the annual report? Beautifully printed on quality paper, designed for framing and distribution? In a brochure or pamphlet? As a wallet-size card? Embedded in a Lucite paperweight? Printed on a company calendar or coffee mugs? Silk-screened on T-shirts? Emblazoned on a banner? Engraved in granite? Displayed at the front door?

If you're proud of your official mission statement, you'll want to communicate its message in a variety of ways that reflect your company's distinctive culture.

Like most any task, breaking down the process into smaller steps makes it easier to accomplish. Ultimately, by focusing on your company's goals, you'll achieve this one, as well:

"Be fruitful and multiply..."

The ancient mission statement, also mentioned at the beginning of this section, is still very much to the point. In fact, it's an excellent place from which to begin writing your own mission. Consider the ways and means your company can be fruitful in the sense of growing your business. Determine the strategies to multiply your profitability.

And you're on your way toward the creation of a successful mission statement.

LET ME HEAR FROM YOU

I welcome the opportunity to consider the mission statements of other companies, non-profit organizations, colleges and universities, municipalities, and government agencies for future editions of *The Mission Statement Book*. Submissions should include a description of the organization, revenue and employee data, a specific contact's name, and a brief statement that grants me permission to use the submitted material. Submissions should be mailed to me at:

Jeffrey Abrahams
c/o Ten Speed Press
P. O. Box 7123
Berkeley, CA 94707

PART II

THE COMPANIES
AND THEIR STATEMENTS

THE MORE THAN 300 companies presented here represent a wide variety of industries. But in order to present each one in a consistent manner, I have included the company's statement(s) and a profile of the company, comprised of a corporate description plus statistics for annual revenues and number of employees, when available.

I put this data to use in Part III. There you'll find a series of indexes that arrange companies by industry, number of employees, and state, as well as an index that lists all the companies that have a mission statement of one sentence in length.

The corporate descriptions are most often presented in the companies' own words found in their annual reports. Sources for the statements and statistics are listed with each company entry.

In categorizing each company, I had the dilemma of placing companies that contributed to more than one type of industry. In some cases, the company has been placed in an industry category that was listed *first* by the company itself in its own corporate description. In other cases, I categorized the company by the industry it was most closely associated with (for instance, General Motors makes locomotives as well as cars, but it seemed most logical to place it in the Motor Vehicles and Related category.) You may wish to refer to several related headings in Part III to find companies that straddle industry categories.

Most of these companies are publicly owned. Some are cooperatives. Many of the privately held companies do not release statistics for revenues. This has been noted where applicable.

Please note: No attempt has been made to analyze whether or not companies actually "practice what they preach" and conduct business by the terms of their mission statements, vision, values, objectives, goals, etc. That is an entirely different kind of book. My intention here is to focus on the nature and content of the mission statement genre and provide a reference resource for people attempting to write a statement for their company or organization.

COMPANY | *Ace Hardware Corporation*

STATEMENT | Ace Mission Statement

The Ace corporate mission is to be a retail support company… providing independent Ace dealers with quality products, programs and services that focus on retail success. The philosophies of low up-front pricing and highly efficient, productive management will always guide our basic operating decisions.

We are committed to offering the best overall program to Ace retailers. To do so, we must maintain our market share and expand it where possible by supporting our existing dealers, as well as broadening our dealer base, where appropriate.

We also are committed to understanding the dynamics of retailing, the effects of intense competition, and the importance of improving communication with Ace dealers. We are here to serve the Ace dealer, we know our success is based on our independent retailer's success, and we are committed to that success.

ADDRESS   2200 Kensington Ct.
Oak Brook, IL 60521

INDUSTRY CATEGORY   Retail

CORPORATE DESCRIPTION

Ace Hardware Corporation operates as a wholesaler of hardware and related products, and manufactures paint products. As a dealer-owned cooperative, Ace sells its products retail to the public through 4,100 individual retailers who own 5,000 Ace stores.

SIZE REVENUES $2,018,000,000 (gross sales) as of 1993

NUMBER OF EMPLOYEES   3,405 as of 1993

SOURCE   *1993 Annual Report*

◆ ◆ ◆ ◆ ◆ ◆ ◆

COMPANY | *Adia Personnel Services*

STATEMENT | Vision
Passion for quality.
Dedication to innovation.
Commitment to employees.

| Goal
To translate Adia's vision into increased market share, long-term profitability and employee loyalty.

| Mission Statement
Adia will be recognized as the industry leader by consistently providing service excellence to our customers. We will be our clients' first choice for personnel services.

Adia will be known as the easiest personnel services company to do business with. We are committed to removing barriers between us and our customers.

Adia will be identified as a company which improves client productivity by providing highly skilled temporary and full-time workers.

Adia will be perceived as the preferred company to work for in the industry. Our commitment to management and staff autonomy, extensive training, internal promotions and generous benefits will translate into unparalleled ownership and pride by our employees. These programs will result in high staff retention, positive morale and exceptional company loyalty.

Adia will provide franchisees with a high level of support resulting in an appreciation of their Adia affiliation and recognition of the value of services provided by Adia. Adia will actively solicit franchisees' advice and suggestions.

Adia will be regarded as the industry leader for innovation throughout its operations. We will integrate successful industry traditions with progressive programs and management.

Adia will attract and retain the highest level of temporary employees by providing benefits and programs customized for the unique requirements of this segment of our work force. Worker satisfaction will result in outstanding Adia representation.

Adia will achieve significant market share while consistently producing operating results and profits that exceed industry norms.

ADDRESS   100 Redwood Shores Parkway
                Redwood City, CA 94065

INDUSTRY CATEGORY   Business Services

CORPORATE DESCRIPTION
Adia is in the personnel services business, providing temporary and full-time workers.

SIZE REVENUES   Not available

NUMBER OF EMPLOYEES   Not available

SOURCE   Company representative

COMPANY | *Advest, Inc.*

STATEMENT

Advest's mission is to be the best at helping people build wealth, primarily toward retirement, through the highest quality, most effective professionals in the industry.

ADDRESS 280 Trumbull St.
Hartford, CT 06103

INDUSTRY CATEGORY Financial, Investment Services

CORPORATE DESCRIPTION

Advest, Inc., one of the country's leading regional investment brokerage firms, is a subsidiary of The Advest Group, Inc., a diversified, publicly-traded financial services firm. Through a network of some 90 offices in 17 states and the District of Columbia, Advest offers a comprehensive range of investment products and services to individuals, business owners and corporations.

SIZE REVENUES $202,031,000 as of 1993

NUMBER OF EMPLOYEES 1,600 as of October 15, 1994

SOURCE *1993 Annual Report*

STATEMENT | **Airborne Express
Statement of Values**

Airborne Express is its people, teamed to satisfy the world-wide shipment and delivery needs of their customers. Every employee is an important and valued member of the Airborne team. Each strives to perform with excellence and to ensure reliable, economical, quality service. All take pride in being the industry's premier provider of customer satisfaction, in fact and by reputation.

Airborne Values are the foundation for the corporate drive to excel.

Customer satisfaction is the top priority of every employee and the purpose of every job. Cost effective ongoing achievement of customer satisfaction is the foundation of our business.

◈ ❖ ◈

Strategies, goals and objectives, established to ensure consistent customer satisfaction, corporate financial health, and employee development and support, are clearly defined, communicated and understood.

◈ ❖ ◈

Management believes in, promotes and pursues excellence through-out the organization. Excellence is expected in the quality and quantity of work done by every employee in every function, both for our customers and our fellow employees. "Doing it right the first time" is the dominant pattern in every activity.

◈ ◈ ◈

Initiative and ingenuity applied to the conduct of business and the resolution of problems are encouraged and supported throughout the organization.

⟡ ✦ ❦

The roles and responsibilities of every employee are clearly defined. Aggressive cooperative fulfillment on behalf of our customers and in support of Airborne strategies and goals is valued and commendable.

✦ ❦ ⟡

Reward structures recognize contribution to and achievement of results that enhance customer satisfaction, improve cost effectiveness and strengthen profitability.

✦ ❦ ⟡

The outcomes of living the Airborne Values are:

Quality service for our customers.
A rewarding work environment for our people.
Adequate return to our shareholders.

ADDRESS   3101 Western Ave.
P. O. Box 662
Seattle, WA 98111

INDUSTRY CATEGORY   Package Delivery Service

CORPORATE DESCRIPTION
Airborne Express provides door-to-door express delivery of small packages and documents throughout the United States and to most foreign countries. The company also acts as an international and domestic freight forwarder for shipments of any size. Most of the company's domestic shipments are transported on its own airline and fleet of ground transportation vehicles through its company-owned airport and central sorting facility in Wilmington, Ohio. Airborne Express' responsibility begins with pickup at point of origin and extends through delivery to the consignee. Throughout all transactions, the customer has access to progress reports every step of the way.

SIZE REVENUES $1,719,981,000 as of 1993

NUMBER OF EMPLOYEES   15,774 as of 1993

SOURCES   *1992 Annual Report, 1993 Annual Report,* company representative

◆ ◆ ◆ ◆ ◆ ◆ ◆

COMPANY | *Alliant Techsystems, Inc.*

STATEMENT | Mission

The mission of Alliant Techsystems is to be the leading supplier of defense products and services to the U. S. government and its allies. We will:

❖ Be an outstanding employer

❖ Lead in the markets we serve

❖ Continuously improve the quality of everything we do

❖ Be a positive force in the communities where we live and work

And by so doing, we will achieve customer satisfaction, superior financial performance, and enhanced shareholder value.

ADDRESS   600 Second St. NE
Hopkins, MN 55343-8384

INDUSTRY CATEGORY   Industrial, Specialized

CORPORATE DESCRIPTION

Alliant Techsystems' businesses have supplied high-quality defense products and systems to the U. S. government and its allies for more than 50 years. Today, the company ranks as the largest munitions supplier to the U. S. Department of Defense and the world's leading developer and manufacturer of lightweight torpedoes.

SIZE REVENUES $775,329,000 as of 1994

NUMBER OF EMPLOYEES   4,900 as of 1994

SOURCE   *1994 Annual Report*

◆ ◆ ◆ ◆ ◆ ◆ ◆

COMPANY | *Allied Signal Inc.*

STATEMENT | **Our Vision**

We will be one of the world's premier companies, distinctive and successful in everything we do.

Our Commitment

We will become a Total Quality Company by continuously improving all our work processes to satisfy our internal and external customers.

Our Values

CUSTOMERS Our first priority is to satisfy customers.
INTEGRITY We are committed to the highest level of ethical conduct wherever we operate. We obey all laws, produce safe products, protect the environment, practice equal employment, and are socially responsible.

PEOPLE We help our fellow employees improve their skills, encourage them to take risks, treat them fairly, and recognize their accomplishments, stimulating them to approach their jobs with passion and commitment.

TEAMWORK We build trust and worldwide teamwork with open, candid communications up and down and across our organization. We share technologies and best practices, and team with our suppliers and customers.

SPEED We focus on speed for competitive advantage. We simplify processes and compress cycle times.

INNOVATION We accept change as the rule, not the exception, and drive it by encouraging creativity and striving for technical leadership.

PERFORMANCE We encourage high expectations, set ambitious goals, and meet our financial and other commitments. We strive to be the best in the world.

ADDRESS   101 Columbia Rd.
Morristown, NJ 07962-1057

INDUSTRY CATEGORY   Industrial, Specialized

CORPORATE DESCRIPTION
Allied Signal Inc. manufactures a variety of specialized materials for the Aerospace, Automotive, and Engineered Materials markets serving the needs of consumer, military and commercial customers. Allied has more than 400 facilities in the United States and 40 other countries and territories.

SIZE REVENUES $11,827,000,000 as of 1993

NUMBER OF EMPLOYEES   86,400 as of 1993

SOURCE   *1993 Annual Report*

COMPANY | *American Protective Services, Inc.*

STATEMENT | **American Protective Services, Inc.**
Company Philosophy

QUALITY SERVICE

To provide the finest service that money can buy, yet still be affordable to our market.

STANDARDS OF ETHICS

To conduct ourselves with unfailing commitment to the highest ethical and professional standards. To always treat others as we would like to be treated.

OUR MOST IMPORTANT RESOURCE

To place maximum emphasis on our uniformed personnel...our most important resource. To keep the profit motive of our free enterprise system in harmony with the needs of our people, and when necessary, to err in favor of human considerations rather than monetary ones.

PROFESSIONAL DEVELOPMENT

To provide good jobs for our people; jobs that are challenging, but safe, and that provide a realistic expectation of career development.

REASONABLE PROFIT

To realize a reasonable profit for all our hard work and for the risks that we assume in providing our service.

JOB SATISFACTION

To be proud that we have given our work our best effort and had fun along the way.

ADDRESS   7770 Pardee Ln.
Oakland, CA 94621-1454

INDUSTRY CATEGORY   Security

CORPORATE DESCRIPTION

American Protective Services is a privately-held contract security company. It provides security officers for a wide variety of businesses, including ships, warehouses, shopping centers, high-rise office buildings, hospitals, airports, construction projects, radio, television and motion picture studios, hotels, country clubs, residential communities, hi-tech and research facilities, government and public utilities, factories, and retail stores.

Their business is to assist their clients in theft prevention, access control, safety and a host of other essential services.

SIZE REVENUES $251,000,000+ as of 1993

NUMBER OF EMPLOYEES 13,000+ as of 1993

SOURCE Company representative

◆ ◆ ◆ ◆ ◆ ◆ ◆

COMPANY | *American United Life Insurance Company*

STATEMENT | **Mission Statement**

AUL's mission is to take care of people and their concerns about financial security. AUL provides peace of mind by sheltering its customers from the risk of loss caused by premature death, sickness, disability or outliving financial resources after retirement.

AUL's mission is to be a financially strong mutual insurance company that provides quality products and services to its customers. AUL is organized into four product divisions—Group, Individual, Pensions and Reinsurance—to best meet the insurance needs of individuals and businesses by offering life, health and annuity products.

ADDRESS P.O. Box 368
Indianapolis, IN 46206-0368

INDUSTRY CATEGORY Insurance

CORPORATE DESCRIPTION

American United Life Insurance Company® is a mutual company with headquarters in Indianapolis. It was founded in 1877 and currently is licensed to sell in 45 states and the District of Columbia.

AUL has $5.7 billion in assets and is a diversified company with four major product lines.

SIZE REVENUES $1,102,600,000 as of 1993

NUMBER OF EMPLOYEES 1,000 as of November, 1994

SOURCES *1993 Annual Report*; company representative

COMPANY | *Ameritas Life Insurance Corp.*

STATEMENT | Ameritas Vision Statement

Ameritas is, and will remain, among the most financially secure insurance companies in America. Building on this strength, we will consistently achieve competitive returns on surplus from diversified revenue streams from national and regional sources.

We will achieve this goal by enhancing our four core businesses that we are committed to, Individual, Group, Pension and Investment, and by entering related businesses that reinforce our core businesses and provide superior returns.

We are committed to providing products and exemplary service that are valuable to our customers.

Our strategies will build on the competitive strengths that distinguish Ameritas:

—more than a century of service to the public
—financial strength and relative size
—breadth of products and services
—multiple distribution channels
—investment and fiduciary skills

We will be progressive and market-oriented, providing quality products that fulfill customer needs. We will operate efficiently through distinct businesses, targeting specific market segments with defined strategies and coordinated activities. We will emphasize accountability and reward accomplishment, while stressing ethical behavior. We will continue Ameritas' tradition of social responsibility.

We will always act in the long-term interests of our policyowners.

We will measure our performance by sustaining balanced growth of earnings and revenues and by our competitive rankings.

Our greatest assets are our customers and our people who serve them. We are dedicated to both, and proud of our tradition of providing quality products and services, acting with integrity, and helping our customers achieve financial security.

ADDRESS   5900 O St.
PO Box 81889
Lincoln, NE 68501

INDUSTRY CATEGORY   Insurance

CORPORATE DESCRIPTION
Ameritas Life Insurance Corp. is a mutual company offering a full line of life insurance, pensions and group dental insurance. In 1993, the corporation had assets of $1.9 billion.

SIZE REVENUES $26,900,000 (net income) as of 1993

NUMBER OF EMPLOYEES   850 as of November 1, 1994

SOURCES   *1993 Annual Report*; company representative

◆　◆　◆　◆　◆　◆　◆

COMPANY | *Ameritech*

STATEMENT | **Our Vision**
Ameritech will be the world's premier provider of full-service communications for people at work, at home or on the move. Our goal will be to improve the quality of life for individuals and to increase the competitive effectiveness of the businesses we serve.

As we move and manage information for our customers, we will set standards for value and quality.

Ameritech's competence will reach worldwide, building on our strength in America's vibrant upper Midwest. Customers can be assured that we will assume no task we cannot do exceedingly well.

ADDRESS   30 S. Wacker Dr.
Chicago, IL 60606

INDUSTRY CATEGORY   Telecommunications

CORPORATE DESCRIPTION
Ameritech is one of the world's leading information companies, providing full service communications and advanced information services to about 12 million customers in the Midwest. Ameritech also has operations in New Zealand, Poland and other international markets.

SIZE REVENUES $11,710,400,000 as of 1993

NUMBER OF EMPLOYEES   67,192 as of 1993

SOURCE   *1993 Annual Report*

◆ ◆ ◆ ◆ ◆ ◆ ◆

COMPANY | *AMETEK Inc.*

STATEMENT | **AMETEK'S Mission**
To achieve enhanced, long-term shareholder value by building a strong operating company serving diversified markets to earn a superior return on assets and to generate growth in cash flow.

❖ Succeed with the shareholder value enhancement plan, including reducing the cost of capital with debt levels consistent with AMETEK's strong cash flow.

❖ Realize over the long term a 30% Return on Assets (Operating Profit divided by Assets) for all operating businesses.

❖ Optimize cash flow for investment in growth and debt reduction.

❖ Build competitive advantages by investing in the growth of current businesses to evolve and extend core products and manufacturing technologies into new products, niche markets and new applications.

❖ Continue to apply Total Quality Management throughout the Company to nurture new product development, manage change and continual improvement, and make cost reductions an integral part of planning and control.

❖ Capitalize on the competitive advantages of floor care, specialty metals and water filtration products. Build on unique advantages in other product lines and other niche markets.

❖ Multiply the benefit of operational resources with a global market expansion, especially in Europe and the Pacific Rim. Employ strategic alliances and joint ventures to manage risk, especially for international growth.

❖ Maintain a flat, decentralized organization focused on the customer. Seek business synergies that create strength and reduce costs.

❖ Link incentive compensation with qualitative and quantitative business performance.

ADDRESS   Corporate Office
Station Square
Paoli, PA 19301

INDUSTRY CATEGORY   Manufacturing

CORPORATE DESCRIPTION
AMETEK designs, builds and sells:

- ❧ Motors for vacuum cleaners, furnaces, electric lawn tools, computers and business machines;
- ❧ Water filtration systems for home, commercial and industrial use;
- ❧ High-purity metal in strip and powder form for electronics and telecommunications industry;
- ❧ Instruments for aerospace, automotive, manufacturing, utility and petrochemical industries.

SIZE REVENUES $732,000,000 (net sales) as of 1993

NUMBER OF EMPLOYEES   6,100 (worldwide) as of 1993

SOURCES   *1993 Annual Report*; company representative

◆ ◆ ◆ ◆ ◆ ◆ ◆

COMPANY | **AMP Incorporated**

STATEMENT | **OUR MISSION**
AMP Incorporated is in the business of designing, manufacturing, marketing and selling interconnection components, subassemblies and services for electrical, electronic and optical applications. These are supplied both direct to customers and through distributors and subcontractors.

AMP's customer base includes original equipment manufacturers and businesses which install and maintain electrical and electronic equipment throughout the world.

AMP's business is customer-driven, technology-influenced and engineering-oriented, coupled with world-class manufacturing.

In order to achieve the core company goals, various business units have been created. These business units consist of sectors, groups, divisions, departments, companies and strategic alliances, which have the responsibility for developing cohesive missions, quantifiable objectives and comprehensive strategies through adopting the guiding principles within the following key result areas:

Total Customer Satisfaction
Continuous Quality Improvement
Human Resource Excellence
Growth
Profitability
Cost Reduction
Innovation/Technological Leadership
Public Responsibility/Corporate Citizenship

OUR VISION

We share a vision of AMP Incorporated as a Worldwide Team of People who are:

Motivated to pursue the path to excellence through continuous improvement in all that we do.

Empowered to think globally and act locally as we address the true needs of our markets.

Inspired to provide our customers with products and services so outstanding that we will be the supplier of choice.

OUR VALUES

At AMP we believe in...

Earning our leadership position in the interconnection industry by continuing to develop innovative products and services and by meeting and surpassing our customers' expectations.

Maintaining steadfast commitment to excellence in every product and every service we provide as a means of earning the confidence and loyalty of our customers.

Serving our customers' global needs by offering them our foundation of worldwide support.

Encouraging personal and team ownership of problem identification, prevention, and solution.

Creating a climate of trust and respect that empowers our people to develop to the fullest, while sharing the responsibilities of success and the rewards of achievement.

Keeping each individual and function informed about AMP, its customers, suppliers, and competitors.

Forming lasting, mutually beneficial relationships with our customers and suppliers, based on fairness and integrity.

Achieving the growth and profit that guarantee our financial stability and competitive strength to maximize the long-term return to shareholders.

Fulfilling our responsibilities as a good corporate citizen by being a positive, powerful force in our communities worldwide and helping conserve our natural environment.

ADDRESS   P. O. Box 3608
Harrisburg, PA 17105-3608

INDUSTRY CATEGORY   Electronics

CORPORATE DESCRIPTION
The world leader in electrical/electronic connection devices, AMP supplies well over 100,000 types of and sizes of devices to 200,000 electrical/electronic equipment makers—and tens of thousands of customers who install and maintain equipment. AMP has 160 facilities in 32 countries.

SIZE REVENUES $3,451,000,000 as of 1993

NUMBER OF EMPLOYEES   26,900 (worldwide) as of 1993

SOURCES   *1992 Annual Report*, "The Fortune 500," *Fortune* 129, no. 8 (April 8, 1994)

◆   ◆   ◆   ◆   ◆   ◆   ◆

COMPANY | *AMR Corporation (American Airlines)*

STATEMENT | **AMR Corporate Vision**
We will be the global market leader in air transportation and related information services.
That leadership will be attained by:
   ❖ Setting the industry standard for safety and security.
   ❖ Providing world class customer service.
   ❖ Creating an open and participative work environment which seeks positive change, rewards innovation, and provides growth, security and opportunity to all employees.
   ❖ Producing consistently superior financial returns for shareholders.

ADDRESS   P. O. Box 619616
Dallas/Fort Worth Airport
Dallas, TX 75261-9616

INDUSTRY CATEGORY   Transportation

CORPORATE DESCRIPTION
AMR Corporation is the parent company of American Airlines. One of the largest scheduled passenger airlines in the world, American provides jet service to approximately 180 destinations worldwide.

SIZE REVENUES $15,820,000,000 as of 1993

NUMBER OF EMPLOYEES 118,422 as of May, 1994

SOURCE Company representative

◆　◆　◆　◆　◆　◆　◆

COMPANY | *Anheuser-Busch Companies, Inc.*

STATEMENT

[Author's note: The following Mission Statement from Anheuser-Busch was its Statement through 1993. In 1994, the company revised the Statement. However, it was not available at the time this manuscript went to press. I am presenting the current version because it merits your attention for its structure, language, tone, breadth, and spirit.]

A Mission Statement for Anheuser-Busch Companies, Inc.

This mission statement clarifies the direction and general goals of Anheuser-Busch Companies, enabling employees at all levels to better understand their company and the role they play in its success. Additionally, by looking beyond any one product or operating company, this statement provides a reference point from which specific business strategies can be assessed and progress can be measured.

In the broadest sense, our field of competition is the leisure industry. Our place in that industry is clear...

❖ Beer is our core business and always will be.

❖ Other businesses complementary to beer will be needed over the long-term to maintain our status as a growth company.

BEER

Our goals are to:

❖ Maintain our reputation for the highest quality products and services in the brewing industry.

❖ Market our products aggressively, successfully and responsibly. At no time will we encourage the abusive consumption of our products, or their consumption by minors.

❖ Sustain and enhance our competitive position within the United States through continued market share growth.

❖ Increase our share of global brewing industry sales through our historic emphasis on quality products, and by adapting our marketing and distribution expertise to meet the cultural demands of the local marketplace.

COMPANY | *Aztech Controls Corporation*

STATEMENT | **Vision Statement**

To be recognized by our customers, vendors, and employees as the industry leader.

Mission Statement

To exceed our goals by embracing the changes in technology and distribution that results in growth and reinvestment.

Guiding Principles

♦ Integrity is the foundation of our business
♦ Anticipate and create new ways to add value
♦ Teamwork is vital throughout our company
♦ Quality is what the customer states it is

DIVERSIFICATION EFFORTS

Our goals are to:

❖ Broaden the business base of our company and maintain its strong growth trends by successfully developing opportunities in the entertainment, packaging and food products industries.

❖ Focus on businesses that permit us to earn a premium on our investment by providing superior products and services; that have substantial room for financial and market share growth; that complement our beer business, and that are compatible with our existing corporate culture.

❖ Rely on technical expertise, investment spending and careful management to achieve and maintain the position

♦ Change is essential for our growth
♦ Empower all employees to manager
♦ Customer relations
♦ Vendor relationships
♦ Commitment to profitable growth and reinvestment
♦ Commitment to employee personal well being

CORPORATE DESCRIPTION

Aztech Controls is an industrial distributor in the valve and fitting business. Aztech's 1994 revenues are $10 million and they have 32 employees.

ADDRESS   2451 W. Birchwood Ave., Ste. 101
Mesa, AZ 85202

SOURCE   Company representative

of low-cost-producer in commodity businesses which we have entered to support our brewing operations.

❖ Provide approximately one-third of our company's earnings, including financial contributions from international brewing, by the end of this century.

STAKEHOLDERS

In discharging our responsibility to the various stakeholders we serve, Anheuser-Busch must translate its business strategies to more specific objectives. Our goals are to provide:

❖ Our **employees** at all levels with satisfying and financially rewarding work, and with continuing opportunities for personal development and advancement.

❖ Our **shareholders** with a superior return on their investment in our company.

❖ Our **consumers** with premium quality products and services that have the highest value-to-cost ratio in their category.

❖ Our **wholesalers** with a commitment to our ongoing and mutually beneficial relationship, including opportunities for profitable growth, supporting services and financing.

❖ Our **suppliers** with the opportunity for a long-term relationship built on open negotiations to provide state-of-the-art products and services capable of meeting our quality standards at the lowest possible price.

❖ Our **society** with an exemplary demonstration of corporate social responsibility and good citizenship in all areas, but with particular attention to the reduction of alcohol abuse through research and education, the protection of our environment, and the full integration of all peoples into the life of our nation.

ADDRESS One Busch Pl.
St. Louis, MO 63118-1852

INDUSTRY CATEGORY   Food/Beverage

CORPORATE DESCRIPTION
Anheuser-Busch Companies, Inc., is a St. Louis-based diversified corporation whose subsidiaries include the world's largest brewing organization, the country's second-largest producer of fresh-baked goods and the country's second-largest theme park operator.

SIZE REVENUES $11,505,300,000 (net sales) as of 1993

NUMBER OF EMPLOYEES   43,345 as of 1993

SOURCES   *1993 Annual Report;* company representative

◆　◆　◆　◆　◆　◆　◆

COMPANY | *ANTHONY INDUSTRIES, INC.*

STATEMENT | Mission Statement

Anthony Industries is dedicated to the continuous improvement of all products and services to meet our customers' needs, allowing us to prosper as a business and to provide an attractive return for our stockholders, the owners of our business.

Improvement of products and services will be accomplished by focusing on the processes that make up our business and through the involvement of all employees to help with the improvement of these processes.

We will strive to provide innovative and improved products and services to our customers by understanding their requirements and anticipating their future needs.

We recognize that our people are our most valuable resource. We are committed to providing training and fostering a work environment of teamwork and shared values that will allow our objective of continuous improvement to be achieved.

We will endeavor to be a good corporate citizen at all times by engaging in activities that have a positive social and economic impact on the communities in which we work and the world at large.

ADDRESS   4900 S. Eastern Ave., Ste. 200
Los Angeles, CA 90040

INDUSTRY CATEGORY   Manufacturing

CORPORATE DESCRIPTION
Anthony Industries and its subsidiaries manufacture and sell recreational and industrial products. The recreational products include alpine and nordic skis and apparel; athletic jackets; imprintable shirts and bowling shirts; personal flotation devices; construction of residential concrete swimming pools; manufacture of swimming pool equipment and covers; mountain bikes; rods, reels and other fishing tackle items. Industrial products include the manufacture and sale of extruded monofilament used by the paperweaving industry and for cutting line, fishing line and sewing thread; fiberglass marine antennas, communication and navigation equipment and light poles; and laminated and coated paperboard products.

SIZE REVENUES $431,640,000 (net sales) as of 1993

NUMBER OF EMPLOYEES   Not available

SOURCE   *1993 Annual Report*

COMPANY | *Applied Materials, Inc.*

STATEMENT | Mission

To be the world's largest supplier of semiconductor wafer processing systems and services worldwide through product innovations and enhancement of customer productivity.

| **Values and Vision Statement**

Close to Customer
More than technology, customers define our accomplishments.

Achievement Oriented
Aggressive goals and meeting commitments drive our success.

Respect for the Individual
Mutual trust and respect are shared by all.

Honesty and Integrity
Honesty and integrity are essential for building trust.

Teamwork
Effectiveness increases when we exchange ideas and share responsibilities.

Performance and Rewards
Commitment and performance ensure growth.

Professional Management
Professional managers lead employees to translate values into action.

Excellence and Quality
Every task can be continually improved.

Global Awareness
Embracing different perspectives leads to a wealth of opportunities.

Obligations to Stockholders
Return long-term value to our investors.

Positive Social Contribution
Make a meaningful contribution in our communities.

ADDRESS   3050 Bowers Ave.
Santa Clara, CA 95054

INDUSTRY CATEGORY   High Technology

CORPORATE DESCRIPTION
Applied Materials is a global growth company and the largest producer of wafer fabrication systems for the worldwide semiconductor industry.

SIZE REVENUES $1,080,047,000 as of 1993

NUMBER OF EMPLOYEES   4,739 as of 1993

SOURCE *1993 Annual Report*

◆ ◆ ◆ ◆ ◆ ◆ ◆

COMPANY │ *Aristech Chemical Corporation*

STATEMENT │ **ARISTECH CHEMICAL CORPORATION**
STATEMENT OF MISSION
Aristech Chemical Corporation is a diversified producer of chemicals and plastics serving a large number of industrial and consumer firms.

We dedicate our efforts to the responsible development, production, marketing, and delivery of products of the highest quality and uniformity meeting our customers' needs.

In order to meet our obligations to our customers, suppliers, employees, owners and the public, we will continually improve the reliability, uniformity and quality of our resources, products and services.

While doing so, we will also constantly strive to improve health, safety and environmental performance, with sensitivity and responsiveness to public concerns.

(Signed)

Thomas Marshall
Chief Executive Officer
Aristech Chemical Corporation

ADDRESS　　600 Grant St.
　　　　　　　Pittsburgh, PA 15219-2704

INDUSTRY CATEGORY　　Chemicals

CORPORATE DESCRIPTION
Aristech Chemical Corporation is a diversified producer of chemicals and plastics serving a large number of industrial and consumer firms.

SIZE REVENUES　　Not available (privately held)

NUMBER OF EMPLOYEES　　1,800 as of 1993

SOURCE　　"Capabilities" brochure

STATEMENT | **OUR OPERATING PRINCIPLES**

To respect the dignity and inherent rights of the individual human being in all dealings with people.

To maintain high moral and ethical standards and to reflect honesty, integrity, reliability and forthrightness in all relationships.

To reflect the tenets of good taste and common courtesy in all attitudes, words and deeds.

To serve fairly and in proper balance the interests of all groups associated with the business—customers, stockholders, employees, suppliers, community neighbors, government and the general public.

OUR CORPORATE MISSION

We will be a fast and flexible learning organization committed to ever-improving the value of Armstrong for our employees, customers and shareholders.

We will be a world leader in all our businesses by excelling in customer satisfaction, innovation, marketing and manufacturing.

These capabilities, our people, and our commitment to quality will be our global platform for growth.

OUR STRATEGIES FOR SUCCESS

Build a human resource and leadership development program that will assure continuous learning, agile thinking and positive change.

Develop marketing expertise that will give us a competitive advantage year after year.

Forge strong and superior relationships with all our customers.

Improve our process to understand consumers and other end users and to create compelling offers for them.

Invest in the tools of technology and the methods of world-class manufacturing.

Invest in capital, innovation and marketing where returns are in line with our shareholders' expectations.

Seek alliances, products and brands which will gain strength from our capabilities in customer relationships, innovation, marketing and manufacturing.

ADDRESS   P. O. Box 3001
Lancaster, PA 17604-3001

INDUSTRY CATEGORY   Manufacturing

CORPORATE DESCRIPTION
Armstrong is primarily a manufacturer and marketer of interior furnishings. Its products include floor coverings, building products and furniture.

SIZE REVENUES $2,525,400,000 as of 1993

NUMBER OF EMPLOYEES   20,500 as of July, 1994

SOURCE   *1993 Annual Report*

COMPANY | *AT&T Corp.*

STATEMENT | **Mission Statement**
We are dedicated to being the world's best at bringing people together—giving them easy access to each other and to the information and services they want and need—anytime, anywhere.

ADDRESS   32 Avenue of the Americas
New York, NY 10013-2412

INDUSTRY CATEGORY   Telecommunications

CORPORATE DESCRIPTION
AT&T is a global company that provides communications services and products, as well as network equipment and computer systems, to businesses, consumers, telecommunications service providers and government agencies. AT&T Bell Laboratories engages in basic research as well as product and service development. AT&T also offers a general-purpose credit card and financial and leasing services. AT&T does business in some 200 countries.

SIZE REVENUES $67,156,000,000 as of 1993

NUMBER OF EMPLOYEES   308,700 as of 1993

SOURCE   *1993 Annual Report*

COMPANY | *Atlanta Gas Light Company*

STATEMENT | **Our Company's Vision**

Atlanta Gas Light Company will become America's **leading** natural gas and energy services company by being the **provider of choice** for customers, employees, and investors.

To be the provider of choice…Atlanta Gas Light Company must change…

❖ For Customers
—From…Emphasis on regulation…to emphasis on competition
—From….Offering what we think customers want… to providing what customers value

❖ For Employees
—From…Being "good enough"…to being the best
—From…Rewarding for longevity…to rewarding for performance

❖ For Investors
—From…"We have always done it this way"…to "How can it be done better?"
—From…Business as usual…to increasing shareholder value

ADDRESS   P. O. Box 4569
Atlanta, GA 30302

INDUSTRY CATEGORY   Utility

CORPORATE DESCRIPTION

Atlanta Gas Light Company is the largest natural gas distribution company in the southeastern United States, serving more than 1.2 million customers in 228 cities and communities in Georgia.

Through its subsidiary, Chattanooga Gas Company, the Company serves more than 40,000 customers in Chattanooga and Cleveland, Tennessee.

SIZE REVENUES $1,130,300,000 as of 1993

NUMBER OF EMPLOYEES   3,764 as of 1993

SOURCE   *1993 Annual Report*

◆ ◆ ◆ ◆ ◆ ◆ ◆

COMPANY | *Autodesk, Inc.*

STATEMENT | **VISION**
To create software tools that transform ideas into reality.

| **MISSION**
To create quality software solutions and support services that foster innovation, creativity and productivity for customers and partners around the world.

| **PHILOSOPHY/VALUES**
At Autodesk we work to excite and inspire our CUSTOMERS worldwide with INNOVATIVE software that defines the market. We strive to produce the best QUALITY products and processes. We're committed to our employees, customers, partners and vendors, as we consider them an integral part of our business. We are flexible in our approaches, practice responsible risk-taking and learn from our mistakes. We're

alert to PROFITABLE ideas, and are able to forego short-term gain in favor of long-term vitality for our shareholders.

We are direct, clear and ETHICAL in our communication and actions. We will not deceive anyone—not even our competitors. We speak with HONESTY, courage and care. We're accountable for our words, our work and our processes—building a challenging and rewarding work environment.

We RESPECT individuality both inside and outside the corporation, honoring diverse lifestyles and workstyles. We believe our vitality depends on capitalizing on everyone's unique talents. Through collaboration and TEAMWORK we continually create ourselves, our company and our success.

May 1994

ADDRESS   2320 Marinship Way
Sausalito, CA 94965

INDUSTRY CATEGORY   High Technology

CORPORATE DESCRIPTION
Autodesk, Inc. develops, markets and supports a family of design automation and multimedia software products for use on personal computers and workstations. The Company distributes its products primarily through a network of dealers and distributors and has operations in the Americas, Europe and Asia/Pacific.

SIZE REVENUES $405,596,000 (net) as of 1994

NUMBER OF EMPLOYEES   1,788 as of 1994

SOURCE   *1994 Annual Report*

COMPANY | *Avon Products, Inc.*

STATEMENT | **OUR VISION**
To be the Company that best understands and satisfies the
product, service and self-fulfillment needs of women—globally.

ADDRESS   9 W. 57th St.
New York, NY 10019

INDUSTRY CATEGORY   Consumer Goods and Services

CORPORATE DESCRIPTION
Avon is the world's leading direct seller of beauty and related products,
with $4.0 billion in annual revenues. Avon markets to women in more
than 100 countries through 1.7 million independent representatives.

SIZE REVENUES $4,007,600,000 (net sales) as of 1993

NUMBER OF EMPLOYEES   30,000 as of 1993

SOURCE   *1993 Annual Report*

COMPANY | *Baldor Electric Company*

STATEMENT | **TO BE THE BEST, AS DETERMINED BY OUR CUSTOMERS...**

Our mission is: To be the best (as determined by our customers) marketers, designers and manufacturers of electric motors and drives. To achieve this, we must:

❖ Provide better value to our customers than any of our competitors,

❖ Attract and retain competent employees dedicated to reaching our goals and objectives,

❖ Produce good, long-term results for our shareholders.

ADDRESS   P. O. Box 2400
Fort Smith, AR 72902

INDUSTRY CATEGORY   Manufacturing

CORPORATE DESCRIPTION

Baldor Electric Company designs, manufactures and markets a broad line of energy-efficient electric motors and electronic drives. From the home office in Fort Smith, Arkansas, the Company supports the sales offices and warehouses that stock Baldor products worldwide to supply distributors and original equipment manufacturers. Baldor does business in more than 55 countries.

SIZE REVENUES $356,595,000 (net sales) as of 1993

NUMBER OF EMPLOYEES   3,000 as of 1994

SOURCES   *1993 Annual Report*; company representative

COMPANY | *Ball Corporation*

STATEMENT | **"The Company's Mission"**

Ball Corporation's mission, as a manufacturing and services company, is to provide consistent customer value through competitive levels of technology, quality and service, while maintaining high standards of integrity, ethical conduct and social responsibility.

| **THE COMPANY'S OBJECTIVE**

Ball Corporation's overall objective is to maximize long-term shareholder wealth by providing an attractive total return to investors in the form of dividends and increase in share price.

ADDRESS   345 S. High St.
P.O. Box 2407
Muncie, IN 47307-0407

INDUSTRY CATEGORY   Manufacturing

CORPORATE DESCRIPTION

Ball Corporation manufactures metal and glass containers for the beverage and food industries and provides aerospace and communications systems to government and commercial customers.

The company produces metal beverage containers and ends for brewers and softdrink fillers plus metal cans and ends for food processors. Glass containers are manufactured, primarily for the food, juice, wine and liquor markets. Also, light-gauge steel is slit, cut, coated and lithographed, primarily for the food can market.

Ball serves the electro-optics and cryogenics, space and systems engineering and telecommunications products markets through its aerospace and communications segment.

SIZE REVENUES $2,440,900,000 as of December 31, 1993

NUMBER OF EMPLOYEES 13,954 as of December 31, 1993

SOURCE *1993 Annual Report*

◆ ◆ ◆ ◆ ◆ ◆ ◆

COMPANY | *Banta Corporation*

STATEMENT | **BANTA CORPORATE MISSION**
Banta Corporation, a leader in the graphic communications industry, provides quality printing and other image services to publishers, merchandisers and consumer products companies. The vitality of this business depends upon providing targeted products and services on a timely basis, in a quality manner, at a competitive value.

Banta's very existence depends on providing superior products and services to customers. Banta businesses serve a broad spectrum of graphic communication needs for educational, general book and magazine publishers, and for advertising, catalog, other direct marketing and consumer products companies. The Corporation delivers professionalism, accuracy, timeliness, quality products, appropriate technology and value. It has built credibility, relationships and reputation that distinguish it from the competition. Banta will not knowingly compromise its value by promulgating inappropriate graphics or content.

As a publicly owned corporation, Banta's ultimate responsibility is to its shareholders. Banta's goal, in this regard, is to earn a superior return on investment through profit improvement and growth. Corporate focus and strategic positioning consistent with prudent yet aggressive asset management create the value placed on Banta common stock in the securities market.

Banta's success depends on honest, thoughtful, hard-working people who work as a team and are dedicated to the importance of setting and achieving higher goals. Banta feels a deep, personal responsibility to all its associates and will reward employees commensurate with their contributions to the success of the business. As an equal opportunity employer, it seeks to create and maintain an environment where every person has the opportunity to reach his or her potential.

Banta is committed to honesty and integrity in its relationship with suppliers of raw materials, goods and services. The Corporation evaluates suppliers on the basis of quality, price, service and innovation.

Banta encourages associates to become involved in activities that make their communities a better place to live and do business. Support of worthwhile projects in areas where the Corporation operates enhances the general health, education and well-being of the communities. Banta's Corporate Foundation selectively supports national, regional and community civic and cultural activities and educational institutions.

Banta Corporation's stated objective is to perform at superior levels. Profit increases the value of shareholder's investment and is essential to business reinvestment and employee security. Growth is necessary to provide opportunities on an ever-increasing scale for all associates. Banta Corporation, therefore, is committed to achieving profitable growth.

ADDRESS   225 Main St., River Place
P. O. Box 8003
Menasha, WI 54952-8003

INDUSTRY CATEGORY   Media/Printing/Publishing

CORPORATE DESCRIPTION
Banta Corporation is one of North America's leading providers of printing and graphic services. It serves publishers of educational and general books, special-interest magazines, consumer and business catalogs, and direct marketing materials. Its other businesses offer pre-press services, computer software packages, multimedia kits, point-of-purchase displays, product labels, postage stamps and single-use products.

SIZE REVENUES $691,244,000 (net sales) as of 1993

NUMBER OF EMPLOYEES   4,204 as of December, 1993

SOURCE   *1993 Annual Report*

COMPANY | *Bard (C. R. Bard, Inc.)*

STATEMENT | **MISSION**
Bard's Mission is to be the most respected worldwide health care company by profitably developing, manufacturing and marketing outcome-based health care products and exceeding the quality, integrity and service expectations of our customers. In the execution of this Mission, Bard will create opportunities for its employees, be a respected community citizen and optimize shareholder value.

ADDRESS   730 Central Ave.
Murray Hill, NJ 07974

INDUSTRY CATEGORY   Health Care

CORPORATE DESCRIPTION
C. R. Bard, Inc. is a leading multinational developer, manufacturer and marketer of health care products. Bard holds strong positions in cardiovascular, urological and surgical products.

SIZE REVENUES $970,800,000 as of 1993

NUMBER OF EMPLOYEES   8,450 as of 1993

SOURCE   *1993 Annual Report*

COMPANY | *Barnett Banks, Inc.*

STATEMENT | **MISSION STATEMENT**

The mission of Barnett is to create value for its owners, customers and employees as a major financial services provider in the United States.

We will strengthen our position in existing markets by providing a full range of financial services, by acquiring other financial institutions, and by capitalizing on our market knowledge and our commitment to entrepreneurial market ownership.

Our focus will be on satisfying our customers' total financial needs by offering differentiated benefits driven by a sales and service process that solidifies and expands the total customer relationship.

Barnett will aggressively pursue diversified income opportunities which include internal initiatives, acquisitions, and alliances in attractive markets throughout the country which complement, leverage, and expand our core capabilities.

By the year 2000, Barnett will be a fully diversified financial services organization with the acknowledged leadership position in the evolving banking business in its markets and with a diversified group of other financial businesses throughout the nation.

ADDRESS 50 North Laura St.
P. O. Box 40789
Jacksonville, FL 32203-0789

INDUSTRY CATEGORY Banking

CORPORATE DESCRIPTION
Barnett Banks, Inc. operates 616 banking offices in Florida and Georgia. With $38 billion assets, it is the leading financial institution in Florida and the 22nd-largest in the United States.

SIZE REVENUES $421,000,000 (net income) as of 1993

NUMBER OF EMPLOYEES   18,400 as of June 30, 1994

SOURCE   *1993 Annual Report*

◆ ◆ ◆ ◆ ◆ ◆ ◆

COMPANY | *Bausch & Lomb Incorporated*

STATEMENT
(From the company booklet entitled "The Values We Share at Bausch & Lomb")

Value Defined
val'ue (val'yoo) n.—
belief, principle or conviction that has fundamental worth to people. For instance, loyalty to one's family is a value many share. Honesty or sincerity is another common value.

The Importance of Values
The concept of values is vital in most areas of society. Our standards of behavior, even our laws, spring from our values. If we accept certain values as important, then we will strive to protect and defend them, even when they are rejected or ignored by others.

Shared values bind the members of a group together. Individual and group activities are thus directed along a common path. Values jointly shared also provide a framework for making decisions, encourage constructive patterns of behavior and define avenues for personal and business success.

The Role of Values at Bausch & Lomb

At Bausch & Lomb, we've inherited a strong company whose values have shaped a tradition of excellence and quality that spans more than 135 years. A clear understanding of those values will help us meet the obligation we have to preserve and enhance what we have inherited, especially the Bausch & Lomb name and all that it represents. It also enables us to pass on a company that continues to reach its highest potential for future generations of employees and shareholders.

Although our company operates in an ever-changing environment, our values remain constant. They don't shift with time or circumstance. They don't yield to whim or convenience. They apply to all areas of our business. Bausch & Lomb's values are clearest when viewed in relation to these elements: customers and quality; employees; profits; innovation; and community.

We'll discuss these areas in the pages to follow.

The Importance of Customers & Quality

The trust, respect and loyalty of customers worldwide is vital to Bausch & Lomb's long-term success. We earn and maintain these attributes by making conformance to customer's expectations our number one priority, as expressed in two ways.

❖ First, we totally commit ourselves to our customers, including those within the company, by identifying their expectations; remaining attuned and responding to changing demands; developing relationships based on trust and mutual respect; and by assuming a leadership role in advancing their knowledge and skills and championing the success of their activities or business.

❖ Second, we pursue quality as a way of life at Bausch & Lomb. Quality is more than a word used to describe our products and services. It's an attitude that affects everything we do. Since 1853, Bausch & Lomb products have been known throughout the world for their quality. To continue this tradition we will:

❖ Require strict attention to quality in every department and every functional area, at all levels.

❖ Provide the highest quality products and services.

❖ Select suppliers according to their quality and total cost, not just price.

Our commitment to our customers and to quality is constant and consistent. We define Quality as consistently conforming to the expectations of our Customers.

A Partnership with Employees

Bausch & Lomb's employees are the company's most important corporate resource. Their efforts produce more than products and services—they produce the company's success and lead it towards the future. Bausch & Lomb and its

COMPANY | *BYERS & HAPPEL IOWA REALTY*

STATEMENT

To be market dominant in Eastern Iowa through an elite team of professionals setting new standards for ethics, service and accomplishment.

employees have a partnership, built upon mutual trust and respect. To maintain this relationship, the company and the employee must be committed to upholding certain principles...on every level, worldwide.

The first and most important principle is that every employee's contribution is valuable. Each individual is necessary to the success of the company as a whole.

In recognition of that principle, we are committed to helping each employee reach his or her full potential by providing job opportunities and salary advancement on the basis of merit, without bias or discrimination of any kind. We are further committed to diversity throughout the company, and to implementing specific programs to increase the representation of women and minorities, especially in senior management.

As individuals, we must be committed to upholding high standards of personal conduct at work and to carrying out our responsibilities in the best possible manner. In addition, we must treat our fellow employees with trust, respect and dignity.

We are committed to encouraging creativity and initiative by providing an environment for all employees to develop

CORPORATE DESCRIPTION
Byers & Happel Iowa Realty is an Iowa real estate company with more than 145 Realtors®.

ADDRESS   211 First Ave. S.E.
                Cedar Rapids, IA 52401

SOURCE   Company representative

skills and abilities. As individuals, we are asked to contribute ideas and suggestions continually to seek a better way to improve the company, its products and its work methods.

As partners, the company and employees must be sensitive to each other's needs and concerns. We believe in recognizing the achievements of individual employees and in compensating employees fairly. We will recognize employees' concerns for employment continuity by making layoffs and position eliminations measures of last resort.

Together, we will support a positive image of Bausch & Lomb in its worldwide community. We will also show sensitivity to the needs of the company's customers at all times.

Finally, the company and employees, as partners, will join together to make Bausch & Lomb a safe, healthy place to work.

The Role of Profits

Bausch & Lomb is in business to make a profit. That is the only way the company can pay its employees a fair wage, provide an attractive return to shareholders, and invest in future growth. It is also the only way the company can sustain itself to carry out its business mission and citizenship responsibilities.

The company has become known in recent years for high standards of growth and profitability. The company will be managed with the intent of maintaining such high standards, and management and employees will be challenged to contribute toward these goals.

Although we remain focused on the need to maximize performance, Bausch & Lomb will balance its needs for current earnings with its desire for consistent long-term growth. The company will not mortgage its future for the sake of short-term gain.

Innovation and Finding a Better Way

Innovation and creativity are essential catalysts for Bausch & Lomb's future success. Our search for new products and services, and for business methods which better meet the needs of our customers must reach into every sector of our company.

Bausch & Lomb is committed to encouraging the teamwork, initiative and entrepreneurial spirit which fosters innovation, and to nurturing emerging businesses which creates significant growth for the company. This requires the company to provide an atmosphere which allows individuals to challenge the status quo and to assume reasonable risk, and which permits new ideas to surface in an unrestricted manner. It further obligates Bausch & Lomb to adequately fund the process of discovery, to provide the tools of research and to find progress in ideas which have failed as well as in those which succeed.

Our Company and Our Community

Bausch & Lomb believes that the company and its employees have a shared responsibility to work for the betterment of their communities. When the company and the community work together, there can be significant benefits for both parties.

To reinforce this commitment, the company will operate in an ethical manner, carefully observing all laws and regulations; will be sensitive to community needs; and will act in partnership with other businesses, agencies of government, and civic organizations to improve the quality of life for everyone.

Accordingly, the company encourages individual employee involvement in community activities at all levels. Utilizing corporate resources, Bausch & Lomb will engage in a selected range of philanthropic activities in its home communities, seek appropriate leadership roles, and remain in close contact with other private sector and governmental leaders.

ADDRESS   One Chase Square
P. O. Box 54
Rochester, NY 14601-0054

INDUSTRY CATEGORY   Health Care

CORPORATE DESCRIPTION
Bausch & Lomb manufactures and distributes products for the
Healthcare and Optics business.

The Healthcare segment consists of three sectors:

> ❧ The Personal Health Sector: Consists of branded products
purchased directly by consumers. Products include contact lens
solutions, oral care products, eye care products, and non-pre-
scription medications.

> ❧ The Medical Sector: Consists of contact lenses, ophthalmic
pharmaceuticals, hearing aids, dental implants, and other products sold to healthcare professionals, or which are obtainable by
consumers only through a prescription.

> ❧ The Biomedical Sector: Includes products and services sup-
plied to customers engaged in the research and development
of pharmaceuticals and the production of genetically engineered
materials.

The Optics Segment consists primarily of products used by
consumers for the protection or enhancement of vision, such as sun-
glasses, binoculars and telescopes.

SIZE REVENUES $1,872,000,000 as of 1993

NUMBER OF EMPLOYEES   15,900 (worldwide) as of 1993

SOURCES   *1993 Annual Report;* "The Values We Share" company
publication

COMPANY | *Baxter Healthcare Corporation*

STATEMENT | Mɪssɪon

We will be the leading health-care company by providing the best products and services for our customers around the world, consistently emphasizing innovation, operational excellence and the highest quality in everything we do.

| Sᴛʀᴀᴛᴇɢʏ

Service: Provide the undisputed best service to customers in both distribution and manufacturing.
Technological Innovation: Bring to market a stream of innovative new products in selected areas of medical technology, through internal development and external partnerships.
International Expansion: Increase global market penetration.

| Vᴀʟᴜᴇs

Respect: We will treat all individuals with dignity and respect and be honest, open and ethical in all our dealings with customers, with shareholders and with each other.
Responsiveness: We will strive continually to understand and meet the changing requirements of our customers through teamwork, empowerment and innovation.
Results: We will consistently keep our commitment to provide value to our customers, to shareholders and to one another.

ADDRESS   One Baxter Pkwy.
Deerfield, IL 60015-4633

INDUSTRY CATEGORY   Medical Products and Services

CORPORATE DESCRIPTION
Baxter is the world's leading manufacturer and marketer of products and services for use in hospitals and other health-care settings. The

company operates in two industry segments: medical specialties and medical/laboratory products and distribution.

SIZE REVENUES $8,879,000,000 (net sales) as of 1993

NUMBER OF EMPLOYEES 60,400 as of 1993

SOURCE *1993 Annual Report*

◆　◆　◆　◆　◆　◆　◆

COMPANY | *Bay View Capital Corporation*
(Bay View Federal Bank)

STATEMENT | **Mission Statement**
The mission of Bay View Federal Bank is to operate a successful, safe and sound regional bank serving the financial needs of the California communities in which it is located.

| **Directional Statements**
To accomplish this mission, management and the staff will, with respect to the following constituencies:
1. Shareholders – Generate through earnings sufficient capital to sustain the growth objectives of the Bank and achieve equitable returns to shareholders. Increase the value of the retail franchise through expansion of products, services and markets served. Prudently manage the risk components of the balance sheet in order to ensure the long term viability of the Bank.

2. Customers – Meet customer needs by investing prudently in research, development and sales programs that increase market penetration. Emphasize quality of service in all dealings with customers.

3. Regulators – Maintain favorable regulatory ratings that will allow the Bank to pursue its business plan.

4. Employees – Invest in the human resources of the Bank to accomplish corporate objectives and enhanced career opportunities for employees.

ADDRESS   2121 S. El Camino Real
San Mateo, CA 94403

INDUSTRY CATEGORY   Banking

CORPORATE DESCRIPTION
Bay View Capital Corporation is the holding company for Bay View Federal Bank, a federally-chartered savings bank with $2.6 billion in assets. Bay View operates 25 branches and 4 loan production offices principally in the San Francisco Bay Area.

SIZE REVENUES $12,500,000 (profits) as of 1993

NUMBER OF EMPLOYEES   476 as of 1993

SOURCES   *1992 Annual Report*; "The Fortune Service 500," *Fortune* 129, no. 11 (May 30, 1994)

COMPANY | *Becton Dickinson and Company*

STATEMENT | **AT BECTON DICKINSON, SUPERIOR QUALITY IS THE ONLY WAY**

Our mission as a Company is to provide the many markets we serve with products of consistently superior quality at price levels that are fair and competitive. Achieving this mission is a responsibility we all share and is necessary to meet the expectations of our customers, ourselves, and our shareholders. With this uncompromising dedication to superior quality, we have a focus for our actions that unifies us, adds value to our work, and enriches our lives.

ADDRESS   1 Becton Dr.
Franklin Lakes, NJ 07417-1880

INDUSTRY CATEGORY   Medical Products and Services

CORPORATE DESCRIPTION
Becton Dickinson and Company manufactures and sells a broad range of medical supplies and devices and diagnostic systems for use by health care professionals, medical research institutions and the general public.

SIZE REVENUES $2,465,000,000 as of September, 1993

NUMBER OF EMPLOYEES   19,100 as of September, 1993

SOURCE   *1993 Annual Report*

COMPANY | *Ben & Jerry's Homemade, Inc.*

STATEMENT | **Ben & Jerry's Statement of Mission**

Ben and Jerry's is dedicated to the creation and demonstration of a new corporate concept of linked prosperity. Our mission consists of three interrelated parts:

PRODUCT MISSION:

To make, distribute and sell the finest quality all-natural ice cream and related products in a wide variety of innovative flavors made from Vermont dairy products.

SOCIAL MISSION:

To operate the company in a way that actively recognizes the central role that business plays in the structure of society by initiating innovative ways to improve the quality of life of a broad community: local, national, and international.

ECONOMIC MISSION:

To operate the company on a sound financial basis of profitable growth, increasing value for our shareholders and creating career opportunities and financial rewards for our employees.

Underlying the mission of Ben & Jerry's is the determination to seek new and creative ways of addressing all three parts, while holding a deep respect for individuals, inside and outside the company, and for the communities of which they are a part.

ADDRESS   P. O. Box 240
Waterbury, VT 05676

INDUSTRY CATEGORY   Food/Beverage

CORPORATE DESCRIPTION

Ben & Jerry's Homemade, Inc., a Vermont corporation, makes Ben & Jerry's super-premium ice cream, Ben & Jerry's lowfat frozen yogurt, and ice cream novelties. The company's products are available in unique as well as traditional flavors, and are marketed through supermarkets, grocery stores, convenience stores, and restaurants. The company also franchises Ben & Jerry's ice cream scoop shops.

SIZE REVENUES $140,328,000 as of 1993

NUMBER OF EMPLOYEES   600 as of 1993

SOURCE   *1993 Annual Report*

◆ ◆ ◆ ◆ ◆ ◆ ◆

COMPANY | *Best Products Co., Inc.*

STATEMENT | **OUR MISSION IS TO BE A**

Customer-Driven Retailer.

We will exceed our customers' expectations every day in every way.

We will provide friendly, courteous, knowledgeable and prompt service in all areas of our business.

We will provide an environment in which our associates are offered opportunities for growth and recognized for their accomplishments.

We will provide destination assortments of quality brand name merchandise at exceptional value.

We will provide an attractive return on investment.

ADDRESS   1400 Best Plaza
Richmond, VA 23260-6303

INDUSTRY CATEGORY   Retail

CORPORATE DESCRIPTION
Best Products is the second largest catalog showroom retailer in the United States, selling jewelry and nationally advertised brand name hardlines merchandise in 157 stores in 22 states. The Company also operates 12 Best Jewelry stores and a nationwide mail order service.

SIZE REVENUES $1,459,300,000 (net sales) as of January 29, 1994

NUMBER OF EMPLOYEES   11,500 as of 1994

SOURCES   *1993 Annual Report*; company representative

COMPANY | *Betz Laboratories, Inc.*

STATEMENT | **Betz Corporate Strategies**

The primary mission of Betz Laboratories, Inc. is to utilize value-added services and concepts to promote growth of its basic businesses profitably while maintaining existing net margins:

Betz will continue to provide its customers a return on their Betz investment through value added programs and concepts.

Betz will continue to build on its strengths and focus most of its resources into the basic businesses and product lines.

Betz will continue to specialize through decentralization wherever it makes sense from a marketing or technology standpoint as a method to improve its market penetration and profit growth.

Betz will continue to strive to be the highest quality company in all aspects of its people, products, services, and technology.

Betz will continue to help preserve the environment and maintain our dedication to the safe and prudent use of our chemicals in our technical and commercial programs.

ADDRESS   4636 Somerton Rd.
Trevose, PA 19053-6783

INDUSTRY CATEGORY   Chemicals

CORPORATE DESCRIPTION

Betz is a multinational company that is a technological leader in the worldwide specialty chemical market. The Company's business is the engineered chemical treatment of water, wastewater, and process systems operating in a wide variety of industrial and commercial applications, with particular emphasis on the chemical, petroleum refining, paper, automotive, electrical utility and steel industries.

SIZE REVENUES $684,872,000 (net sales) as of 1993

NUMBER OF EMPLOYEES 4,115 as of 1993

SOURCES *1993 Annual Report*; "Who We Are—Our Corporate Mission" company publication, 1992

◆　◆　◆　◆　◆　◆　◆

COMPANY | *Blockbuster Entertainment Group*

STATEMENT | Mission Statement
The mission of Blockbuster Entertainment Group, is to be the best provider of entertainment options that meet consumer needs. We will accomplish this by:
1. Understanding the entertainment interests of the consumer better than anyone else.
2. Delivering unique products with the highest level of customer service.
Our resolve to consistently provide the best customer entertainment experience will result in exciting opportunities for our employees and an exceptional return for our investors.

ADDRESS One Blockbuster Plaza
Fort Lauderdale, FL 33301-1860

INDUSTRY CATEGORY Consumer Goods and Services

CORPORATE DESCRIPTION
Blockbuster Entertainment Group, a division of Viacom Inc., operates a chain of video rental stores.

SIZE REVENUES $2,900,000,000 as of December 31, 1993

NUMBER OF EMPLOYEES   55,000 as of October 31, 1994

SOURCE   Company representative

◆ ◆ ◆ ◆ ◆ ◆ ◆

COMPANY | *Boise Cascade Corporation*

STATEMENT | **OUR MISSION**
To continuously improve the Company's long-term value to customers, employees, shareholders, and society.

ADDRESS   One Jefferson Square
P. O. Box 50
Boise, ID 83728-0001

INDUSTRY CATEGORY   Manufacturing

CORPORATE DESCRIPTION
Boise Cascade Corporation, an equal opportunity employer, is an integrated paper and forest products company headquartered in Boise, Idaho, with operations located in the United States and Canada. The Company manufactures and distributes paper and paper products, office products, and building products and owns and manages timberland to support these operations.

SIZE REVENUES $3,958,300,000 as of 1993

NUMBER OF EMPLOYEES   17,362 as of 1993

SOURCE   *1993 Annual Report*

STATEMENT

Any business is a member of a social system, entitled to the rights and bound by the responsibilities of that membership.

Its freedom to pursue economic goals is constrained by law and channeled by the forces of a free market. But these demands are minimal, requiring only that a business provide wanted goods and services, compete fairly, and cause no obvious harm.

For some companies that is enough. It is not enough for Borg-Warner.

We impose upon ourselves an obligation to reach beyond the minimal. We do so convinced that by making a larger contribution to the society that sustains us, we best assure not only its future vitality, but our own.

This is what we believe...

We believe in the dignity of the individual.

However large and complex a business may be, its work is still done by people dealing with people. Each person involved is a unique human being, with pride, needs, values, and innate personal worth. For Borg-Warner to succeed we must operate in a climate of openness and trust, in which each of us freely grants others the same respect, cooperation, and decency we seek for ourselves.

We believe in our responsibility to the common good.

Because Borg-Warner is both an economic and social force, our responsibilities to the public are large. The spur of competition and the sanctions of the law give strong guidance to our behavior, but alone do not inspire our best. For that we must heed the voice of our natural concern for others. Our challenge is to supply goods and services that are of superior value to those who use them; to create jobs that provide meaning for those who do them; to honor and enhance human life; and to offer our talents and our wealth to help improve the world we share.

We believe in the endless quest for excellence.

Though we may be better today than we were yesterday, we are not as good as we must become. Borg-Warner chooses to be a leader—in serving our customers, advancing our technologies, and rewarding all who invest in us their time, money and trust. None of us can settle for doing less than our best, and we can never stop trying to surpass what already has been achieved.

We believe in continuous renewal.

A corporation endures and prospers only by moving forward. The past has given us the present to build on. But to follow our visions to the future, we must see the difference between traditions that give us continuity and strength, and conventions that no longer serve us—and have the courage to act on that knowledge. Most can adapt after change has occurred; we must be among the few who anticipate change, shape it to our purpose, and act as its agents.

We believe in the commonwealth of Borg-Warner and its people.

Borg-Warner is both a federation of businesses and a community of people. Our goal is to preserve the freedom each of us needs to find personal satisfaction while building the strength that comes from unity. True unity is more than a melding of self-interests; it results when values and ideals also are shared. Some of ours are spelled out in these statements of belief. Others include faith in our political, economic, and spiritual heritage; pride in our work and our company; the knowledge that loyalty must flow in many directions; and a conviction that power is strongest when shared. We look to the unifying force of these beliefs as a source of energy to brighten the future of our company and all who depend on it.

About these statements

In September 1981, Borg-Warner chairman James E. Beré asked about 100 senior managers to help him define the company's basic business principles. He asked each of them to reflect on what values and beliefs should underlie Borg-Warner's business decisions, to send him these ideas in writing, and to take part in interviews on the subject.

This testimony was compiled by the corporate staff throughout the winter of 1981–82, and interwoven with Beré's own ideals for the company. Beré and staff then grouped the ideas into major themes and developed these into the five statements listed inside [above]. The preamble was added to sum up both the philosophy that launched this process and the goal the five tenets are meant to serve.

The statements are intended to help guide all who act on Borg-Warner's behalf. As Beré said in announcing them at a management meeting in May 1982, the beliefs are "our promise to the future."

(Copyright © 1982 Borg-Warner Corporation)

ADDRESS   200 S. Michigan Ave.
Chicago, IL 60604

INDUSTRY CATEGORY   Consumer and Business Services

CORPORATE DESCRIPTION
Borg-Warner Security Corporation is the nation's largest security company, with 87,000 employees serving more than 150,000 customers from nearly 600 offices located throughout the United States and in Canada, the United Kingdom and Colombia. Guard, alarm, armored and courier services are provided under the Wells Fargo®, Burns®, Pony Express® and Bel-Air names, which represent the best in technology, service and performance.

SIZE REVENUES $1,764,600,000 as of 1993

NUMBER OF EMPLOYEES   87,000 as of 1994

SOURCES: Company representative; "The Beliefs of Borg-Warner," company publication, 1982

COMPANY | *Bruno's, Inc.*

STATEMENT | **Mission Statement**

Bruno's Inc. is a leading southeastern supermarket chain that utilizes multiple store formats to cater to all consumers. We will always offer our customers the best possible values. Our perishable departments will be superior, offering the freshest and highest quality products unmatched by any competitor. We will treat our family of employees fairly, and we will be customer and community minded. We will use selected technology to enhance our efficiencies and to support our future growth. Through these means we will continue to provide added value to our customers, our shareholders, our employees, and our communities.

ADDRESS   800 Lakeshore Pkwy.
Birmingham, AL 35211

INDUSTRY CATEGORY   Food/Beverage

CORPORATE DESCRIPTION

Bruno's, Inc. is a leading regional food retailer, operating a total of 258 supermarkets in Alabama, Georgia, Mississippi, Florida, South Carolina, and Tennessee.

SIZE REVENUES $2,834,688,000 (net sales) as of 1994

NUMBER OF EMPLOYEES   27,000 as of 1994

SOURCE   Company representative

COMPANY | *Burlington Northern Inc.*

STATEMENT | **Burlington Northern Mission**
Our goal is to provide high-quality transportation and information services that exceed customers' expectations, maximize our return to shareholders and offer all BN people growth and opportunity in an injury-free workplace.

ADDRESS   3800 Continental Plaza
777 Main St.
Fort Worth, TX 76102

INDUSTRY CATEGORY   Transportation

CORPORATE DESCRIPTION
Burlington Northern Inc., headquartered in Fort Worth, Texas, is the parent company of Burlington Northern Railroad, one of the world's leading providers of high-quality rail and transportation services. It operates the longest U. S. rail system based on miles of road and second main track, with 24,500 miles reaching across 25 states and two Canadian provinces. BN is the only western railroad with direct service to Canada, and the only U. S. rail carrier with both land and water access to Mexico. The company generates its revenues by transporting coal, grain, intermodal containers and a variety of industrial, consumer, automotive and forest products.

SIZE REVENUES $4,699,000,000 as of 1993

NUMBER OF EMPLOYEES   30,502 as of 1993

SOURCE   *1993 Annual Report*

COMPANY | *Burnett (Leo Burnett Company, Inc.)*

STATEMENT | **Our Corporate Mission**

The mission of the Leo Burnett Company is to create superior advertising.

In Leo's words: Our primary function in life is to produce the best advertising in the world, bar none.

"This is to be advertising so interrupting, so daring, so fresh, so engaging, so human, so believable and so well-focused as to themes and ideas that, at one and the same time, it builds a quality reputation for the long haul as it produces sales for the immediate present."

ADDRESS   35 W. Wacker Dr.
Chicago, IL 60613

INDUSTRY CATEGORY   Advertising

CORPORATE DESCRIPTION

A worldwide advertising agency network of 61 full-service offices in 51 countries, the privately-held Leo Burnett Company was founded in 1935 by Leo Burnett.

SIZE REVENUES $4,200,000,000 as of 1993

NUMBER OF EMPLOYEES   6,300 as of 1993

SOURCE   Company representative

COMPANY | *Butler Manufacturing Company*

STATEMENT | **CORPORATE MISSION STATEMENT**

Butler Manufacturing Company's mission is to be the value and service leader for building systems, specialty components, and construction services for nonresidential construction customers.

ADDRESS   BMA Tower, Penn Valley Park
P. O. Box 419917
Kansas City, MO 64141-0917

INDUSTRY CATEGORY   Construction

CORPORATE DESCRIPTION

Butler Manufacturing Company is a leader in the marketing, design, and production of systems and components for nonresidential structures. Products and services are provided within the commercial, community, industrial, and agricultural markets.

Butler was founded in 1901, and currently operates manufacturing, engineering, and service centers throughout the United States and twelve foreign countries. The Company's products are primarily sold, installed, and serviced through approximately 4,000 independent dealers in the United States and throughout the world. Butler also provides complete design/build construction services directly to large customers with multiple sites or with projects of unusual size or complexity.

SIZE REVENUES $575,847,000 (net sales) as of 1993

NUMBER OF EMPLOYEES   2,562 as of 1993

SOURCE   1993 *Annual Report*

STATEMENT | **CABOT CORPORATION
STATEMENT OF STRATEGY**

Vision/Mission Statement

To build successful businesses by developing and using our market knowledge, and our operating, financial, and technical competencies.

To lead in quality, safety, innovation, employee involvement, operating standards, and financial performance.

To be recognized as the preferred supplier, customer, and employer; as a valued member of the community; and as a quality company by stockholders and the financial community.

Operating Cultures

❖ Principles, which require adherence to ethical, legal, and environmental standards and the maintenance of decent, safe, and healthy working conditions in all facilities.

❖ Employees, who are accountable, creative, entrepreneurial, profit-conscious, highly skilled, and quick.

❖ Management, which is customer-focused, urgent, empowering, simple, and governed by mutual respect and Total Quality methods.

Strategies for Base Business Development

❖ Total cost improvement, declining real unit costs

❖ Market segmentation, creative margin improvement, Market Driven Management (MDM)

❖ Customer/supplier partnerships where possible/appropriate

❖ Basic technology improvement and protection

❖ Employee development

❖ Sharing of knowledge and competence within the company

❖ Task alignment, Added Value Analysis (AVA)

Strategies for Related Business Development

❖ Exploitation of global position
❖ Creation of interdivisional opportunities
❖ Development of sales/distribution skills
❖ Development of business unit extensions
❖ Expansion of existing commercial relationships

ADDRESS   75 State St.
Boston, MA 02109-1806

INDUSTRY CATEGORY   Chemicals

CORPORATE DESCRIPTION
Cabot Corporation has operations in specialty chemicals and materials, and energy.

SIZE REVENUES $1,614,000,000 as of 1993

NUMBER OF EMPLOYEES   5,400 as of 1993

SOURCES   Financial Report; company representative

COMPANY | *Carpenter Technology Corporation*

STATEMENT | Mission

It is the mission of Carpenter Technology to satisfy the specialty materials and service needs of our customers 100% of the time through excellence in technology, manufacturing, fabrication, marketing, and distribution.

Through Company-wide Continuous Improvement in the quality of everything we do, we will strengthen our leadership position with our customers worldwide. We will promote

COMPANY | *BUSINESS PSYCHOLOGY ASSOCIATES*

STATEMENT | CORE VALUES AND BELIEFS

- The quality of each associate's lifestyle, both at and away from work, is of primary importance.
- The associate is entitled to the opportunity to maximize their individual and collective potential
- Each associate is expected to utilize the opportunity to develop his or her potential
- Our service must contribute to the welfare of both the individuals and organizations we serve and to society as a whole
- Our efforts must reflect the highest standard of ethics and quality
- To be viable an organization must produce a profit, but profit is a natural outgrowth of doing things right

PURPOSE

To help individuals and organizations maximize their potential by providing and managing Behavioral Healthcare that is:

organizational effectiveness and provide an open and partici-pative work environment with opportunity for personal growth for all employees.

We will maintain the highest levels of integrity in business conduct, a strong sense of public responsibility, and earn a competitive return on investment for our shareholders.

ADDRESS   101 W. Bern St.
Reading, PA 19607

INDUSTRY CATEGORY   Industrial, Specialized

- of the highest quality
- the most effective
- the most efficient

MISSION
Revolutionize Behavioral Healthcare!

CORPORATE DESCRIPTION
Business Psychology Associates provides Employee Assistance Programs, Preferred Provider Organizations (PPOs) and Managed Behavioral Health Care services to employers and other mental health care purchasers.

Revenues for 1993 were 1.6 million. The company has 27 employees and 210 subcontractors.

ADDRESS   1501 Tyrell Land
Boise, ID 83706

SOURCE   Company representative

CORPORATE DESCRIPTION

For more than a century, Carpenter Technology Corporation has been applying its experience and honing its skills in developing and manufacturing high-performance alloys that provide such essential properties as strength, durability and corrosion resistance in the countless number of products made with specialty steels.

Today, Carpenter manufactures more than 400 grades of specialty steel products for some 14,000 customers. Users span virtually all major industries—transportation, aviation, aerospace, chemical, petrochemical, electrical, electronic—and include numerous companies making a host of consumer and industrial products.

SIZE REVENUES $628,795,000 as of 1994

NUMBER OF EMPLOYEES   3,697 as of 1994

SOURCE   *1994 Annual Report*

◆ ◆ ◆ ◆ ◆ ◆ ◆

COMPANY | *Caterpillar Inc.*

STATEMENT | **Our Mission**

❖ Provide customers worldwide with differentiated products and services of recognized superior value.

❖ Pursue businesses in which we can be a leader based on one or more of our strengths.

❖ Create and maintain a productive work environment in which employee satisfaction is attained with high levels of personal growth and achievement while conforming to our

"Code of Worldwide Business Conduct and Operating Principles."

❧ Achieve growth and provide above-average returns for stockholders resulting from both management of ongoing businesses and a studied awareness and development of new opportunities.

[Note: The Caterpillar Inc. Mission Statement is reprinted with the expressed written permission of Caterpillar Inc.]

ADDRESS   100 N.E. Adams St.
Peoria, IL 61629

INDUSTRY CATEGORY   Construction

CORPORATE DESCRIPTION
Caterpillar Inc. together with its consolidated subsidiaries operates in three principal business segments:

1. Machinery—Design, manufacture, and marketing of earth-moving, construction, and materials handling machinery.

2. Engines—Design, manufacture, and marketing engines for earthmoving and construction machines.

3. Financial Products—Provides financing alternatives for Caterpillar and noncompetitive related equipment sold through Caterpillar dealers, and extends loans to Caterpillar customers and dealers.

SIZE REVENUES $11,615,000,000 as of 1993

NUMBER OF EMPLOYEES   51,250 as of 1993

SOURCE   *1993 Annual Report*

STATEMENT | Purpose

CBI Industries is a world-wide business enterprise whose purpose is to enhance shareholder value by safely and profitably providing products and services of the highest value through its contracting, industrial gases and terminaling businesses principally to customers who process, store and/or use liquids and gases. To achieve this purpose, CBI's decisions focus on sustaining customer satisfaction, maximizing employee contribution and maintaining the highest degree of integrity in its conduct.

Guiding Principles

1 To prudently manage our assets to provide a fair return to our shareholders.

2 To be continually responsive to the changing needs of our customers.

3 To emphasize the importance of our employees by: Providing an environment where people realize their full potential, where they feel good about their work, are challenged and well trained, and are able to grow both professionally and personally, thereby maximizing their contributions.

Promoting employee ownership to enhance a mutuality of interest with other shareholders.

Developing and maintaining appropriate compensation, benefit and retirement programs to promote long-term employment.

4 To encourage innovation which improves our business processes, practices, and products and services, in order to achieve a clear competitive advantage.

5 To foster a work environment which emphasizes integrity, quality, safety, training and productivity as important and ongoing practices throughout CBI.

6 To develop close relationships with our suppliers, treating them with fairness and respect, enabling them to support our commitments to our customers.

7 To carry out work consistent with responsible behavior toward the environment.

8 To encourage and support the activities of our employees in civic, social and professional organizations where they live and work.

ADDRESS   800 Jorie Blvd.
Oak Brook, IL 60521-2268

INDUSTRY CATEGORY   Industrial, Specialized

CORPORATE DESCRIPTION
CBI Industries has subsidiaries operating in the construction of metal plate structures and other contracting services, industrial gases, oil blending and storage, and other investments.

SIZE REVENUES $1,671,744,000 as of 1993

NUMBER OF EMPLOYEES   14,100 as of December 31, 1993

SOURCE   *1993 Annual Report*

COMPANY | *Cenex, Inc.*

STATEMENT | **Cenex Purpose**
To strengthen the economic well-being of our member-owners.

| **Our Mission**
To anticipate and meet the agronomy, petroleum and related product and service needs of farmers, ranchers and rural communities through local cooperatives.
To be the preferred supplier of those products and services through local cooperatives.
To build and maintain a financially strong cooperative system.

ADDRESS   P. O. Box 64089
St. Paul, MN 55164-0089

INDUSTRY CATEGORY   Agriculture

CORPORATE DESCRIPTION
Cenex serves 320,000 farmers and ranchers through more than 1,800 local cooperatives in 15 states from the Great Lakes to the Pacific Northwest. Through the Cenex/Land O'Lakes marketing joint venture, essential supplies are provided to rural America including refined fuels, lubricants, propane, tires and vehicle accessories, plant food, crop protection products and information/technology services.

SIZE REVENUES $2,047,992,000 (net sales) as of 1993

NUMBER OF EMPLOYEES   3,000 as of 1994

SOURCE   *1993 Annual Report*

COMPANY | *Centerbank*

STATEMENT | **Our Company Vision**

Our company will continue to endeavor to be a provider of financial services and products that customers need and want. The company will maintain strategic and organizational flexibility to meet the challenges associated with the dynamics of the changing industry landscape.

In pursuing its vision, the company will endeavor to maintain an environment which encourages employee integrity, creativity, a spirit of excitement, and personal growth; rewards high performance; and ensures a high level of customer satisfaction.

ADDRESS 60 N. Main St.
Waterbury, CT 06702

INDUSTRY CATEGORY Banking

CORPORATE DESCRIPTION

Centerbank is a diversified financial services company committed to enhancing long-term profitability and increasing shareholder value. Incorporated in 1850, it comprises banking and commercial finance operations in Connecticut as well as nationwide mortgage banking and equipment leasing businesses. With assets of $2.8 billion, deposits of $2.2 billion, a $6.0 billion mortgage servicing portfolio, and shareholders' equity of $173.6 million, Centerbank is one of the larger independent financial institutions based in Connecticut.

SIZE REVENUES $2,800,000,000 (assets) as of June 30, 1994

NUMBER OF EMPLOYEES 1,500 as of November, 1994

SOURCES *1993 Annual Report;* company representative

COMPANY | *Centura Banks, Inc.*

STATEMENT | **THE CENTURA COMMITMENT**

WE ARE COMMITTED to helping our customers achieve all of their financial goals. Customers are the reason we exist, and we must go above and beyond their expectations to create positive, memorable experiences for them. We must listen to their needs, provide them with creative, appropriate financial solutions and serve them in a friendly, caring way.

WE ARE COMMITTED to doing what's right, without exception. Every decision we make, and every action we take, must follow the highest ethical and moral standards. We must tell the truth, keep all commitments and use our time and resources to make our world a better place to live.

WE ARE COMMITTED to creating an exceptional place to work. The power of each individual must be allowed to grow and develop to its potential. We must respect human dignity, reward outstanding performance and empower our people to make the most beneficial decisions for their customers, the company and themselves.

WE ARE COMMITTED to excellence in everything we do. There is always a better way. We must think creatively, continuously improve and pursue new ideas to achieve uncommon breakthroughs. We must thrive on change, shun bureaucracy and strive to surpass our competitors. We must grow our knowledge, learn from our mistakes and emphasize quality in all aspects of our work.

WE ARE COMMITTED to following these principles to make a profit. We must profit to remain in business, grow and meet our responsibilities to all who have a stake in our success— namely our employees, our customers, our communities and our shareholders.

ADDRESS   134 N. Church St.
P. O. Box 1220
Rocky Mount, NC 27802

INDUSTRY CATEGORY   Banking

CORPORATE DESCRIPTION
Centura is a bank holding company headquartered in Rocky Mount, North Carolina, which provides a full range of financial services for businesses and individuals. At year 1993, Centura had $4,139,365,000 in assets.

SIZE REVENUES $41,066,000 (net income) as of 1993

NUMBER OF EMPLOYEES   1,870 as of 1993

SOURCE   *1993 Annual Report*

◆   ◆   ◆   ◆   ◆   ◆   ◆

COMPANY │ *Chase Manhattan Corporation*

STATEMENT │ THE CHASE MANHATTAN VISION

│ PURPOSE
We provide financial services that enhance the well-being and success of individuals, industries, communities and countries around the world.

│ MISSION
Through our shared commitment to those we serve, we will be the best financial services company in the world.

❖ Customers will choose us first because we deliver the highest quality service and performance.

❖ People will be proud and eager to work here.

❖ Investors will buy our stock as a superior long-term investment.

| **VALUES**

To be the best for our customers, we are team players who show respect for our colleagues and commit to the highest standards of quality and professionalism.

❖ Customer Focus

❖ Respect for Each Other

❖ Teamwork

❖ Quality

❖ Professionalism

ADDRESS   1 Chase Manhattan Plaza
New York, NY 10081-0001

INDUSTRY CATEGORY   Banking

CORPORATE DESCRIPTION

The Chase Manhattan Corporation is a bank holding company that was incorporated in 1969 and whose principal subsidiary is The Chase Manhattan Bank, N.A.

In addition to the bank, the Corporation holds investments in other subsidiaries that provide a variety of financial services, including commercial and consumer financing, investment banking, securities trading and investment advisory services.

SIZE REVENUES $966,000,000 (net income) as of 1993

NUMBER OF EMPLOYEES   34,000 as of 1993

SOURCE   *1993 Annual Report*

COMPANY | *Chemfab Corporation*

STATEMENT | **MISSION STATEMENT**
Our mission is to deliver superior value to our customers through preeminence in polymer-based flexible advanced materials and related manufacturing process technologies.

ADDRESS   701 Daniel Webster Hwy.
P. O. Box 1137
Merrimack, NH 03054-1137

INDUSTRY CATEGORY   Manufacturing

CORPORATE DESCRIPTION
Chemfab Corporation and its consolidated subsidiaries is an international advanced performance materials company. It designs, manufactures, and markets a wide range of products for use in extreme service environments. These products are based on the Company's flexible composite materials and specialty films which exhibit exceptional thermal, chemical, electrical, mechanical and release characteristics. The Company's flexible composite materials typically consist of woven fiberglass or other high-strength reinforcements coated or laminated with thermoplastics and elastomers. Worldwide end-use applications are in aerospace, architectural, chemical processing, communications, electronics, food processing, military, protective clothing, and other industrial markets.

SIZE REVENUES $52,151,000 as of 1994

NUMBER OF EMPLOYEES   427 as of 1994

SOURCE   *1994 Annual Report*

COMPANY | *Chemical Banking Corporation*

STATEMENT | **Chemical Banking Corporation**
1992 Mission Statement

"Our mission is to be the best brand-based financial institution, a leader in our chosen markets.

We value the highest ethical standards and leadership, excellence and quality in everything we do while creating and maintaining mutually valuable customer relationships.

We are committed to an environment marked by teamwork, accountability, innovation, openness and empowerment that provides an opportunity for personal challenge and growth."

© 1992 Chemical Banking Corporation
All Rights Reserved. Reprinted by Permission.

ADDRESS   270 Park Ave.
New York, NY 10017

INDUSTRY CATEGORY   Banking

CORPORATE DESCRIPTION
Chemical Banking Corporation is a broad-based financial institution with three core business franchises—the Global Bank, the Regional Bank and Texas Commerce Bancshares. Chemical's Global Bank is a leading bank for large U. S. corporations and foreign-based multinationals, with significant product franchises.

SIZE REVENUES $1,604,000,000 (profits) as of 1993

NUMBER OF EMPLOYEES   41,567 as of 1993

SOURCES   *1992 Annual Report;* "The Fortune Service 500," *Fortune* 129, no. 11 (May 30, 1994)

COMPANY | *Chevron Corporation*

STATEMENT | **Chevron Corporation**
Our Mission, Vision, Values, Strategies

MISSION

Chevron is an international petroleum company. Our mission is to achieve superior financial results for our stockholders, the owners of our business.

VISION

Our vision is to be Better than the Best, which means:
- *All employees are proud of their work.*
- *Competitors respect us.*
- *Customers and Suppliers prefer us.*
- *Investors are eager to invest in us.*
- *Communities welcome us.*
Continuous Quality Improvement is the process we will use to achieve our vision.

VALUES

How we pursue our mission, building on our basic values, is as important as the mission itself.
- *Employees*—the key to success—providing the fundamental strength, vitality and reputation of our Company.
- *Customers*—our basic focus—achieving a lasting partnership means a commitment to excellence in everything we do.
- *Community*—the respect of the community is critical—requiring the highest ethical standards of business, social and environmental responsibility.

STRATEGIES

Our primary objective is to achieve superior operating and financial results so that our stockholders' return exceeds the performance of our strongest competitors. Our goal for the period 1994–1998 is to be number one relative to our competitors in Total Stockholder Return. We believe a 15% per year average return will be required to achieve this goal. In pursuing this objective we will balance long-term growth and short-term profits.

Guided by Chevron's Corporate Strategic Plan we will reach this objective by:

❖ *Building a committed team to accomplish the Corporate mission.* Built on mutual trust and respect for our differences, we will foster a work environment where communication is open and effective, our maximum contributions are valued and rewarded and teamwork is practiced in support of the common good. We will accept our individual responsibility for personal growth, alignment of our goals with the Company's strategies and the success of the business.

❖ *Focusing attention on customers.* We will anticipate and respond quickly to the changing needs of our customers— providing quality products and services to customers inside and outside the Company.

❖ *Ensuring that all operations meet the challenge of the strongest competitors.* We will gain a competitive edge through superior asset management, effective cost control and effective use of technology.

❖ *Identifying and improving our key work processes.* We will continuously benchmark best practices, improve productivity, measure progress, and communicate results and experiences.

❖ *Decentralizing decision making and accountability.* We will effectively communicate Corporate objectives and policies, move operational goals and decision making to strategic business units and stress the importance of meeting specific goals.

❖ *Giving high priority to environmental, public and government concerns.* Compliance is not enough—we will look ahead, anticipate change and develop innovative responses to safety, environmental, public and governmental concerns.

ADDRESS   225 Bush St.
San Francisco, CA 94104

INDUSTRY CATEGORY   Oil and Gas

CORPORATE DESCRIPTION
Chevron is an international petroleum company.

SIZE REVENUES $37,882,000,000 as of 1993

NUMBER OF EMPLOYEES   47,576 as of 1993

SOURCE   *1993 Annual Report*

◆   ◆   ◆   ◆   ◆   ◆   ◆

COMPANY | ***Chicago And North Western Transportation Co.***

STATEMENT | **Mission Statement**

The <u>mission</u> of the Chicago and North Western Transportation Company is to provide quality rail service at a competitive cost to businesses which can ship their products on our railroad. We believe our rail service makes a significant contribution to the strength of the nation's economy and is a great benefit to our customers who primarily ship coal, grain, other agricultural commodities, motor vehicles, containerized merchandise, iron ore, steel, petrochemicals, paper and lumber.

In support of this mission, management has established the following <u>corporate goals:</u>

◈ Increase the value of the company by growing the business and efficiently managing costs.

◈ Continuously improve the total transportation service provided to our customers.

❖ Fulfill and improve our commitment to our customers by means of fostering collaborative relationships which recognize and support our mutual goals and interests.

❖ Enhance our leadership role in the railroad industry as an aggressive promoter of productivity improvement and of a corporate climate which encourages open communication, teamwork and innovation.

❖ Foster a rewarding work environment where employees can earn excellent pay and benefits, have an opportunity for growth, reasonable expectation of job security, competent supervision and working conditions that are perceived as humane, just, and encouraging.

❖ Ensure that the company honors its responsibility to operate safely and provide a safe work environment.

❖ Meet societal obligations as a corporate citizen of the communities in which we operate.

Taken together, these corporate goals establish a set of beliefs, or creed, to serve as a guide in choosing our business methods as we pursue our operational objectives.

ADDRESS   165 N. Canal St.
Chicago, IL 60606

INDUSTRY CATEGORY   Transportation

CORPORATE DESCRIPTION
Chicago and North Western Transportation Company is the nation's eighth-largest freight railroad in terms of revenues and miles operated.

SIZE REVENUES $1,043,200,000 as of 1993

NUMBER OF EMPLOYEES   6,158 as of 1993

SOURCES   *1993 Annual Report* and 10K

COMPANY | *Chrysler Corporation*

STATEMENT | Chrysler Corporation

Purpose

To produce cars and trucks that people will want to buy, will enjoy driving, and will want to buy again.

Core Beliefs and Values

Customer Focus

Delighting our customers stands above all other values and requires:

- *Exceptional products*
- *Exceeding expectations in quality, service, value and things gone right*
- *Pleasing purchase experience*
- *Quick, satisfactory redress of grievances*
- *Effective, responsive communication*
- *Building trust through integrity*

Inspired People

Our success will be achieved only through inspired people, operating in an environment based on:

- *Mutual trust and respect*
- *Openness and candor*
- *Empowerment and teamwork*
- *Innovation and risk taking*
- *Encouraging and valuing diversity*
- *Integrity*

Continuous Improvement

Our culture must be based on the continuous improvement of core processes in all aspects of the business by:

- *Embracing change*
- *Eliminating waste and bureaucracy*

Financial Success

To pursue our other values we must make enough money to ensure our vitality in good times and bad.

Our Reputation

Our reputation is important. It will be determined by the standards and behaviors of all our people.

Mission

To be the premier North American car and truck company by 1996, and worldwide by 2000.

ADDRESS   12000 Chrysler Dr.
Highland Park, MI 48288

INDUSTRY CATEGORY   Motor Vehicles and Related

CORPORATE DESCRIPTION
Chrysler Corporation produces passenger cars, minivans, sport-utility vehicles and light-duty trucks for sale to customers in nearly 100 countries. In North America, the company markets vehicles through three divisions: Chrysler/Plymouth, Dodge/Dodge Truck and Jeep®/Eagle. Chrysler's major subsidiaries are Chrysler Financial Corporation, which provides financing for Chrysler dealers and customers; Chrysler Technologies Corporation, which manufactures high-technology electronic products; and Pentastar Transportation Group, Inc., which includes Thrifty Rent-A-Car System, Inc., Snappy Car Rental, Inc. and Dollar Rent A Car Systems, Inc.

SIZE REVENUES $43,600,000,000 as of 1993

NUMBER OF EMPLOYEES   128,000 as of 1993

SOURCE   *1993 Annual Report*

COMPANY | *Ciba-Geigy Corporation*

STATEMENT | **Our Vision**

By striking a balance between our

economic

social

environmental

responsibilities we want to ensure the prosperity of our enterprise beyond the year 2000.

Responsibility for long-term economic success

We aim to generate appropriate financial results through sustainable growth and constant renewal of a balanced business structure, so that we justify the confidence of all those who rely on our company—stockholders, employees, business partners and the public.

We will not put our long-term future in danger by taking short-term profits.

Social responsibility

Ciba is open and trustworthy toward society. Through our business activities we wish to make a worthwhile contribution to the solution of global issues and to the progress of mankind. We recognize our responsibility when turning new discoveries in science and technology into commercial reality; we carefully evaluate benefits and risks in all our activities, processes and products.

Responsibility for the environment

Respect for the environment must be part of everything we do.

We design products and processes to fulfill their purpose safely and with as little environmental impact as possible. We use natural resources and energy in the best possible way and reduce waste in all forms. It is our duty to dispose of all unavoidable waste using state of the art technology.

ADDRESS   444 Saw Mill River Rd.
Ardsley, NY 10502-2699

INDUSTRY CATEGORY   Chemicals

CORPORATE DESCRIPTION
Ciba is a leading worldwide biological and chemical group, based in Switzerland, dedicated to satisfying needs in healthcare, agriculture and industry with innovative value-adding products and services.

SIZE REVENUES   Not available (in U. S. dollars)

[Author's note: as the company's annual sales are reported in Swiss Francs, no statistic for annual revenues is listed.]

NUMBER OF EMPLOYEES   87,480 (worldwide) as of 1993

SOURCE   *1993 Annual Report*

♦　♦　♦　♦　♦　♦　♦

COMPANY | *Citicorp*

STATEMENT | CITICORP'S VISION
To be a global bank, unique in worldwide presence...dedicated to our customers...financially strong...consistent...committed to our staff and its development...delivering sustained superior performance to investors.
Unique, Global
Unique in being global, operating both locally and collectively around the world in delivering financial services for the

benefit of both individual and corporate customers; unique also in spirit.

Customer Dedication

Dedicated to serving the financial needs of customers. Our success depends upon our importance to them. Customer needs define position, product and service offerings. We seek to build sustained relationships and recognize the importance of continuity of people. We are committed to competitive excellence, delivering customer satisfaction, and investing in the business, people and technology required to meet our customer needs.

Financially Strong

Our balance sheet and earnings will be a source of strength; recognized internally, by customers, investors, competitors, rating agencies, and regulators. Control, executional excellence and productivity improvements are acknowledged objectives.

Consistent

Consistent and dependable: in our commitment to our people, with our customers, in the development and execution of our strategy, and in our risk profile.

Staff and its Development

We seek to recruit, develop and retain the most talented people from around the world. We will reward people based on merit, teamwork, results, and shared values. We are accountable: We will take responsibility for our actions and the exercise of judgment. We treat people with trust, openness and respect, and maintain the highest ethical standards in dealing with customers, the community and each other.

Delivering Sustained Superior Performance to our Investors

Our objective is to achieve superior return on shareholders' equity. We seek the reality and reputation of being well-managed, being consistently sound in our risk-taking judgments, and being seen as one of the most respected financial institutions in the world; a unique global bank.

ADDRESS   399 Park Ave.
New York, NY 10043

INDUSTRY CATEGORY   Banking

CORPORATE DESCRIPTION
Citicorp, with its subsidiaries and affiliates, is a global financial services organization. Its staff of 81,500 serves individuals, businesses, governments, and financial institutions in over 3,300 locations,

COMPANY │ *Cerner®*

STATEMENT │ **OUR VISION:**
Cerner believes that all clinical information within a community should interrelate to create the foundation for high quality, efficient healthcare.

Cerner's vision is that our patient-focused system will empower healthcare enterprises to establish this foundation. Our vision is embodied in Cerner's Healthcare Network Architecture (HNA).

♦ ♦ ♦ ♦ ♦ ♦ ♦ ♦ ♦   ♦ ♦ ♦ ♦ ♦ ♦ ♦ ♦ ♦

HNA is not a product but a benefit of combining Cerner products and other clinical information technologies. HNA enables healthcare enterprises to achieve benefits greater than the sum of their investments in clinical information technology.

including branch banks, representative offices, and subsidiary and affiliate offices in 93 countries throughout the world.

Citicorp, a U. S. bank holding company, is the sole shareholder of Citibank, N.A. (Citibank), its major subsidiary.

SIZE REVENUES $16,075,000,000 as of 1993

NUMBER OF EMPLOYEES   81,500 (worldwide) as of 1993

SOURCE   *1993 Annual Report*

| **OUR MISSION:**
"To automate the process of healthcare"

CORPORATE DESCRIPTION

Cerner creates clinical information systems designed to automate the patient care process for diagnosing and treating patient medical problems. Cerner's revenues were $101.1 million in 1992. The company has a workforce of more than 1,100 associates with offices and implementation sites around the world.

ADDRESS   2800 Rockcreek Pkwy.
Kansas City, MO 64117

SOURCE   Company representative

STATEMENT

The Mission of Clark Equipment Company is to design, manufacture and market the finest equipment in the world for our customers, to provide the most satisfying careers for our employees, and to earn high returns and growth for our stockholders.

We seek to become a great company. On the path to greatness, we must:

❖ Develop the best design engineering skills.

❖ Develop the best manufacturing operations.

❖ Develop the best marketing and sales capability.

❖ Integrate these abilities into the best products and services.

The principles of the company are to conduct itself with honesty and integrity, provide value to its customers, treat all employees with fairness, behave responsibly with respect to the environment and with respect to the safety of its employees and the users of its products, and operate at all times ethically and well within the laws of all the countries of the world.

ADDRESS   100 N. Michigan St.
P. O. Box 7008
South Bend, IN 46634

INDUSTRY CATEGORY   Manufacturing

CORPORATE DESCRIPTION
Clark Equipment Co. designs and manufactures skidsteer loaders, construction machinery, paving equipment (Blaw-Knox), and axles and transmissions for off-highway equipment.

SIZE REVENUES $874,900,000 as of 1993

NUMBER OF EMPLOYEES   5,948 as of 1993

SOURCES   *Financial Report;* "The Fortune 500," *Fortune* 129, no. 8 (April 8, 1993)

◆ ◆ ◆ ◆ ◆ ◆ ◆

COMPANY | *Clorox (The Clorox Company)*

STATEMENT | **Organization**

We recognize that our continued success as a company depends upon the abilities and best efforts of the people at our U. S. and International operations.

We strive, therefore, to maintain the kind of organization in which our people can perform to the best of their ability to help the Company achieve its objectives. A number of principles guide us in structuring the organization for managing our business and for encouraging the performance necessary for the Company's success.

| **Principles**

We will maintain within the organization the flexibility to take full advantage of our opportunities and make the best use of our strengths and resources.

To most effectively develop, manufacture and market our products, we have established profit centers and the centralized staff functions to support them. When justified by promising business opportunities, we will establish new profit centers and sales organizations, and new central staff services groups.

We will delegate responsibility with accountability to the lowest practical level with the proper balance of management control to assure optimum coordination and use of our resources worldwide.

We will encourage an innovative spirit throughout the organization.

We will encourage our people to take the initiative in their work, understanding that some risk is involved, but also recognizing that the potential benefits to the business often outweigh such risks.

We continually will focus on productivity improvement, cost reduction, and quality in our operations.

We will strive for and encourage throughout the entire Company a working alliance among all levels of the organization to achieve our common goals. We will use the "team approach" in all our work.

Every job in our organization should permit us to earn respect and recognition, to maintain individuality and dignity, and to experience the deep satisfaction of working with others for a common purpose.

ADDRESS   1221 Broadway
Oakland, CA 94612

INDUSTRY CATEGORY   Consumer Goods and Services

CORPORATE DESCRIPTION

The Clorox Company is a dynamic international organization whose principal business is developing, manufacturing and marketing products that provide excellent value for consumers. These products are sold primarily in grocery stores and other retail outlets in many parts of the world.

The Company's line of domestic retail products includes many of the country's best known brands of laundry additives, home cleaning products, cat litters, insecticides, charcoal briquets, salad dressings, sauces and water filter systems. The great majority of the Company's brands either lead or are a strong second in their categories.

The Company's Professional Products unit is focused on expanding many of its successful retail franchises in cleaning and food products into new channels of distribution such as the institutional and professional markets and the food service industry.

SIZE REVENUES $1,836,949,000 as of ending June 30, 1993

NUMBER OF EMPLOYEES   4,850 as of June 30, 1993

SOURCES   *1993 Annual Report;* "Our Beliefs" company publication

♦ ♦ ♦ ♦ ♦ ♦ ♦

COMPANY | *CMS Energy*

STATEMENT | **OUR STRATEGIC PLAN**

Our Vision, Goals, Strategies and Creed Join Together to Form Our Strategic Plan.

❧ Our Vision declares how we as a company will operate in philosophical terms—in decision making, serving customers and measuring success.

❧ Our Goals describe what we will do to cement positive relationships with our stakeholders.

❧ Our Strategies explain how we will reach our goals.

❧ Finally, the company Creed is our pledge of performance. Good service and value to our customers is a must.

| **OUR VISION**

CONSUMERS POWER COMPANY improves the quality of life and prosperity of its customers by providing energy and related services that are reliable, attractively priced and tailored to the needs of the customer.

The FOUNDATION of our growth is the *territory that we serve.* We improve the vitality of our customer base by providing rates and services that meet our customers' needs. We bring energy-related technology and services to our customers that improve their ability to compete and thrive in the global marketplace. We accomplish this by being highly efficient, by fostering innovation, and by maximizing our ability to work and learn together.

As EMPLOYEES, we are *skilled* in carrying out the actions necessary to serve our customers, and we are *expected to participate* in the creation and execution of processes, policies and procedures with the flexibility to meet changing customer needs.

Our INVESTMENT decisions are made with a priority on *reducing product price, improving the quality of service* we provide our customers, and expanding our services portfolio to meet changing customer needs.

The measure of our SUCCESS is *shareholder return.* As our service territory prospers and as our customers benefit from competitive rates, reliable energy and innovative services, our shareholders are rewarded by earning an outstanding return on their investment, by receiving a dividend that is predictable, sustainable and substantial, and by continued growth in the value of their investment.

GOAL 1 | MAINTAIN A POSITIVE MPSC WORKING RELATIONSHIP.

STRATEGIES

❖ Resolve issues with MPSC on a timely basis.

❖ Share plans regularly with MPSC and staff.

❖ Openly acknowledge acceptance of MPSC authority.

❖ Utilize careful, limited judicial appeal strategy.

❖ Review work plan accomplishments quarterly with MPSC staff.

❖ Work closely and openly with Commission and staff on issues and trends of general industry interest, with emphasis on regulatory impacts of competitive issues.

GOAL 2 | **EARN EMPLOYEE TRUST AND CONFIDENCE.**
STRATEGIES

❖ Create an environment where decisions are expected to meet the criteria implicit in the Strategic Plan (Corporate Vision, Creed, Goals and Strategies).

❖ Establish general behavior consistent with the Corporate Creed (as determined by subordinates, peers, supervisors and customers) as important to continued career success.

❖ Establish and maintain a constructive union relations environment by working with union leadership to develop mutually beneficial goals, strategies and timetables for improved employment practices which enable employees to better meet the changing needs of our customers.

❖ Maintain a focus on wellness and family to promote healthy lifestyles.

❖ Promote a learning environment where employees understand the changing nature of the utility business, contribute to defining the company's responses to these changes, and receive fair access to career development opportunities.

❖ Establish equitable compensation programs which recognize and reward individual and team performance and appropriately reflect increased responsibility.

GOAL 3 | **ACHIEVE CUSTOMER SATISFACTION THROUGH SUPERIOR SERVICE AT COMPETITIVE RATES.**
STRATEGIES

❖ Focus corporate resources on understanding and meeting the needs of customers from the customers' perspective.

❖ Aggressively work to retain and add customers within profitability criteria.

❖ Engage all employees in the identification of customer service, margin growth and cost-saving opportunities.

❖ Reengineer business processes to improve our ability to add, serve and retain customers.

❖ Develop rates and pricing structures which enhance Consumers Power Co.'s flexibility and competitive position.

❖ Aggressively manage production costs to attain competitive advantage over alternative power suppliers.

❖ Expand customer service beyond the meter.

GOAL 4 | **CONTINUALLY ACHIEVE AUTHORIZED SHAREHOLDER RETURN.**

STRATEGIES

❖ Successfully market uncommitted MCV capacity.

❖ Establish performance-based incentive regulation with balanced incentives for customer and shareholder.

❖ Obtain MPSC acceptance of financial goals and strategies that are attractive to investors.

❖ Reduce debt and achieve a balanced capital structure.

❖ Make financially prudent capital investments that reduce product price, improve service quality and expand our services portfolio to meet changing customer needs.

❖ Maximize the value of our utility-related core competencies in current and new markets.

GOAL 5 | **MAINTAIN SAFETY LEADERSHIP.**

STRATEGIES

❖ Build individual and collective employee commitment to achieve an injury-and incident-free work place.

❖ Increase public safety and customer safety education programs.

❖ Work with regulators and other stakeholders to develop clear definitions of safety requirements, and meet those requirements.

❖ Involve employees who use the tools/equipment in purchase decisions and in operating procedure development.

❖ Increase the understanding by management and all employees of the technical, procedural and cost aspects of safety issues.

❖ Implement electric shock task force recommendations.

GOAL 6 | **ENHANCE THE ECONOMIC, SOCIAL AND ENVIRONMENTAL PROGRESS OF THE COMMUNITIES WE SERVE.**

STRATEGIES

❖ Encourage and recognize the community leadership positions and volunteer efforts of employees and retirees.

❖ Support and implement programs and activities which enhance the quality of education with emphasis on math and science studies.

❖ Assist the communities we serve in achieving improved economic attractiveness and prosperity.

❖ Develop and pursue a corporate-wide strategy for environmental stewardship.

❖ Develop a communication and education strategy to address emerging energy issues of public concern (EMF, stray voltage, rad-waste, etc.).

❖ Improve Michigan business climate to enhance economic development.

OUR CREED

We, The People of CMS Energy and Consumers Power, believe that providing superior service and excellent value to our customers, in a safe way, are our most important priorities.

In doing so, we maximize the likelihood of a prosperous company that can provide substantial benefits to our shareholders, employees, and the communities we serve.

In conducting our business, we pledge the following to our customers, employees, shareholders, regulators and other government officials, suppliers, and neighbors:

❖ **TO COMMUNICATE** honestly and conduct our business with the highest standards of ethics, trust, and integrity.

❖ **TO RESPECT** the dignity of the individual, nurture diversity, facilitate training and career development, and promote employee fulfillment.

❖ **TO PROMOTE** a sense of ownership, accountability, and responsibility for the company's success by recognizing and encouraging achievement and excellence.

❖ **TO STRIVE** constantly to improve our performance by encouraging innovation, responsible risk-taking, and teamwork among all who contribute to our success.

❖ **TO STRIVE** to achieve a superior return to our share-holders to encourage their continued support and investment.

❖ **TO PROVIDE** a safe, clean, and productive work environment.

❖ **TO PROTECT** the environment, and the locations where we operate to preserve them for the benefit of the communities we serve.

❖ **TO BE GOOD** corporate citizens through charitable giving and voluntary service to our communities, our state and our nation.

ADDRESS   212 W. Michigan Ave.
Jackson, MI 49201-2277

INDUSTRY CATEGORY   Utility

CORPORATE DESCRIPTION
CMS Energy is a $7 billion (asset) group of **Growing** energy companies with operations in electric generation and distribution, natural gas distribution and storage, oil and gas exploration, independent power and utility services. Its principal subsidiary, Consumers Power, is the nation's fourth-largest combination electric and gas utility.

SIZE REVENUES $3,481,664,000 as of 1993

NUMBER OF EMPLOYEES   9,811 as of 1993

SOURCES   *1993 Annual Report*, "Our Strategic Plan" company publication

Introduction

The insurance contract, at its heart, is a specific commitment on CNA's part that allows our customers to better fulfill their own diverse commitments. Recognition of this fact has led us to adopt the phrase For All the Commitments You Make as a reflection of our view of the basic value we provide our customers. In the process of serving our customers, we also make commitments to many others, such as producers, employees, stockholders, and our communities. By their very nature, commitments must be kept. We believe that the following values and strategies allow us to make our commitments with confidence that we will indeed keep them, now and in the future.

VALUES

1. Integrity

We believe in maintaining the utmost integrity in dealing with our policyholders, producers, employees, stockholders and communities where we do business.

2. Focus on Underlying Economic Value

We manage our business to maximize its underlying economic value. We do not let short-term profit considerations override long-term profit opportunities.

3. Long-term Relationships

We value long-term relationships with our customers, producers, reinsurers and employees. We pursue strategies designed to foster long term relationships with customers and with producers. We recognize loyalty among employees in our personnel management practices.

4. Excellence in Execution

We are committed to being the best in what we do. In planning or in execution, we want our people to be the best they can be. Our decision-making process requires solid information and rigorous analysis. We provide an environment that allows every one of our employees an opportunity to realize his or her potential to the fullest extent.

5. Organizational Responsibility

We believe that great plans are most surely achieved in the long run by an organizational system of checks and balances (thereby minimizing the probability of big mistakes), by taking controlled risks and by reducing our risk through not depending too much on any one business.

6. Pre-eminence of the Customer

We recognize that any business can succeed only if it can create and keep customers. While the insurance product alone provides a valuable service that is in the public interest, we must provide more than just another insurance product. Cost-effective methods of doing business; cost containment; value-added, caring service all are needed to fully serve and satisfy our customers.

STRATEGIES

1. Insurance Rather than Financial Services

In the absence of market need, we do not want to be a broad-based financial services company. We want to focus on risk management needs. For example, we do not want to provide stock brokerage or real estate brokerage services.

2. Multi-line Operation

We want to pursue segments of both the commercial and individual markets. We also want to meet selected needs in property, liability, life, health and pension areas.

Our strategy of being a multi-line company follows from our desire to maximize the value of our businesses in place and our desire to control the risk from changes in the environment.

3. Capitalizing on Strengths

We want to focus our efforts and resources on businesses where we have strong competitive position and management expertise. This requires that we focus on businesses where we have or can build large enough volume to be competitive. Wherever CNA's expertise and competitive position allow, we want to provide products to meet all the risk management needs for our customers.

4. Partnership with Distributors
We want to cultivate long term, genuine partnership relationships with our distributors. HPA (High Performance Agency) and LSA (Life Select Agency) programs are examples of this strategy.

5. Cost-effective Methods of Doing Business
We seek cost-effective methods of doing business by maintaining a lean functional organization and by improving productivity through work flow streamlining and automation. Expense reduction can provide significant competitive advantages as long as other goals, such as excellence in execution, are not compromised.

6. Cost Containment
We feel a responsibility to our customers to bring about changes in the costs of goods and services that make up the underlying price of the insurance product. We recognize that the insurance consumer today seeks more than just spread of risk in an insurance product. In order to make products more affordable, we are willing to take an assertive, public position.

7. Value-added, Quality Service
We want to provide our customers value-added, quality, caring service; individual attention; and positive, meaningful communications. More than most, insurance is a people business. Our product is intangible. We seek to differentiate CNA by the quality of individual contacts with our customers.

ADDRESS   CNA Plaza
Chicago, IL 60685

INDUSTRY CATEGORY   Insurance

CORPORATE DESCRIPTION

CNA Financial Corporation is the parent company of the multi-line CNA Insurance Companies, which rank among the 15 largest insurance organizations in the United States, with 1993 property-casualty and life-health premium of $8.9 billion.

SIZE REVENUES $11,010,800 as of 1993

NUMBER OF EMPLOYEES   15,000 as of 1993

SOURCE   *1993 Annual Report*

♦ ♦ ♦ ♦ ♦ ♦ ♦

COMPANY | *Coachmen Industries, Inc.*

STATEMENT | **CORPORATE MISSION & GUIDING PRINCIPLES**

MISSION:

Coachman Industries, Inc. is a leading manufacturer of recreational vehicles, manufactured homes, specialty vehicles, and related products. Our mission is to design, market and continually advance our products to be the value leader in the industries we serve. This, in turn, allows us to prosper as a business and to offer opportunities to our employees as well as provide a reasonable return to our shareholders.

PRINCIPLES:

How we accomplish our mission is as important as the mission itself. Fundamental to success for the Company are those basic values which have guided our progress since our founding.

❖ **Our Corporate motto is "Dedicated to the Enrichment of Your Life."**
This means we will do our best to provide quality products and services which will improve the lifestyle of our users.

❖ **Our word is our bond.**
Our dealers and suppliers are our partners. We endeavor to practice the Golden Rule in all of our relations with others.

❖ **Quality is our first priority.**
We must achieve customer satisfaction by building quality products. This will allow us to compete effectively in the marketplace. We will always remember: No sale is a good sale for Coachmen unless it fulfills our customers' expectations.

❖ **Customers are the focus of everything we do.**
As a Company we must never lose sight of the commitment we make to those who buy our products. Our deep-seated philosophy is that "Business goes where it is invited and stays where it is well cared for."

❖ **Integrity is our commitment.**
The conduct of our Company's affairs must be pursued in a manner that commands respect for its honesty and integrity.

❖ **Profits are required for the company to grow and flourish.**
Profits are our report card of how well we provide customers with the best products for their needs.

Our doors are always open to men and women who can contribute to our fulfillment of these goals.

ADDRESS   P. O. Box 3300
Elkhart, IN 46515

INDUSTRY CATEGORY   Motor Vehicles and Related

CORPORATE DESCRIPTION

Coachmen Industries, Inc., manufactures a full line of recreational vehicles and van conversions through five divisions with manufacturing facilities located in Indiana, Georgia and Michigan. These products are marketed through a nationwide dealer network. The Company's housing divisions, with locations in Indiana and Iowa, supply modular housing to builder/dealers in nine adjoining states. The Company's three parts and supply divisions concentrate primarily on providing parts and supplies to the recreational vehicle and van conversion industries, and also have an important interest in the office furniture market.

SIZE REVENUES $193,955,328 (net sales) as of six months ended June 30, 1993

NUMBER OF EMPLOYEES   2,486 as of 1993

SOURCES   *1993 Second Quarter Report; 1993 Annual Report*

◆ ◆ ◆ ◆ ◆ ◆ ◆

COMPANY | *ColumbialHCA Healthcare Corp.*

STATEMENT | Mission

To attain international leadership in the health care field.

⬧ ⬧ ⬧

To provide excellence in health care.

⬧ ⬧ ⬧

To improve the standards of health care in communities in which we operate.

❧ ❧ ❧
To provide superior facilities and needed services to enable physicians to best serve the needs of their patients.

❧ ❧ ❧
To generate measurable benefits for:
The Community
The Employee
The Medical Staff
and, most importantly, The Patient.

ADDRESS   One Park Plaza
P. O. Box 550
Nashville, TN 37202-0550

INDUSTRY CATEGORY   Health Care

CORPORATE DESCRIPTION
Columbia/HCA is a leading hospital management company committed to the delivery of quality patient care at a reasonable cost.

SIZE REVENUES $10,000,000,000+ as of 1993

NUMBER OF EMPLOYEES   130,000 as of 1994

SOURCES   *1993 Annual Report*; company representative

COMPANY | *Comerica Incorporated*

STATEMENT | **Mission**

To forge a cohesive team dedicated to being the standard for exceptional customer service.

| **Vision**

We define ourselves as a relationship-driven financial services organization. Our customers are our first priority. Our employees will be known for their teamwork and will be faithful to our core values and beliefs. We are leaders in the communities we serve. Our board of directors are the shareholders' representatives; we are accountable to them. We will consistently produce returns on equity in the top quintile of the top U. S. bank holding companies.

| **Purpose**

We are in business to enrich peoples' lives.

| **Core Values and Beliefs**

Comerica is a company where...integrity, trust and open communication prevail; customer needs drive our business—we strive to exceed their expectations; we value lasting relationships with our customers, employees, communities and shareholders; we are colleagues, respecting each other and working as a team; we are innovative, flexible and constantly striving to improve; we are entrusted with our responsibilities, held accountable and rewarded fairly; and, we are proud to be members of the team and enjoy coming to work.

ADDRESS   P. O. Box 75000
Detroit, MI 48275-3352

INDUSTRY CATEGORY   Banking

CORPORATE DESCRIPTION

Comerica Incorporated is a bank holding company headquartered in Detroit. It operates financial institutions under the Comerica name in Michigan, California, Florida, Illinois and Texas.

SIZE REVENUES $340,600,000 (profits) as of 1993

NUMBER OF EMPLOYEES   11,424 as of 1993

SOURCES   *1992 Annual Report;* "The Fortune Service 500," *Fortune* 129, no. 11 (May 30, 1993)

♦ ♦ ♦ ♦ ♦ ♦ ♦

COMPANY | *Commercial Federal Corporation*

STATEMENT | **COMMERCIAL FEDERAL CORPORATE PHILOSOPHY**

INVESTOR RELATIONS/EARNINGS

❖ Will achieve consistent long term growth in earnings which will provide above average returns to our investors in relation to the financial industry.

❖ Will achieve and maintain widespread ownership of capital stock.

❖ Will consider positive investor relations as important to our business.

CUSTOMERS

❖ Will serve individuals, families, and professional entities concentrating on the broad middle class.

❖ Will be driven by customer needs in terms of the business we conduct and the services we offer.

HUMAN RESOURCES

❖ Will recognize the human resource as our most valuable asset.

❖ Will seek to attract, develop and retain a quality staff with high productivity and a broad mixture of skills.

❖ Will hold individuals and groups within the staff accountable for results in line with corporate and unit objectives and provide rewards commensurate with performance.

SERVICE

❖ Will provide quality services at a fair value designed to serve the needs of our customers.

❖ Will be innovative, anticipatory, and technologically predisposed in the development and delivery of services.

❖ Will provide services that are profitable and supportive of overall corporate direction.

LEADERSHIP

❖ Will promote a sense of urgency; the ability to respond in a timely fashion to changes in the marketplace.

❖ Will make decisions no higher in the organization than is necessary.

❖ Will provide leadership and management processes that promote:

Planning—The importance of corporate objectives.

Innovation—Questing new ideas and supportive of productive new services.

Accountability—Acceptance of personal responsibility from beginning to completion.

Trust—Mutual at all levels.

Teamwork—Supports productivity and reduces stress.

Open-mindedness—Supports good communication, internal strength, and rank and file enthusiasm.

Integrity—Fairness and honesty with our employees and customers.

Role Models—Provide an example for success.

GROWTH AND DIVERSIFICATION

❖ Will seek growth through retail and wholesale activity on a regional basis.

❖ Will complement long term earnings strategies with growth and diversification. This will provide expanding opportunities for employees.

ADDRESS   2120 S. 72nd St.
Omaha, NE 68124

INDUSTRY CATEGORY   Banking

CORPORATE DESCRIPTION
Commercial Federal Corporation is among the largest retail financial institutions in the Midwest and among the 16 largest thrift institutions in the country. Founded in 1887, Commercial Federal has 67 retail locations serving Nebraska, Colorado, Kansas and Oklahoma.

In addition to its savings bank subsidiary, the Company has other major subsidiary operations: Commercial Federal Mortgage Corporation, a mortgage banking subsidiary with offices in Nebraska, Colorado, Oklahoma and Kansas; Commercial Federal Investment Services, Inc., which offers brokerage and other investment services to consumers; and Commercial Federal Insurance Corporation, offering a variety of consumer insurance products.

SIZE REVENUES $38,300,000 (net income) as of June 30, 1993

NUMBER OF EMPLOYEES   1,150 as of 1993

SOURCES   *1992 Annual Report*; company representative

COMPANY | *Comptek Research, Inc.*

STATEMENT | **Our Mission**

Our mission is to provide innovative electronic and telecommunications products and services which distinguish Comptek on the basis of quality and commitment

ADDRESS   2732 Transit Rd.
Buffalo, NY 14224-2523

INDUSTRY CATEGORY   Telecommunications

CORPORATE DESCRIPTION

Comptek Research, Inc. includes three wholly owned subsidiaries which provide advanced technology products and services to customers throughout the world.

Comptek Federal Systems, Inc. provides electronic warfare and battle management systems to the U. S. Department of Defense and allied military services.

Comptek Telecommunications, Inc. provides data communications products and services to the financial industry and other commercial customers.

Industrial Systems Service, Inc. manufactures electronic assemblies and systems for a broad range of military and commercial applications.

SIZE REVENUES $63,073,000 as of March 31, 1994

NUMBER OF EMPLOYEES   660 as of March 31, 1994

SOURCE   *1994 Annual Report*

STATEMENT | **CSC'S Mission**

✧ Leadership in the solution of client problems in information systems technology

—Offer a full spectrum of services from business reengineering and I. T. strategy to systems integration, operations management outsourcing and professional services

—Respond to each client with the combination of services that is best for him

| **MANAGEMENT PRINCIPLES**

The corporate purpose of Computer Sciences Corporation is to be preeminent in the solution of client problems in information systems technology. This demands that we make an absolute commitment to excellence in our contract performance and products. We will achieve our purpose by observing these principles:

We commit to client satisfaction as our most important business objective.

We recognize that CSC's accomplishments are the work of the people who comprise CSC. We will encourage initiative, recognize individual contribution, treat each person with respect and fairness, and afford ample opportunity for growth in CSC.

We in turn will require of our people the highest standards of professionalism and technical competence.

We will maintain the highest standards of ethics and business conduct, and operate at all times within the laws of the United States and all other countries in which we do business.

We will identify and respond aggressively to new opportunities, and commit to success in each undertaking.

Finally, our success as a company requires that we achieve profits and growth commensurate with a leadership position in our industry.
(Signed)

William R. Hoover
Chairman and CEO

ADDRESS 2100 E. Grand Ave.
El Segundo, CA 90245

INDUSTRY CATEGORY Computer Services

CORPORATE DESCRIPTION
Computer Sciences Corporation (CSC) solves client problems in information systems technology. Its broad-based services include management consulting in the strategic use of information technology; the development and implementation of complete information systems; and outsourcing, covering the full range of a client's information technology activities.

SIZE REVENUES $2,582,670,000 as of 1994

NUMBER OF EMPLOYEES 30,000 as of 1993

SOURCE *1993 Annual Report*

COMPANY | *Computervision Corporation*

STATEMENT
Computervision's Customer Commitment is to help customers gain a time-to-market advantage by continuously improving the productivity of their people, processes and technologies.

ADDRESS   100 Crosby Dr.
Bedford, MA 01730

INDUSTRY CATEGORY   High Technology

CORPORATE DESCRIPTION
Computervision Corporation is a leading international supplier of desktop and enterprise-wide product development software and services. For more than 25 years, the company's product and process data management (PDM) and design automation (CAE/CAD/CAM) software solutions have helped manufacturers improve product quality and reduce time to market. Computervision Services provides best practices consulting programs to support product development process reengineering and technology implementation. Computervision Services also supports applications, systems and networks in heterogeneous computing environments.

SIZE REVENUES $827,315,000 as of 1993

NUMBER OF EMPLOYEES   3,800 as of December 31, 1993

SOURCE   Form 10-K (1993)

COMPANY | *Conner Peripherals, Inc.*

STATEMENT | **MISSION**
Conner's mission is to be the leading supplier of computer storage solutions by providing a comprehensive line of disk drives, tape drives, disk arrays and data protection and storage management software for the entry, value, performance and portable market segments.

ADDRESS   3081 Zanker Rd.
San Jose, CA 95134

INDUSTRY CATEGORY   High Technology

CORPORATE DESCRIPTION
Conner is a leading supplier of storage solutions for the computer industry.

SIZE REVENUES $2,151,672,000 as of December 31, 1993

NUMBER OF EMPLOYEES   10,000 as of December 31, 1993

SOURCE   *1993 Annual Report*

STATEMENT | **[For MotorFreight]**
Mission Statement

CF MotorFreight will continue to distinguish itself as the premier long-haul LTL motor carrier in North America. The Company will maintain this position by embracing a no-compromise philosophy of customer satisfaction. Evidence of our success is the marketplace perception that CF MotorFreight is a preferred service company with which to do business.

[For Con-Way Transportation Services]
Mission Statement

The Con-Way Transportation Services Mission is to expand and diversify its transportation and support services, including LTL regional trucking, full truckload transportation and international shipping.

Con-Way Transportation Services will balance short and long range objectives, optimize profitability, and develop dominant market position through product leadership and effective integration of human, capital and material resources.

Key Elements

❖ People
❖ Service
❖ Capacity
❖ Technology
❖ CFI Support

[For Emery Worldwide]
Mission Statement

Our mission is to exceed our customers' expectations. We believe they deserve nothing less. Whether we meet in the customer's office, on the dock or over the telephone, we're honest and professional. Individually, we are proud of our work and our history of innovations. Together, we are a team of dedicated people working to satisfy our customers.

Emery Worldwide is an international and domestic transporter of packages, parcels and freight. We also will handle envelopes for customers who require transportation of packages, parcels and freight. No shipment is too large to be handled by Emery Worldwide. The company serves business customers.

Emery Worldwide strives to provide total freight transportation to customers. Inbound packages, parcels and freight are as important as our outbound.

We clearly understand each location's expense of performing service on behalf of each of our customers and govern our sales efforts and operational activities accordingly.

ADDRESS   3240 Hillview Ave.
Palo Alto, CA 94304

INDUSTRY CATEGORY   Transportation

CORPORATE DESCRIPTION
Consolidated Freightways, Inc. is a $4.1 billion diversified transportation company specializing in the movement of less-than-truckload freight through 11 independent companies that provide transportation services for commercial and industrial shipments by land, sea and air throughout North America and the world. The principal operating companies are: CFMotor Freight, Con-Way Transportation Services, and Emery Worldwide.

SIZE REVENUES $4,191,811,000 as of 1993

NUMBER OF EMPLOYEES   39,100 as of 1993

SOURCE   *1993 Annual Report*

COMPANY | *Continental Airlines*

STATEMENT | **Corporate Vision**
To Be Recognized as the Best Airline in the Industry by our
Customers, Employees and Shareholders.

ADDRESS   2929 Allen Pkwy., Ste. 2010
Houston, TX 77019

INDUSTRY CATEGORY   Transportation

CORPORATE DESCRIPTION
Continental Airlines was the nation's fifth largest air carrier in 1992,
as measured by revenue passenger miles.

SIZE REVENUES $5,775,300,000 as of 1993

NUMBER OF EMPLOYEES   43,140 as of 1993

SOURCES   Company representative; "The Fortune Service
500," *Fortune* 129, no. 11 (May 30, 1994)

COMPANY | *Continental Medical Systems, Inc.*

STATEMENT | **Mission Statement**

Acting as a diversified provider of medical rehabilitation and physician services, the Mission of **Continental Medical Systems** is to ensure high quality and cost effective outcomes to those we serve while providing a favorable return to our stockholders.

ADDRESS   P. O. Box 715
Mechanicsburg, PA 17055

INDUSTRY CATEGORY   Health Care

CORPORATE DESCRIPTION
The Company is a diversified provider of comprehensive medical rehabilitation and physician services. The Company has a significant presence in each of the rehabilitation industry's three principal sectors—inpatient rehabilitation care, contract services and outpatient rehabilitation care. Additionally, the Company is the largest provider of physician locum tenens services in the United States.

SIZE REVENUES $1,004,839,000 as of 1994

NUMBER OF EMPLOYEES   14,000 as of 1994

SOURCE   *1994 Annual Report*

COMPANY | *Cooper Tire & Rubber Company*

STATEMENT | **Business Creed**

Over the years, Cooper Tire & Rubber Company has maintained a consistent style of doing business. This reliability and steadiness is rooted in the Company's rich history as one of America's pioneer tire and rubber products manufacturers.

In a 1926 interview, I. J. Cooper, former president for whom the Company is named, outlined three planks in Cooper's business platform:

❧ Good Merchandise—because it doesn't pay to make, sell or use an inferior article.

❧ Fair Play—prices that satisfy the user, leave the dealer with a profit and the maker with a margin to cover his labor, thought and investment.

❧ Square Deal—to everyone, every time because you can't beat a natural law and still progress and prosper.

ADDRESS Findlay, OH 45840-2315

INDUSTRY CATEGORY Motor Vehicles and Related

CORPORATE DESCRIPTION

Cooper Tire & Rubber Company, founded in 1914, specializes in the manufacturing and marketing of rubber products for consumers and industrial users. Products include automobile and truck tires, inner tubes, vibration control products, hoses and hose assemblies, automotive sealing systems and specialty seating components.

SIZE REVENUES $1,193,647,544 as of 1993

NUMBER OF EMPLOYEES 7,607 as of 1993

SOURCE *1993 Annual Report*

COMPANY | *Copperweld Corporation*

STATEMENT | **MISSION STATEMENT**
Copperweld Corporation is recognized worldwide as a leading manufacturer of mechanical and structural tubing and bimetallic wire products. Our mission is to provide superior products and services in response to our customers' needs. By continuous improvement of all aspects of our performance, we anticipate our customers' critical requirements and maintain competitive advantage in the markets we serve. Our goal is to be an ever-vital and prosperous business providing an innovative, productive, and rewarding environment for our people; real value for our customers and suppliers; and a reasonable ongoing return for our shareholders.

COMPANY   CETAC TECHNOLOGIES INC.

STATEMENT   CETAC MISSION STATEMENT
To develop and provide the best analytical product solutions to meet the needs of customers in our primary markets at an unequaled value.

CORPORATE DESCRIPTION
CETAC is a world leader in sample introduction and sample pretreatment technologies for chemical analysis. The Company develops, manufactures, and markets a family of products and services that provide essential solutions to customers around the globe.

In accomplishing our business mission, we are guided by the following basic principles:

Customers are the ultimate focus of all of our business activities.

Quality in product, services, and all of our business transactions is first priority.

Integrity is never compromised.

People provide the strength, energy, and essential resource to ensure a successful business.

Employee involvement, trust, recognition and teamwork, drive, personal growth, contribution, accomplishment, and sustained superior performance.

Continuous Improvement is our way of life; change is valued for the competitive opportunities it presents.

CETAC and its associated companies provide a comprehensive range of product based solutions for the analysis of elements in samples ranging from drinking water and high purity acids to radio-active waste.

CETAC's 1993 annual revenues were $6 million. They have 50 employees.

ADDRESS   5600 S. 42nd St.
              Omaha, NE 68107

SOURCE   Company representative

Value created for our customers and suppliers is a prerequisite to the continuing generation of value for our enterprise.

Critical Appraisal of the Competitive Environment is essential for ongoing success to provide clear focus on necessary change and to define the associated resource deployment.

ADDRESS   Four Gateway Center, Ste. 2200
Pittsburgh, PA 15222-1211

INDUSTRY CATEGORY   Manufacturing

CORPORATE DESCRIPTION
Copperweld Corporation is a manufacturer of structural, mechanical and welded-mechanical steel tubing, and bimetallic rod, wire, and strand.

SIZE REVENUES   Not available

NUMBER OF EMPLOYEES   1,350 as of 1994

SOURCE   Company representative

Our Purpose

Our purpose is to deliver superior, long-range economic benefits to our customers, our employees, our shareholders, and to the communities in which we operate. We accomplish this by living our corporate values.

Our Strategy

Corning is an evolving network of wholly and jointly owned businesses which owes its continued existence to shared values, a core competence in science and technology, and an unending spirit of innovation in all aspects of our corporate life.

Corning will focus on four strategies that will enable the corporation to reach its long-term financial goals:

Growth Markets. Invest aggressively in growing markets in which we are or expect to be #1 or #2 and in which we are the high-quality, low-cost supplier. These markets are: Communications, Environment, Life Sciences.

Traditional Businesses. Manage our traditional businesses for cash to support these growth investments.

Core Science and Technology. Nurture our science and technology so that it drives our growth markets and also creates as-yet undefined future opportunities.

Corporate Investments. Hold our investments in Dow Corning and Pittsburgh Corning for optimal growth and cash generation over time.

Our corporate network adds value to its component parts through our company's name and reputation, a common dedication to our core values, a coherent overall strategy, and shared financial and human resources.

What we value

Our Values

We have a set of enduring beliefs that are ingrained in the way we think and act. These values guide our choices, defining for us the right courses of action, the clearest directions, the preferred responses. Consistent with these values we set our objectives, formulate our strategies, and judge our results. By living these values we will achieve our purpose.

Quality

Total Quality is the guiding principle of Corning's business life. It requires each of us, individually and in teams, to understand, anticipate, and surpass the expectations of our customers. Total Quality demands continuous improvement in all our processes, products, and services. Our success depends on our ability to learn from experience, to embrace change, and to achieve the full involvement of all our employees.

Integrity

Integrity is the foundation of Corning's reputation. We have earned the respect and trust of people around the world through more than a century of behavior that is honest, decent, and fair. Such behavior must continue to characterize all our relationships, both inside and outside the Corning network.

Performance

Providing Corning shareholders a superior long-term return on their investment is a business imperative. This requires that we allocate our resources to ensure profitable growth, maintain an effective balance between today and tomorrow, deliver what we promise, and tie our own rewards directly to our performance.

Leadership

Corning is a leader, not a follower. Our history and our culture impel us to seek a leadership role in our markets, our multiple technologies, our manufacturing processes, our management practices, and our financial performance. The goods and services we produce are never merely ordinary and must always be truly useful.

Innovation

Corning leads primarily by technical innovation and shares a deep belief in the power of technology. The company has a history of great contributions in science and technology, and it is this same spirit of innovation that has enabled us to create new products and new markets, to introduce new forms of corporate organization, and to seek new levels of employee participation. We embrace the opportunities inherent in change, and we are confident of our ability to help shape the future.

Independence

Corning cherishes—and will defend—its corporate freedom. That independence is our historic foundation. It fosters the innovation and initiative that has made our company great, and will continue to provide inspiration and energy to all parts of our network in the future.

The Individual

We know that in the end the commitment and contribution of all our employees will determine our success. Corning believes in the fundamental dignity of the individual. Our network consists of a rich mixture of people of diverse nationality, race, gender, and opinion, and this diversity will continue to be a source of our strength. We value the unique ability of each individual to contribute, and we intend that every employee shall have the opportunity to participate fully, to grow professionally, and to develop to his or her highest potential.

Where we want to go

Our Financial Goals

Performance

We will be consistently in the top 25 percent of the Fortune 500 in financial performance as measured by return on equity and long-term growth in earnings per share.

Capital Structure

We will maintain a debt-to-capital ratio of approximately 30 percent and a long-term dividend payout of 33 percent.

We will issue new shares of stock on a limited basis in connection with employee ownership programs and acquisitions with a clear strategic fit, and we will repurchase shares on the open market as appropriate.

ADDRESS   One Riverfront Plaza
Corning, NY 14831

INDUSTRY CATEGORY   Manufacturing

CORPORATE DESCRIPTION
Corning Incorporated is a diversified products and services company with a strong tradition of technological innovation. Although historically a glass and specialty materials manufacturer, Corning today concentrates on the three key global markets that account for 60 percent of its revenues: optical communications, life sciences and the environment.

SIZE REVENUES $4,004,800,000 as of 1993

NUMBER OF EMPLOYEES   39,200 as of 1993

SOURCE   *1993 Annual Report*

COMPANY | *Corporate Child Care Management Services*

STATEMENT | **Mission Statement**

❖ To be the nation's leading company helping employers create child care solutions for their employees.

❖ To deliver excellence in child care services that improves the standards of child care in communities in which we operate.

❖ To achieve measurable benefits for:

our clients,

their employees,

our employees,

our investors,

and, most importantly, **the children and their parents**.

OUR PURPOSE

We support parents and create value for their employer by providing a nurturing environment where children are safe, happy, growing and learning.

OUR VALUES

TRUST

HONESTY

EXCELLENCE

CREATIVITY

RESPONSIVENESS

EMPATHY

ENTHUSIASM

DEDICATION

ADDRESS   631 Second Ave. South
                 Nashville, TN 37210

INDUSTRY CATEGORY   Business Services

CORPORATE DESCRIPTION

Corporate Child Care Management Services is a national leader in employer-sponsored child care. The company develops and manages child care centers for employers which are tailored to meet the unique needs of the workplace. The company also provides consultation services to companies interested in exploring the feasibility of child care and other family and work solutions.

The company currently works in partnership with more than 50 companies in 18 states.

SIZE REVENUES $25,000,000 as of 1994

NUMBER OF EMPLOYEES   1200 as of 1994

SOURCE   Company representative

COMPANY | **Comprehensive Technologies International Incorporated**

STATEMENT | **CORPORATE MISSION STATEMENT**

Developing CTI's Mission Statement and communicating it throughout the entire company is critical for the overall success of CTI. Understanding where CTI wants to go as a company will be the foundation for achieving organizational alignment. The cornerstone of that alignment will involve employees working together and focusing their efforts in the same direction to achieve common goals and objectives which support CTI's Corporate Mission Statement.

"CTI's Corporate Mission is to be the nationally recognized partner of choice for government and commercial clients as they seek to improve their business processes, products, and services. This will be

COMPANY | *CRAY RESEARCH, INC.*

STATEMENT | **CRAY'S MISSION STATEMENT**

Cray Research provides the leading supercomputing tools and services to help solve our customers' most challenging problems.

ADDRESS   655 Lone Oak Dr.
Eagan, MN 55121

INDUSTRY CATEGORY   High Technology

CORPORATE DESCRIPTION

Cray Research produces supercomputers with very powerful computational capacities.

accomplished by maintaining a top-quality workforce, enhancing professional services with technology applications, and continuing to be on the leading edge of innovation in the development of "electronic business" applications solutions. To achieve these complementary goals, CTI will augment its traditional professional services with technology applications that increase the productivity of and reduce costs for its clients. Additionally, CTI will develop software products that integrate electronic data interchange (EDI), imaging, relational databases, multimedia, networking, and other emerging technologies to improve the competitiveness of its technology professional services. CTI is committed to a corporate synergistic relationship between and among its areas of specialization that will require a new forward-thinking corporate culture that thrives on innovation and technological change, respects the dignity of each and every employee, and embraces total quality leadership."

SIZE REVENUES $895,000,000 as of 1993

NUMBER OF EMPLOYEES 4,960 as of 1993

SOURCES *1992 Annual Report;* "The Fortune 500," *Fortune* 129, no. 8 (April 8, 1994)

◆ ◆ ◆ ◆ ◆ ◆ ◆

COMPANY | *CSX Corporation*

STATEMENT | **CSX Mission Statement**

CSX is a transportation company committed to being a leader in railroad, inland water and containerized distribution markets.

HOW TO DO IT

We must practice what we preach. We must internally integrate our technical/management services and the software products lines of business to improve our own productivity and efficiency while reducing operational costs. We will establish an Institute for Technology Innovation and Networking (ITIN) to educate and train our employees to use our new technologies and methods. We will establish a company-wide Total Quality Management (TQM) Program. Where appropriate, we will introduce our new services and products to our existing contracts. Our ultimate goal is to provide our clients with best-value pricing, customer-oriented professional services and tailored software solutions

To attract the human and financial resources necessary to achieve this leadership position, CSX will support our three major constituencies:

❖ For our customers, we will work as a partner to provide excellent service by meeting all agreed-upon commitments.

❖ For our employees, we will create a work environment that motivates and allows them to grow and develop and perform their jobs to the maximum of their capacity.

❖ For our shareholders, we will meet our goals to provide them with sustainable, superior returns.

CSX Values Statement

The primary responsibility of every CSX employee is to serve customers in the spirit of partnership in order to understand and satisfy their needs.

We must provide quality execution on a consistent basis over the long term through:

❖ An organization that values its employees and respects their dignity.

❖ A commitment to teamwork, openness and candor.

─────────────────────────────── ◆

supported by highly motivated employees. This goal is nurtured by a corporate culture that encourages innovation, rewards initiative, and fosters the psychological and spiritual growth of every person. (Signed)

Celestino Beltran, Chairman and CEO
May 12, 1993

CORPORATE DESCRIPTION

Comprehensive Technologies International, Inc. (CTI) is a diversified technology based professional services and "Electronic Commerce"

❖ A commitment to increased quality and continuous improvement.

❖ Increased empowerment and personal accountability.

❖ A commitment to ethical conduct.

❖ A willingness to innovate and change in well-planned ways that yield a competitive advantage.

❖ A sense of urgency and bias for action.

Only by carrying out these values will CSX be able to fulfill our ultimate responsibility to provide sustainable, superior returns to our shareholders.

ADDRESS   One James Center
901 E. Cary St.
Richmond, VA 23219-4031

INDUSTRY CATEGORY   Transportation

CORPORATE DESCRIPTION

CSX Corporation is an international transportation services company offering a wide variety of rail, container-shipping, intermodal, barging, trucking, contract logistics and related services worldwide. Business units include: CSX Transportation Inc., Sea-Land Service

◆ ══════════════════════════════ ◆

software development company formed in 1980 and now headquartered in Fairfax County, Virginia. The fiscal year ending July 31, 1994, CTI generated $31.6 million in revenue and employed 410 employees in 8 offices nationwide.

ADDRESS   11350 Random Hills Rd., Ste. 300
Fairfax, VA 22030

SOURCE   Company representative

Inc., CSX Intermodal Inc., American Commercial Lines Inc., and Customized Transportation Inc.

SIZE REVENUES $8,940,000,000 as of 1993

NUMBER OF EMPLOYEES 47,063 as of 1993

SOURCE *1993 Annual Report*

◆ ◆ ◆ ◆ ◆ ◆ ◆

COMPANY | *CUNA Mutual Insurance Group*

STATEMENT | Mission

THE CUNA MUTUAL GROUP

To promote the credit union concept as the practical approach to the financial well-being of people, to pursue quality and innovation in insurance and finance-related products and excellence in service, to provide services directed to building and supporting the credit union system, to provide a dynamic organization for employee growth and public respect while maintaining the highest ethical standards.

OPERATING PRINCIPLES:

TO PROMOTE the credit union idea as the best financial alternative for the consumer;

TO SUPPORT the Credit Union National association, the leagues and all associated organizations and to build with them a unified, national credit union system;

TO MARKET insurance and finance-related services within the credit union movement and to no other financial institution and only to individual non-members when marketing is in furtherance of the interests of credit unions, such as building potential membership or creating favorable recognition of the credit union idea;

TO PROVIDE credit unions with innovative and creative services and continued strong leadership within the credit union movement; **TO PROVIDE** quality life and disability insurance and finance-related services with good consumer value; **TO PROVIDE** broad fidelity, property, casualty, and liability insurance coverage for the credit union movement at low cost, consistent with sound actuarial and risk management principles; **TO RECOGNIZE AND ENCOURAGE** the individual employee contribution to the success and growth of the CUNA Mutual Group and to encourage a sense of social responsibility toward the communities in which we reside; **TO CONTINUE** the emphasis on financial strength through growth of capital and surplus;

All of which shall be supported by a program of excellence in product quality and service while maintaining high standards of ethics and integrity.

ADDRESS   5910 Mineral Point Rd.
Madison, WI 53705

INDUSTRY CATEGORY   Insurance

CORPORATE DESCRIPTION
CUNA Mutual Insurance Society (CUNA Mutual) is a mutual life insurance company organized under the laws of the State of Wisconsin. The CUNA Mutual Insurance Group serves only credit unions and credit union members.

The CUNA Mutual Group had 1993 assets of $2,462,593,000.

SIZE REVENUES $1,472,604,000 as of 1993

NUMBER OF EMPLOYEES   5,500 as of 1993

SOURCES   *1993 Annual Report*; company representative

The Dana Style Will Be Fully Implemented.

❖ Dana people are our most important asset.

❖ The Dana Style is the key to our global success.

Dana Will Be A World Leader In Quality, Service, And Technology For Each Of Our Products.

❖ We will be the best at what we do.

❖ Our customers will want our products and services because they are the best value available anywhere.

Dana Will Obtain 50% Of Our Total Sales From Distribution Markets.

❖ We will increase distribution sales by growing at a rate faster than our other markets through acquisitions, market penetration, and new product introduction.

❖ We will broaden our customer base by emphasizing sales through distributor channels, including service parts sales and industrial distribution.

Dana Will Obtain 50% Of Our Total Sales Outside The United States.

❖ We will increase non-U. S. sales by growing our international activities at a rate faster than our domestic operations.

❖ U. S. operations will grow and emphasize exports.

❖ We will achieve international growth through acquisitions, increased exports, market penetration, and new ventures commensurate with corporate financial objectives.

Dana's Financial Performance Will Consistently Exceed The Standard and Poor's 500.

❖ We will exceed the price-earnings ratio of the Standard and Poor's 500 Composite Index by continuous improvement of earnings per share, by minimizing cycles in earnings, and by achieving a 20% corporate return on equity.

The Policy Committee

5/1/94

ADDRESS   P. O. Box 1000
Toledo, OH 43697

INDUSTRY CATEGORY   Motor Vehicles and Related

CORPORATE DESCRIPTION
Dana is a global leader in the manufacturing and marketing of vehicular and industrial components.

SIZE REVENUES $5,460,000,000 as of 1993

NUMBER OF EMPLOYEES   36,000 as of 1993

SOURCES   *1992 Annual Report;* "The Fortune 500," *Fortune* 129, no. 8 (April 8, 1994)

COMPANY | *Delta Air Lines, Inc.*

STATEMENT | **Vision for the Future**

**OUR VISION IS FOR DELTA TO BE THE
WORLDWIDE AIRLINE OF CHOICE.**

Worldwide....We provide our customers access to the world, and we will be an innovative, aggressive, ethical and successful competitor committed to profitability and superior customer service. Looking ahead, we will consider opportunities to expand through new routes and alliances.

Airline....We will stay in the business we know best and where we are leaders—air transportation and related services. We believe air transportation will grow worldwide, and we will focus our time, attention and investment in building on our leadership position.

Of Choice....We will be the airline of choice for customers, investors and Delta people. For experienced business and leisure travelers, we will provide value and a superior travel experience from the time a reservation is made to when baggage is claimed. For air shippers, we will provide service and value. For our stockholders, we will earn a consistent, superior financial return. For Delta people, we will offer challenging, rewarding, results-oriented work in an environment that respects and values their contributions.

ADDRESS   1050 Delta Blvd.
Atlanta, GA 30320-6001

INDUSTRY CATEGORY   Transportation

CORPORATE DESCRIPTION

Delta Air Lines, Inc., has been engaged in the air transportation business since 1929. Based on calendar 1993 data, Delta is the third largest U. S. airline as measured by operating revenues and revenue passenger miles flown, and the largest U. S. airline as measured by passengers enplaned.

The Company provides scheduled air transportation over an extensive route network. At September 12, 1994, Delta served 153 domestic cities in 43 states, the District of Columbia, Puerto Rico, and the U. S. Virgin Islands, and 57 cities in 32 foreign countries. Service over most of Delta's routes is highly competitive. In addition to scheduled passenger service, Delta also provides air freight, mail and other related aviation services.

SIZE REVENUES $12,359,000,000 as of 1994

NUMBER OF EMPLOYEES 71,412 as of 1994

SOURCE *1994 Annual Report*

◆ ◆ ◆ ◆ ◆ ◆ ◆

COMPANY | *Deluxe Corporation*

STATEMENT | **OUR CORPORATE GOALS**
Our corporate goals consist of: satisfying the needs of our customers; providing meaningful work for our employees; producing a quality return to our shareholders; and preserving the health of our business.

| **OUR MISSION**
Our mission is to serve our customers as the best supplier of products and services in the markets we serve.

OUR COMMITMENT

To Customers:

We offer customers superior products and services. We believe we are successful because of our commitment to customer service—service that emphasizes quality products, prompt order handling and follow-up, dependable information processing, and strict security. If we fail to provide total satisfaction, we forfeit the right to that customer's business.

To Employees:

We recognize that our success depends upon the attitudes and performance of all Deluxers. Therefore, we select qualified employees and try to create an atmosphere conducive to quality performance—by sharing information, opportunities, and the rewards of a successful operation. We are concerned about and sensitive to family issues and the diversity of our work force, and we respect the dignity and rights of each person in our organization. We strive to provide equal opportunity, fair treatment, a safe work environment, and meaningful employment for all employees.

To Shareholders:

We are committed to maintaining a healthy company so our shareholders will profit from their investment. We prefer to focus on corporate health, rather than growth, because we recognize that growth generally accompanies a healthy organization.

To The Community:

We endeavor to be sensitive to the well-being of our employees and their communities by sharing responsibility for the economic, social, physical, and cultural environments of those communities.

OUR OBJECTIVES

Financial:

We intend to maintain the company's financial strength. We are committed to attaining a healthy balance sheet, positive cash flow, and earnings growth that equals or exceeds sales growth. We also strive to provide regular cash dividends to shareholders.

Marketing:

We serve the needs of our customers with quality products and services. Although our primary focus is on health, we expect our efforts to result in sales growth that equals or exceeds the growth rate of our markets. Our strategy is to differentiate ourselves in the marketplace by providing superior value at competitive prices. We also strive to maintain a reputation for integrity in our communications with customers.

Manufacturing:

We endeavor to produce high-quality products and maintain established service schedules on all orders. We are committed to state-of-the-art technology, the highest standards of workmanship and accuracy, ample production capacity, and an efficient distribution system.

Information Systems:

We use up-to-date computer technology to support customer and company needs for accurate, secure, and convenient retrieval of data. Meeting this objective commits us to providing protected, high-integrity hardware, software, and telecommunications.

ADDRESS   P. O. Box 64399
St. Paul, MN 55164-0399

INDUSTRY CATEGORY   Business Products

CORPORATE DESCRIPTION

Deluxe Corporation is an industry leader in providing products and services to the financial payment systems industry. The Company is the nation's largest check printer and also provides electronic funds transfer (EFT) processing services and software, debit and credit card services, internal bank forms, consumer credit products, and account verification services to financial institutions. The Company also provides check authorization and collection services to retailers. Deluxe's Business Systems Division produces a variety of computer and business forms and related products for small businesses and professional practices; and also tax forms and electronic tax filing services to tax preparation professionals. The Company's Consumer Specialty Products Division markets greeting cards, gift wrap, stationery and a variety of related products to households.

SIZE REVENUES $1,581,767,000 (net sales) as of 1993

NUMBER OF EMPLOYEES   17,748 as of 1993

SOURCES   *1993 Annual Report;* "Commitment" company publication

◆　◆　◆　◆　◆　◆　◆

COMPANY | *Deposit Guaranty Corp.*

STATEMENT | **Mission Statement**
The mission of Deposit Guaranty Corp. is to increase shareholder value by providing financial services in our areas of operation with balanced emphasis on customer sales and service, credit quality, operational efficiency, and profitability.

Amplification
"…financial services…": our core business is providing basic banking services, gathering deposits and extending credit. In addition to traditional banking, Deposit Guaranty provides a broad range of financial services designed to meet more completely our customers' financial needs. Basic deposit and credit products are complimented [sic] by the asset management

services of our Trust Division, full and discount brokerage services, a family of private label mutual funds, select insurance products, and cash management services. These ancillary products and services are designed to strengthen existing customer relationships, enhance our competitive advantages, and provide additional cross-selling opportunities. All of the products and services we provide must add profit on their own or through synergy with other products. The broader range of financial services will strengthen the value of the Deposit Guaranty franchise, as well as enhance and diversify our stream of earnings.

"...areas of operation...": we are part of a regional banking organization serving markets in Mississippi and the Shreveport, LA, metropolitan area, and offer corporate and financial services in contiguous states and on a nationwide basis to companies with Mississippi and Ark-La-Tex operations. While we are not seeking to acquire for expansion's sake, when conditions are correct, we will consider acquiring other financial institutions. These conditions include acquisition candidates that have markets with favorable characteristics and acquisition prices which can increase our profits over time. Geographic proximity to where we operate, as well as an organizational culture that can mesh with ours are important considerations.

"...balanced emphasis...": customer sales and service, credit quality, and operational efficiency are musts for profitability, and adequate profitability does not exist without excellent customer sales and service, excellent credit quality, and operational efficiency.

"...customer sales and service...": excellent customer sales and service is vital to attracting and retaining customers, who are our reason to exist. Treating customers in an exceptional manner is the goal of Service Vision—"Win One for the

Customer," both internal and external, results in winning one for all of us.

"...credit quality...": low credit losses are essential to soundness and profitability. Making credit available to a borrower, when it is not sound to do so, results in harm to the customer and to the bank; making credit available on a sound basis will help a customer grow and help our bank. While some losses are part of doing business, we need to strive for low charge-offs.

"...operational efficiency...": with declining interest rate spreads and increased competition, being efficient is a must in the banking industry of the present and the future. Only banks which are lean from a staffing standpoint with proficient, trained employees, judicious with their use of branch offices, and who use technology to deliver products and services in a cost effective, customer pleasing way will service and prosper.

"...profitability...": adequate profits are essential to our growth and continued viability as a financial organization and are the necessary ingredient to regard our shareholders and have competitive wages, benefits and personal growth opportunities for our employees. We endeavor to pass a portion of our profits and efforts back into our communities to help the areas in which we operate develop economically and in the long term help our profitability because of a better market in which to operate.

Increasing profitability is a function of superior customer service, sound credit quality, and operational efficiency. Deposit Guaranty is committed to increasing shareholder value and profitability by effectively balancing the often competing needs of customer sales and service, credit quality and operating efficiency.

ADDRESS   P. O. Box 730
Jackson, MS 39205

INDUSTRY CATEGORY   Banking

CORPORATE DESCRIPTION
Deposit Guaranty Corp. is a Jackson, Mississippi–based financial services company with over $5 billion in assets. Its primary subsidiaries are Deposit Guaranty National Bank, Mississippi's largest financial institution with 130 banking locations across the state, and Commercial National Bank, Louisiana's fifth largest bank with 12 branches in the Shreveport area.

Other subsidiaries include Deposit Guaranty Mortgage Company, one of the largest mortgage loan servicers in Mississippi; Deposit Guaranty Investments Inc., a full-service broker dealer subsidiary; and G & W Life Insurance Company, a 79 percent–owned subsidiary which provides credit life insurance.

SIZE REVENUES $66,552,000 (net income) as of 1993

NUMBER OF EMPLOYEES   2,575 as of 1993

SOURCES   *1993 Annual Report*; "The Fortune Service 500," *Fortune* 129, no. 11 (May 30, 1994)

◆　◆　◆　◆　◆　◆　◆

COMPANY | *Diamond Shamrock, Inc.*

STATEMENT | **"BE THE BEST—GROW AND WIN"**
OUR VISION
As a cohesive team we will grow and achieve superior financial results for our company.
We will consistently:
◈ Focus On Our Customers

- ❧ Continuously Improve Everything We Do
- ❧ Produce Quality Products And Service
- ❧ Out-Perform Competition
- ❧ Create Opportunities Out Of Change
- ❧ Value, Respect, And Develop Every Employee
- ❧ Encourage Each Employee's Participation And Ideas
- ❧ Be Ethical, Responsible, And Protective Of The Environment
- ❧ Be Safe, Have Fun, And Take Pride In Our Work

ADDRESS   P. O. Box 696000
San Antonio, TX 78269-6000

INDUSTRY CATEGORY   Oil and Gas

CORPORATE DESCRIPTION
Diamond Shamrock, Inc. is a highly focused, regional refiner and marketer of petroleum products. Its two efficient refineries in Texas have a combined throughput capacity of 205,000 barrels per day and operate at near capacity levels producing quality products such as gasoline, diesel, and jet fuel. Approximately 4,600 miles of crude oil and refined products pipelines bring crude oil into the refineries and connect these refineries to 14 products terminals throughout the company's Southwest markets. Annually, the company sells over two billion gallons of performance tested gasoline through nearly 2,000 branded outlets—776 company-operated Corner Stores in Texas, Colorado, Louisiana, and New Mexico, and 1,194 branded stations in eight states supplied by jobbers. Other businesses include petro-chemical processing and natural gas liquids marketing and storage.

SIZE REVENUES $2,555,300,000 as of 1993

NUMBER OF EMPLOYEES   6,000+ as of 1993

SOURCE   *1993 Annual Report*

COMPANY | *Digi International Inc.*

STATEMENT | Mission Statement

To develop and market connectivity products for networked systems.

ADDRESS   6400 Flying Cloud Dr.
Eden Prairie, MN 55344

INDUSTRY CATEGORY   High Technology

CORPORATE DESCRIPTION
Digi International is a leading provider of data communications hardware and software products that deliver solutions for multiuser environments, remote access and wide area networks. The company produces the communications subsystems under the DigiBoard, Arnet, Star Gate and MiLAN tradenames and markets its products to a broad range of worldwide distributors, systems integrators, value added resellers (VARs) and original equipment manufacturers (OEMs).

SIZE REVENUES $93,400,000 as of 1993

NUMBER OF EMPLOYEES   333 as of 1993

SOURCE   *1993 Annual Report*

COMPANY | *Donnelly Corporation*

STATEMENT | **Corporate Values Statements**
VALUES

All companies have goals, plans and standards by which they measure their performance. Donnelly's corporate identity has always been shaped by the values that are listed in this document. As we continue to operate in a rapidly changing environment, it is essential that we clearly express and understand our values. This ensures that we accept personal responsibility for upholding them and that they guide our actions.

We invite you to join us in the exploration of the issues that these values raise and in the work of making them a visible part of everyday life at Donnelly. While this may not be easy work, it is very exciting and rewarding. Let's make it happen!

Dwane Baumgardner
Chairman of the Board

We believe these elements to be essential in operating our business.
ONE
We serve our customers with excellence. Our existence depends on them.

TWO
We respect people. They are important and we empower them.

THREE
We are highly productive through participation, teamwork and accountability.

FOUR
We demonstrate integrity, high ethical standards, and respect for the community and environment in all of our actions.

FIVE
We are a manufacturing organization thriving on change, committed to continuous improvement, and achieving zero defects in all areas.

SIX

We have strong leadership at all levels which is critical to our success.

SEVEN

We expand and strengthen synergistic core competencies.

EIGHT

We select products based on strong competitive advantage, high profitability, and global potential.

NINE

We grow profitably to achieve security and above average returns for employees and shareholders.

TEN

We support long-term cooperative relationships with excellent suppliers.

ADDRESS   414 E. 40th St.
Holland, MI 49423-5368

COMPANY | *Computer Media Technology*

STATEMENT | **CMT Values & Mission**

- ◆ Effective leadership that creates stability and profit, assuring an exceptional work environment.
- ◆ Give the customer more than he or she expects—everytime.
- ◆ Don't over-commit and under-produce.
- ◆ Each of us must strive to do the very best we can—everyday, that usually wins!
- ◆ Everyone must display a sincere, infectious customer-oriented attitude—"How can I help you?"
- ◆ Practice Quality, Quality, Quality.

INDUSTRY CATEGORY   Motor Vehicles and Related

CORPORATE DESCRIPTION
Donnelly Corporation is a supplier to the global automotive industry. In North America, Europe, and Asia...nearly every major auto maker in the world receives products from Donnelly. The company operates from 19 facilities worldwide.

SIZE REVENUES $337,262,000 (net sales) as of 1994

NUMBER OF EMPLOYEES   2,704 as of 1994

SOURCES   *1994 Annual Report*; "Corporate Values Statements" company brochure

- ◆ Have respect for the individual.
- ◆ Everyone at CMT is a Salesperson.

CORPORATE DESCRIPTION
CMT is a software industry-oriented supplier of magnetic media, CD-ROM services, computer supplies and recycling/returned materials processing services. In 1994, the company had 15 employees and revenues approached $6 million.

ADDRESS   257 Humbolt Ct.
Sunnyvale, CA 94089

SOURCE   Company representative

STATEMENT

[Excerpts from the company publication "Vision: and Strategy for the Nineties"]

Vision

A premier global company...dedicated to growth...driven by quality performance and innovation...committed to maximizing our customers' successes...always living our Core Values.

Strategy

TECHNOLOGY

To realize our Vision, we will be the leader in chemistry-related technologies, which are the foundation for all of our businesses. It is the application of all technologies by every function to create real solutions to important customer problems that will create the growth our Vision demands.

We will search for and find additional technologies and products from both internal and external sources to enhance those already in place.

STRATEGIC BUSINESS MIX

Our six Global Business Groups will provide the foundation for growth and diversification to pursue our Vision through the end of this century. We will continue to search for strategic acquisitions as a part of our commitment to growth. Top priority will be given to further expand value-added products, services and technologies.

GEOGRAPHIC EMPHASIS

The Areas, in concert with the Global Business Groups, will continuously prioritize geographic opportunities and devote resources only to those with satisfactory potential for profits and growth. In general, and in the long term, production should be placed in the market it supports.

ORGANIZATION

We will continue to refine the concept of globally integrated businesses, operating in a matrix organization with geographic implementation of global business strategies, through functional centers of technical expertise. Emphasizing and sharpening our marketing efforts will improve our ability to identify and meet customer needs.

A lean organization with a minimum of managerial layers is central to our organizational style.

PEOPLE

Our employees are the source of Dow's success. We treat them with respect, promote teamwork, and encourage personal freedom and growth. Excellence in performance is sought and rewarded.

We will foster an environment in which people look forward to change and are committed to improvement through a life-long pursuit of continuous personal development. We will emphasize respect for the individual through:

- Encouragement of entrepreneurialism.
- Training and development programs.
- Decentralization of responsibility and authority.
- Liberation and utilization of talent and experience.
- Recognition of individual initiative in the achievement of team success.

Dow Core Values

If you can't do it better, why do it?
—H. H. Dow, Founder

Long-term profit growth is essential to ensure the prosperity and well-being of Dow employees, stockholders, and customers. How we achieve this objective is as important as the objective itself. Fundamental to our success are the core values we believe in and practice.

Employees are the source of Dow's success. We treat them with respect, promote teamwork, and encourage personal freedom and growth. Excellence in performance is sought and rewarded.

Customers will receive our strongest possible commitment to meet their needs with high quality products and superior service.

Our Products are based on continuing excellence and innovation in chemistry-related sciences and technology.

Our Conduct demonstrates a deep concern for ethics, citizenship, safety, health and the environment.

ADDRESS   2030 Dow Center
Midland, MI 48674

INDUSTRY CATEGORY   Chemicals

CORPORATE DESCRIPTION
Dow manufactures and supplies more than 2,000 products and services, including chemicals and performance products, plastics, hydrocarbons and energy, and consumer specialties—which include agricultural products, pharmaceuticals and consumer products. The company operates 183 manufacturing sites in 33 countries and employs about 55,400 people around the world.

SIZE REVENUES $18,060,000,000 as of 1993

NUMBER OF EMPLOYEES   55,400 as of 1993

SOURCES   "Dow at a Glance" company publication, "Vision" company publication

COMPANY | *Dreyer's Grand Ice Cream, Inc.*

STATEMENT | **Mission**

To become the leading premium ice cream company in America.

ADDRESS   5929 College Ave.
Oakland, CA 94618

INDUSTRY CATEGORY   Food/Beverage

CORPORATE DESCRIPTION

Dreyer's Grand Ice Cream, Inc. and its subsidiaries are engaged in the business of manufacturing and distributing premium ice cream and other frozen dairy products.

SIZE REVENUES $470,665,000 (net sales) as of 1993

NUMBER OF EMPLOYEES   1,800 as of August, 1994

SOURCES   *1993 Annual Report*; company representative

STATEMENT | **Our Shared Vision**

We will be the supplier of choice by our customers, the employer of choice by our co-workers and our communities, the investment of choice by our owners and the model of integrity and excellence for business and industry.

Our Mission

We produce and supply electricity, provide related products and services and pursue opportunities that complement our business. We will continually improve our products and services to better meet our customers' needs and expectations, helping our customers, employees, owners and communities to prosper.

Our Guiding Principles

We pursue excellence in all we do.

We strive continually to improve our products and services, our human and community relations, the safety of our operations and our financial performance.

Customers are our focus.

We anticipate, understand and meet our customers' changing needs and expectations.

Involved employees are our most important asset.

We give our best and work to create an environment that provides each of us the opportunity to reach our potential.

Financial success keeps us in business.

To prosper, both as employees and as a corporation, we maintain the financial strength of our company and provide a competitive return to our owners.

We are involved, responsible citizens.

We maintain our tradition of citizenship and service through actions that demonstrate our care for the people and environment around us.

Teamwork is our way of life.
We work in partnership with our co-workers, and with our customers, suppliers, owners and governments to achieve mutual goals. Trust and respect are the foundations of our team approach.
Integrity is never compromised.
Our actions and decisions reflect the highest ethical and professional standards.

ADDRESS   P. O. Box 1005
Charlotte, NC 28201-1005

INDUSTRY CATEGORY   Utility

CORPORATE DESCRIPTION
Headquartered in Charlotte, NC, Duke Power supplies electricity to more than 1.7 million residential, commercial and industrial customers in a 20,000-square-mile service area in North Carolina and South Carolina. Since its founding nearly 90 years ago, the Company has grown to become the nation's sixth-largest investor-owned electric utility as measured by kilowatt-hour sales.

SIZE REVENUES $4,281,876,000 as of 1993

NUMBER OF EMPLOYEES   18,274 as of 1993

SOURCE   *1993 Annual Report*

COMPANY | *Duriron (The Duriron Company, Inc.)*

STATEMENT | **FULFILLING THE MISSION**

The mission of Duriron is to serve the needs of the worldwide process industries for fluid handling products, systems and services. This will be accomplished through our ability to identify and meet the market requirements now and in the future. We will focus our efforts toward specialized applications where there is a need for high value products that can be differentiated through application know-how, engineering design and/or materials expertise. It is our intent to be among the leaders in the markets we serve through a Company-wide commitment to the philosophy of total quality and through continued advancement of our product development, manufacturing and marketing skills.

ADDRESS   3100 Research Blvd.
Dayton, OH 45420

INDUSTRY CATEGORY   Manufacturing

CORPORATE DESCRIPTION

The Duriron Company, Inc. designs and manufactures engineered products including valves and automation equipment, pumps, filtration and chemical waste systems for the movement and control of corrosive and difficult to manage fluids and vapors. Its customers include those who make, process or use chemicals, petroleum, and the products from it, pharmaceuticals, textiles, pulp and paper, and food and beverages.

SIZE REVENUES $313,920,000 (net sales) as of 1993

NUMBER OF EMPLOYEES   2,350 (worldwide) as of 1993

SOURCE   *1993 Annual Report*

COMPANY | *Eastern Enterprises*

STATEMENT | **EASTERN'S MISSION STATEMENT**

Eastern's primary objective is to maximize total return to its shareholders, by investing in companies which provide their customers with quality products and services, and managing those businesses in a manner that achieves, over time, sustainable earnings growth and an above average return on invested capital.

ADDRESS 9 Riverside Rd.
Weston, MA 02193

INDUSTRY CATEGORY Diversified

CORPORATE DESCRIPTION

Eastern Enterprises is comprised of three business segments:
1) Boston Gas Company: New England's largest gas distribution company serving over 500,000 residential, commercial and industrial customers in Boston and 73 other cities and towns throughout eastern and central Massachusetts.
2) Midland Enterprises Inc.: The nation's leading carrier of coal on the inland waterways.
3) WaterPro Supplies Corporation: The largest U. S. distributor of components for repairing and expanding municipal water supply and wastewater collection systems.

SIZE REVENUES $1,099,800,000 as of 1993

NUMBER OF EMPLOYEES 3,600 as of 1993

SOURCE *1993 Annual Report*

COMPANY | *Eaton Corporation*

STATEMENT | **Mission Statement**

Producing the highest quality products at costs which make them economically practical in the most competitively priced markets.

To be achieved by our global commitment to:

- ❖ Customer satisfaction
- ❖ Profitable growth
- ❖ Total quality leadership
- ❖ Continuous productivity improvement
- ❖ The Eaton Philosophy of excellence through people
- ❖ Concern for our communities and environment, and
- ❖ The highest standard of integrity

ADDRESS   Eaton Center
1111 Superior
Cleveland, OH 44114-2584

INDUSTRY CATEGORY   Manufacturing

CORPORATE DESCRIPTION

Eaton manufactures a variety of components and controls for automobiles, trucks, appliances, military equipment, industrial products, hydraulics, and semiconductor equipment.

SIZE REVENUES $4,400,000,000 as of 1993

NUMBER OF EMPLOYEES   50,000 as of September 1, 1994

SOURCE   *1992 Annual Report;* company representative

Our Mission, Philosophy and Standards of Performance

Our Mission. Our business is to be a leading innovator, developer and marketer of worldwide services, products and systems, which provide superior value to our customers in meeting their cleaning, sanitizing and maintenance needs, while conserving resources and preserving the quality of the environment and providing a fair profit for our shareholders.
Our Shareholders. We will be a growth company. We will provide our shareholders with a 15% annual growth in per share earnings while continually investing in product research and business development to assure a reliable future. Dividends will be consistent and recognize shareholders' needs for an adequate return and the company's need for growth capital. Our financial objectives also include a minimum 20% return on beginning of the year shareholders' equity and an "A" rated balance sheet.

We intend to remain an independent company. We believe that, to effectively maximize our shareholders' equity, positive customer service attitudes are critical to our success. This can best be provided in a flexible and entrepreneurial environment.

We encourage all employees to be long-term shareholders.

Recognizing that the quality of our shareholders' investment is built and measured over time, we will not sacrifice long-term growth in sales and earnings for short-term results.
Employees. We are dedicated to the belief that the most important resource is people who respond positively to recognition, involvement and opportunities for personal and career development. We are most productive and fulfilled in an environment where we empower and are empowered to

act. We will address problems and mistakes constructively, learn from them and contribute to their solution. We encourage a team approach with mutually supportive relationships based on objectivity, integrity, openness and trust.

We will judge ourselves on our ability to be self-critical and to provide an atmosphere encouraging open and constructive communication. We will share the information needed to do our jobs and provide a sense of direction and purpose required to face up to problems and take appropriate actions and risks. We will communicate our goals clearly, assure that decisions are made by those people closest to the situation, and encourage and support them in those decisions.

Our workplaces will be functional, clean and safe. Our working environment will foster mutual values, goals and goodwill. We will constantly strive for excellence, satisfaction and, occasionally, joy. Enthusiasm at all levels of our company is important to us.

People will be hired, paid and promoted based on qualifications, teamwork and performance. We believe that everyone benefits when the most capable person is promoted. People will be compensated fairly and rewarded well for their extra contributions to the company's success. We will not need a third party to protect our fair rights and interests.

People are encouraged to participate in setting their own goals and judging their own performance with regular supervisory reviews. We prefer promotion from within and support active programs of training and self-development that complement the corporation's philosophies and objectives.

We seek talented, action-oriented people who are enthusiastic, honest, open and hardworking, who want to do their jobs well and who expect their co-workers to do likewise. We want men and women who use the company's equipment and money as carefully as if it were their own, who suggest ways to be more productive and who help each other. We want and will encourage people to go the extra mile, work the added hour, make the additional call! Above all, we want associates who accept responsibility and accountability for their own growth, behavior and performance.

Our Customers. The company that fails its customers, fails! We will be superior to our competitors in providing the highest value to our customers at a fair price. We will constantly listen to our customers, respond quickly to their current needs and anticipate future needs.

We will stay close to our customers, tell them the truth and earn their business every day. Superior service built this company. Superior service will continue to be our central policy and philosophy. We will be vigorous, tough, ethical competitors.

We will supply our customers with superior services, specialty products and systems that are safe and reliable. We will advertise and promote our services and products in a professional and ethical manner and support them with well-trained people.

Our Organization. We seek an organization that is flexible, innovative, responsive and entrepreneurial. To accomplish this, we will create decentralized business units which have great freedom, within corporate strategy and policy limits, to develop their own business strategies and plans and to achieve agreed upon objectives. Actions will be judged on the extent to which they promote the overall good of the corporation over the separate interests of groups.

We will anticipate a changing environment. We are committed to the concept of continual improvement.

We seek to concentrate our efforts on providing services and products which have measurable benefits over state-of-the-art.

We will organize around the needs of our business units and provide only those central services which are essential to our growth, the protection of our corporate assets or provide significant advantages in terms of quality and cost.

We will observe uniform accounting practices and prompt disclosure of operating results, with no surprises.

We favor simplicity; we want action. We are results-oriented. We favor substance over form and quality over quantity. We believe in the free flow of candid, objective information, up, down and across organizational lines. We insist on "homework" and planning. We want overachievement.

Our Society. We recognize the importance of service to society and will contribute positively to the communities in which we operate. Our company's business will be conducted in accordance with the law and stated corporate and societal standards of conduct.

This statement is an expression of our mission and shared values, the achievement of which is an ongoing challenge and a never-ending process. It requires us to respond effectively to an ever-changing environment. It requires pragmatism and dreams, courage and confidence, trust and commitment— our mutual Quest for Excellence.

ADDRESS　　Ecolab Center
370 Wabasha St. N.
St. Paul, MN 55102-1390

INDUSTRY CATEGORY　　Business Services

CORPORATE DESCRIPTION
Ecolab is the leading global developer of premium cleaning, sanitizing and maintenance products and services for the hospitality, institutional and industrial markets. Customers include hotels and restaurants, foodservice and healthcare facilities, dairy plants and farms, and food and beverage processors around the world.

SIZE REVENUES　　$1,041,518,000　as of 1993

NUMBER OF EMPLOYEES　　7,586 as of 1993

SOURCE　　*1993 Annual Report;* "Quest for Excellence" company publication

Our purpose is to furnish financial services of value to our clients. We should act as their agents, putting their interests before our own.

We are confident that if we do our jobs well and give value for what we charge, not only will mutual trust and respect develop, but satisfaction and a fair reward will result.

Ethics Statement

The highest standard of ethical conduct is expected of all A. G. Edwards personnel. When faced with possible conflicts of interests, we should give preference to the client and the firm over our personal interests. We should not, without management approval, use the firm or our positions in it for personal gain other than our direct compensation.

Operating Philosophies

During 1968 and '69, our top management team spent two days a month for 24 months developing a model of the firm we wanted to be and to which we were determined to commit our careers and our capital. We agreed that building this firm would take precedence over our concerns for our personal estates or positions.

We committed ourselves to delivering financial services of value to a market we called the "mass, class market" through a network of retail branches acting as agent for the customer. We wanted to be customer-driven, and the agency relationship meant that our first allegiance had to be to the client. We should eliminate any profit centers or incentives that conflicted with the welfare or interest of the client. We realized that this plan would not allow us to manufacture our own financial products.

We recognize that the most important relationship in our business is a bond of trust between the client and the investment broker, and we should build and strengthen this relationship. If we are to be customer-driven, we must listen to our customers and be conscious of their interests in all our decisions.

Our growth should come naturally and involve only people of high character who share our philosophy of putting the customer first. Only after we have found better-than-average quality and a philosophical fit should we then look toward viability.

Profit is not the purpose of our business and should not be sought for its own sake. Rather, it is a necessity if we are to be able to continue to deliver value to our clients, so we must be careful to do what we have chosen to do in a manner that is efficient and cost-effective. We should be more concerned with the client than with the competitor.

It is one of our corporate objectives to have fun. To enjoy what we are doing, we must like those with whom we work. In order to do this, we must respect each other and work together in mutual trust. To encourage trust, we must strive for completely open communication: management must not keep secrets and must not be defensive when criticized. We must foster an atmosphere that encourages fellow employees to speak candidly and without fear of reprisal. How else can we learn?

It is important for all of us to remember why we are here and to be careful to deliver value to our customers for what we charge them. We should try to do our jobs better each week and to have fun doing them.

Ben Edwards
December 1991

ADDRESS One North Jefferson
St. Louis, MO 63103-2287

INDUSTRY CATEGORY Financial Investment services

CORPORATE DESCRIPTION

A. G. Edwards, Inc. is a holding company whose subsidiaries provide securities and commodities brokerage, investment banking, trust, asset management, and insurance services. Its principal subsidiary, A. G. Edwards & Sons, Inc., is a St. Louis-based financial services company with more than 450 locations in 48 states and the District of Columbia. A. G. Edwards & Sons provides a full range of financial products and services to individual and institutional investors, and offers investment banking services to corporate, governmental and municipal clients.

SIZE REVENUES $1,278,641,000 as of 1994

NUMBER OF EMPLOYEES 10,206 as of 1994

SOURCE *1994 Annual Report*

COMPANY | *Energen Corporation*

STATEMENT | **ENERGEN STATEMENT OF PRINCIPLES**
We will conduct our business and earn a profit based on ethical standards and values which recognize:

❖
The dignity and worth of all individuals

❖
Commitment to excellence in performance

❖
Personal and business integrity and

❖
Courage of convictions and action.

ADDRESS   2101 Sixth Ave. N.
Birmingham, AL 35203

INDUSTRY CATEGORY   Oil and Gas

CORPORATE DESCRIPTION
Energen is a diversified energy company based in Birmingham, Alabama. The Company has two major lines of business:
— Natural gas distribution through Alagasco
— Oil and gas exploration and production through Taurus Exploration

SIZE REVENUES $357,116,000 as of 1993

NUMBER OF EMPLOYEES   1,568 as of 1993

SOURCE   *1993 Annual Report*

COMPANY | *Entergy Corporation*

STATEMENT | **Entergy Corporation Vision Statement**
Entergy will be a world-class performer in the increasingly competitive electric energy business through aggressive leadership by customer-focused, highly productive, empowered employees.

ADDRESS   P. O. Box 61005
New Orleans, LA 70161

INDUSTRY CATEGORY   Utility

CORPORATE DESCRIPTION
Entergy Corporation is one of the larger investor-owned public utility holding companies in the United States, and the leading electricity supplier in the Middle South region. Headquartered in New Orleans, Entergy serves more than 1.7 million retail customers through its operating companies in Arkansas, Louisiana, and Mississippi. Entergy also provides wholesale electricity off-System to other utilities, and markets its energy expertise worldwide.

SIZE REVENUES $4,485,300,000 as of 1993

NUMBER OF EMPLOYEES   11,914 as of 1993

SOURCES   *1993 Annual Report*; "The Fortune Service 500," *Fortune* 129, no. 11 (May 30, 1994)

STATEMENT | **Ethyl Corporation Vision And Values**

OUR VISION

To Be At The Top of Customers' Lists of Suppliers

In the markets we serve, Ethyl will be at the top of existing and potential customers' lists of companies from which they will choose to do business.

To achieve this vision, we will operate according to the following values:

Respect for People

Achieving our vision depends entirely on the ability of Ethyl's people to contribute individually and collectively, to develop new skills, to work in an environment that fosters pride and to share in the contributions they make toward the success of the company. This success requires a culture that makes it possible for Ethyl people to achieve full potential. Such a culture is based on mutual trust and respect.

Unquestionable Integrity

Personal and corporate integrity are the foundations for all our activities. Integrity is a cherished possession we want never to lose.

Continually Improving Quality

Quality means satisfying customers' needs now and in the future. To do this, we must continually improve the quality of everything we make or do.

Our Partners—Customers and Suppliers

To be at the top of customers' lists, we must become their partners. This means we must share their business goals, champion their interests and link our resources to theirs in anticipation of their future needs. We need and will encourage the partnership of our suppliers in support of our customers' needs and goals as well.

Safety and Environmental Responsibility
It is Ethyl's goal to provide workplaces for employees that are safe, healthy and environmentally sound. Likewise, our presence in communities will not adversely affect the safety, health or environment of our neighbors. Finally, we will participate in ongoing activities, like Responsible Care®, that improve the health, safety and environment of the world.

Good Citizenship
We intend to be good citizens wherever we have a presence throughout the world. Good citizens do more than simply comply with laws; they support causes that help to improve the community. We will support such causes as a corporation and encourage Ethyl people to take active roles in answering community needs.

Economic Viability
To realize this vision, Ethyl must be an economically viable and profitable organization. As we operate according to our vision and values, Ethyl will enjoy long-term growth with continually improving performance.

ADDRESS 330 S. Fourth St.
P. O. Box 2189
Richmond, VA 23217

INDUSTRY CATEGORY Chemicals

CORPORATE DESCRIPTION
Ethyl Corporation develops, manufactures and blends performance-enhancing fuel and lubricant additives marketed worldwide to refiners and others who sell petroleum products for use in transportation and industrial equipment. Ethyl additives increase the value of gasoline, diesel and heating fuels as well as lubricants for engines, automatic transmissions, gears and hydraulic and industrial equipment.

Ethyl spun-off its chemicals business in February 1994. Ethyl Corporation Vision and Values was created to reflect the values of the newly focused corporation.

SIZE REVENUES $1,019,022,000 as of December 31, 1994

NUMBER OF EMPLOYEES   1,500 as of December 31, 1994

SOURCES   *1994 Annual Report*; company representative

◆   ◆   ◆   ◆   ◆   ◆   ◆

COMPANY | *Federal Express Corporation*

STATEMENT | Corporate Mission

Federal Express is committed to our People-Service-Profit philosophy. We will produce outstanding financial returns by providing totally reliable, competitively superior global air-ground transportation of high priority goods and documents that require rapid, time-certain delivery. Equally important, positive control of each package will be maintained utilizing real-time electronic tracking and tracing systems. A complete record of each shipment and delivery will be presented with our request for payment. We will be helpful, courteous, and professional to each other and the public. We will strive to have a completely satisfied customer at the end of each transaction.

—Frederick K. Smith, Chairman and Chief Executive Officer

ADDRESS   2005 Corporate Ave.
Memphis, TN 38132

INDUSTRY CATEGORY   Transportation

CORPORATE DESCRIPTION
Federal Express Corporation offers a wide range of customized services for the time-definite transportation and distribution of goods and documents throughout the world, using an extensive fleet of aircraft and vehicles.

SIZE REVENUES $8,479,456,000 as of 1994

NUMBER OF EMPLOYEES   103,900+ (worldwide) as of 1994

SOURCE   *1993 Annual Report;* company representative

◆ ◆ ◆ ◆ ◆ ◆ ◆

COMPANY | *Federal-Mogul Corporation*

STATEMENT | **Federal-Mogul Mission Statement**

Federal-Mogul's primary strategic focus is the manufacturing and distribution of products into the global vehicular and industrial aftermarket. The company is committed to providing these markets with world class quality products and adding value through the interdependence of our manufacturing and distribution operations.

We will also continue our history of support to the original equipment market. In fact, we will strive to be a leader in all OEM products in which the company participates.

Through this integrated approach, we will create sufficient value to be rewarded by our customers. This unique value created will result in profits for our investors, and help meet our commitment of providing job satisfaction and a pleasant work environment for all our employees.

Our product development, manufacturing and distribution systems will be designed for flexibility, high quality and fast customer response. This will create Federal-Mogul's time-based competitive advantage of supplying low volume/high variety products.

Corporate Strategy

The elimination of time in dealing with the development, manufacturing, distribution and administrative needs of our customers is our major priority.

Guiding Principles

1. Quality

Complete customer satisfaction in products and service is crucial to our continued survival in a global environment.

COMPANY | *Eriez Magnetics*

STATEMENT | **Fundamental Principle**

"Using the Golden Rule as a guide—to build a worldwide organization that will give our CUSTOMERS high-quality products and services at a favorable price commensurate with good service before and after sale; our ASSOCIATES the best possible job opportunity to sell their products and services in an atmosphere of courtesy and trust and at prices that will allow them to make a fair profit; and our STOCKHOLDERS a reasonable continuing return on their investment. Recognizing our social responsibilities to the COMMUNITIES in which we operate, we will strive to conduct our affairs in such an efficient, capable, and friendly manner that everyone with whom we come in contact will be happy to be associated with us."

2. Customer Response

Our customers are our reason for being. All our efforts must be directed towards providing them with the best products and services.

3. Continuous Improvement

We must never be satisfied with our performance. We must strive to provide the very best in products, services and value.

4. Respect for all Individuals

Employee involvement means trust and respect for each other as members of a team.

5. Ethical Conduct

Our integrity in the marketplace and with each other must never be compromised. Our conduct must be socially responsible. We are committed to equal opportunities for all individuals.

Corporate Description

Eriez develops and markets a variety of magnetic devices for use in industry. The Eriez product line includes a wide range of separation, purification, vibratory, metal detection, and automated magnetic devices to help improve productivity and profits for customers around the world. As of 1994, the company had 450 employees and annual revenues of $60 million. The company's Fundamental Principle statement presented here was introduced in 1948.

ADDRESS   P. O. Box 10608
Erie, PA 16514

SOURCES   "From Pioneer To World Leader" company publication; company representative

ADDRESS 26555 Northwestern Hwy.
Southfield, MI 48034

INDUSTRY CATEGORY Manufacturing

CORPORATE DESCRIPTION
Federal-Mogul Corporation is a global distributor and manufacturer of a broad range of precision parts, primarily components for automobiles, light and heavy duty trucks, farm and construction vehicles, and industrial products.

SIZE REVENUES $1,575,500,000 as of 1993

NUMBER OF EMPLOYEES 14,400 as of 1993

SOURCE *1993 Annual Report*

◆ ◆ ◆ ◆ ◆ ◆ ◆

COMPANY | *Federated Department Stores, Inc.*

STATEMENT | **CORPORATE PHILOSOPHY**
Federated clearly recognizes that the customer is paramount, and that all actions and strategies must be directed toward providing an enhanced merchandise offering and better service to targeted consumers through dynamic department stores.

Aggressive implementation of the company's strategies, as well as careful and thorough planning, will provide Federated's department stores with a competitive edge.

Federated is committed to open and honest communications with employees, shareholders, vendors, analysts and the news media. The company will be pro-active in sharing information and in keeping these audiences up-to-date on important and material developments.

CORPORATE OBJECTIVES

The corporate objectives of Federated Department Stores, Inc. are:

❧ To accelerate comp-store sales growth and identify strategic growth opportunities that are consistent with the company's business objectives.

❧ To continue moving the company toward performance levels that are consistent with the results produced by the nation's top department store retailers. This will be accomplished through a more coordinated, centralized and common approach to running the business, and through disciplined, consistent and undiverted attention to execution in all aspects of the company's department store operation.

ADDRESS   7 W. Seventh St.
Cincinnati, OH 45202

INDUSTRY CATEGORY   Retail

CORPORATE DESCRIPTION
Federated Department Stores, Inc. is one of the nation's largest operators of premier department stores located in the eastern, midwestern, northwestern and southeastern regions of the United States. Federated conducts its retail business through its operating divisions, which among them operate 232 department stores in 26 states.

SIZE REVENUES $7,229,000,000 as of 1993

NUMBER OF EMPLOYEES   67,000+ as of 1993

SOURCE   *1994 Corporate Fact Book*

COMPANY | *Ferro Corporation*

STATEMENT | FERRO's CORPORATE MISSION

Ferro is organized and managed to achieve steady growth in operating profits, enhancement of shareholder value, and dividend payments commensurate with earnings growth.

Operations are directed to meeting the needs of customers for high-performance specialty materials, engineered products and services worldwide. These businesses will have sufficient size, technical scope and market position to provide opportunities for current and future growth.

Because a company's reputation is one of its most valued assets, Ferro conducts its business on sound ethical principles, based upon integrity and fairness to all constituencies.

While the Company's ultimate responsibility is to its shareholders, Ferro also has a deep commitment to employees, whose skills, attitudes and efforts are essential to the Company's continued success.

ADDRESS 1000 Lakeside Ave.
Cleveland, OH 44114-1183

INDUSTRY CATEGORY Industrial, Specialized

CORPORATE DESCRIPTION

Ferro Corporation is a leading worldwide producer of specialty materials for industry. These materials include specialty coatings, colors, ceramics, plastics and chemicals.

The Company's major markets encompass building and renovation, home appliances, household furnishings, transportation, industrial products, packaging and leisure applications. The Company's strong worldwide status is based upon its manufacturing presence in 22 countries and its marketing and customer service operations in over 100 nations.

SIZE REVENUES $1,065,748,000 as of 1993

NUMBER OF EMPLOYEES   6,627 as of December 31, 1993

SOURCES   *1992 Annual Report;* "1992 Profile" company publication; company representative

♦ ♦ ♦ ♦ ♦ ♦ ♦

COMPANY | *First American Corporation*

STATEMENT | **First American Mission Statement**
Our primary responsibility is to manage the company soundly, profitably and with adequate growth to serve the needs of our customers, our employees and our communities, thereby increasing the value of our SHAREHOLDERS' investment.

We believe that by providing our CUSTOMERS with convenient access to high-quality products, coupled with superior service, we can excel and be a leader in our priority markets: individual consumers and small to mid-sized businesses of Tennessee.

We view our EMPLOYEES as partners. We are committed to providing a fair and challenging workplace, one that respects and empowers the individual; encourages professional growth; and recognizes and rewards outstanding performance.

We take seriously our responsibility to our COMMUNITIES. We endeavor to foster their success by offering appropriate financial services to all economic segments and by actively demonstrating our role as a caring corporate citizen. We invest our capital in Tennessee and build strong relationships with our Tennessee suppliers.

ADDRESS   First American Center
300 Union
Nashville, TN 37237

INDUSTRY CATEGORY   Banking

CORPORATE DESCRIPTION
First American Corporation is a bank holding company which was incorporated under the laws of Tennessee in 1968. First American's largest subsidiary is First American National Bank. First American is also the parent of First American Trust Company, N.A. On the basis of total deposits and total assets, First American Corporation is the largest bank holding company headquartered in Nashville, Tennessee, and the second largest in Tennessee.

SIZE REVENUES $101,813,000 (net income) as of 1993

NUMBER OF EMPLOYEES   3,100 as of 1993

SOURCE   *1993 Annual Report*

COMPANY | *First Bank System*

STATEMENT | **THE FBS VISION**
| **MISSION**

We build high-performing banking franchises where we can create and sustain market leadership.

| **GOAL**

We will be one of the top-performing banks, measured in terms of market share and long-term profitability. We will achieve this goal through:

Customer service commitment
Cost control
Credit quality
Capital strength
Core business concentration
Cross-selling aggressively and effectively
Community commitment
Communicating clearly and honestly

| **VALUES**

As a company, we value:

Integrity
We are honest, ethical and fair. We tell the truth and expect to hear the truth from others.
Leadership
As a company and as individuals, we take positions and lead by example in all things important to us.
Performance
We know there is no substitute for outstanding performance. We continually seek ways to reward excellence.
Quality
We understand that our customers define quality and we strive to consistently meet their expectations.

Diversity
We value individual differences and work to leverage their inherent creative potential.
Cooperation
We will work together to achieve our common goals. Openness and flexibility are important.

ADDRESS   601 2nd Ave. S.
Minneapolis, MN 55402

INDUSTRY CATEGORY   Banking

CORPORATE DESCRIPTION
First Bank System, Inc. is a regional bank holding company headquartered in Minneapolis. The company is comprised of 9 banks and trust companies and several nonbank subsidiaries with 220 offices primarily in Minnesota, Colorado, Montana, North Dakota, South Dakota, Wisconsin and Illinois.

SIZE REVENUES $1,702,500,000 as of 1993

NUMBER OF EMPLOYEES   12,300 as of 1993

SOURCE   *1993 Annual Report*

COMPANY | *First Financial Corporation*

STATEMENT

"We will efficiently build shareholder value by providing a broad line of high-quality financial services to the residents of the Midwest through conveniently located retail banking offices, innovative programs and products, and friendly, professional employees. An important part of this mission is to deepen our relationship with existing customers by exceeding their expectations in helping them meet their housing and related financial needs."

"We will set ourselves apart through our responsiveness and reliability which we demonstrate every day through every action with our customers and each other."

ADDRESS   1305 Main St.
Stevens Point, WI 54481

INDUSTRY CATEGORY   Banking

CORPORATE DESCRIPTION

First Financial Corporation is the holding company for two consumer banking companies—First Financial Bank, FSB and First Financial–Port Savings Bank, FSB. First Financial Bank had assets of $5 billion as of mid-year 1994 and operated 124 banking offices in Wisconsin and Illinois.

SIZE REVENUES $45,215,000 (net income) as of 1993

NUMBER OF EMPLOYEES   1,320 as of 1993

SOURCES   "The Fortune Service 500," *Fortune* 129, no. 11 (May 30, 1994); company representative

STATEMENT | **MISSION STATEMENT**

First Financial Management Corporation's corporate mission is:

To provide information processing services which support consumer and commercial transactions.

In accomplishing this mission, FFMC subscribes to the following Statement of Beliefs:

❖ FFMC shall be a market-driven company.

❖ FFMC believes that the Customer is the most important asset of the Corporation and as such, should be treated with the highest level of respect and attention.

❖ FFMC believes that a high quality level of service delivered on a consistent basis is essential in maintaining satisfied Customers.

❖ FFMC believes that its Customers deserve competitive technology and high quality products that allow them to be competitive in their markets.

❖ FFMC believes that to provide long-term stability for its Customers and Shareholders, it must remain financially sound and produce consistent profits that maintain or improve returns from year to year.

❖ FFMC believes that its Employees must have high professional ethics, high moral standards, and good business practices to maintain the confidence and respect of its Customers, Shareholders and fellow Employees.

❖ FFMC believes that it and its Employees should be judged and rewarded on the results of their actions (performance) rather than on the actions themselves.

❖ FFMC believes that all Employees should be given the opportunity to develop their skills and realize their maximum potential. To this end FFMC believes that, whenever possible, promotions should be from within and that programs should be in place to train Employees and broaden their experience.

❖ FFMC believes in a decentralized style of management: delegating responsibilities, authorities and accountabilities to the lowest practical level in our organization—where control can be maintained.

❖ FFMC believes that its management must provide the leadership necessary to achieve Customer satisfaction, Employee satisfaction, improvement of earnings, and business growth.

ADDRESS 3 Corporate Square, Ste. 700
Atlanta, GA 30329

INDUSTRY CATEGORY Financial Investment services

CORPORATE DESCRIPTION
First Financial Management Corporation is a national leader in information services, offering a vertically integrated set of data processing, storage and management products for the capture, manipulation and distribution of data. Services include merchant credit card authorization, processing and settlement; check guarantee and verification; debt collection and accounts receivable management; data imaging, micrographics and electronic data base management; integrated care management services; and the development and marketing of data communications and information processing systems.

SIZE REVENUES $1,659,800,000 as of 1993

NUMBER OF EMPLOYEES 11,500 as of 1993

SOURCES *1993 Annual Report*, "The Fortune Service 500," *Fortune* 129, no. 11 (May 30, 1994)

STATEMENT | **Mission Statement**

At First Interstate Bank, our mission is to provide superior value and exceptional service to our customers.

To accomplish this:

We believe in being a preferred employer.

We believe in the importance of maintaining superior asset quality.

We believe in actively supporting the communities we serve.

We believe in maintaining the highest levels of professional integrity and personal ethics.

We believe in rewarding our shareholders with returns that consistently meet their expectations.

As a result, we will be recognized as a leader in the financial services industry.

Values and Strategies

VALUE

We provide superior value and exceptional service to our customers.

STRATEGY

We are building relationships with customers to become their primary financial services provider.

We provide a diverse range of financial products and services that meet a variety of customer needs. Our employees accurately assess our customers' financial requirements and recommend the appropriate products and services.

We differentiate ourselves from our competitors through quality service. We acknowledge the difficulty of maintaining and improving service levels while building a lower cost structure, but can manage this challenge.

First Interstate will be a banking company of common products marketed at the local level. We foster a strong sales and service culture that understands our local markets and works to expand our share of individual and business customers in all of our regions.

VALUE

We believe in being a preferred employer.

STRATEGY

We provide our employees with an environment that recognizes their value as individuals and as members of the team. We are a caring employer and treat all employees with respect, creating a climate of trust, pride, and positive empowerment.

We encourage teamwork, open, two-way communication and personal development to reinforce our commitment to our employees.

We seek to attract the highest quality individuals whose personal values and professional skills are consistent with our strategy of providing exceptional service to our customers.

Our employees are encouraged to accept accountability for personal development. The company provides educational opportunities that enhance individual and team effectiveness.

We are strongly committed to fair compensation and recognition which demonstrate to our employees our desire to reward their effort and commitment.

We encourage and reward teamwork within and between regions and the corporate staff.

VALUE

We believe in the importance of maintaining superior asset quality.

STRATEGY

Credit quality will be one of our highest priorities. Decisions will demonstrate adherence to the company's policies and guidelines.

We continuously improve our lending processes. We utilize standard credit policies and procedures across the corporation. We monitor and control concentrations of credit portfolio, and borrower risk. The skills of our lenders are enhanced through their participation in our Exemplary Credit Program.

VALUE
We believe in actively supporting the communities we serve.

STRATEGY
We invest financial and human support to improve the quality of life in our communities.

We affirm our responsibility to be a valued corporate citizen, sensitive to community needs and concerns. We actively encourage and support the involvement of all employees in volunteer organizations.

We strongly support the aims and objectives of the Community Reinvestment Act and seek to exceed regulatory requirements.

VALUE
We believe in maintaining the highest levels of professional integrity and personal ethics.

STRATEGY
We evaluate all of our decisions and actions against an ethical framework based on openness, honesty, and fairness.

We emphasize the importance of behavior that consistently reflects our values and mission. We are measured by the integrity and ethics we demonstrate in our relationships with internal and external customers.

VALUE
We believe in rewarding our shareholders with returns that consistently meet their expectations.

STRATEGY
We will achieve long-term, sustainable profitability by focusing on relationships and transactions that will produce predictable and consistent earnings streams.

We will deliver excellent financial results as measured by return on equity while maintaining a conservative balance sheet and strong capital position.

We are committed to outstanding credit quality, proper revenue and expense management, and prudent fixed asset investments. We will enhance our revenue stream by increasing our share of core deposits, capitalizing on appropriate lending opportunities, continuing to expand noninterest income sources, and promoting the sales of alternative investment products that fit our customers' needs.

We recognize the importance of short- and long-term planning and accept accountability for achieving planned results.

VALUE

We will be recognized as a leader in the financial services industry.

STRATEGY

As we consistently adhere to our values and strategies and achieve our goals, we will demonstrate our leadership position in the industry.

We emphasize continuous improvement as we pursue quality in every aspect of our business.

ADDRESS   633 W. 5th St.
Los Angeles, CA 90071

INDUSTRY CATEGORY   Banking

CORPORATE DESCRIPTION

First Interstate is the 14th largest commercial banking company in the U. S. and the largest based in Southern California. Its 1,093 domestic offices in 13 western states serve individuals, small businesses, middle market companies and selected large corporations and financial institutions. First Interstate provides quality common financial products and services marketed at the local level to nearly five million households in over 500 western U. S. communities.

As of June 30, 1994, First Interstate Bancorp had total assets of $53,303,400,000.

SIZE REVENUES $3,000,000,000 as of 1993

NUMBER OF EMPLOYEES   28,128 as of March 31, 1994

SOURCES   *1993 Annual Report;* "Second Quarter 1994 Fact Sheet;" "Our Mission, Values and Strategies" company publication

◆　◆　◆　◆　◆　◆　◆

COMPANY | *First of America Bank Corporation*

STATEMENT | **FIRST OF AMERICA BANK CORPORATION MISSION STATEMENT**

We will compete in the financial services market by serving the needs of our customers first as we strive to maximize the value of our shareholders' investment. As we compete, our highest guiding values will remain CARING, LEADERSHIP, QUALITY, and PROFESSIONALISM.

CARING: We will guide our business activities by a sense of genuine caring as we serve our customers, fellow employees and our communities. We will treat our employees with fairness and provide them with opportunities for development to be their best. We will contribute to the economic vitality and quality of life in all of our communities.

LEADERSHIP: We will achieve or maintain a leading position within our markets and our industry, in market share, growth, return on investment, efficiency and innovative products and services.

QUALITY: We will remain committed to a superior level of quality in the development, design, sales and delivery of products and services to our individual, commercial, governmental and agricultural customers.

PROFESSIONALISM: We will conduct ourselves and our business in a way that creates confidence in First of America among customers, shareholders and our communities. We will apply expertise to serving the financial needs of our customers and maintain high ethical standards in all situations.

ADDRESS   211 S. Rose St.
Kalamazoo, MI 49007

INDUSTRY CATEGORY   Banking

CORPORATE DESCRIPTION
First of America Bank Corporation, headquartered in Kalamazoo, Michigan, is one of the largest bank holding companies in the Midwest with assets over $23 billion. First of America has 611 offices in Michigan, Indiana, Illinois, and Florida that serve over 350 communities. The banks engage in commercial banking, retail banking and mortgage banking, and provide trust, and other financial services. Based on net income, profitability and size of franchise, First of America is ranked among the top 36 banking companies in the United States.

SIZE REVENUES $247,385,000 (net income) as of 1993

NUMBER OF EMPLOYEES   13,472 as of September 30, 1994

SOURCES   *1993 Annual Report*; company representative

COMPANY | *First Tennessee National Corporation*

STATEMENT
Be the best at serving our customers, one opportunity at a time.

ADDRESS   P. O. Box 84
Memphis, TN 38101-0084

INDUSTRY CATEGORY   Banking

CORPORATE DESCRIPTION
First Tennessee National Corporation (FTNC) is one of the nation's 75 largest banking companies, with assets of $10.7 billion as of 3/31/94.

SIZE REVENUES $72,218,000 (net income) as of three months ended June 30, 1994

NUMBER OF EMPLOYEES   7,074 as of 1994

SOURCES   *Second Quarter Report 1994*; company representative

COMPANY | *First Virginia Banks, Inc.*

STATEMENT

[*Author's note:* The following appears to be addressed to the company's employees]

| **The First Virginia Creed**

Our goal is to provide friendly and professional service. We must continually strive to make our customers feel welcome. As an individual, you can accomplish this goal by greeting customers by name whenever possible, and by always thanking them for banking with us. And, when customers have questions, you should attempt to answer them as quickly and as accurately as possible. Collectively, we must carefully evaluate the needs of all customers and be sure to provide them with all the financial services they need.

Finally, we must realize that, individually and as a whole, we are responsible for creating the atmosphere that will make customers feel at home. Our fundamental responsibility is to consider how our attitudes and actions will affect customer opinion and satisfaction. Along with being fiscally responsible and earning an acceptable return for our stockholders, providing friendly, helpful service is a fundamental part of our business philosophy.

(Signed)
Robert H. Zalokar
Chairman and Chief Executive Officer

ADDRESS   One First Virginia Plaza
6400 Arlington Blvd.
Falls Church, VA 22042-2336

INDUSTRY CATEGORY   Banking

CORPORATE DESCRIPTION
First Virginia Banks, Inc., with assets of approximately $7.04 billion, is the oldest bank holding company headquartered in Virginia.

SIZE REVENUES $116,024,000 (net income) as of 1993

NUMBER OF EMPLOYEES   4,727 as of December 31, 1993

SOURCE   *1993 Annual Report*

◆ ◆ ◆ ◆ ◆ ◆ ◆

COMPANY | *Firstar Corporation*

STATEMENT | **The Vision We Share**
Firstar will create and retain mutually beneficial long-term relationships with our customers, employees, communities, and shareholders.

We will consistently provide outstanding customer satisfaction by conveniently delivering financial products and services that are valued for features, quality, and price. We will listen to our customers and use their insights to make continuous improvements.

The success of Firstar and its employees is interdependent. As an employer, Firstar will create a challenging environment that emphasizes professional growth, rewards performance, and affords equal opportunity to all of our people. As employees, we will work together in a spirit of teamwork and mutual respect. We will always adhere to the highest standards of ethics and integrity.

Firstar will be a good corporate citizen. We will actively support the economic, social and cultural well-being of our communities.

We will provide our shareholders a competitive return on their investment by consistently performing in the top quartile of our peer group.

We realize that the only way we can achieve this vision is to be a financially strong, consistently profitable, and growing organization. As we prioritize our activities, soundness is first, then profitability, and finally growth.

By fulfilling this vision, we will assure our future as one of the nation's most successful and respected financial institutions.

ADDRESS   777 E. Wisconsin Ave.
Milwaukee, WI 53202

INDUSTRY CATEGORY   Banking

CORPORATE DESCRIPTION
Firstar Corporation is a $13.8 billion bank holding company, headquartered in Milwaukee, Wisconsin. The company delivers a comprehensive range of financial products and services to consumers and businesses through a three-tiered distribution system consisting of a large lead bank, member banks and correspondent customers.

Businesses include:

❖ 36 banks and 200 offices in Wisconsin, Iowa, Minnesota, Illinois, Arizona and Florida.

❖ Other business units engaged in trust and investment management, mortgage banking, insurance, securities brokerage, and related financial services. Credit cards and a variety of other consumer financial products are marketed under the name Elan.

SIZE REVENUES $204,294,000 (net income) as of 1993

NUMBER OF EMPLOYEES   9,000 as of 1993

SOURCES   *1993 Annual Report*

COMPANY | *Flagstar Companies, Inc.*

STATEMENT

[*Author's note:* the following statements are excerpted from the "Chairman's Letter," which appeared in the company's 1992 Annual Report and was written by Chairman and Chief Executive officer, Jerome J. Richardson.]

To be the best food service company in the world by the year 2000. Mission 2000 is the process we are using to achieve this goal.

As part of Mission 2000, we are measuring our success in the following key areas:

❖ **Competition.** Increasing customer traffic more rapidly than our competitors.

❖ **Employment.** Achieving measurable reductions in employee turnover, improving productivity and maximizing customer satisfaction.

❖ **Citizenship.** Monitoring the commitment of employee knowledge and time, corporate contributions and in-kind gifts to priority needs in the communities we serve, as well as progress toward specific goals in the hiring and advancement of women and minorities and the development of business relationships with firms owned by women and minorities.

❖ **Shareholder value.** Achieving an investment grade rating on our debt securities and a 2:1 long-term debt to equity ratio, and annual improvements in operating income of 10 percent or more.

ADDRESS   203 E. Main St.
Spartanburg, SC 29319

INDUSTRY CATEGORY   Food/Beverage

CORPORATE DESCRIPTION

Flagstar Companies, Inc. through its wholly-owned subsidiary, Flagstar Corporation, is one of the largest food service enterprises in the United States, operating (directly and through franchisees) more than 2,400 moderately-priced restaurants. These restaurants are Denny's, Hardee's, Quincy's Family Steakhouse, and El Pollo Loco.

SIZE REVENUES $3,970,000,000 as of 1993

NUMBER OF EMPLOYEES   123,000 as of December 31, 1993

SOURCE   *1993 Annual Report*

♦ ♦ ♦ ♦ ♦ ♦ ♦

COMPANY | *Fleming Companies, Inc.*

STATEMENT | **Fleming's Mission**
is to...

Become a World-Class Marketing and Distribution Company
Our primary focus will be on the efficient and effective marketing and distribution of food and related products. We are committed to achieving sound growth, outstanding business results and a superior return for our shareholders.

We will seek to expand our business both domestically and in global markets, and will make selective investments in retail niche operations and excellent wholesale operations to further augment a world-class marketing and distribution system.

Position the Customers We Serve to Win at Retail
State-of-the-art services must be offered to the retailers we serve. Major investments in technology will be made to create a competitive edge in distribution and retailing. We must provide the cost-effective support necessary to assure the long-term success of our retailers because our success is directly related to theirs.

Always Remember that Individuals Make the Difference
We will strive to attract, motivate and retain the most talented people in our industry. Innovation and risk taking will be encouraged at every level. We will maintain a highly productive environment based on teamwork, individual initiative, mutual trust and respect for our fellow associates. Our business will be conducted according to the highest ethical standards.

Maintain a Clear Vision of Our Future Direction
To accomplish our objectives, we recognize the importance of setting priorities and executing plans consistent with our strategic goals. This requires strong leadership and the pursuit of excellence in every aspect of our business.

ADDRESS   P. O. Box 26647
6301 Waterford Blvd.
Oklahoma City, OK 73126

INDUSTRY CATEGORY   Food/Beverage

CORPORATE DESCRIPTION
Fleming supplies food and related products to more than 4,800 stores in 36 states, the Caribbean, Mexico, and other Central and South American countries.

SIZE REVENUES $13,092,100,000 as of 1993

NUMBER OF EMPLOYEES   23,000 as of 1993

SOURCES *1992 Annual Report;* "Vision 2000" company publication; "The Fortune Service 500," *Fortune* 129, no. 11 (May 30, 1994)

◆ ◆ ◆ ◆ ◆ ◆ ◆

COMPANY | *Forest Oil Corporation*

STATEMENT | **MISSION STATEMENT**
To enhance shareholder value through application of the company's existing technical expertise and operating capabilities by making selected oil and gas investments whose business risk characteristics and return potentials are consistent with the financial risk capacity of the corporation.

ADDRESS 950 17th St., Ste. 1500
Denver, CO 80202

INDUSTRY CATEGORY Oil and Gas

CORPORATE DESCRIPTION
Forest Oil Corporation is engaged in the acquisition and exploitation of, exploration for and development and production of oil and natural gas. The Company's principal reserves and producing properties are located in the Gulf of Mexico and in Texas, Oklahoma and Wyoming.

SIZE REVENUES $105,148,000 as of 1993

NUMBER OF EMPLOYEES 187 (salaried and hourly) as of 1993

SOURCES *1993 Annual Report;* 10-K Report

COMPANY | *FPL Group, Inc.*

STATEMENT

"We will be the preferred provider of safe, reliable, and cost-effective products and services that satisfy the electricity-related needs of all customer segments."

ADDRESS

P. O. Box 14000
Juno Beach, FL 33408

INDUSTRY CATEGORY   Utility

COMPANY   *Flying Colors Painting, Inc.*

STATEMENT   **The Flying Colors Mission statement**

To give each homeowner a terrific paint job.
To build great skills and bring out great attitudes in all our people.
To make money by running a value-based business.

CORPORATE DESCRIPTION

Flying Colors is a residential housepainting company that teaches and supports talented college students in all aspects of running their own-

CORPORATE DESCRIPTION

FPL Group, Inc. is a holding company, the principal subsidiary of which is Florida Power & Light Company (FPL), one of the largest investor-owned electric utilities in the nation. FPL provides electric service to more than 6 million people—about half the population of Florida. FPL's service area covers almost the entire eastern seaboard of mainland Florida and the state's west coast south of Tampa.

SIZE REVENUES $5,316,294,000 as of 1993

NUMBER OF EMPLOYEES   12,406 as of 1993

SOURCE   *1993 Annual Report*

businesses. As of the summer of 1994, Flying Colors had 310 employees and brought in revenues of $1.6 million.

ADDRESS   P. O. Box 538
New Canaan, CT 06840

SOURCE   Company representative

COMPANY | *Fuller (H. B. Fuller Company)*

STATEMENT | **THE COMPANY'S MISSION**

The H. B. Fuller corporate mission is to be a leading and profitable worldwide formulator, manufacturer and marketer of quality specialty chemicals, emphasizing service to customers and managed in accordance with a strategic plan. H. B. Fuller Company is committed to its responsibilities, in order of priority, to its customers, employees, stockholders and communities. H. B. Fuller will conduct business legally and ethically, support the activities of its employees in their communities and be a responsible corporate citizen.

ADDRESS   2400 Energy Park Dr.
Saint Paul, MN 55108-1591

INDUSTRY CATEGORY   Manufacturing

CORPORATE DESCRIPTION

H.B. Fuller Company is a 107-year-old worldwide manufacturer and marketer of adhesives, sealants, coatings, paints and other specialty chemicals. These are used in a wide range of industries, including packaging, woodworking, automotive, aerospace, graphic arts, appliances, filtration, windows, nonwoven/hygienic, sporting goods, shoes and ceramic tile.

SIZE REVENUES $975,000,000 as of 1993

NUMBER OF EMPLOYEES   6,000 as of 1993

SOURCES   *1993 Annual Report;* "The Fortune 500," *Fortune* 129, no. 8 (April 8, 1994)

COMPANY | *Gannett Company, Inc.*

STATEMENT | **Gannett's Basic Game Plan**

Business Definition

Gannett is a $3.6 billion news, information and communications company.

We operate with the belief that improving products and sound management will lead to higher profits for our shareholders. The underlying theme in our ads is: "A world of different voices where freedom speaks."

Our assets include:

❖ USA TODAY;

❖ Daily and weekly community newspapers and specialty publications;

❖ Television and radio stations in Top 25 and growth markets;

❖ Out-of-home and in-home media products.

Strategic Vision

❖ Create and expand quality products through innovation;

❖ Make acquisitions in news, information and communications and related fields that make strategic and economic sense.

Operating Principles

❖ Provide effective leadership and efficient management.

❖ Achieve a positive return on new and acquired products and properties in a reasonable period of time, while recognizing those with high growth potential may take more time.

❖ Increase profitability and increase return on equity and investment over the long term.

❖ Enhance the quality and editorial integrity of our products, recognizing that quality products ultimately lead to higher profits.

❖ Guarantee respect for and fairness in dealing with employees.

❖ Offer a diverse environment where opportunity is based on merit.

❖ Show commitment and service to communities where we do business.

❖ Deliver customer satisfaction.

❖ Dispose of assets that have limited or no potential.

❖ In all activities, we show respect for the First Amendment and our responsibility to it.

(January 25, 1994)

ADDRESS   1100 Wilson Blvd.
Arlington, VA 22234

INDUSTRY CATEGORY   Media/Printing/Publishing

CORPORATE DESCRIPTION
Gannett is a $3.6 billion media and information company whose assets include USA TODAY, daily and weekly newspapers, specialty publications, television and radio stations in Top 25 or growth markets, as well as out-of-home media products in the belief that improving products and good management will lead to higher profits.

SIZE REVENUES $3,641,621,000 as of 1993

NUMBER OF EMPLOYEES   36,500 as of 1993

SOURCE   *1993 Annual Report*

COMPANY | *Gates Rubber Company*

STATEMENT | **Quality Commitment**

Everyone in every function involved, empowered and committed to continuous quality improvement using systematic approaches and processes.

Quality Definition

Meet or exceed customer expectations with products, services and experiences that are superior to the competition.

Gates Rubber Company Values

At The Gates Rubber Company, we value...

- ethical behavior.
- quality and service to our customers, both internal and external.
- open and effective communication.
- innovation.
- contribution of both the individual and the team.
- results.
- continuous improvement in everything we do.
- being the best in all we do, and
- trusting and respecting all stakeholders
- in working with our customers, suppliers, each other and our communities.

The Mission of The Gates Rubber Company

- Satisfy our customers' expectations by manufacturing and marketing engineered products for original equipment and replacement markets.
- Continually improve all business processes by involving all employees in GQC.
- Grow faster than our markets by introducing better products and systems, producing them consistently and marketing them aggressively.

❖ Be recognized for our quality values by customers, suppliers, employees, shareholders and friends.

❖ Generate profits sufficient to provide adequate growth, reward to employees and acceptable return on investments.

| The Vision of The Gates Rubber Company

The vision we have for The Gates Rubber Company as we progress into the 21st century:

❖ **CUSTOMER SATISFACTION:**

an innovative, technological leader dedicated to customer satisfaction with constantly improving products and services of superior quality and value.

❖ **HUMAN RESOURCES:**

a progressive and open place to work which views the individual as the most important asset for success, thereby continually improving the individual's capabilities through training, systems improvements and empowerment, stressing a teamwork environment while also recognizing individual contribution, providing consistent personnel policies and populated by highly skilled individuals with a perspective of being the best in all they do.

❖ **VALUES:**

a successful, prudent, efficient company with ethical standards, recognized as a quality leader.

❖ **COMPETITIVENESS:**

a competitive company striving to be the best in the industry, controlling costs while growing in sales and profits, constantly expanding product offerings, serving customers on a global basis and being the highest value producer.

❖ **PUBLIC IMAGE:**

an ethical and environmentally conscious manufacturer responsive to customers, employees and community, recognized internally and externally for quality and value, welcome wherever we go and constantly striving to improve.

❖ FINANCIAL:

a financially-sound institution with the financial strength necessary to support the strategic direction, emphasizing long-term benefits of investments and recognized as the best value company by all stakeholders.

ADDRESS   900 S. Broadway
P. O. Box 5887
Denver, CO 80217

INDUSTRY CATEGORY   Industrial, Specialized

CORPORATE DESCRIPTION

The Gates Rubber Company is a subsidiary of The Gates Corporation. The Gates Corporation, with annual sales exceeding $1.3 billion, is among the 300 largest industrial companies in the United States, and is one of the larger industrials in the world, ranked by sales. Gates ranks in the top 100 privately-owned companies in the United States in terms of sales, and is one of the largest private firms in the world.

The Gates Rubber Company is primarily in the fluid and mechanical power transmission, motion control, and material transfer businesses. Gates manufactures automotive and industrial belts and hose, and hydraulic hose, assemblies and connectors, both for original equipment manufacturers and replacement markets.

The company also make custom rubber footwear, carpet underlay, and rubber sheeting and matting. Manufacturing, automotive and transportation, agriculture, mining, construction, office equipment, computer technology, and food processing and handling are the primary industries it serves.

SIZE REVENUES $1,000,000,000+ as of 1993

NUMBER OF EMPLOYEES   12,000 as of 1993

SOURCE   "The Gates Corporation At A Glance" company publication

STATEMENT | **VISION STATEMENT**

GenCorp will be one of the most respected diversified companies in the world.

MISSION STATEMENT

Our mission is to continuously improve the company's value to shareholders, customers, employees, and society.

STRATEGIC STATEMENT

We will pursue our vision through focused growth based on our technologies and our strong positions in aerospace, automotive, and polymer products.

This strategy of focused diversification will be implemented through effective management processes which assure that consistent corporate interests and values are brought to decentralized decisions.

VALUES STATEMENT

We are committed to this set of core values:

❖ Quality is our primary objective in everything we do. We will strive for quality in our products, people, technology, financial results, management processes, and our relations with all of our constituents.

❖ We will respond effectively to our customers' needs by—

—Pursuing continuous improvement.

—Encouraging innovation.

—Delivering what we promise.

—Valuing our suppliers.

❖ The people of GenCorp will determine our success by—

—Maintaining the highest ethical standards.

—Placing primary emphasis on safety.

—Involving all employees by creating an environment which enhances teamwork, personal growth, achievement, and recognition.

—Treating each other with respect and trust.

—Integrity will govern our conduct.

❖ We will demonstrate respect for the environment and our neighbors by—

—Meeting our responsibilities as citizens.

—Operating our facilities in an environmentally responsible manner.

ADDRESS 175 Ghent Rd.
Fairlawn, OH 44333-3300

INDUSTRY CATEGORY Diversified

CORPORATE DESCRIPTION

GenCorp is a technology-based company with strong positions in aerospace, automotive, and polymer products.

SIZE REVENUES $1,900,000,000 as of 1993

NUMBER OF EMPLOYEES 13,300 (worldwide) as of 1993

SOURCES *Financial Report*; company representative

COMPANY | *General American Life Insurance Company*

STATEMENT

Our mission is to provide life insurance, health insurance, retirement plans, and related financial services to individuals and groups of employees as well as reinsurance to other insurance companies. Our objective is to do a superior job of meeting the needs of an ever increasing number of clients and to do so by outperforming our competitors in products, services, marketing, administration, and financial results.

ADDRESS   P. O. Box 396
St. Louis, MO 63166

INDUSTRY CATEGORY   Insurance

CORPORATE DESCRIPTION

General American is among the nation's 50 largest life insurance companies. A mutual company, it is owned by its policyholders.

SIZE REVENUES $2,600,000,000 as of 1993

NUMBER OF EMPLOYEES   2,691 (salaried) as of July 1, 1994

SOURCE   *1993 Annual Report*

COMPANY | *General Electric Company*

STATEMENT | **GE VALUES**
GE LEADERS, ALWAYS WITH
UNYIELDING INTEGRITY:

Create a clear, simple, reality-based, customer-focused vision and are able to communicate it straightforwardly to all constituencies.

Set aggressive targets, understanding accountability and commitment, and are decisive.

Have a passion for excellence, hating bureaucracy and all the nonsense that comes with it.

Have the self-confidence to empower others and behave in a boundaryless fashion. They believe in and are committed to Work-Out as a means of empowerment and are open to ideas from anywhere.

Have, or have the capacity to develop, global brains and global sensitivity and are comfortable building diverse global teams.

Stimulate and relish change and are not frightened or paralyzed by it, seeing change as opportunity, not threat.

Have enormous energy and the ability to energize and invigorate others. They understand speed as a competitive advantage and see the total organizational benefits that can be derived from a focus on speed.

ADDRESS   3135 Easton Turnpike
Fairfield, CT 06431

INDUSTRY CATEGORY   Diversified

CORPORATE DESCRIPTION
GE is a diversified technology, manufacturing and services company with a commitment to achieving worldwide leadership in each of its 13 major businesses: aerospace, aircraft engines, broadcasting (NBC), electrical distribution equipment, electric motors, financial services, industrial and power systems, information services, lighting, locomotives, major appliances, medical systems and plastics. John F. Welch, Jr. is Chairman and Chief Executive Officer of GE.

SIZE REVENUES $60,562,000,000 as of 1993

NUMBER OF EMPLOYEES   222,000 (worldwide) as of 1993

SOURCE   *1993 Annual Report*

◆ ◆ ◆ ◆ ◆ ◆ ◆

COMPANY | *General Mills, Inc.*

STATEMENT | GENERAL MILLS
THE COMPANY OF CHAMPIONS
STATEMENT OF CORPORATE VALUES
CONSUMERS

Consumers choose General Mills because we offer competitively superior products and services.

EMPLOYEES

Employees choose General Mills because we reward innovation and superior performance and release their power to lead.

INVESTORS

Investors choose General Mills because we consistently deliver financial results in the top 10 percent of all major companies.

Our heritage and commitment to outstanding accomplishment has made General Mills "The Company of Champions." Each of us at General Mills must strive to exemplify the values that distinguish us as a unique and special company.

PRODUCTS AND SERVICES

We will provide competitively superior products and services to our customers and consumers. This superiority will be measured by rigorous, comparative testing versus the best competitive offerings and by growth in market shares.

Providing championship products and services is a never-ending job requiring continuous improvement ahead of competition.

PEOPLE AND ORGANIZATION

General Mills' people will be the best in our industries— people who are winners, ever striving to exceed their past accomplishments. Exceptional performance is the result of these people working together in small and fluid teams on those issues where success will clearly widen our competitive advantage.

We value diversity and will create workplaces where people with diverse skills, perspectives, and backgrounds can exercise leadership and help those around them release their full power and potential.

We will minimize organizational levels and have broad spans of responsibility. We will drive out bureaucracy and parochialism. We will trust each other and have the self-confidence to challenge and accept challenge.

INNOVATION

Innovation is the principal driver of growth. Innovation requires a bias for action. To be first among our competitors, we must constantly challenge the status quo and be willing to experiment. The anticipation and creation of change, both in established businesses and in new products and services, is essential for competitive advantage.

We recognize that change—and risk—are inherent to innovation. Our motivation system will strongly reward successful risk-taking, while not penalizing an innovative idea that did not work.

SPEED

We will be the fastest moving and most productive competitor. We will set specific goals to improve our speed and productivity each year compared to our own past performance and to the competition.

COMMITMENT

Our commitment to our shareholders is to deliver financial results that place us in the top 10 percent of all major companies. This can only be accomplished with the personal commitment of each of us.

The persistency to bounce back from disappointments, the intensity to pursue the exceptionally difficult, and the reliability to deliver promised results are all part of our commitment to our shareholders, to each other, and to our pride in "The Company of Champions." This commitment is demonstrated by substantial and increasing levels of employee stock ownership.

CITIZENSHIP

We will have significant positive impact on our communities. We will focus on specific projects where our efforts will make a difference in direct philanthropy, in our corporate investment in nonprofit ventures, and through our own personal involvement in civic and community affairs.

ADDRESS   P. O. Box 1113
Minneapolis, MN 55440

INDUSTRY CATEGORY   Food/Beverage

CORPORATE DESCRIPTION
General Mills manufactures a variety of breakfast cereals. The consumer food group includes Betty Crocker Desserts, Bisquick, Helper Dinner Mixes, Yoplait Yogurt, Fruit Snacks, Gorton's Frozen Seafood and Pop Secret Popcorn. Restaurant operations include Red Lobster and The Olive Garden. General Mills also manufactures and markets food products in foreign countries.

SIZE REVENUES $8,135,000,000 as of 1993

NUMBER OF EMPLOYEES   121,290 as of 1993

SOURCES   *1991 Annual Report*; "Statement of Corporate Values" company publication; "The Fortune 500," *Fortune* 129, no. 8 (April 8, 1994)

◆　◆　◆　◆　◆　◆　◆

COMPANY | *General Motors Acceptance Corporation (GMAC)*

STATEMENT | **The GMAC Mission:**
We are dedicated to providing financial services to GM dealers and their customers in such form and of such quality as to **enhance** the marketing of GM cars and trucks, **enable** our employees to share in General Motors Acceptance Corporation's success and **provide** our shareholder, General Motors, with a superior return on investment.

ADDRESS   3044 W. Grand Blvd.
Detroit, MI 48202

INDUSTRY CATEGORY   Financial Investment services

General Motors Acceptance Corporation (GMAC) is the finance and insurance subsidiary of General Motors.

SIZE REVENUES $12,483,500,000 (gross) as of 1993

NUMBER OF EMPLOYEES   18,300 as of 1993

SOURCE   *1993 Annual Report*

◆ ◆ ◆ ◆ ◆ ◆ ◆

COMPANY | *General Motors Corporation*

STATEMENT | **Our Vision: Industry Leadership through Customer Enthusiasm**

Our vision is for GM to be the world leader in transportation products and services. We'll know we've achieved the vision when we have the most satisfied and enthusiastic customers in all market segments where we compete. Customer enthusiasm in the marketplace is what ultimately translates into leadership in sales, earnings, and returns on investment and assets.

And we will build customer enthusiasm by focusing our people and our processes on teamwork and continuous improvement in all areas of the business.

ADDRESS   3044 W. Grand Blvd.
Detroit, MI 48202

INDUSTRY CATEGORY   Motor Vehicles and Related

CORPORATE DESCRIPTION
General Motors Corporation is best known as the world's largest full-line vehicle manufacturer. It makes and sells cars, trucks, and

locomotives worldwide. GM's other substantial business interests include GM Hughes Electronics Corporation, involved in automotive electronics, commercial technologies, telecommunications and space, and defense electronics; Electronic Data Systems Corporation, applying information technologies around the globe; and General Motors Acceptance Corporation and its subsidiaries, providing financing and insurance to GM customers and dealers.

SIZE REVENUES $138,219,500,000 as of 1993

NUMBER OF EMPLOYEES   710,800 (average, worldwide) as of 1993

SOURCE   *1993 Annual Report*

◆　◆　◆　◆　◆　◆　◆

COMPANY | *General Public Utilities Corporation*

STATEMENT | **PURPOSE**
People providing people with energy to meet today's needs and realize tomorrow's dreams.

MISSION
To be a premier supplier of energy and energy-related services through the skills of our employees and the excellence of our customer service.

GPU SYSTEM'S VALUES
RESPECT
❖ Be a good listener; encourage diverse opinions and be willing to accept them

- Recognize the achievements of others
- Don't prejudge another person's qualities or intentions
- Respect confidences
- Recognize each individual's human dignity and value

HONESTY & OPENNESS

- Be forthright and never use information as a source of power
- Strive for clarity, avoid "slippery" words
- Focus on issues, not personalities
- Carry no hidden agendas
- Be willing to admit your own mistakes and be tolerant of others' mistakes.

TEAMWORK

- Acknowledge all co-workers in the GPU System companies as valuable team members

COMPANY | *Globe Metallurgical Inc.*

STATEMENT | **The Company Mission of Globe Metallurgical**

is to provide products and services that lead the silicon metal and ferroalloy industries in the highest quality at the lowest manufacturing costs. To maintain our lead, we must continually improve our products and services.

We will meet our customers' needs with products, services, and technologies that represent true value. This will ensure long-term profits for growth, job security for our employees, and give our owners and shareholders sustained, high investment returns.

(Signed)
Arden C. Sims, President & CEO

- ❖ Practice solidarity by respecting and supporting team decisions
- ❖ Encourage initiative and participation
- ❖ Demand excellence from yourself and seek it from others
- ❖ Be accountable to the team.

INTEGRITY & TRUST
- ❖ Act and speak ethically
- ❖ Show confidence in the character and truthfulness of others
- ❖ Keep commitments
- ❖ Be accountable for your own actions and expect accountability of others as well
- ❖ Accept responsibility for your own mistakes and give credit to others for their accomplishments.

COMMITMENT
- ❖ Seek opportunities for positive and appropriate change

CORPORATE DESCRIPTION
Globe Metallurgical Incorporated manufactures and markets silicon metal, specialty ferroalloys and their related by-products. The company's products are used by chemical manufacturers, foundries, aluminum manufacturers, specialty ceramic and refractory manufacturers, and concrete manufacturers.

ADDRESS   P. O. Box 157
Beverly, OH 45715

SOURCE   Company representative

❖ Be clear in describing what needs to be changed and why, and how that change can be accomplished

❖ Challenge and change inappropriate policies

❖ Recognize that taking and accepting reasonable risks is necessary business conduct

❖ Lead by example

❖ Demonstrate a sense of urgency in all that we do.

ADDRESS   100 Interpace Pkwy.
Parsippany, NJ 07054-1149

INDUSTRY CATEGORY   Diversified

CORPORATE DESCRIPTION
GPU is a Pennsylvania corporation and was organized in 1946 as a holding company registered under the Public Utility Holding Company Act of 1935. GPU does not operate any utility properties directly, but owns all the outstanding common stock of three electric utilities serving customers in New Jersey—Jersey Central Power & Light Company (JCP&L)—and Pennsylvania—Metropolitan Edison Company (Met-Ed) and Pennsylvania Electric Company (Penelec). The business of these subsidiaries consists predominately of the generation, transmission, distribution and sale of electricity. GPU also owns all of the common stock of GPU Service Corporation (GPUSC), a service company; GPU Nuclear Corporation (GPUN) which operates and maintains nuclear units of the subsidiaries; and Energy Initiatives, Inc. (EI) and EI Power, Inc. (EI Power), which develop and operate non-utility generating facilities.

SIZE REVENUES $3,596,090,000 as of 1993

NUMBER OF EMPLOYEES   11,963 as of 1993

SOURCES   *1993 Annual Report*; company representative

COMPANY | *Georgia Gulf*

STATEMENT | **MISSION**

Georgia Gulf will continue to be an efficient, integrated manufacturer and marketer of quality chemical and plastic products to users worldwide and will be dedicated to continuous improvement of the processes, products and services required to meet our customers' changing needs. We will strive to earn a superior long-term return for our shareholders while providing meaningful work for our employees and always operating with the highest regard for environmental protection, safety and the overall well-being of the communities in which we operate.

(September 1994)

GUIDING PRINCIPLES

All applicable laws and regulations will be adhered to with special emphasis on meeting or exceeding environmental and safety standards.

Relationships with customers, stockholders, employees, suppliers and the communities in which we operate will be conducted in a fair, open and ethical manner. Never ending process improvement will be practiced in order to provide quality products and services which meet the needs of our customers.

Equal opportunity for advancement will be provided to all employees in an atmosphere of open communication, trust, respect and support.

Competitive compensation and benefits, including incentive and equity programs based upon company profitability and long-term growth, recognizing both team work and individual achievement, will be offered to all employees.

(May 1994)

ADDRESS 400 Perimeter Center Terrace, Ste. 595
Atlanta, GA 30346

INDUSTRY CATEGORY Chemicals

CORPORATE DESCRIPTION
Georgia Gulf is an efficient, integrated manufacturer and marketer
of quality chemical and plastic products.

SIZE REVENUES $768,902,000 as of 1993

NUMBER OF EMPLOYEES 1,124 as of 1993

SOURCE 1993 *Annual Report*

◆　◆　◆　◆　◆　◆　◆

COMPANY | *Geraghty & Miller, Inc.*

STATEMENT | **COMPANY MISSION STATEMENT**
CREATING ENVIRONMENTAL VALUE
From day-to-day activities through long-term planning,
Geraghty & Miller is guided by this simple and clear mission.
The creation of *environmental value* for clients, the Company,
its employees, and its stockholders is achieved by adhering to
a set of principles which, taken together, define *environmental value.*

◈• Anticipate and Respond to Client Needs.
◈• Cost Effective Solutions.
◈• Broad Range of Applied Expertise.

❧ Dynamic and Seamless National and International Network of People and Skills.

❧ Staff Driven by Personal Integrity, Trust, Communication and Cooperation.

❧ Staff Empowered to Meet Client Needs.

❧ Quality Processes to Produce Quality Results.

❧ Maintenance of Financial Integrity of Projects and the Firm.

❧ Maximizing Employee and Stockholder Benefits by Maximizing Product Value.

❧ Improvement of Environmental Quality.

ADDRESS   1099 18th Street, Ste. 2950
Denver, CO 80202

INDUSTRY CATEGORY   Environmental Engineering

CORPORATE DESCRIPTION
Geraghty & Miller, Inc. is a full-service environmental company that provides a wide spectrum of consulting, engineering, hydrocarbon and remediation services. The Company enjoys a preeminent reputation in the development, management, and protection of ground-water resources and the correction of soil and ground-water contamination.

SIZE REVENUES $135,000,000 (gross) as of 1993

NUMBER OF EMPLOYEES   1,200 as of 1993

SOURCES   *1991 Annual Report*; company representative

COMPANY | *Gibson Greetings, Inc.*

STATEMENT | **OUR MISSION**

Our mission is to provide the highest quality products that communicate personal expression; to support our retailers' business objectives through innovation, responsiveness and productivity; and to achieve the goals of our shareholders and our associates.

© Gibson Greetings, Inc.

Reprinted with Permission of Gibson Greetings, Inc., Cincinnati, Ohio 45237.

ALL RIGHTS RESERVED.

OUR VALUES

WHO WE ARE AND WHAT WE STAND FOR:

❖ We are a TEAM committed to achieving our mission.

❖ WE strive to be the best in everything we do.

❖ We seek open communication and feedback by listening and responding to our customers, our shareholders and our associates.

❖ We adhere to a stringent code of honor and integrity.

❖ We trust, respect and care for each other.

❖ We mutually establish clear accountability and goals.

❖ We seek to attack the problem and not the person.

❖ We encourage our associates to become prudent risk takers, to grow, to contribute and to accomplish.

❖ We take satisfaction from winning and having fun in the process.

© Gibson Greetings, Inc.

Reprinted with Permission of Gibson Greetings, Inc., Cincinnati, Ohio 45237.

ALL RIGHTS RESERVED.

ADDRESS   2100 Section Rd.
Cincinnati, OH 45237

INDUSTRY CATEGORY   Retail

CORPORATE DESCRIPTION
Gibson Greetings, Inc. produces greeting cards, gift wrap and related social expression items.

SIZE REVENUES $547,000,000 (net sales) as of December 31, 1993

NUMBER OF EMPLOYEES   6,500 (full and part time) as of September 30, 1993

SOURCE   Company representative

◆ ◆ ◆ ◆ ◆ ◆ ◆

COMPANY | *Gillette (The Gillette Company)*

STATEMENT | MISSION
Our mission is to achieve or enhance clear leadership, worldwide, in the existing or new core consumer product categories in which we choose to compete.
Current core categories are:
❖ Male grooming products including blades and razors, electric shavers, shaving preparations, and deodorants and antiperspirants.

◆ Selected female grooming products including wet shaving, hair removal and hair care appliances, deodorants and antiperspirants and party plan skin care and cosmetic products.

◆ Writing instruments and correction products.

◆ Certain areas of the oral care market including toothbrushes, interdental devices and oral care appliances.

◆ Selected areas of the high-quality small household appliance business, including coffeemakers and food preparation products.

To achieve this mission, we will also compete in supporting product areas that enhance the company's ability to achieve or hold the leadership position in core categories.

Values

In pursuing our mission, we will live by the following values:

People. We will attract, motivate and retain high-performing people in all areas of our business. We are committed to competitive, performance-based compensation, benefits, training and personal growth based on equal career opportunity and merit. We expect integrity, civility, openness, support for others and commitment to the highest standards of achievement. We value innovation, employee involvement, change, organizational flexibility and personal mobility. We recognize and value the benefits in the diversity of people, ideas and cultures.

Customer Focus. We will invest in and master the key technologies vital to category success. We will offer consumers products of the highest levels of performance for value. We will provide quality service to our customers, both internal and external, by treating them as partners, by listening, understanding their needs, responding fairly and living up to our commitments. We will be a valued customer to our suppliers, treating them fairly and with respect. We will provide these quality values consistent with improving our productivity.

Good Citizenship. We will comply with applicable laws and regulations at all government levels wherever we do business. We will contribute to the communities in which we operate and address social issues responsibly. Our products will be safe to make and to use. We will conserve natural resources and we will continue to invest in a better environment.

We believe that commitment to this mission and to these values will enable the Company to provide a superior return to our shareholders.

(Courtesy, The Gillette Company)

ADDRESS   Prudential Tower Bldg.
                 Boston, MA 02199

INDUSTRY CATEGORY   Consumer Goods and Services

CORPORATE DESCRIPTION

Founded in 1901, The Gillette Company is the world leader in blades and razors. The Company holds a major position in North America in sales of toiletries and is the world's top seller of writing instruments. Braun is the number one marketer of electric shavers in Germany and is among the leaders in Europe, North America and Japan. Oral-B is among the top sellers of toothbrushes in the United States and is the leader in several international markets.

Manufacturing operations are conducted at 62 facilities in 28 countries, and products are distributed through wholesalers, retailers and agents in over 200 countries and territories.

SIZE REVENUES $5,410,800,000 as of 1993

NUMBER OF EMPLOYEES   33,400 as of December 31, 1993

SOURCE   *1993 Annual Report*

STATEMENT

OUR MISSION is constant improvement in products and services to meet our customers' needs. This is the only means to business success for Goodyear and prosperity for its investors and employees. QUALITY IS THE KEY TO CUSTOMER SATISFAC- TION

| **GUIDING PRINCIPLES**

CUSTOMER SATISFACTION—Everything we do is directed to the satisfaction of present and future customers. Quality is defined by the current expectations, as well as by future needs and desires of our customers.

PROCESS IMPROVEMENT—Results are achieved through the management of processes. All processes—and the resulting products and services—can be improved, forever. The improvements may take the form of revolutionary changes, innovations or the accumulation of many small steps. The improvements may involve such areas as quality, cost, delivery or time.

PEOPLE—We value the commitment, knowledge and cre- ativity of the men and women of Goodyear. Everyone has the ability to contribute to our mission of constant improvement. Cooperation and respect among individuals and departments are fundamental to success.

ACTION BASED ON FACTS—Sound business decisions are based on sound data and rigorous analysis. Facts are reviewed in an atmosphere without blame. Understanding and use of data collection and analysis is vital in all areas.

ADDRESS   1144 E. Market St.
Akron, OH 44316-0001

INDUSTRY CATEGORY   Motor Vehicles and Related

CORPORATE DESCRIPTION
Goodyear's principal business is the development, manufacture, distribution, marketing and sale of tires for most applications throughout the world. In addition to being a leading tire manufacturer, the company manufactures and sells several lines of rubber products for the transportation industry and various industrial and consumer markets and numerous rubber-related chemicals for various applications. Goodyear also provides automotive repair and other services.

SIZE REVENUES $11,643,000,000 as of 1993

NUMBER OF EMPLOYEES   90,384 as of 1993

SOURCES   *1992 Annual Report;* "The Fortune 500," *Fortune* 129, no. 8 (April 8, 1994)

◆   ◆   ◆   ◆   ◆   ◆   ◆

COMPANY | *Grace (W. R. Grace & Co.)*

STATEMENT | **Mission**
  Grace's mission is to maximize long-term value to shareholders while balancing value to other stakeholders—our employees, customers, suppliers and communities.

ADDRESS   One Town Center Rd.
  Boca Raton, FL 33486-1010

INDUSTRY CATEGORY   Chemicals

CORPORATE DESCRIPTION
Grace is the world's largest specialty chemical company and holds a leadership position in specialized health care.

SIZE REVENUES $4,408,400,000 as of 1993

NUMBER OF EMPLOYEES   34,000 as of 1993

SOURCE   *1993 Annual Report*

◆   ◆   ◆   ◆   ◆   ◆   ◆

COMPANY | *Haemonetics Corporation*

STATEMENT | Mission
❖ Enhance the safety and quality of the world's blood supply
❖ Increase the availability of blood components from a shrinking donor population

Haemonetics Quality Statement
Quality is...conformance to our customer requirements with an absolute, measurable yes or no.

ADDRESS   400 Wood Rd.
P. O. Box 9114
Braintree, MA 02184-9114

INDUSTRY CATEGORY   Medical Products and Services

CORPORATE DESCRIPTION

Haemonetics pioneered, and is the world leader in the design, manufacture, and marketing of blood processing equipment and related disposables.

SIZE REVENUES $248,449,000 as of 1994

NUMBER OF EMPLOYEES   1,109 as of 1994

SOURCE   *1994 Annual Report*

◆   ◆   ◆   ◆   ◆   ◆   ◆

COMPANY | *Hanna (M. A. Hanna Company)*

STATEMENT | Mission

M. A. Hanna's mission is to create an international specialty chemicals company that:

Builds and maintains leadership in its markets by delivering superior value to its customers, as measured by customer service and responsiveness, product quality, product offering, technology and product development capability;

Attracts and retains qualified and productive associates by providing a challenging work environment, decision-making authority consistent with responsibility, continuous training, competitive compensation and opportunities to share in the financial success of the business through pay-for-performance and stock ownership;

Develops long-term partnerships with its suppliers and customers because of its unparalleled market access, market knowledge and value-added capabilities;

Commands respect as a corporate citizen by enforcing high ethical, legal, social and safety standards and preserving and protecting the environment;

And rewards investors with a consistently superior return on investment.

ADDRESS   200 Public Square, Ste. 36-5000
Cleveland, OH 44114-2304

INDUSTRY CATEGORY   Chemicals

CORPORATE DESCRIPTION
M. A. Hanna Company is a leading international specialty chemicals company whose products and services extend to a wide range of markets in the polymers industry.

SIZE REVENUES $1,519,728,000 as of 1993

NUMBER OF EMPLOYEES   6,334 as of 1993

SOURCE   *1993 Annual Report*

◆　◆　◆　◆　◆　◆　◆

COMPANY | *Harsco Corporation*

STATEMENT | NEW MISSION STATEMENT
The Mission of Harsco Corporation is to achieve consistent, superior financial returns from operations complemented by targeted and prudent growth in markets and technologies familiar to the Company. Enhanced shareholder value will be

obtained by developing and maintaining lead industry positions in the markets served through the delivery of products and services that provide the best value to the customer.

ADDRESS   P. O. Box 8888
              Camp Hill, PA 17001-8888

INDUSTRY CATEGORY   Manufacturing

CORPORATE DESCRIPTION
Harsco, a diversified industrial manufacturing and service company, conducts its business through 10 Divisions and has 16 varied classes of products and services. Its operations fall into three Operating Groups: Metal Reclamation and Mill Services; Infrastructure, Construction and Transportation; and Process Industry Products. Harsco has over 175 major facilities in 30 countries, including the United States. Harsco also holds a 40% ownership in United Defense, L.P., a $1.0 billion joint venture with FMC Corporation, which principally manufactures ground combat planes for the U.S. and international governments.

SIZE REVENUES $702,800,000 (net sales) as of first six months in 1994

NUMBER OF EMPLOYEES   12,900 as of 1993

SOURCE   *1993 Annual Report*

COMPANY | *Hershey Foods Corporation*

STATEMENT | **Mission Statement**

Hershey Foods Corporation's mission is to be a focused food company in North America and selected international markets and a leader in every aspect of our business. In North America, our goal is to enhance our number one position in confectionery and achieve number one positions in pasta and chocolate-related grocery products.

ADDRESS   Hershey, PA 17033

INDUSTRY CATEGORY   Food/Beverage

CORPORATE DESCRIPTION

Hershey Foods Corporation, which celebrated its centennial in 1994, is a leading North American producer of chocolate and confectionery products, a major U. S. producer of dry pasta products, and has international interests in Germany, Italy, The Netherlands, Belgium, Mexico and the Far East.

SIZE REVENUES $3,488,000,000 as of 1993

NUMBER OF EMPLOYEES   14,300 as of 1993

SOURCES   *1993 Annual Report*; company representative; "The Fortune 500," *Fortune* 129, no. 8 (April 8, 1994)

STATEMENT | **Corporate Objectives**

The organizational framework for our objectives

The achievements of an organization are the result of the combined efforts of each individual in the organization working toward common objectives. These objectives should be realistic, should be clearly understood by everyone in the organization and should reflect the organization's basic character and personality.

At Hewlett-Packard, we have five underlying organizational values that guide us as we work toward our common objectives.

❖ **We have trust and respect for individuals.** We approach each situation with the understanding that people want to do a good job and will do so, given the proper tools and support. We attract highly capable, innovative people and recognize their efforts and contributions to the company. HP people contribute enthusiastically and share in the success that they make possible.

❖ **We focus on a high level of achievement and contribution.** Our customers expect HP products and services to be of the highest quality and to provide lasting value. To achieve this, all HP people, but especially managers, must be leaders who generate enthusiasm and respond with extra effort to meet customer needs. Techniques and management practices which are effective today may be outdated in the future. For us to remain at the forefront in all our activities, people should always be looking for new and better ways to do their work.

❖ **We conduct our business with uncompromising integrity.** We expect HP people to be open and honest in their dealings to earn the trust and loyalty of others. People at every level are expected to adhere to the highest standards of business ethics and must understand that anything less is totally unacceptable. As a practical matter, ethical conduct cannot be assured by written HP policies and codes; it must be an integral part of the organization, a deeply ingrained tradition that is passed from one generation of employees to another.

We achieve our common objectives through team work. We recognize that it is only through effective cooperation within and among organizations that we can achieve our goals. Our commitment is to work as a worldwide team to fulfill the expectations of our customers, shareholders and others who depend upon us. The benefits and obligations of doing business are shared among all HP people.

COMPANY | *L. Norman Howe & Associates*

STATEMENT | **The Mission of L. Norman Howe & Associates: (Under the corporate banner of F&P Inc.)**

To provide opportunities and support for all Associates to achieve personal growth and total well-being.

Some of his guidelines for this new business philosophy were:

❖ To use "work" to support each associate's quest for personal growth.

❖ To erase the line between work and play.

❖ To have leaders view leadership as service rather than status.

❖ To have integrity and aliveness be inherent in company goals.

❖ To gain alignment through common understanding, not edicts.

❖ To emphasize shared responsibility.

❖ To focus on the individual's well-being as well as job performance.

❖ **We encourage flexibility and innovation.** We create a work environment which supports the diversity of our people and their ideas. We strive for overall objectives which are clearly stated and agreed upon, and allow people flexibility in working toward goals in ways which they help determine are best for the organization. HP people should personally accept responsibility and be encouraged to upgrade their skills and capabilities through ongoing training and development. This is especially important in a technical business where the rate of progress is rapid and where people are expected to adapt to change.

❖ To support learning from failure rather than blaming for failure.

❖ To have it be okay to express feelings.

❖ To pay attention to process as well as objective and results.

❖ To encourage the recognition of the context for the conditions.

❖ To encourage cooperative, ecological thinking.

❖ To have an organic rather than a static structure.

❖ To emphasize being open and questioning, rather than just doing it "by the book."

CORPORATE DESCRIPTION
L. Norman Howe & Associates is in the business of the design and management of promotion events and systems.

ADDRESS   95 N. Marengo Ave., Ste. #1
Pasadena, CA 91101

SOURCE   Company representative

The Hewlett-Packard objectives which follow were initially published in 1957. Since then they have been modified from time to time, reflecting the changing nature of our business and social environment. This version represents the latest updating of our organizational framework and objectives. We hope you will find this informative and will look to these objectives and underlying values to guide your activities as part of the HP team.

(Signed)
Dave Packard
Chairman of the Board

(Signed)
Bill Hewlett
Director Emeritus

(Signed)
John Young
President and Chief Executive Officer

Profit

To achieve sufficient profit to finance our company growth and to provide the resources we need to achieve our other corporate objectives. ...

Customers

To provide products and services of the highest quality and the greatest possible value to our customers, thereby gaining and holding their respect and loyalty....

Fields Of Interest

To participate in those fields of interest that build upon our technology and customer base, that offer opportunities for continuing growth, and that enable us to make a needed and profitable contribution. ...

Growth

To let our growth be limited only by our profits and our ability to develop and produce innovative products that satisfy real customer needs. ...

Our People

To help HP people share in the company's success which they make possible; to provide employment security based on their performance; to ensure them a safe and pleasant work environment; to recognize their individual achievements; and to help them gain a sense of satisfaction and accomplishment from their work. ...

Management

To foster initiative and creativity by allowing the individual great freedom of action in attaining well-defined objectives. ...

Citizenship

To honor our obligations to society by being an economic, intellectual and social asset to each nation and each community in which we operate. ...

ADDRESS P. O. Box 1301
Palo Alto, CA 94303-0890

INDUSTRY CATEGORY High Technology

CORPORATE DESCRIPTION
Hewlett-Packard designs, manufactures and services electronic products and systems for measurement, computation and communications.

SIZE REVENUES $20,317,000,000 as of 1993

NUMBER OF EMPLOYEES 96,200 as of 1993

SOURCES *1992 Annual Report;* "The Fortune 500," *Fortune* 129, no. 8 (April 8, 1994); *1993 Annual Report;* "Corporate Objectives" company publication

COMPANY | *Hibernia Corporation*

STATEMENT | **PURPOSE STATEMENT**

Hibernia's purpose is to make it possible for people to achieve their financial goals and realize their dreams.

MISSION STATEMENT

Hibernia's mission is to be recognized by 1996 as the best provider of financial services throughout Louisiana.

This will be achieved by:

❖ Becoming the employer of choice by providing a challenging and rewarding work environment.

❖ Being acclaimed by customers as the service leader.

❖ Targeting a minimum 15% deposit share in each of the markets in which we compete, while seeking the leading position.

❖ Building on our position as the leading commercial lender in the state and becoming the dominant retail lender.

❖ Expanding client relationships with traditional and non-traditional fee-based products and services.

❖ Securing a position in the top quartile of our peer group—as measured by returns on assets and equity and the key indicators of asset quality.

❖ Being an outstanding corporate citizen.

ADDRESS   P. O. Box 61540
New Orleans, LA 70161

INDUSTRY CATEGORY   Banking

CORPORATE DESCRIPTION

Hibernia Corporation, through its subsidiary, Hibernia National Bank, provides a wide range of banking services for businesses, individuals, and public bodies, including checking and savings accounts, lending, international banking activities, trust services, mutual funds, annuities, brokerage services, cash management and mortgage banking.

SIZE REVENUES $263,000,000 (net interest income and non-interest income) as of December 31, 1993

NUMBER OF EMPLOYEES   2,522 as of December 31, 1993

SOURCE   *1993 Annual Report*

◆　◆　◆　◆　◆　◆　◆

COMPANY | *Hoechst Celanese Corporation*

STATEMENT | **Mission**

We are a large, international company based in the United States. We operate a broad spectrum of chemistry-related businesses within the worldwide Hoechst organization.

We will be the recognized leader in our target markets.

We will be the preferred employer in our industry.

We recognize that people are our most valuable asset.

We will be the partner of choice for customers, suppliers, and other creators of innovative concepts.

We will be a major contributor to and take full advantage of the strong technological base of the Hoechst Group.

We will continually increase the long-term value of our company.

We operate in a decentralized manner, allowing each business to develop within our Values.

Vision

Hoechst Celanese will leverage core competencies to grow market value faster than any of the five largest chemical companies in North America. We will be a publicly traded company with values-based leadership, strategically managing a balanced portfolio of businesses to achieve consistent excellent performance.

ADDRESS   Route 202-206
P. O. Box 2500
Somerville, NJ 08876-1258

INDUSTRY CATEGORY   Chemicals

CORPORATE DESCRIPTION
Hoechst Celanese Corporation is a subsidiary of Hoechst AG of Germany, with leading positions in chemicals, fibers, advanced materials and technologies, and the life sciences.

Products include commodity and specialty chemicals; textiles and technical fibers; polyester resins and films; engineering and high performance plastics; branded prescription, generic and bulk pharmaceuticals; crop protection and animal health products.

SIZE REVENUES $6,900,000,000 (sales) as of 1993

NUMBER OF EMPLOYEES   29,900 (worldwide) as of 1993

SOURCES   *1993 Annual Report*; 1993 Facts and Figures sheet

COMPANY | *HON Industries, Inc.*

STATEMENT | **Our Vision**

HON INDUSTRIES and its members are dedicated to achieving excellence through the pursuit of a philosophy, strategies, and day-to-day actions aimed at achieving rapid continuous improvement. We continuously strive to develop a culture where members, customers, suppliers, shareholders, and the public experience fairness and respect in their relations with the company.

Achieving excellence depends on individual and collective integrity and the relentless pursuit of the following long-standing beliefs:

HON INDUSTRIES SHALL BE PROFITABLE.

The Company pursues mutually profitable partnerships with customers and suppliers. Only when the company achieves an adequate profit can the other elements of this Vision be realized.

HON INDUSTRIES SHALL BE ECONOMICALLY SOUND.

The company safeguards and grows the shareholders' equity by attaining superior financial performance and maintaining a strong balance sheet. This allows us greater flexibility to respond in a continuously changing market and business environment.

HON INDUSTRIES SHALL PURSUE SOUND GROWTH.

The company pursues profitable growth in order to continue providing increased job and financial opportunities for members, customers, suppliers, shareholders, and the public.

HON INDUSTRIES SHALL BE A SUPPLIER OF QUALITY PRODUCTS AND SERVICES.

The company provides reliable products and services of high quality and value to our end-users which exceed our customers' expectations and allow the distributor and the company to make a fair profit.

HON INDUSTRIES SHALL BE A GOOD PLACE TO WORK.

The company pursues a participative environment and culture that nurture the active involvement of each member, and that attract and retain the most capable people who work safely, are motivated, and are devoted to making the company and themselves jointly prosper.

HON INDUSTRIES SHALL BE A RESPONSIBLE CORPORATE CITIZEN.

The company and its members actively participate in the civic, cultural, educational, environmental, and governmental affairs of our society. The company follows, and requires all members to follow, ethical and legal business practices.

When the company is appreciated by its members, favored by its customers, supported by its suppliers, respected by the public, and admired by its shareholders, this Vision is fulfilled.

ADDRESS 414 E. Third St.
P. O. Box 1109
Muscatine, IA 52761-7109

INDUSTRY CATEGORY Business Products

CORPORATE DESCRIPTION
HON Industries, Inc. is a manufacturer and marketer of office furniture, office products, and home building products.

SIZE REVENUES $780,326,000 (net sales) as of 1993

NUMBER OF EMPLOYEES 6,257 as of 1993

SOURCES *1993* Form 10-K; company representative

"To be a leader in the food field with highly differentiated quality products that attain optimum share of market while meeting established profit objectives."

Quality Policy

"We will supply defect-free products and services which conform to clearly defined requirements to meet the needs of our customers, employees and others we serve."

The five principles of quality management form the foundation of this policy. They are:

❖ The Definition of Quality is Conformance to Customer Requirements

❖ The System of Quality is Prevention and Continuous Improvement

❖ The Performance Standard is Zero Defects

❖ The Measurement of Quality is the Price of Nonconformance

❖ All Work is a Process

© Hormel Foods Corporation 1994

Company Values

Our mission will be accomplished by focusing on values relating to our consumers, customers, employees, shareholders, suppliers and the communities we serve.

Consumers—We strive to:

❖ anticipate, listen and respond to consumer desires for innovative new products.

❖ develop loyal consumers through continuous improvement of product quality and consistency.

❖ be a trustworthy provider of wholesome, nutritious and good tasting food products of excellent value.

❖ provide service that is innovative, responsive, reliable, courteous and professional.

❖ develop partnerships with our customers to assure mutual success.

❖ provide quality products supported by innovative and effective marketing programs.

Employees—We seek to provide an environment in which:

❖ all employees trust and respect one another.

❖ teamwork and positive attitudes are commonplace.

❖ all ideas are valued, respected and recognized.

❖ continuous improvement, innovation and prevention are a way of life.

❖ everyone strives to satisfy customers at all times.

Shareholders—We are committed to:

❖ long-term profitability and growth.

❖ providing optimum economic value for our shareholders.

❖ a satisfactory return on assets employed.

❖ making sound economic decisions based on thorough risk and return assessments.

Suppliers—We develop mutually beneficial supplier relationships built on:

❖ trust and respect.

❖ optimization of total value through innovation, technology and process involvement.

❖ quality, price and service.

Communities—We serve our communities by:

❖ operating modern, clean, safe and efficient facilities which add value to the community.

❖ our active participation and leadership in community affairs.

❖ leading and supporting community and national efforts to improve the environment.

© Hormel Foods Corporation 1994

ADDRESS   1 Hormel Place
Austin, MN 55912

INDUSTRY CATEGORY   Food/Beverage

CORPORATE DESCRIPTION
Having served the needs of generations of consumers for more than a century, Hormel Foods Corporation continues to successfully build upon its role as one of the leading processors and marketers of branded, value-added meat and food products. Hormel Foods competes nationally and internationally.

Hormel Foods and its family of subsidiaries manufacture, market and distribute thousands of processed food products which are known and respected by consumers, retail grocers, foodservice operators and industrial customers.

A majority of the Company's products are sold under the Hormel brandmark. The company also has at least 26 other well-established brandmarks.

SIZE REVENUES $2,853,997,000 as of 1993

NUMBER OF EMPLOYEES   9,500 as of 1994

SOURCES   *1993 Annual Report; 1994 Annual Report;* company representative

COMPANY | *Household International, Inc.*

STATEMENT | Mission Statement

The business objectives of Household International are established within the framework of our corporate mission:

"We will be a premier financial services organization meeting the needs of individuals and companies through consumer banking, consumer finance, commercial finance, insurance, investments and related services.

We will treat our customers with dignity and respect as we deliver the best service in the industry. We will develop and maintain long-term relationships with our customers by offering a broad line of high quality products and services which meet their needs. We will be vigorous, innovative and a leading participant in the markets we serve.

We view our employees as our greatest resource and will provide every opportunity for them to achieve their hopes, goals and career aspirations. We will encourage our employees to be involved in the civic affairs of their communities.

We will be exemplary corporate citizens, always conducting ourselves in an ethical and honest manner.

We will accomplish these goals while providing our shareholders with a superior return on their investment."

ADDRESS   2700 Sanders Rd.
Prospect Heights, IL 60070

INDUSTRY CATEGORY   Financial Investment Services

CORPORATE DESCRIPTION
Household International is the nation's largest and oldest consumer finance company.

SIZE REVENUES $248,700,000 (net income) as of 1993

NUMBER OF EMPLOYEES   17,300 as of 1993

SOURCE   *1993 Annual Report*

◆　◆　◆　◆　◆　◆　◆

COMPANY | *Houston Industries Incorporated*

STATEMENT | Mission Statement
The mission of Houston Industries Incorporated is to maximize shareholder value and satisfy its customers' needs, while providing its employees a rewarding and productive work environment and conducting its affairs responsibly in the community.

Houston Industries will accomplish this mission by creating a corporate vision of successful growth, by carefully managing its assets and by integrating its businesses through effective planning and allocation of resources.

ADDRESS   P. O. Box 4567
Houston, TX 77210

INDUSTRY CATEGORY   Utility

CORPORATE DESCRIPTION
Houston Industries Incorporated is a diversified holding company involved in the electric utility, cable television and non-regulated power businesses.

SIZE REVENUES $4,323,930,000 as of 1993

NUMBER OF EMPLOYEES   11,350 as of 1993

SOURCE   *1993 Annual Report*

◆   ◆   ◆   ◆   ◆   ◆   ◆

COMPANY | *Huntington Bancshares Incorporated*

STATEMENT | **Mission Statement**
The mission of Huntington Bancshares Incorporated is to meet the financial services needs of individuals and businesses. We seek dominant position in the markets where we choose to compete by providing high quality, differentiated products, and legendary customer service. Our thrust for business development is to penetrate existing markets, deliver products and services to new geographic markets, and strategically manage our business mix to achieve superior results.

ADDRESS   41 S. High St.
Columbus, OH 43287

INDUSTRY CATEGORY   Banking

CORPORATE DESCRIPTION
Huntington Bancshares Incorporated is an $18 billion regional bank holding company headquartered in Columbus, Ohio. The company's banking subsidiaries operate 352 offices in Ohio, Florida, Illinois, Indiana, Kentucky, Michigan, Pennsylvania, and West Virginia. In addition, mortgage, trust, investment banking and automobile finance subsidiaries manage 89 offices in the eight states mentioned

as well as Connecticut, Delaware, Maryland, Massachusetts, New Jersey, North Carolina, Rhode Island and Virginia.

SIZE REVENUES $1,542,089,000 as of 1993

NUMBER OF EMPLOYEES   8,395 as of December 31, 1993

SOURCE   *1993 Annual Report*

♦ ♦ ♦ ♦ ♦ ♦ ♦

COMPANY | *IBM*
(International Business Machines Corporation)

STATEMENT | **IBM PRINCIPLES**
The marketplace is the driving force behind everything we do.

♦ ♦ ♦ ♦

At our core, we are a technology company with an overriding commitment to quality.

♦ ♦ ♦ ♦

Our primary measures of success are customer satisfaction and shareholder value.

♦ ♦ ♦ ♦

We operate as an entrepreneurial organization with a minimum of bureaucracy and a never-ending focus on productivity.

♦ ♦ ♦ ♦

We never lose sight of our strategic vision.

♦ ♦ ♦ ♦

We think and act with a sense of urgency.

◆ ❧ ❦ ◆

Outstanding, dedicated people make it all happen, particularly when we work together as a team.

◆ ❧ ❦ ◆

We are sensitive to the needs of all employees and to the communities in which we operate.

◆ ❧ ❦ ◆

ADDRESS   Corporate Headquarters
One Old Orchard Rd.
Armonk, NY 10549

INDUSTRY CATEGORY   High Technology

CORPORATE DESCRIPTION
IBM develops, manufactures and sells advanced information processing products, including computers and microelectronic technology, software, networking systems and information technology-related services.

SIZE REVENUES $62,716,000,000 as of 1993

NUMBER OF EMPLOYEES   256,207 as of 1993

SOURCE   *1993 Annual Report*

COMPANY | *ICN Pharmaceuticals, Inc.*

STATEMENT | **THE ICN MISSION**
OUR GOALS

❖ **Quality Products**

To make health care products that improve the quality of life for mankind

❖ **Financially Strong**

To deliver a strong and consistent financial performance that provides a fair return to our investors

❖ **Global Leader**

To become one of the largest and most successful health care companies in the world

❖ **Customer-Driven**

To deliver friendly professional service fully responsive to the needs of our customers

❖ **Good Employer**

To sustain a working environment that attracts, retains and develops committed employees who take pride in the success of the company

❖ **Good Neighbor**

To be a good global citizen responsive to the needs of our communities and constituencies

To achieve these goals, we must:

Deliver friendly, professional service consistently through well-trained and motivated employees

Search continuously for improvement through innovation and the use of technology

Employ planning and decision-making processes that provide clear direction and sense of purpose

Foster a leadership style throughout the organization which encourages respect for individuals, teamwork and close identification with customers

Strive constantly to achieve agreed standards of quality at competitive cost levels

ADDRESS   ICN Plaza
3300 Hyland Ave.
Costa Mesa, CA 92626

INDUSTRY CATEGORY   Pharmaceutical/Biotechnology

CORPORATE DESCRIPTION
ICN Pharmaceuticals, Inc. is the parent company for SPI Pharmaceuticals, Inc., which manufactures, markets, and distributes over 600 pharmaceutical products in over 60 countries throughout the world, serving the U. S., Eastern and Western Europe, Canada, Mexico and the Far East. Major products include a variety of prescription and nonprescription pharmaceutical products, including antivirals, antibiotics, dermatologicals, cardiovasculars, analgesics, antirheumatics, central nervous system compounds and vision care lines. SPI products are marketed under the ICN tradename.

SIZE REVENUES $364,358,000 as of 1991

NUMBER OF EMPLOYEES   Not available as of 1994

SOURCE   *1991 Annual Report*

COMPANY | *Illinois Power Company*

STATEMENT | **Mission**
Illinois Power will be a low-cost provider of electricity and natural gas service with an unparalleled commitment to the needs of its customers.

Critical Success Factors
Six factors critical to the success of Illinois Power are:
- Leadership and Cultural Change
- Customer Focus
- Cost Control
- Market Expansion
- Regulatory Reform
- Strategic Alliances

ADDRESS   500 S. 27th St.
Decatur, IL 62525

INDUSTRY CATEGORY   Utility

CORPORATE DESCRIPTION
Illinois Power Company is a public utility engaged principally in the generation, transmission, distribution, and sale of electric energy and the distribution, transportation, and sale of natural gas solely in the State of Illinois. The Company's territory is one-quarter of the state. The Company serves approximately 560,000 customers.

SIZE REVENUES $1,581,200,000 as of December 31, 1993

NUMBER OF EMPLOYEES   4,540 as of December 31, 1993

SOURCE   *1993 Annual Report*

COMPANY | *Inland Container Corporation*

STATEMENT | Mission

To be the preferred supplier of containerboard and corrugated by delivering the highest value in products and service to our customers. We will accomplish this by fully involving our people in the process of continuous improvement through quality and the elimination of waste. We believe that the pursuit of continuous improvement will earn our shareholders a sustained high rate of return on investment and provide our people with safe and rewarding employment.

ADDRESS
4030 Vincennes Rd.
Indianapolis, IN 46268

INDUSTRY CATEGORY
Manufacturing

CORPORATE DESCRIPTION
Inland Container Corporation is a subsidiary and business unit of Temple-Inland, a Diboll, Texas-based holding company with major interests in paper, packaging, building products and financial services.

Inland Container Corporation currently operates seven paper mills, four of which are 100% recycle mills, 39 corrugated box manufacturing plants, and a tape plant. In 1993, this group produced 2.5 million tons of containerboard (linerboard and corrugating medium), and shipped 1.98 million tons of corrugated boxes. The company ranks among the top four in the United States in both containerboard and corrugated box production.

SIZE REVENUES $1,248,500,000 (container and containerboard manufacturing net sales) as of 1993

NUMBER OF EMPLOYEES   Not available as of 1993

SOURCE   1993 *Annual Report*

COMPANY | *Inland Steel Industries*

STATEMENT | **Mission Statement for Inland Steel Industries**

To be a market-oriented, quality-driven management company focused on distribution of industrial materials and production of high quality steel products and other engineered materials.

Market-oriented: Inland Steel Industries will serve selected customer groups in the industrial materials market and will focus on improving the long-term competitive position of its customers. Inland will achieve competitive advantage by strategically positioning its businesses in targeted segments of the industrial materials market.

The Inland business units pursue competitive advantage based upon superior knowledge of their customers' products, markets and economics. They seek to improve the competitive position of their customers by providing superior products and services.

Quality-driven: Inland is committed to continuous improvement in the quality of all of its products and services provided to customers, internal as well as external. All line and staff operations will measure quality by how well they anticipate and satisfy customer needs.

Management company: Inland competes as an interrelated group of businesses designed to increase shareholder value by sustained superior profitability. It is not a loose holding of independent businesses. Each business receives competitive benefits through sharing of financial resources, information, technology, plant and equipment, personnel, know-how, and markets with related business units. Inland provides strategic direction to its businesses units; creates strategic alliances; stimulates change; performs the financial functions; sets the standards for and evaluates performance; allocates resources; directs and coordinates the interactivities among units; and defines the specific mix of businesses at any point in time.

Distribution of industrial materials: Inland has an excellent foundation of experience in servicing the industrial market with its existing distribution businesses. The distribution segment concentrates on customers who require just-in-time delivery, processing and broad product selection, and who value service. Inland will grow this business group through internal development and acquisition of new businesses.

COMPANY | *Insight Direct, Inc.*

STATEMENT | **Our Goal**

Insight's goal is to be the best direct marketer in the World.

| **Mission Statement**

The mission of Insight Direct, Inc. is to be the industry leader in the volume direct marketing of technology products to the end user; to have a base of very satisfied customers and to remain profitable for the benefit of the employees and shareholders.

While currently focused on steel, aluminum, and plastic products, Inland will seek profitable opportunities in distribution of other industrial materials.

Production of high quality steel products: Inland's business focus in manufacturing is on carbon steel. Its vision for the steel segment is to produce efficiently sophisticated sheet and bar products, fully competitive with the best producers in the world. The principal steel market focus is the automotive, appliance, electric motor and office furniture segments of the industrial materials market. Our steel businesses will serve customers who are leaders in their markets, that need sophisticated products made to exacting standards, and who value technical service and long-term relationships.

…and other engineered materials: The Company believes that the industrial market offers excellent opportunities to expand into manufacturing and processing of other engineered materials in concert with or separate from carbon steel.

CORPORATE DESCRIPTION
Insight is one of the nation's largest direct marketers of computer products. Customers include Fortune 500 companies, the U. S. Government, small businesses, and end-users worldwide. As of 1994, the company had annual sales of $200 million and 550 employees.

ADDRESS   1912 W. 4th St.
Tempe, AZ 85281

SOURCE   Company representative

ADDRESS   30 W. Monroe St.
Chicago, IL 60603

INDUSTRY CATEGORY   Manufacturing

CORPORATE DESCRIPTION
Inland Steel Industries, Inc. is a holding company whose businesses
are leaders in value-added steel and materials distribution. It owns
Inland Steel Company, the fifth largest integrated steel producer in
the United States, and Inland Materials Distribution Group, Inc.,
the nation's largest metal distribution network.

SIZE REVENUES $3,888,000,000 as of 1993

NUMBER OF EMPLOYEES   16,152 as of 1993

SOURCE   Company representative

◆　◆　◆　◆　◆　◆　◆

COMPANY │ *International Dairy Queen, Inc.*

STATEMENT │ **IDQ Mission Statement**
We are in the business of managing diverse franchise systems,
with current emphasis on those in the fast-food, treat and
snack areas.

It is our intention to continue to grow in the franchising
business, providing financial, management, marketing, operational, training, equipment, engineering, insurance and supply systems to franchisees. We will continue to expand within
the food franchise industry through the growth of existing
systems and the acquisition of systems which complement the

existing systems, and outside that industry through franchise systems in non-food categories.

We will maintain strong financial standards which will facilitate enhanced return to our stockholders, capital for our further business growth and market growth for our franchises.

In each system we manage, we will be as professionally informed and skilled as the best operators within the category, so that the revenues we earn result from leadership, innovation and genuine service to our franchisees.

We will operate our business professionally and ethically, with appropriate concern for our franchisees, employees and the communities in which we conduct business.

ADDRESS   7505 Metro Blvd.
Minneapolis, MN 55439

INDUSTRY CATEGORY   Food/Beverage

CORPORATE DESCRIPTION
International Dairy Queen, Inc. is engaged in the business of developing, licensing and servicing a system of more than 5,400 Dairy Queen stores in the United States, Canada and other foreign countries featuring hamburgers, hot dogs, various dairy desserts and beverages; more than 480 Orange Julius stores in the United States, Canada and other foreign countries featuring blended drinks made from orange juice, fruits and other fruit flavors, along with various snack items; more than 90 Karmelkorn stores featuring popcorn and other treat items; and more than 115 Treat Center stores serving a combination of Dairy Queen, Orange Julius and/or Karmelkorn products.

SIZE REVENUES $241,612,000 as of 1993

NUMBER OF EMPLOYEES   538 as of 1993

SOURCE   *1993 Annual Report*

STATEMENT | **IGT Mission Statement**

IGT is in business to provide for the needs of our customers, our employees and our shareholders, while recognizing our responsibility to the communities in which we operate.

❖ IGT is committed to providing our customers with quality products at a competitive price which, together with excellent service and support, will assist them in maximizing their profitability.

❖ IGT is committed to providing our employees with a stable and rewarding work environment, the opportunity to grow to the extent of their talents, and the opportunity to share in the success of the company which they make possible.

❖ IGT is committed to providing our shareholders with an above average return on their investment, since our ability to serve the needs of our customers and employees is made possible only through their support.

❖ IGT is committed to being a responsible corporate citizen in the communities in which we operate, and encourages our employees to individually be an asset to the community in which they live.

ADDRESS   520 S. Rock Blvd.
Reno, NV 89510-0580

INDUSTRY CATEGORY   Hotel, Hospitality, and Related

CORPORATE DESCRIPTION
International Game Technology is an industry leader in the design, manufacture and marketing of gaming machines and proprietary software systems for computerized wide-area gaming machine networks. IGT is the only gaming machine manufacturer licensed to do business in every regulated gaming jurisdiction in the world.

SIZE REVENUES $478,030,000 (gross revenues) as of 1993

NUMBER OF EMPLOYEES 3,000 (worldwide) as of 1993

SOURCES *1993 Annual Report*, company representative

◆ ◆ ◆ ◆ ◆ ◆ ◆

COMPANY | *Johnson Controls, Inc.*

STATEMENT | JOHNSON CONTROLS VISION

OUR CREED

We believe in the free enterprise system. We shall consistently treat our customers, employees, shareholders, suppliers and the community with honesty, dignity, fairness and respect. We will conduct our business with the highest ethical standards.

OUR MISSION

Continually exceed our customers' increasing expectations.

WHAT WE VALUE

INTEGRITY: Honesty and fairness are essential to the way we do business and how we interact with people. We are a company that keeps its promises. We do what we say we will do, and we will conduct ourselves in accordance with our code of ethics.

CUSTOMER SATISFACTION: Customer satisfaction is the source of employee, shareholder, supplier and community benefits. We will exceed customer expectations through continuous improvement in quality, service, productivity and time compression.

OUR EMPLOYEES: The diversity and involvement of our people is the foundation of our strength. We are committed to their fair and effective selection, development, motivation and recognition. We will provide employees with the tools, training and support to achieve excellence in customer satisfaction.

IMPROVEMENT AND INNOVATION: We seek improvement and innovation in every element of our business.

SAFETY AND THE ENVIRONMENT: Our products, services and workplaces reflect our belief that what is good for the environment and the safety and health of all people is good for Johnson Controls.

OBJECTIVES

CUSTOMER SATISFACTION: We will exceed customer expectations through continuous improvement in quality, service, productivity and time compression.

TECHNOLOGY: We will apply world-class technology to our products, processes and services.

GROWTH: We will seek growth by building upon our existing businesses.

MARKET LEADERSHIP: We will only operate in markets where we are, or have the opportunity to become, the recognized leader.

SHAREHOLDER VALUE: We will exceed the after-tax, median return on shareholders' equity of the Standard & Poor's Industrials.

ADDRESS   5757 N. Green Bay Ave.
P. O. Box 591
Milwaukee, WI 53201-0591

INDUSTRY CATEGORY   Business Services

CORPORATE DESCRIPTION
Johnson Controls is a global market leader in facility services and control systems, automotive seating systems, plastic packaging, and automotive batteries.

SIZE REVENUES $6,182,000,000 as of 1993

NUMBER OF EMPLOYEES   50,100 (worldwide) as of 1993

SOURCE   *1993 Annual Report*, "The Fortune 500," *Fortune* 129, no. 8 (April 8, 1994)

♦ ♦ ♦ ♦ ♦ ♦ ♦

COMPANY | *Johnson Wax (S. C. Johnson & Sons, Inc.)*

STATEMENT | **THIS WE BELIEVE**
OUR GUIDING PRINCIPLES

Our company has been guided by certain basic principles since its founding in 1886.

These principles were first summarized in 1927 by H. F. Johnson, Sr., in his Christmas Profit Sharing speech:

"The goodwill of the people is the only enduring thing in any business. It is the sole substance. ... The rest is shadow!"

In 1976, we formally stated these basic principles in "**This We Believe**." Since then, our statement of corporate philosophy has been translated and communicated around the world—not only within the worldwide company, but also to key external audiences. It has served us well by providing all employees with a common statement of the basic principles which guide the company in all the different cultures where we operate. It has also provided people outside the company with an understanding of our fundamental beliefs. It communicates the kind of company we are.

Now, more than ten years after "**This We Believe**" was developed and following the celebration of our 100th anniversary, it is appropriate to restate, clarify and reaffirm our commitment to uphold these principles, because our company, like most others in these highly volatile times, has had to adjust its business strategies worldwide. This restatement and clarification is important to assure that our corporate policies and the actions of our managers and other employees continue to be fully supportive of our beliefs.

"**This We Believe**" states our beliefs in relation to the five groups of people to whom we are responsible and whose trust we have to earn:

EMPLOYEES

We believe that the fundamental vitality and strength of our worldwide company lies in our people.

CONSUMERS AND USERS

We believe in earning the enduring goodwill of consumers and users of our products and services.

GENERAL PUBLIC

We believe in being a responsible leader within the free market economy.

NEIGHBORS AND HOSTS

We believe in contributing to the well-being of the countries and communities where we conduct business.

WORLD COMMUNITY

We believe in improving international understanding.

These beliefs are real and we will strive to live up to them. Our commitment to them is evident in our actions to date.

The sincerity of our beliefs encourages us to act with integrity at all times, to respect the dignity of each person as an individual human being, to assume moral and social responsibilities early as a matter of conscience, to make an extra effort to use our skills and resources where they are most needed, and to strive for excellence in everything we do.

Our way of safeguarding these beliefs is to remain a privately held company. Our way of reinforcing them is to make profits through growth and development, profits which allow us to do more for all the people on whom we depend.

We believe that the fundamental vitality and strength of our worldwide company lies in our people, and we commit ourselves to:

❧ **Maintain good relations among all employees around the world based on a sense of participation, mutual respect, and an understanding of common objectives, by:**

—Creating a climate whereby all employees freely air their concerns and express opinions with the assurance that these will be fairly considered.

—Attentively responding to employees' suggestions and problems.

—Fostering open, two-way communications between management and employees.

—Providing employees with opportunities to participate in the process of decision-making.

—Encouraging employees at all levels and in all disciplines to work as a team.

—Respecting the dignity and rights of privacy of every employee.

❧ **Manage our business in such a way that we can provide security for regular employees and retirees, by:**

—Pursuing a long-term policy of planned, orderly growth.

—Retaining regular employees, if at all possible, as conditions change. However, this may not always be possible, particularly where major restructuring or reorganization is required to maintain competitiveness.

—Retraining employees who have acceptable performance records and are in positions no longer needed, provided suitable jobs are available.

❧ **Maintain a high level of effectiveness within the organization, by:**

—Establishing clear standards of job performance.

—Ensuring that the performance of all employees meets required levels by giving appropriate recognition to those whose performance is good and by terminating those whose performance, despite their managers' efforts to help, continues below company standards.

❧ **Provide equal opportunities in employment and advancement, by:**

—Hiring and promoting employees without discrimination, using qualifications, performance, and experience as the principal criteria.

❧ **Remunerate employees at levels that fully reward their performance and recognize their contribution to the success of their company, by:**

—Maintaining base pay and benefit programs both of which are fully competitive with those prevailing within the relevant marketplaces.

—Maintaining, in addition to our fully competitive pay and benefit programs, our long-standing tradition of sharing profits with employees.

❧ **Protect the health and safety of all employees, by:**

—Providing a clean and safe work environment.

—Providing appropriate safety training and occupational health services.

❧ **Develop the skills and abilities of our people, by:**

—Providing on-the-job training and professional development programs.

—Helping employees qualify for opportunities in the company through educational and development programs.

❧ **Creative environments which are conducive to self-expression and personal well-being, by:**

—Fostering and supporting leisure-time programs for employees and retirees.

—Developing job-enrichment programs.

—Maintaining the long tradition of high quality and good design in our office and plants.

❧ **Encourage initiative, innovation, and entrepreneurism among all employees, thereby providing opportunities for** greater job satisfaction while also helping the worldwide company achieve its objectives.

We believe in earning the enduring goodwill of consumers and users of our products and services, and we commit ourselves to:

❖ **Provide useful products and services throughout the world, by:**

—Monitoring closely the changing wants and needs of consumers and users.

—Developing and maintaining high standards of quality.

—Developing new products and services which are recognized by consumers and users as being significantly superior overall to major competition.

—Maintaining close and effective business relations with the trade to ensure that our products and services are readily available to consumers and users.

—Continuing our research and development commitment to provide a strong technology base for innovative and superior products and services.

❖ **Develop and market products which are environmentally sound and which do not endanger the health and safety of consumers and users, by:**

—Meeting all regulatory requirements or exceeding them where worldwide company standards are higher.

—Providing clear and adequate directions for safe use, together with cautionary statements and/or symbols.

—Incorporating protection against misuse where this is appropriate.

—Researching new technologies for products which favor an improved environment.

❖ **Maintain and develop comprehensive education and service programs for consumers and users, by:**

—Disseminating information to consumers and users which promotes full understanding of the correct use of our products and services.

—Handling all inquiries, complaints, and service needs for consumers and users quickly, thoroughly, and fairly.

We believe in being a responsible leader in the free market economy, and we commit ourselves to:

❖ **Ensure the future vitality of the worldwide company, by:**

—Earning sufficient profits to provide new investment for planned growth and progress.

—Maintaining a worldwide organization of highly competent, motivated, and dedicated employees.

❖ **Conduct our business in a fair and ethical manner, by:**

—Not engaging in unfair business practices.

—Treating our suppliers and customers both fairly and reasonably, according to sound commercial practice.

—Packaging and labeling our products so that consumers and users can make informed value judgments.

—Maintaining the highest advertising standards of integrity and good taste.

—Not engaging in bribery.

❖ **Share the profits of each local company with those who have contributed to its success, by:**

—Rewarding employees through a profit sharing program.

—Allocating a share of the profits to enhance the well-being of communities where we operate.

—Developing better products and services for the benefit of consumers and users.

—Providing to shareholders a reasonable return on their investment.

❖ **Provide the general public with information about our activities so that they have a better understanding of our worldwide company.**

We believe in contributing to the well-being of the countries and communities where we conduct business, and we commit ourselves to:

❧ **Seek actively the counsel and independent judgment of citizens of each country where we conduct business to provide guidance to local and corporate management, by:**

—Selecting independent directors to serve on the board of each of our companies worldwide.

—Retaining distinguished associates and consultants to assist us in conducting our business according to the highest professional standards.

❧ **Contribute to the economic well-being of every country and community where we conduct business, by:**

—Ensuring that new investment fits constructively into the economic development of each host country and local community.

—Encouraging the use of local suppliers and services offering competitive quality and prices.

❧ **Contribute to the social development of every country and community where we conduct business, by:**

—Providing training programs for the development of skills.

—Staffing and managing with nationals from those countries wherever practicable.

—Involving ourselves in social, cultural, and educational projects which enhance the quality of life.

❧ **Be a good corporate citizen, by:**

—Complying with and maintaining a due regard for the laws, regulations, and traditions of each country where we conduct business.

We believe in improving international understanding, and we commit ourselves to:

❧ Act with responsible practices in international trade and investment, by:

—Retaining earnings necessary for reinvestment in our local companies and remitting dividends on a consistent basis.

—Making royalty, licensing, and service agreements which are fair and reasonable and which do not result in any hidden transfer of profits.

—Limiting foreign exchange transactions to normal business requirements and for the protection of our assets.

◈ Promote the exchange of ideas and techniques, by:

—Encouraging the rapid diffusion of new technology to our local companies and licensees, while protecting our ownership rights and investment in such technology.

—Organizing worldwide and regional meetings for the dissemination and exchange of information.

—Providing support and assistance, especially in technical and professional fields, to develop skills throughout the organization.

—Following a balanced approach between transferring people to new jobs to gain experience and leaving people on the job long enough to make positive contributions in their assignments.

—Participating actively in non-political national and international activities with the objective of improving the global business climate.

ADDRESS　　1525 Howe St.
Racine, WI 53403

INDUSTRY CATEGORY　　Consumer Goods and Services

CORPORATE DESCRIPTION

SC Johnson Wax is one of the world's leading manufacturers of chemical specialty products for home, personal care and insect control. It is also a leading supplier of products and services for commercial, industrial and institutional facilities. In the area of financial services, the corporation has interests in venture capital and insurance.

SIZE REVENUES   Not available (privately held)

NUMBER OF EMPLOYEES   13,100 (worldwide) as of June, 1994

SOURCES   "Profile" company publication; company representative; "This We Believe" company publication

◆ ◆ ◆ ◆ ◆ ◆ ◆

COMPANY | *Jostens, Inc.*

STATEMENT | **Jostens Strategic Plan 1994–1996**
| **JOSTENS' MISSION STATEMENT**

Jostens' mission is to enhance the development and motivation of individuals and organizations. Through a strong customer focus Jostens will be the foremost marketer of programs and services which address instructional, recognition, identity, tradition, training and achievement needs.

Jostens will adhere to certain basic principles in fulfilling this mission. These are:

❧ Enhancing stakeholders' interests through superior sales and earnings growth and responsible financial management.

❧ Adhering to the highest level of ethical standards and corporate citizenship.

❧ Creating and maintaining a challenging and rewarding work environment.

❧ Participating in businesses in which we either have or expect to attain, a market leadership position.

Jostens' primary objective is to provide our shareholders a superior return on their investment. In order to accomplish this, we adopt the following goals:

◈ Attain double-digit compounded annual growth in sales and earnings per share. Improve after-tax margins and maintain positive net operating cash flow.

◈ Maintain and/or improve market share and penetration in all markets. Adopt a marketing orientation which focuses on programs to serve our customers, not just products.

◈ Be an environmentally responsible company.

◈ Achieve a diverse and committed work force, maximizing the potential of all Jostens employees and sales representatives through diversity, quality involvement, training, and motivation programs.

ADDRESS   5501 Norman Center Dr.
Minneapolis, MN 55437

INDUSTRY CATEGORY   Consumer Goods and Services

CORPORATE DESCRIPTION
Jostens' products and services include: yearbooks, class rings, graduation products, student photography packages, technology-based educational products and services, customized sales and service awards, sports awards, and customized products for university alumni.

SIZE REVENUES $827,000,000 as of June 30, 1994

NUMBER OF EMPLOYEES   8,000 as of June 30, 1994

SOURCE   *1994 Annual Report*

COMPANY | *Kansas City Life Insurance Company*

STATEMENT | **purpose**
of Kansas City Life Insurance Company

Kansas City Life Insurance Company exists to provide present and future financial security to people, thereby assuring them a dignity and a quality of life that they and their beneficiaries might otherwise not enjoy, and

To sustain Kansas City Life's own growth and prosperity through good management and reasonable profit, thus enabling the Company to continue to serve people for as long as their needs exist.

business philosophies
of Kansas City Life Insurance Company

The People Who are Kansas City Life Believe That:

Life Insurance is unequalled as a means of providing guaranteed financial protection to people, and Kansas City Life strives to promote and sell life insurance fairly and at a reasonable cost to meet the real needs of people.

The highest order of integrity and business ethics must be practiced in every transaction, and the protection of funds entrusted to the Company by policyowners for their future financial security is a basic responsibility of each person who makes up the Company.

Every Kansas City Life customer, whether policyowner, beneficiary, or loan customer, deserves the finest service and consideration from every Kansas City Life associate.

Kansas City Life stockholders are entitled to earn as good a return on their investments as the Company can produce, and they expect the management to conduct the Company's business in a manner that will be in the stockholders' best interest.

Kansas City Life recognizes that its own people are the primary reason for its continuing success, and these people always will be fairly compensated and advanced for their contributions to the Company's success. The Company and its general agencies are interdependent; both must succeed in order for each to grow and prosper.

Kansas City Life must be a good corporate citizen, participating in civic, community and business affairs with both money and personal involvement. The Company is and should continue to strive to be a highly regarded leader in the national life insurance business, participating in and supporting the activities of the industry as a whole. As such a leader, Kansas City Life should serve as an example of a company that will operate as honestly and efficiently without stringent governmental regulation as it would with such regulation.

Kansas City Life is a company concerned with and dedicated to improving the quality of human life.

ADDRESS   3520 Broadway
Kansas City, MO 64111

INDUSTRY CATEGORY   Insurance

CORPORATE DESCRIPTION
Kansas City Life Insurance Company markets individual life, annuity and group products through approximately 145 career general agencies.

The Kansas City Life corporate group includes Kansas City Life and two major subsidiaries—Old American Insurance Company and Sunset Life Insurance Company of America.

SIZE REVENUES $396,552,000 as of 1993

NUMBER OF EMPLOYEES   2,000 as of 1993

SOURCES   *1993 Annual Report*; company representative

COMPANY | *Kansas City Power & Light Company*

STATEMENT | **Mission Statement**
To be the regional energy supplier of choice.

ADDRESS   P. O. Box 418679
               Kansas City, MO 64141-9679

INDUSTRY CATEGORY   Utility

CORPORATE DESCRIPTION
Kansas City Power & Light Company is a medium-size electric utility and the corporate successor to one of the world's first electric companies, generating electricity since 1882. Headquartered in downtown Kansas City, Missouri, the Company generates and distributes electricity to over 419,000 customers in a 4,700-square-mile area located in 23 counties in western Missouri and eastern Kansas. Customers include 368,000 residences, 49,000 commercial firms, and over 2,000 industrials, municipalities and other electric utilities.

SIZE REVENUES $857,450,000 as of 1993

NUMBER OF EMPLOYEES   2,340 as of September 30, 1994

SOURCES   *1993 Annual Report*; company representative

COMPANY | *Kaufman and Broad Home Corporation*

STATEMENT | **Kaufman and Broad Mission Statement**
"We build homes to meet people's dreams."

OBJECTIVES

We are fiercely determined to continue to succeed. We intend to provide the best quality housing for our customers, a superior return to our shareholders, and a chance for every employee to make a difference and share in our success.

VISION

We strive to be the leading home builder in each market in which we operate. We intend to lead the way in home building well into the 21st century.

CORE VALUES

It is our intention to deliver a quality product...100% of the time.

We believe the true test of quality is customer satisfaction. There are no good excuses.

We treat each customer specially and each situation individually.

We strive to be at the cutting edge of product development and innovative design.

We reward innovation and encourage reasonable and prudent risk taking.

We don't just build homes, we build neighborhoods.

This business is built around people. We want self-directed winners who have high personal integrity.

This is a team business where we depend on one another. We expect each person to make a contribution.

All people at Kaufman and Broad have clout. We all work for the same ultimate boss, our customers.

Our subcontractors and suppliers are our partners. We demand a lot from them, especially high quality work. We expect to work and prosper together.

We respect the dignity of those with whom we deal. We always try to be fair.

While we are committed to steady growth and improved earnings, we will not over-emphasize short-term results.

We view land as a raw material for use in the building process, not as a speculative investment.

We believe in long-range planning. It is nonsense to say you can't plan the future in this business.

Our company's success is built on conservative financial policies, a strong capital base and superior earnings capacity. We believe a sustained level of solid profitability is critical to our future.

Autonomous regions are the cornerstone of our operational success. We have pioneered a divisional structure that links entrepreneurial executives with a lean headquarters group.

We are constantly striving to conduct our business in a way that will enable us to prosper in both good and lean times.

ADDRESS   10877 Wilshire Blvd., 12th Floor
Los Angeles, CA 90024

INDUSTRY CATEGORY   Construction

CORPORATE DESCRIPTION
Kaufman and Broad Home Corporation is the West's largest home builder and one of the largest builders in metropolitan Paris, France.

SIZE REVENUES $1,237,850,000 as of 1993

NUMBER OF EMPLOYEES   1,241 as of 1993

SOURCE   *1993 Annual Report*

STATEMENT | **A STRATEGIC STATEMENT**

KAYDON designs, manufactures and sells custom-engineered products for a broad and diverse customer base. Kaydon's principal products include antifriction bearings, bearing systems, filters, filter housings, high-performance rings, sealing rings, specialty retaining rings and balls, shaft seals and slip-rings. These products are used by our customers in a wide variety of medical, instrumentation, material handling, machine tool positioning, aerospace, defense, construction and other industrial applications. Kaydon is customer-focused and concentrates on providing a cost-effective solution to the customer's problem, through a close engineering relationship with leading manufacturers throughout the world.

KAYDON's strategy is to function as an extension of our customers' businesses through a commitment to identify and provide engineered solutions to design problems. We seek to blend technical innovation with cost-effective manufacturing and outstanding service.

KAYDON manufactures custom engineered components with significant complexity, usually in small lot sizes, which are sold directly to a broad spectrum of customers who incorporate the component into their end product. Kaydon services the replacement market for these components directly to the users, through the OEM or through an array of traditional distributors particular to the industry served.

KAYDON strives to develop growth opportunities by expanding our range of technical capabilities through both internal developments and selected acquisitions. This permits us to pursue our strategy of customized technical solutions beyond our current products into expanded product and market areas.

KAYDON avoids the high volume, commodity markets such as transportation and appliances. We also avoid businesses which are heavily dependent upon electronics, distribution, consumer products, software development or which provide services.

KAYDON's successful implementation of this strategy will result in superior earnings growth and return on capital. Management's long-term objectives are to achieve a 15% compound rate of growth in earnings; a minimum 20% return on stockholders' investment; and a 15% return on total capital employed.

ADDRESS   Arbor Shoreline Office Park
193459 U. S. 19 North, Ste. 500
Clearwater, FL 34624

INDUSTRY CATEGORY   Manufacturing

CORPORATE DESCRIPTION
Kaydon designs, manufactures and sells custom-engineered products for a broad and diverse customer base. Kaydon's principal products include antifriction bearings, bearing systems, filters, filter housings, high-performance rings, sealing rings, specialty retaining rings, shaft seals and slip-rings. These products are used in a variety of industrial applications. (See "A Strategic Statement.")

SIZE REVENUES $184,060,000 as of 1993

NUMBER OF EMPLOYEES   1,661 as of 1993

SOURCES   *1991 Annual Report*; company representative

COMPANY | *Kellogg's (Kellogg Company)*

STATEMENT | **KELLOGG COMPANY PHILOSOPHY**

OUR MISSION

Kellogg is a global company committed to building long-term growth in volume and profit and to enhancing its worldwide leadership position by providing nutritious food products of superior value.

OUR SHARED VALUES

Profit and Growth: Profitable growth is our primary purpose. We are committed to consistent, long-term growth in earnings and to superior returns for our shareholders. We want to be, and be recognized as, a growth company.

People: Kellogg people are our company's greatest competitive advantage. Each and every individual will be given the

COMPANY | *Ketchum Communications*

STATEMENT | Our Mission

To create innovative communications for clients who appreciate the value fresh ideas add to their business.

CORPORATE DESCRIPTION

Ketchum Communications Inc. (KCI) is the eighteenth-largest communications firm in the world, with billings in excess of $1 billion and 1,160 employees (as of 1994).

The operating units provide a full range of marketing and communications services in 14 major U. S. markets and in 21 countries.

opportunity to contribute to and share in the company's success. We are committed to helping Kellogg people reach their full potential and to recognizing their achievements.

Consumer Satisfaction and Quality: The consumer is the ultimate judge of our success. Kellogg people, together with our suppliers and trade partners, will provide consumers with products and services of superior value. We are committed to excellence in everything we do.

Integrity and Ethics: Integrity is the cornerstone of our business practice. We will conduct our affairs in a manner consistent with the highest ethical standards.

Social Responsibility: Social responsibility is an integral part of our heritage. We are committed to be, and be recognized as, an economic, intellectual and social asset in each community, region and country in which we operate.

Ketchum Advertising, headquartered in New York City, is the fourth-largest independent advertising agency in the U. S. and ranks sixteenth-largest overall. Ketchum Public Relations, also headquartered in New York City, is the seventh-largest public relations agency in the U. S.

ADDRESS   Six PPG Place
Pittsburgh, PA 15222-5488

SOURCE   Company representative

ADDRESS   One Kellogg Sq.
Battle Creek, MI 49016-3599

INDUSTRY CATEGORY   Food/Beverage

CORPORATE DESCRIPTION
Kellogg Company, headquartered in Battle Creek, Michigan, is the world's leading producer of ready-to-eat cereal products. The Company also manufactures frozen waffles, toaster pastries, cereal bars, and other convenience foods.

SIZE REVENUES $6,295,400,000 as of 1993

NUMBER OF EMPLOYEES   16,151 as of 1993

SOURCES   *1993 Annual Report, 1992 Annual Report,* company representative

◆ ◆ ◆ ◆ ◆ ◆ ◆

COMPANY | *Kellwood Company*

STATEMENT | **KELLWOOD'S MISSION**

To continue to be a leading international marketer, merchandiser and manufacturer of value-oriented products in each of our portfolios of soft goods companies.

To maintain a strong customer focus, building partnerships with superior products and services that meet or exceed the present and future needs of the retailer.

To encourage and support our employees, recognizing that through their high standards, creativity and commitment, our company will prosper.

To achieve long-term growth of profits and return on shareholder investment through sound financial management practices and operating disciplines.

ADDRESS   600 Kellwood Pkwy.
Chesterfield, MO 63017

INDUSTRY CATEGORY   Consumer Goods

CORPORATE DESCRIPTION
Kellwood, a leading marketer, merchandiser and manufacturer of apparel, home fashions, and recreational camping soft goods, sources its products through a global network of company owned and contractor facilities. The Company's products are sold through every channel of distribution in more than 25,000 stores in the United States, and in an increasing number of outlets in Mexico and Canada.

SIZE REVENUES $1,203,086,000 as of 1994

NUMBER OF EMPLOYEES   15,500 (worldwide) as of 1994

SOURCE   *1994 Annual Report*

COMPANY | *Kemper Corporation*

STATEMENT | **MISSION STATEMENT**

Kemper Corporation is a financial services company that gathers, manages and protects the assets of individual, corporate and institutional clients. Our mission is to generate attractive returns and long-term appreciation for our clients and stockholders by developing and distributing high-quality products and services and operating in a highly professional and ethical manner.

ADDRESS   One Kemper Dr.
Long Grove, IL 60049-0001

INDUSTRY CATEGORY   Insurance

CORPORATE DESCRIPTION

Kemper Corporation, with $14.8 billion in consolidated assets at year-end, is a financial services organization with businesses in asset management, life insurance, risk management services, securities brokerage, reinsurance and property-casualty insurance.

SIZE REVENUES $2,304,400,000 as of 1993

NUMBER OF EMPLOYEES   6,335 as of 1993

SOURCES   *1992 Annual Report;* "The Fortune Service 500," *Fortune* 129, no. 11 (May 30, 1994)

COMPANY | *Kent Electronics Corporation*

STATEMENT | **CORPORATE OBJECTIVE**

To become the best national specialty electronics distribution company with sales offices and distribution centers in the major U. S. markets and to establish K*TEC as one of the largest multi-plant specialty electronic custom contract manufacturers.

ADDRESS 7433 Harwin Dr.
Houston, TX 77036

INDUSTRY CATEGORY Electronics

CORPORATE DESCRIPTION

Kent Electronics is a national specialty electronics distributor and a multi-plant custom contract manufacturer. Kent distributes electronic connectors, wire and cable, passive and electromechanical products to original equipment manufacturers and industrial users and provides local area network (LAN) interconnect wiring products to the voice and data communications aftermarket. The Company is a custom contract manufacturer of electronic interconnect assemblies, other subassemblies and custom battery power packs.

SIZE REVENUES $192,887,000 as of 1994

NUMBER OF EMPLOYEES 808 as of 1994

SOURCE *1994 Annual Report*

STATEMENT

Keyport is a customer-focused, premier provider of innovative annuity and life insurance products which enable customers, in selected market segments, to reach their long-term financial goals. We provide outstanding product value and quality service to our customers and a rewarding environment for all employees, while optimizing shareholder value.

ADDRESS   125 High St.
Boston, MA 02110-2712

INDUSTRY CATEGORY   Insurance

CORPORATE DESCRIPTION

Keyport is a specialty life insurance company providing retirement savings products including Fixed Rate Annuities and Variable Annuities. Its ultimate parent company is Liberty Mutual Insurance Company.

SIZE REVENUES $1,775,765,000 as of December 31, 1993

NUMBER OF EMPLOYEES   308 as of June, 1994

SOURCE   Company representative

COMPANY | *Knight-Ridder, Inc.*

STATEMENT | The Knight-Ridder Promise

A Statement Of Knight-Ridder Values

Knight-Ridder is one of the world's leading publishing and information companies. Our enterprise is both a business and a public trust, built on the highest standards of ethics and integrity. We are rooted in our founders' conviction that high-quality newspapers—fair, independent, probing, relevant and compassionate—are indispensable to our free society.

Our moral obligation is to excel in all that we do. We recognize that change is inevitable. We welcome change and intend to benefit from it. Our values, though, do not change. We intend that the name of Knight-Ridder shall be forever synonymous with the best in newspaper publishing, the delivery of business and professional information, and all other activities in which we choose to participate.

The Knight-Ridder Promise

No individual or single group can assure Knight-Ridder's continued success. All who care about this company and count upon its healthy future are dependent on one another. Therefore, we make these promises...

To Our Customers...

We promise to put you first. Unless we satisfy you, we cannot succeed. We are committed to meeting your needs and expectations—and exceeding them whenever possible. You can count on our honesty and fairness, our professionalism, our responsiveness, our courtesy, our dedication to quality—and our passion to serve you well.

To Our Employees...

We promise to help you achieve your full potential. We promise personal respect, fair pay, a clean and safe workplace. We promise equal opportunity for reward and advancement. We promise a role in a great enterprise that is central to our society—and recognition and appreciation for a job well done.

To Our Shareholders...

We promise to work hard, in all parts of our company, to make your investment in Knight-Ridder an attractive one. We are committed to seeing that your money is invested in operations with sound economic prospects. We are committed to consistent growth in profits and a fair return on investment— and not just when the economy is robust.

To Our Communities...

We promise to be good citizens, to contribute to the quality of life and civic betterment of the communities that sustain us. We will do that through searching and sensitive journalism that fully meets our public-service obligations, through ethical and enlightened business practices, through civic participation and financial support.

To Our Society...

We know that ours is not just another business, but one that requires special fidelity to the principles of democracy. We promise to be faithful to those principles and to act always in vigorous support of a free press, freedom of speech and a free flow of information around the globe.

All these commitments are part of The Knight-Ridder Promise...a promise for our people and for our future.

ADDRESS   One Herald Plaza
Miami, FL 33132-1693

INDUSTRY CATEGORY   Media/Printing/Publishing

CORPORATE DESCRIPTION

Knight-Ridder, Inc. is an international information and communications company engaged in newspaper publishing, business news and information services, electronic retrieval services, news, graphics and photo services, cable television and newsprint manufacturing. Knight-Ridder's various information services reach more than 100 million people in 135 countries.

SIZE REVENUES $2,451,000,000 as of 1993

NUMBER OF EMPLOYEES 20,420 (worldwide) as of 1993

SOURCES *1991 Annual Report,* "The Fortune 500," *Fortune* 129, no. 8 (April 8, 1994)

◆ ◆ ◆ ◆ ◆ ◆ ◆

COMPANY | *Kroger (The Kroger Co.)*

STATEMENT | THE KROGER CO.

OUR MISSION is to be a leader in the distribution and merchandising of food, health, personal care, and related consumable products and services. In achieving this objective, we will satisfy our responsibilities to shareowners, employees, customers, suppliers, and the communities we serve.

We will conduct our business to produce financial returns that reward investment by shareowners and allow the Company to grow. Investments in retailing, distribution and food processing will be continually evaluated for their contribution to our corporate return objectives.

We will constantly strive to satisfy consumer needs better than the best of our competitors. Operating procedures will reflect our belief that the organizational levels closest to the consumer are best positioned to respond to changing consumer needs.

We will treat our employees fairly and with respect, openness and honesty. We will solicit and respond to their ideas and reward meaningful contributions to our success.

We value America's diversity and will strive to reflect that diversity in our work force, the companies with whom we do business, and the customers we serve. As a company, we will convey respect and dignity to each individual.

We will encourage our employees to be active, responsible citizens and will allocate resources for activities that enhance the quality of life for our customers, our employees and the communities we serve.

(Signed)

Joseph A. Pichler
Chairman and Chief Executive Officer

ADDRESS   1014 Vine St.
Cincinnati, OH 45202-1100

INDUSTRY CATEGORY   Food/Beverage

CORPORATE DESCRIPTION
The Kroger Company was founded in 1883 and incorporated in 1902. As of December 31, 1993 the Company was the largest grocery retailer in the United States based on annual sales. The Company also manufactures and processes food for sale by its supermarkets.

SIZE REVENUES $22,384,301,000 as of 1993

NUMBER OF EMPLOYEES   190,000 as of 1993

SOURCE   *1993 Annual Report*; company representative

COMPANY | *Lafarge Corporation*

STATEMENT | **Mission:**
To be the best North American company in the cement, construction materials and waste conversion businesses.

| **Principles:**
To be responsive to the needs of our:
  Shareholders—giving them a competitive return on their investment through long-term earnings growth and financial strength;
  Customers—contributing to their success by providing them with quality products and service on a competitive basis;
  Employees—ensuring their fair treatment and helping them develop their skills and dedication;
  Communities—being a good corporate citizen through community involvement and sound environmental practices.

ADDRESS 11130 Sunrise Valley Dr.
Reston, VA 20910

INDUSTRY CATEGORY Construction

CORPORATE DESCRIPTION
Lafarge Corporation was organized in April 1983, bringing together Canada Cement Lafarge Ltd., Canada's largest cement producer, and General Portland Inc., the second-largest cement company in the United States. Lafarge also produces other construction materials.

SIZE REVENUES $1,511,000,000 as of 1993

NUMBER OF EMPLOYEES   7,300 as of 1993

SOURCES   *1992 Annual Report*; company representative

◆ ◆ ◆ ◆ ◆ ◆ ◆

COMPANY | *Landstar Systems, Inc.*

STATEMENT | **Mission Statement**
To be the leading provider of safe, specialized transportation
services through a network of employees, agents, drivers and
owner-operators who deliver safe, specialized services to a
broad range of customers throughout North America.

ADDRESS   First Shelton Place
1000 Bridgeport Ave.
Shelton, CT 06484

INDUSTRY CATEGORY   Transportation

CORPORATE DESCRIPTION
Landstar System, Inc., a transportation services company, operates
the third largest truckload carrier business in North America.

SIZE REVENUES $780,520,000 as of 1993

NUMBER OF EMPLOYEES   2,230 as of 1993

SOURCES   *1993 Annual Report*; "The Fortune Service 500,"
Fortune 129, no. 11 (May 30, 1994)

COMPANY | *Levi Strauss & Co.*

STATEMENT | **BUSINESS VISION**

The Company developed its Business Vision to identify its goals and provide direction for prioritizing all its initiatives and strategies. The Business Vision is as follows:

We will strive to achieve responsible commercial success in the eyes of our constituencies, which include stockholders, employees, consumers, customers, suppliers and communities. Our success will be measured not only by growth in shareholder value, but also by our reputation, the quality of our constituency relationships, and our commitment to social responsibility. As a global company, our businesses in every country will contribute to our overall success. We will leverage our knowledge of local markets to take advantage of the global positioning of our brands, our product and market strengths, our resources and our cultural diversity. We will balance local market requirements with a global perspective. We will make decisions which will benefit the Company as a whole rather than any one component. We will strive to be cost effective in everything we do and will manage our resources to meet our constituencies' needs. The strong heritage and values of the Company as expressed through our Mission and Aspiration Statements will guide all of our efforts. The quality of our products, services and people is critical to the realization of our business vision.

We will market value-added, branded casual apparel with Levi's® branded jeans continuing to be the cornerstone of our business. Our brands will be positioned to ensure consistency of image and values to our consumers around the world. Our channels of distribution will support this effort and will emphasize the value-added aspect of our products. To preserve and enhance consumers' impressions of our brands, the majority of our products will be sold through dedicated distribution, such as Levi's® Only-Stores and in-store shops. We will manage our products for profitability, not volume, generating levels of return that meet our financial goals.

We will meet the service commitments that we make to our customers. We will strive to become both the "Supplier of Choice" and "Customer of Choice" by building business relationships that are increasingly interdependent. These relationships will be based upon a commitment to mutual success and collaboration in fulfilling our customers' and suppliers' requirements. All business processes in our supply chain—from product design through sourcing and distribution—will be aligned to meet these commitments. Our sourcing strategies will support and add value to our marketing and service objectives. Our worldwide owned and operated manufacturing resources will provide significant competitive advantage in meeting our service and quality commitments. Every decision within our supply chain will balance cost, customer requirements, and protection of our brands, while reflecting our corporate values.

The Company will be the "Employer of Choice" by providing a workplace that is safe, challenging, productive, rewarding and fun. Our global work force will embrace a culture that promotes innovation and continuous improvement in all areas, including job skills, products and services, business processes, and aspirational behaviors. The Company will support each employee's responsibility to acquire new skills and knowledge in order to meet the changing needs of our business. All employees will share in the Company's success and commitment to its overall business goals, values and operating principles. Our organization will be flexible and adaptive, anticipating and leading change. Teamwork and collaboration will characterize how we address issues to improve business results.

STATEMENT OF COMPANY MISSION
AND ASPIRATIONS

The Company believes that shared goals are as critical to the Company's success as providing quality products and service and being a leader in the apparel industry. In order to identify and focus these shared goals, the Company adopted the following "Statement of Mission and Aspirations":

Mission Statement

The mission of the Company is to sustain responsible commercial success as a global marketing company of branded casual apparel. We must balance goals of superior profitability and return on investment, leadership market positions, and superior products and service. We will conduct our business ethically and demonstrate leadership in satisfying our responsibilities to our communities and to society. Our work environment will be safe and productive and characterized by fair treatment, teamwork, open communications, personal accountability and opportunities for growth and development.

Aspirations for the Company

We want a Company that our people are proud of and committed to, where all employees have an opportunity to contribute, learn, grow and advance based on merit, not politics or background. We want our people to feel respected, treated fairly, listened to and involved. Above all, we want satisfaction from accomplishments and friendships, balanced personal and professional lives, and to have fun in our endeavors.

When we describe the kind of company we want in the future what we are talking about is building on the foundation we have inherited: affirming the best of our Company's traditions, closing gaps that may exist between principles and practices and updating some of our values to reflect contemporary circumstances. In order to make our aspirations a reality, we need:

New Behaviors: Leadership that exemplifies directness, openness to influence, commitment to the success of others, willingness to acknowledge our own contributions to problems, personal accountability, teamwork and trust. Not only must we model these behaviors but we must coach others to adopt them.

Diversity: Leadership that values a diverse work force (age, sex, ethnic group, etc.) at all levels of the organization, diversity in experience, and a diversity in perspectives. We are committed to taking full advantage of the rich backgrounds and abilities of all our people and to promote a greater diversity in positions of influence. Differing points of view will be sought; diversity will be valued and honesty rewarded, not suppressed.

Recognition: Leadership that provides greater recognition—both financial and psychic—for individuals and teams that contribute to our success. Recognition must be given to all who contribute: those who create and innovate and also those who continually support the day-to-day business requirements.

Ethical Management Practices: Leadership that epitomizes the stated standards of ethical behavior. We must provide clarity about our expectations and must enforce these standards throughout the corporation.

Communication: Leadership that is clear about Company, unit, and individual goals and performance. People must know what is expected of them and receive timely, honest feedback on their performance and career aspirations.

Empowerment: Leadership that increases the authority and responsibility of those closest to our products and customers. By actively pushing responsibility, trust and recognition into the organization we can harness and release the capabilities of all our people.

The Company is providing aspirations training to employees and holds managers and employees accountable for behaviors that are in accordance with these objectives through its employee performance review process.

Consistent with the Company's Mission and Aspirations, the Company sets high goals for responsible environmental stewardship and encourages business partners to do the same.

ADDRESS   Levi's Plaza
P. O. Box 7215
San Francisco, CA 94120

INDUSTRY CATEGORY   Consumer Goods and Services

CORPORATE DESCRIPTION
Levi Strauss Associates Inc. is the world's largest brand-name apparel manufacturer. It designs, manufactures and markets apparel for men, women and children, including jeans, slacks, shirts, jackets, skirts and fleece. Most of its products are marketed under the LEVI'S® and DOCKERS® trademarks and are sold in the United States and in many other countries throughout North and South America, Europe, Asia and Oceania.

SIZE REVENUES $5,900,000,000 as of 1993

NUMBER OF EMPLOYEES   36,400 as of 1993

SOURCE   1993 Form 10K

STATEMENT | **LINCOLN NATIONAL CORPORATION**

VISION:

Lincoln National Corporation will be a high performing financial services company achieving benchmark service, growth and profit.

MISSION:

Lincoln National Corporation exists to satisfy the financial security needs of individuals and businesses. In so doing, LNC must create superior value for shareholders, offer quality products and services to customers, provide satisfying jobs for employees and be a responsible citizen in the communities in which it operates.

GOALS:

To win in the 1990's, LNC will maximize long-term shareholder value through superior operating performance and returns, as measured by:

15% annual return on equity; and

9% annual growth in book value.

CORPORATE STRATEGY:

To establish LNC as the benchmark competitor in each of its businesses and markets through superior execution of core business activities and skills.

Each of LNC's businesses will be a top-tier performer in its respective segment of the financial services industry.

LNC will become the benchmark in each of business [sic], creating long-term value for our shareholders by:

◈ focusing resources and leveraging skills in only those areas where LNC can create substantial value and earn a superior return;

❧ demonstrating a commitment to excellence in customer services through an understanding of the needs and expectations of our customers;

❧ expanding opportunities for employees and maximizing employee satisfaction; and

❧ maintaining and enhancing the security of LNC's capital foundation through superior investment results and management of key risks.

| **STRATEGIC IMPERATIVES:**

Top-tier Performance
Value Creation
Risk Management

ADDRESS   200 E. Berry St.
Fort Wayne, IN 46802

INDUSTRY CATEGORY   Insurance and Financial Services

CORPORATE DESCRIPTION
Lincoln National Corporation owns and operates financial services business with emphasis on annuities, life insurance, property-casualty insurance and life-health reinsurance.

SIZE REVENUES $8,289,800,000 as of December 31, 1993

NUMBER OF EMPLOYEES   11,890 as of December 31, 1993

SOURCES   *1993 Annual Report;* company representative

COMPANY | *Lowe's Companies, Inc.*

STATEMENT | **Lowe's Vision**

Lowe's is in the business of providing the products to help our customers build, improve and enjoy their homes. Our goal is to outservice the competition and be our customers' 1st Choice Store for these products.

ADDRESS   P. O. Box 1111
North Wilkesboro, NC 28656

INDUSTRY CATEGORY   Retail

CORPORATE DESCRIPTION

Lowe's Companies, Inc. is one of America's top forty retailers serving the do-it-yourself home improvement, home decor, home electronics, and home construction markets.

Lowe's more than 320 stores serve customers in 21 states located mainly in the South Atlantic and South Central regions.

SIZE REVENUES $4,538,001,000 as of 1993

NUMBER OF EMPLOYEES   35,000 as of July 1994

SOURCE   *1993 Annual Report*

COMPANY | *LSI Logic Corporation*

STATEMENT | **Mission Statement**

LSI Logic's mission is to offer competitive advantages to our customers worldwide by providing them with the capability required for the rapid design and volume production of electronic systems.

ADDRESS   790 Sycamore Dr.
Milpitas, CA 95035

INDUSTRY CATEGORY   High Technology

CORPORATE DESCRIPTION

LSI Logic is a Fortune 500 designer and manufacturer of high-performance semiconductors. LSI Logic's ASIC (application-specific integrated circuit) technology and CoreWare approach to system-level integration enable customers to create electronic systems on a chip to increase performance and lower costs. The company operates leading-edge manufacturing facilities to produce submicron chips in volume.

LSI Logic has close working relationships with customers in fast-growing vertical markets, including digital video, telecommunications, networking, personal computers, workstations and servers. Using electronic design automation tools, LSI Logic's semiconductors are tailored to the unique requirements of customers in these markets.

SIZE REVENUES $718,812,000 as of 1993

NUMBER OF EMPLOYEES   3,400 as of 1993

SOURCE   *1993 Annual Report*

STATEMENT | **Lyondell Petrochemical Company**
Values For Excellence

Lyondell Petrochemical Company purchases feedstocks and supplies, manufactures and markets refined petroleum products, petrochemicals and polymers.

Our goal is to be the best in every business in which we participate while providing consistent high quality products and services that meet and fully satisfy our customers' requirements and needs. We will provide these products and services at the lowest cost while maximizing value for our shareholders.

We will accomplish our goal through:

❖ Empowerment of all Lyondell employees
❖ Partner relationships with our customers and suppliers
❖ Innovation
❖ Integrity
❖ Continued improvement of our safety, health and environmental performance

COMPANY | *Lens Express Inc.*

STATEMENT | **Mission Statement**

We at Lens Express are committed to fulfilling our customers' needs and expectations by continuing to set the standards for affordable quality eye care products and fast, reliable, convenient service.

- Total quality management
- High equal opportunity standards

We will succeed because maximizing every Lyondell employee's potential and clearly identifying our values will bring out the best of our resources—both people and processes.

ADDRESS   1221 McKinney, Ste. 1600
Houston, TX 77010

INDUSTRY CATEGORY   Chemicals

CORPORATE DESCRIPTION
Lyondell Petrochemical Company is one of the nation's largest and most efficient petrochemical producers and refiners, with manufacturing facilities in Houston, Channelview and Pasadena, Texas and corporate headquarters in downtown Houston. Lyondell's products are primarily basic chemicals or refined products that are used to produce a multitude of consumer goods. Fibers for clothing, ingredients in paint, medicines, carpet, recording tape, trash bags, even automobile components are made from products produced by

CORPORATE DESCRIPTION
Lens Express provides vision care service.

ADDRESS   350 S.W. 12th Ave.
Deerfield Beach, FL 33442

SOURCE   Company representative

Lyondell. In addition, Lyondell has an approximate 90% interest in LYONDELL-CITGO Refining Company Ltd., which operates the nation's eighth largest refinery.

SIZE REVENUES $3,800,000,000 as of 1993

NUMBER OF EMPLOYEES   2,283 as of 1993

SOURCE   Company representative

◆ ◆ ◆ ◆ ◆ ◆ ◆

COMPANY | *Maritz Inc.*

STATEMENT | **Our Maritz Mission**

Our mission is to help our clients improve their performance in critical areas such as sales, marketing, quality, customer satisfaction and cost reduction.

Emphasizing excellence and value, we will create, develop and implement the best possible action plans for our clients through a unique combination of Maritz resources that includes marketing services, employee involvement processes and travel services. We will offer these services worldwide, either separately or in combination, and focus on influencing the behavior of the people who produce, sell, deliver, service and purchase our clients' products and services.

Our Maritz Vision

We will strive to be acknowledged as the best company in the world at helping clients improve performance. We will strive to be the recognized leader in each line of business we pursue.

Through leadership in human resource practices, facilities, information technology and effective business processes, we will strive to be recognized as the best place to work.

Our Maritz Heritage

Above all we value client service, people, teamwork, innovation, sales, profits, working hard, having fun, community service and ethical standards of business conduct.

To aid us in fulfilling our mission and vision, we will remain privately held and financially strong.

ADDRESS   1375 N. Highway Dr.
St. Louis County, MO 63099

INDUSTRY CATEGORY   Business Services

Maritz is privately held but has grown to be a major international corporation providing motivation, travel, research, communications, training, marketing services, business meetings, merchandise fulfillment, management information, and teleservices to clients throughout much of the world. The Company's annual revenues are approaching two billion dollars.

The Company's continuing growth is a direct reflection of the role they play in helping their clients improve the performance of their employees, in order to increase sales and profits, improve productivity, reduce costs and raise employee morale.

Maritz maintains more than 200 offices in 33 states and several foreign countries to serve the needs of their clients, many of which are multinational corporations.

SIZE REVENUES $2,000,000,000 as of 1994

NUMBER OF EMPLOYEES   6,000 as of 1994

SOURCES   *1994 Annual Report*; company representative

COMPANY | *Marriott International, Inc.*

STATEMENT | Mission Statement

We are committed to being the best lodging and management service company in the world, by treating employees in ways that create extraordinary customer service and shareholder value.

ADDRESS   Marriott Dr.
Washington, DC 20058

INDUSTRY CATEGORY   Hotel, Hospitality, and Related

CORPORATE DESCRIPTION

Marriott is a diversified hospitality company with operations and franchises in 50 states and 22 countries. Principal businesses include managing lodging products ranging from full-service hotels and resorts to economy motels and timesharing resorts; management services—including food and facilities management; and a growing number of retirement communities.

SIZE REVENUES $8,062,000,000 as of 1993

NUMBER OF EMPLOYEES   170,000 as of 1993

SOURCE   *1993 Annual Report*

STATEMENT | **Martin Marietta Credo**
Statement of Unifying Principles

In our daily activities we bear important obligations to our country, our customers, our owners, our communities, and to one another. We carry out these obligations guided by certain unifying principles:

❖ **Our foundation is INTEGRITY.** We conduct our business in an open and forthright manner in strict compliance with applicable laws, rules, and regulations so that we are correctly perceived to be an ethical organization of dedicated and competent individuals of high integrity and credibility producing quality products and services that contribute significantly to our communities and to our nation.

❖ **Our strength is our PEOPLE.** The collective talents of our employees comprise our most important asset. Therefore, we provide an organization and operating environment that attracts, nurtures, stimulates, and rewards employee professionalism and creativity, providing a safe workplace and an opportunity for hands-on accomplishment, a criterion highly regarded for promotion and growth.

❖ **Our style is TEAMWORK.** As pioneers and leaders in technology advancement, from design and systems development to manufacturing, testing, and operational integration, the Corporation emphasizes teamwork, recognizing within that framework the critical contribution of the individual. Providing a workplace environment that effectively balances and stimulates the individual and the team is our hallmark.

❖ **Our goal is EXCELLENCE.** Excellence in the form of quality is a shared attribute of the customers and markets we serve and the products we build. Attention to detail and performance are stressed in every line and staff function from the factory floor through the highest levels of management, resulting in a total dedication to mission success.

Code Of Ethics and Standards Of Conduct

Martin Marietta Corporation believes in the highest ethical standards. We demonstrate these beliefs through our commitments—commitments we are dedicated to fulfill.

❧ **To our EMPLOYEES** we are committed to just management and equality for all, providing a safe and healthy workplace, and respecting the dignity and privacy due all human beings.

❧ **To our CUSTOMERS** we are committed to produce reliable products and services at a fair price that are delivered on time and within budget.

❧ **To the COMMUNITIES** in which we live we are committed to be responsible neighbors, reflecting all aspects of good citizenship.

❧ **To our SHAREHOLDERS** we are committed to pursuing sound growth and earnings objectives and to exercising prudence in the use of our assets and resources.

❧ **To our SUPPLIERS** we are committed to fair competition and the sense of responsibility required of a good customer.

ADDRESS   6801 Rockledge Dr.
Bethesda, MD 20817

INDUSTRY CATEGORY   High Technology

CORPORATE DESCRIPTION
Martin Marietta Corporation designs, manufactures, integrates and operates systems and products in leading-edge technologies, including aerospace, electronics, information management and energy, and produces materials for construction and industrial applications.

SIZE REVENUES $9,436,000,000 (sales) as of 1993

NUMBER OF EMPLOYEES   92,000 as of 1993

SOURCES   *1992 Annual Report*; "The Fortune 500," *Fortune* 129, no. 8 (April 8, 1994)

◆ ◆ ◆ ◆ ◆ ◆ ◆

COMPANY | *Mary Kay Cosmetics, Inc.*

STATEMENT | **The Mary Kay Vision**

To be preeminent in the manufacturing, distribution, and marketing of personal care products through our independent sales force.

To provide our sales force an unparalleled opportunity for financial independence, career achievement, and personal fulfillment.

To achieve total customer satisfaction worldwide by focusing on quality, value, convenience, innovation, and personal service.

—Richard C. Bartlett
vice chairman, Mary Kay Corporation

ADDRESS   (as of fall 1995) 16251 Dallas Pkwy.
Addison, TX 75248

INDUSTRY CATEGORY   Consumer Goods and Services

CORPORATE DESCRIPTION

Mary Kay Cosmetics, Inc. is the largest direct selling skin care company in the nation. The Company is an international manufacturer and distributor of premium skin care, glamour, nail care, body and skin care, fragrances, and sun protection products.

While the number of employees is listed here as 2,200, the total number of employees and independent beauty consultants is 350,000 worldwide.

SIZE REVENUES $735,000,000 (wholesale) as of 1993

NUMBER OF EMPLOYEES   2,200 as of 1994

SOURCE   Financial Report

◆　◆　◆　◆　◆　◆　◆

COMPANY | *Maxus Energy Corporation*

STATEMENT | **Vision Statement**
Our aim is to be a successful exploration and production company, generating and pursuing profitable and repeatable investment opportunities with primary emphasis on the areas where we now produce.
June 1994

ADDRESS   717 N. Harwood St.
Dallas, TX 75201

INDUSTRY CATEGORY   Oil and Gas

CORPORATE DESCRIPTION
Maxus Energy Corporation, with headquarters in Dallas, Texas, is one of the largest independent oil and gas exploration and production companies in the world.

SIZE REVENUES $786,700,000 as of December 30, 1993

NUMBER OF EMPLOYEES   825 as of August 1, 1994

SOURCE   *1993 Annual Report*

◆   ◆   ◆   ◆   ◆   ◆   ◆

COMPANY | *MBIA Inc.*

STATEMENT | **MBIA Mission Statement**

Our goal is to be the best and most respected provider of products and services which enhance the efficiency of public finance while selectively expanding our credit enhancement products to other financial obligations.

◈   ◈   ◈   ◈

Our Business—We will make what we do best—enhancing the efficiency of public finance—our blueprint for a successful future. We will continue to build this strong viable business while prudently expanding into new areas where we are able to utilize our existing skills or better serve the changing needs of our traditional customer base.

◈   ◈   ◈   ◈

Our Bondholders—We will provide our securities' holders with a guarantee of unquestioned strength. We will do this by maintaining the most stringent underwriting standards in the industry, by providing the most comprehensive surveillance of our insured credits and by maintaining the financial strength necessary to comfortably meet all of our commitments.

◈   ◈   ◈   ◈

Our Customers—We will provide our customers with innovative value-added solutions and a level of service that is second-to-none.

❖ ❖ ❖ ❖

Our Shareholders—We will achieve strong, sustainable and predictable growth in earnings and in the value of our Company.

❖ ❖ ❖ ❖

Our Employees—We will set high expectations for ourselves and for our business. We will strive to build a culture that is open and treats all fairly. We will create an environment which encourages individual decision-making and working together as a team in the interest of serving our clients and shareholders. We will give of our time, skills and capital to make our community a better place for us all to live and work.

ADDRESS   113 King St.
Armonk, NY 10504

INDUSTRY CATEGORY   Financial Investment services

CORPORATE DESCRIPTION
MBIA Inc., through its wholly owned subsidiary, Municipal Bond Investors assurance Corporation, is the leading insurer of municipal bonds, including new issues and bonds traded in the secondary market. The company also guarantees asset-backed transactions and high-quality obligations offered by qualified financial institutions. In addition, MBIA provides investment management products and services for school districts, municipalities and bond insurers. MBIA Securities Corporation provides fixed-income investment management and trading services for MBIA's municipal cash-management subsidiaries. MBIA Corporation and its French subsidiary, MBIA assurance S.A., have a claims-paying rating of Triple-A from Moody's Investors Service, Inc. and Standard & Poor's.

SIZE REVENUES $429,000,000 as of 1993

NUMBER OF EMPLOYEES   350 as of 1993

SOURCE   *1993 Annual Report*

◆　◆　◆　◆　◆　◆　◆

COMPANY | *MBNA Corporation*

STATEMENT | **MBNA Is A Company Of People Committed To:**
Providing the Customer with the finest products backed by consistently top-quality service.

◆ ◆ ◆ ◆

Delivering these products and services efficiently, thus ensuring fair prices to the Customer and a sound investment for the stockholder.

◆ ◆ ◆ ◆

Treating the Customer as we expect to be treated—putting the Customer first every day—and meaning it.

◆ ◆ ◆ ◆

Being leaders in innovation, quality, efficiency, and Customer satisfaction. Being known for doing the little things and the big things well.

◆ ◆ ◆ ◆

Expecting and accepting from ourselves nothing short of the best. Remembering that each of us, the people of MBNA, makes the unassailable difference.

ADDRESS   400 Christiana Rd.
Newark, DE 19713

INDUSTRY CATEGORY   Banking

CORPORATE DESCRIPTION
MBNA Corporation's primary subsidiary is MBNA America Bank, N.A., a national bank with its principal office in Delaware. It is one of the nation's largest lenders through bank credit cards. All of the company's services are delivered through the mail and by telephone.

SIZE REVENUES $207,800,000 (profits) as of 1993

NUMBER OF EMPLOYEES   9,221 as of 1993

SOURCES   *1992 Annual Report;* "The Fortune Service 500," *Fortune* 129, no. 11 (May 30, 1994)

◆ ◆ ◆ ◆ ◆ ◆ ◆

COMPANY │ *MCI Communications Corporation*

STATEMENT │ **MCI Mission Statement**
MCI provides the full range of basic and advanced telecommunications services domestically and internationally. We are the second largest long distance carrier in the U. S. and the fifth largest carrier of international traffic in the world.

Our key mission through network MCI, our strategic vision, is to continue to grow domestic market share profitably, expand our global capabilities, and take full advantage of emerging technologies to become a leader and meet our customers' needs in the coming world of multimedia.

MCI's strengths in the marketplace are its people, its responsiveness to customers' needs, the development of innovative products based on MCI's flexible, intelligent network platform—integrating the most advanced technologies from the world's leading suppliers.

ADDRESS   1801 Pennsylvania Ave., N.W.
Washington, DC 20006

INDUSTRY CATEGORY   Telecommunications

CORPORATE DESCRIPTION
MCI is a leading Information Age telecommunications company; a global company with broad international presence. It is the second largest long-distance carrier in the U.S. and the fifth largest carrier of international traffic in the world.

SIZE REVENUES $11,921,000,000 as of 1993

NUMBER OF EMPLOYEES   36,235 as of 1993

SOURCE   *1993 Annual Report*

◆　◆　◆　◆　◆　◆　◆

COMPANY | *Medtronic, Inc.*

STATEMENT | MEDTRONIC MISSION STATEMENT
Mission
❖ To contribute to human welfare by application of biomedical engineering in the research, design, manufacture, and sale of instruments or appliances that alleviate pain, restore health, and extend life.

❖ To direct our growth in the areas of biomedical engineering where we display maximum strength and ability; to gather people and facilities that tend to augment these areas; to continuously build on these areas through education and knowledge assimilation; to avoid participation in areas where we cannot make unique and worthy contributions.

❖ To strive without reserve for the greatest possible reliability and quality in our products; to be the unsurpassed standard of comparison and to be recognized as a company of dedication, honesty, integrity, and service.

❖ To make a fair profit on current operations to meet our obligations, sustain our growth, and reach our goals.

❖ To recognize the personal worth of employees by providing an employment framework that allows personal satisfaction in work accomplished, security, advancement opportunity, and means to share in the company's success.

❖ To maintain good citizenship as a company.

ADDRESS   7000 Central Ave. N.E.
Minneapolis, MN 55432

INDUSTRY CATEGORY   Medical Products and Services

CORPORATE DESCRIPTION
Medtronic, Inc. is a leader in producing therapeutic medical devices to improve the cardiovascular and neurological health of patients around the world.

SIZE REVENUES $1,390,922,00 as of April 30, 1994

NUMBER OF EMPLOYEES   10,000 (approximately) as of April 30, 1994

SOURCE   *1994 Annual Report*

COMPANY | *Merck & Co., Inc.*

STATEMENT

Our mission is: to provide society with superior products and services—innovations and solutions that satisfy customer needs and improve the quality of life; to provide employees with challenging work and advancement opportunities, and to provide shareholders with a superior rate of return.

ADDRESS   One Merck Dr.
P. O. Box 100
Whitehouse Station, NJ 08889-0100

INDUSTRY CATEGORY   Pharmaceutical/Biotechnology

CORPORATE DESCRIPTION

Merck & Co., Inc. is the world's largest pharmaceutical company.

SIZE REVENUES $10,498,000,000 as of 1993

NUMBER OF EMPLOYEES   47,100 (worldwide) as of 1993

SOURCES   *1993 Annual Report*; "The Fortune 500," *Fortune* 129, no. 8 (April 8, 1994)

COMPANY | *Meridian Bancorp, Inc.*

STATEMENT | **Statement of Purpose**

Meridian will be a strong, profitable, growth-oriented, diversified provider of financial services that strives aggressively to achieve maximum shareholder and franchise value.

| **OUR VISION**

Our Vision is Meridian's statement of core values that defines the company's culture and the Meridian way of working.

At Meridian, individuals make the difference. Success depends upon a strong customer focus, quality service and continuous improvement by employees who show integrity, caring and initiative.

Our business goes beyond simply meeting customer needs. As a premier provider of financial services, we work together to identify and surpass the expectations of our internal and external customers.

We work together to reach across titles, job responsibilities and organizational structure in order to share information and expertise. Teamwork brings the best of Meridian to our customers.

How we serve our customers is crucial. Each of us enhances relationships with those we serve by being prompt, accurate, professional and by adding a personal touch.

When problems arise, we turn them into opportunities to provide exceptional service. We act decisively, using sound business judgment, creativity and integrity.

We always look for ways to improve. We encourage innovative thinking to find new sources of income, to control costs, to enhance service quality and to work more efficiently.

Improving the quality of our lives as employees is essential to Meridian's success. We are dedicated to providing new approaches that help employees enjoy a balance between commitment to work and life away from work.

The increasing diversity of our workforce in terms of race, gender and cultural background adds richness to our lives. We value diversity, and we encourage an environment where each individual can make a difference in the success of our Company.

Our efforts to enhance the success of our customers, our organization and ourselves depend upon our ability to initiate change and make it work for us. While the forces of change have never been stronger, our opportunities have never been greater.

ADDRESS   10 N. 5th St.
P. O. Box 1102
Reading, PA 19603

INDUSTRY CATEGORY   Banking

CORPORATE DESCRIPTION
Meridian Bancorp, Inc. is a bank and financial services holding company headquartered in Reading, PA.

SIZE REVENUES $157,761,000 (net income) as of December 31, 1993

NUMBER OF EMPLOYEES   6,917 as of December 31, 1993

SOURCE   *1993 Annual Report*

COMPANY | *Meyer (Fred Meyer, Inc.)*

STATEMENT | OUR PHILOSOPHY

At Fred Meyer we are governed by the beliefs that:

❖ Customers are essential, for without them we would have no business. Customers shop most where they believe their wants and needs will be satisfied best.

❖ Satisfactory profits are essential, for without profits our business can neither grow nor satisfy the wants and needs of our Customers, employees, suppliers, shareholders or the community.

❖ Skilled, capable, dedicated employees are essential, for the overall success of our business is determined by the combined ideas, work and effort of all Fred Meyer employees.

Based on these beliefs, we are committed to:

COMPANY | *Mastersoft, Inc.*

STATEMENT | Mastersoft Mission Statement:

"To connect market leading software applications together, for the benefit of the end user."

CORPORATE DESCRIPTION

Mastersoft produces computer software.

ADDRESS 8737 E. Via de Commercio
Scottsdale, AZ 85258

SOURCE Company representative

❖ Serving Customers so well that after shopping with us they are satisfied and want to shop with us again.

❖ Operating our business efficiently and effectively, so we earn a satisfactory profit today and in the future.

❖ Providing an environment that encourages employees to develop their abilities, use their full potential and share ideas that further the success of the business, so they gain a sense of pride in their accomplishments and confidence in their capabilities.

We believe that by following this philosophy we will satisfy Customers and earn their patronage, provide for the profitable growth of our company, and enrich the lives of Fred Meyer employees and their families.

ADDRESS   P. O. Box 42121
                Portland, OR 97242-0121

INDUSTRY CATEGORY   Retail

CORPORATE DESCRIPTION
Fred Meyer, Inc., a Delaware corporation, and its subsidiaries operate a chain of 123 retail stores offering a wide range of food, apparel, fine jewelry, and products for the home, with emphasis on necessities and items of everyday use. The stores are located in Oregon, Washington, Utah, Alaska, Idaho, Northern California, and Montana and include 94 free-standing, multidepartment stores and 29 specialty stores.

SIZE REVENUES $2,979,100,000 (net sales) as of 1993

NUMBER OF EMPLOYEES   25,000 as of 1993

SOURCES   *1992 Annual Report;* "The Fortune Service 500," *Fortune* 129, no. 11 (May 30, 1994)

COMPANY | *Microsoft Corporation*

STATEMENT | Vision

A computer on every desk and in every home.

[Author's note: Microsoft's 1993 Annual Report includes an explanation of their Vision, as follows]

We are single-minded in our commitment to this vision. And we have maintained that singular focus ever since our company was founded in 1975.

This vision has created a revolution that's changed how people around the world do business. We believe that our own success, in large measure, has resulted directly from the effective use of our technology.

This vision is also shaping the future.

While we know that great possibilities lie ahead for us, we also know that the future will make great demands on us. At the same time we commit ourselves to delivering outstanding products today, we are also committing ourselves to creating the infrastructure that will define the information systems of the next 25 years and beyond. In addition, our hope is to make computer technology as indispensable at home as the telephone, and as widespread as the television.

To accomplish these objectives, we hire bright, talented people who share our enthusiasm for technology and our goal of making it easier for people to do more with personal computing.

Ultimately, our dream is to put the power of computers— in business and at home—into people's hands so they can access, integrate, and use information more easily than ever before; what we call Information At Your Fingertips.

It's a dream we believe is within our reach, and within our capabilities.

ADDRESS   One Microsoft Way
Redmond, WA 98052-6399

INDUSTRY CATEGORY   High Technology

CORPORATE DESCRIPTION
Microsoft develops, manufactures, markets, licenses, and supports a wide range of software products, including operating systems for personal computers (PCs), office machines, and personal information devices; applications programs; and languages; as well as personal computer books, hardware, and multimedia products.

SIZE REVENUES $4,649,000,000 as of 1994

NUMBER OF EMPLOYEES   15,257 as of 1994

SOURCES   *1994 Annual Report*; company representative

COMPANY | *Mid-America Dairymen, Inc.*

STATEMENT | **MISSION STATEMENT of**
| **MID-AMERICA DAIRYMEN, INC.**

The mission of Mid-America Dairymen is to provide each member market security by providing a market for all the milk he or she desires to produce and marketing that milk in the form and market channels providing maximum returns consistent with long term stability.

ADDRESS   3253 E. Chestnut Expwy.
Springfield, MO 65802

INDUSTRY CATEGORY   Food/Beverage

CORPORATE DESCRIPTION
Mid-America Dairymen, Inc. is a dairy marketing cooperative, governed by the 13,000 farm families who belong to the cooperative.

SIZE REVENUES $1,826,000,000 as of 1993

NUMBER OF EMPLOYEES   2,932 as of 1993

SOURCES   *1992 Annual Report;* "The Fortune Service 500," *Fortune* 129, no. 11 (May 30, 1994)

COMPANY | *Miller (Herman Miller Inc.)*

STATEMENT | **OUR VISION**

By defining and solving problems of the working and healing environments, we aim to improve the quality of our customers' lives and become their reference point for quality and service. Through personal competence, participation, research, and design we strive for excellence in each aspect of our business.

Our Values: Who We Are

We are a company that values

- ❖ the individual.
- ❖ ownership, participation, and teamwork.
- ❖ excellence.
- ❖ social and environmental responsibility.
- ❖ learning, good design, and new ideas.
- ❖ equity.

Our Expectations: The Way We Work Together

We are an organization of people who expect each other to

- ❖ demonstrate personal integrity, competence, and commitment to excellence.
- ❖ participate and be held accountable for results.
- ❖ work toward an equitable return for investors.

Our Goals: What We Are Working Toward

We are committed to becoming

- ❖ our customers' reference point for excellence in service and quality.
- ❖ a dynamic organization where research, innovation, and good design extend to every business unit and function.
- ❖ an excellent investment opportunity.

Our Strategies: How We Intend to Achieve Our Goals

We intend to achieve our vision by

- ❖ continuously renewing our organization to enable ourselves to learn, grow, change, and improve.

❖ focusing on serving customers in all aspects of our business.

❖ increasing our share of the market.

❖ earning excellent financial results.

ADDRESS   855 E. Main
Zeeland, MI 49464

INDUSTRY CATEGORY   Business Products

CORPORATE DESCRIPTION
Herman Miller is a leading multinational manufacturer of furniture and furniture systems.

SIZE REVENUES $856,000,000 as of 1993

NUMBER OF EMPLOYEES   6,005 as of 1993

SOURCES   Financial Report; "The Fortune 500," *Fortune* 129, no. 8 (April 8, 1994)

◆　◆　◆　◆　◆　◆　◆

COMPANY | *Minnesota Mining and Manufacturing Company (3M)*

STATEMENT | **Statement of 3M Corporate Values**
We are committed to:
—Satisfying our **customers** with superior quality and value,
—Providing **investors** with an attractive return through sustained, high-quality growth,

—Respecting our **social and physical environment**,

—Being a company that **employees** are proud to be a part of.

Satisfying our customers with superior quality and value—

❖ Providing the highest quality products and services consistent with our customers' requirements and preferences.

❖ Making every aspect of every transaction a satisfying experience for our customers.

❖ Finding innovative ways to make life easier and better for our customers.

Providing investors an attractive return through sustained, high-quality growth—

Our goals are:

❖ Growth in earnings per share averaging 10 percent a year or better,

❖ A return on capital employed of 27 percent or better,

❖ A return on stockholders' equity of between 20 and 25 percent,

❖ At least 30 percent of our sales each year from products new in the last four years.

Respecting our social and physical environment—

❖ Complying with all laws and meeting or exceeding regulations,

❖ Keeping customers, employees, investors and the public informed about our operations,

❖ Developing products and processes that have a minimal impact on the environment,

❖ Staying attuned to the changing needs and preferences of our customers, employees and society,

❖ Uncompromising honesty and integrity in every aspect of our operations.

Being a company that employees are proud to be a part of—

❖ Respecting the dignity and worth of individuals,

❖ Encouraging individual initiative and innovation in an atmosphere characterized by flexibility, cooperation and trust,

◈ Challenging individual capabilities,
◈ Valuing human diversity and providing equal opportunity for development.

ADDRESS   3M Center
St. Paul, MN 55144-1000

INDUSTRY CATEGORY   Manufacturing

CORPORATE DESCRIPTION
3M is a worldwide manufacturer serving industrial, commercial, health care and consumer markets. 3M develops, manufactures and markets products through three business sectors: Industrial and Consumer; Information, Imaging and Electronic; and Life Sciences.

SIZE REVENUES $14,020,000,000 (net sales) as of 1993

NUMBER OF EMPLOYEES   86,168 as of 1993

SOURCE   *1993 Annual Report*

COMPANY   *The Mechanics Bank*

STATEMENT   **Mission Statement:**
The Mechanics Bank offers safety and soundness with consistent and fair returns to customers, employees, and shareholders.

CORPORATE DESCRIPTION
Founded in 1905, the Mechanics Bank is a community bank serving the East Bay region of the San Francisco Area with 14 offices. As of 1993,

STATEMENT | **MOBIL CORPORATION**
VISION, MISSION, AND VALUES

OUR VISION:

To be a GREAT, global company. A company, built with pride by all our people, that sets the standard for excellence. A company that brings value to our customers, provides superior returns to our shareholders and respects the quality of life in every one of our communities.

OUR MISSION:

To be a dynamic company that will continually find and develop opportunities for profitable growth in our core businesses, and that will realize the greatest value from our existing assets while keeping tight control of our costs.

WE VALUE:

PEOPLE

To value, trust and empower all of our people to be mutually accountable for Mobil's success; to provide opportunities in a changing environment without boundaries, where each person can develop to be the best that he or she can be.

The Mechanics Bank had net income of $10,059,488 total assets of $822,474,292, and 425 employees

ADDRESS   3170 Hilltop Mall Rd.
Richmond, CA 94806

SOURCE   *1993 Annual Report*; company representative

CUSTOMERS

To understand and satisfy our customers' needs better than anyone and to offer products and services that provide them with the best value.

SHAREHOLDERS

To reward our shareholders by providing a superior long-term total return, which exceeds that of our peers.

ETHICS

To conduct our business to the highest ethical standards and in compliance with all applicable laws and regulations.

TECHNOLOGY

To develop or acquire and then rapidly apply appropriate technology to obtain and sustain competitive advantage.

ENVIRONMENT, HEALTH & SAFETY

To protect the environment and the health and safety of our people and the communities in which we work.

ADDRESS   3225 Gallows Rd.
Fairfax, VA 22037

INDUSTRY CATEGORY   Oil and Gas

CORPORATE DESCRIPTION

Mobil Corporation is a major oil and gas company with operations in over 100 countries. Mobil's other businesses include petrochemicals, plastics, mining and land development. Mobil has a strong base in technology and environmental protection.

SIZE REVENUES $63,975,000,000 as of 1993

NUMBER OF EMPLOYEES   61,900 as of 1993

SOURCES   *1993 Annual Report*; company representative

COMPANY | *Montana Power Company*

STATEMENT | **Objectives**

Corporate: The Montana Power Company and its subsidiaries produce and sell energy and related services and products, at competitive prices, in an environmentally compatible, safe, and reliable manner.

Utility: To create value for the company's customers, employees, shareholders, and our communities, primarily by providing electricity, natural gas, and related services.

Entech: To develop and market energy, technology and related products and services in Montana and other areas, while providing a reasonable profit to our investors.

Independent Power Group: To develop, acquire, operate, purchase, and manage facilities and resources to provide energy services to customers at reasonable prices which provide the Corporation's shareholders with an attractive profit.

ADDRESS   40 E Broadway
Butte, MT 59701-9394

INDUSTRY CATEGORY   Utility

CORPORATE DESCRIPTION

Montana Power Co. has three operating divisions: the Utility Division, Entech Inc., and the Independent Power Group (IPG).

Entech Inc. is the administrative arm for MPC's diversified enterprises in coal mining, oil, and natural gas and technology.

IPG is a wholesale and independent power operation, engaged in cogeneration investments and the marketing of energy.

SIZE REVENUES $1,075,596,000 as of 1993

NUMBER OF EMPLOYEES   4,089 as of January 1, 1994

SOURCES   Company Financial Report, "MPC At A Glance 1994" company publication

◆ ◆ ◆ ◆ ◆ ◆ ◆

COMPANY | *Nalco Chemical Company*

STATEMENT | **Nalco Philosophy of Operation**

Nalco seeks to find customer needs and fill them through the application of specialty chemicals and technology. We enhance the profitability of our customers' business by providing products and services that add value to their operations and provide them an acceptable return on their investment.

Every Nalco employee is expected to do his or her part to help our quality process achieve continuous improvement and greater customer satisfaction.

In doing so, we intend to make a reasonable profit in an ethical manner so that we can reward our shareholders and employees, invest in our future and enrich or improve life in the communities in which we operate. We strive for leadership and continuous growth in serving industry worldwide through practical applied science.

We intend to produce and sell only those chemicals that can be manufactured, distributed, used, and disposed of in a safe manner. We will conduct our operations worldwide in compliance with all applicable laws and regulations; we will make environmental health and safety considerations a priority in order to keep risks at the lowest reasonable level.

No employee shall engage in conduct which results in a conflict of his or her personal interest with that of the company or which reflects unfavorably on the integrity of the company.

All employees are expected to treat one another, suppliers and neighbors within our facility communities with respect. It is our policy that all employees should be able to enjoy a work environment free from all forms of discrimination. In the same fashion, anyone who comes in contact with Nalco should receive the same consideration and fair treatment as though that person were a Nalco employee.

ADDRESS   One Nalco Center
Naperville, IL 60563-1198

INDUSTRY CATEGORY   Chemicals

CORPORATE DESCRIPTION
Nalco Chemical Company is the world's largest producer of specialty chemicals and services for water and industrial process treatment.

SIZE REVENUES $1,389,400,000 as of 1993

NUMBER OF EMPLOYEES   6,802 as of 1993

SOURCE   *1993 Annual Report*

COMPANY | *National City Corporation*

STATEMENT | **What is our Mission?**
The mission of National City Corporation is to achieve levels of performance and profitability within the financial services industry that provide stockholders with an above average rate of return on investment over time. The mission will be accomplished by satisfying customer needs with superior service and quality products at a reasonable cost; remaining financially strong and flexible to take advantage of market opportunities; operating in a socially responsible manner; and attracting, developing and retaining employees who are committed to the Corporation's mission.

ADDRESS   1900 E. 9th St.
Cleveland, OH 44114-3484

INDUSTRY CATEGORY   Banking

CORPORATE DESCRIPTION
National City Corporation is a $29 billion bank holding company headquartered in Cleveland, Ohio. The Corporation's principal banking subsidiaries are located in Cleveland, Columbus, Indianapolis, and Louisville. Other member banks are located in Akron, Dayton, Lexington, and Toledo.

SIZE REVENUES $404,000,000 (profits) as of 1993

NUMBER OF EMPLOYEES   19,960 as of 1993

SOURCE   *1992 Annual Report*; "The Fortune Service 500," *Fortune* 129, no. 11 (May 30, 1994)

COMPANY | *National Semiconductor*

STATEMENT | OUR MISSION AND BELIEFS

Our mission is to excel in serving chosen markets by delivering semiconductor-intensive products and services of the highest quality and value, thereby providing a competitive advantage to our customers worldwide.

TO ACCOMPLISH OUR MISSION, WE BELIEVE WE MUST:

❖ Maintain our integrity and fairness with each other, our customers and suppliers, our investors and the communities in which we live and work.

❖ Exhibit respect for our fellow employees, our environment, and a healthy balance between our work and family.

❖ Enhance our capabilities and skills throughout our careers.

❖ Be curious, imaginative, and courageous in challenging our current thinking.

❖ Create innovative solutions using our technological strengths.

❖ Grow our expertise by learning through teamwork.

❖ Make continuous improvement a way of life.

❖ Strive for excellence in all our efforts.

❖ Reward our shareholders with reasonable profits as a result of exceeding our customers' expectations.

ADDRESS 2900 Semiconductor Dr.
P. O. Box 58090
Santa Clara, CA 95052-8090

INDUSTRY CATEGORY High Technology

CORPORATE DESCRIPTION

National Semiconductor is the fourth largest U. S. semiconductor manufacturer and 12th largest worldwide. National Semiconductor designs, manufactures, and markets high-performance semiconductor products and is a global leader in mixed analog-and-digital technologies. Major market segments are analog-intensive markets, communications-intensive markets, and markets for personal systems.

SIZE REVENUES $2,295,400,000 as of May 29, 1994

NUMBER OF EMPLOYEES   22,300 (worldwide) as of 1994

SOURCE   *1994 Annual Report*

◆ ◆ ◆ ◆ ◆ ◆ ◆

COMPANY | *New England Mutual Life Insurance Company (The New England)*

STATEMENT | **Mission Statement and Operating Principles**

The mission of The New England is to create value for our policyholders and customers through insurance and investment.

Our Operating Principles are:

1. We put our obligations to policyholders first.
2. We respect and value all associates — field and home office.
3. We expect field and home office managers to lead effectively.
4. We are dedicated to customer satisfaction.

5. We pursue quality in all we do.

6. We accept responsibility as a corporate citizen.

ADDRESS　　501 Boylston St.

Boston, MA 02116

INDUSTRY CATEGORY　　Insurance

CORPORATE DESCRIPTION

Founded in 1835, New England Mutual Life Insurance Company (The New England) is the nation's first chartered mutual life insurance company. Based in Boston, Massachusetts, the company is one of the largest life insurers by assets in the U. S., and its investment arm, New England Investment Companies, is one of the country's largest money managers. The New England offers individuals and businesses a full array of insurance, annuities, employee benefit and pension plans, and mutual fund products and services through a national sales network involving 80 general agencies and 3,000 professional representatives. In addition, the company's representatives provide planning and needs analysis to meet many personal financial needs of their customers, including education funding, family, mortgage and income protection, retirement and estate planning.

SIZE REVENUES　　$2,800,000,000 (total) as of 1993

NUMBER OF EMPLOYEES　　2,500 (home office) as of 1993

SOURCE　　Company representative

COMPANY | *Niagara Mohawk Power Corp.*

STATEMENT | Vision

We will become the most responsive and efficient energy services company in the Northeast to achieve maximum value for customers, shareholders and employees.

| Mission

Niagara Mohawk is an energy services company committed to maximizing value to its customers, shareholders and employees.

The Company seeks to satisfy customers' energy needs with high quality, competitively priced electric and gas energy products and services; increase shareholder value through above average growth in earnings; and provide an atmosphere for employees which promotes empowerment and rewards excellence.

Niagara Mohawk promotes safe and efficient practices in the supply, delivery and use of energy. The Company is committed to a cleaner, healthier environment through an active, positive approach to its environmental responsibilities. The Company supports improvement in the social and economic well-being of the communities it serves and seeks cooperative and constructive relationships with all of its regulators.

Niagara Mohawk's business emphasis focuses on results, aggressive and responsible leadership, responsiveness to customer needs and continuous improvement in operations.

ADDRESS   300 Erie Blvd. W.
Syracuse, NY 13202

INDUSTRY CATEGORY   Utility

CORPORATE DESCRIPTION
Niagara Mohawk Power Corp. is an investor-owned utility providing energy to the largest customer service area in New York.

SIZE REVENUES $3,933,400,000 as of 1993

NUMBER OF EMPLOYEES   11,295 as of 1993

SOURCES   *1992 Annual Report*; "Niagara Mohawk Corporate Strategic Plan 1993–1995" company publication; "The Fortune Service 500," *Fortune* 129, no. 11 (May 30, 1994)

◆　◆　◆　◆　◆　◆　◆

COMPANY | *Nike*

STATEMENT | **Corporate Mission**
To maximize profits to shareholders through products and services that enrich people's lives.

ADDRESS   One Bowerman Dr.
Beaverton, OR 97005-6453

INDUSTRY CATEGORY   Consumer Goods and Services

CORPORATE DESCRIPTION
Nike operates predominantly in one industry segmment, that being the design, production, and marketing of athletic and casual footwear, apparel, and accessories.

SIZE REVENUES $3,930,984,000 as of 1993

SIZE EMPLOYEES   9,000 as of 1993

SOURCE   *1993 Annual Report*

◆ ◆ ◆ ◆ ◆ ◆ ◆

COMPANY | *Norfolk Southern Corporation*

STATEMENT | **Our Vision**

Be the safest, most customer-focused and successful transportation company in the world.

Our Mission

Norfolk Southern's mission is to enhance the value of our stockholders' investment over time by providing quality freight transportation services and undertaking any other related businesses in which our resources, particularly our people, give the company an advantage.

Our Creed

We are responsible to our Stockholders, Customers, Employees, and the Communities we serve.

For all our constituencies,
we will make safety our highest priority.

For our Customers,
we will provide quality service, always trying to reduce our costs in order to offer competitive prices.

For our Stockholders,
we will strive to earn a return on their equity investment which will increase the value of their ownership. By generating a reasonable return on invested capital, we will provide

the security of a financially strong company to our customers, employees, stockholders, and communities.

For our Employees,
our greatest asset, we will provide fair and dignified treatment with equal opportunity at every level. We will seek talented Management with the highest standards of honesty and fairness.

For the Communities we serve,
we will be good corporate citizens, seeking to enhance their quality of life through service, jobs, investment, and the energies and good will of our Employees.

ADDRESS   Three Commercial Pl.
Norfolk, VA 23510-2191

INDUSTRY CATEGORY   Transportation

CORPORATE DESCRIPTION
Norfolk Southern Corporation is a Virginia-based holding company that owns all the common stock and controls a major freight railroad, Norfolk Southern Railway Company, and a motor carrier, North American Van Lines, Inc. The railroad system's lines extend over more than 14,500 miles of road in 20 states, primarily in the Southeast and Midwest, and the Province of Ontario, Canada. North American provides household moving, truckload general freight and specialized handling freight services in the United States and Canada, and offers certain motor carrier services worldwide.

SIZE REVENUES $4,460,100,000 as of 1993

NUMBER OF EMPLOYEES   29,304 (average) as of 1993

SOURCE   *1993 Annual Report*

COMPANY | *Northeast Utilities*

STATEMENT | **Corporate Mission Statement**

Northeast Utilities is dedicated to providing safe, dependable, and reasonably priced energy and related services as an ethical, environmentally responsible, and financially sound private enterprise committed to the efficient use of resources, responsive to the needs of customers and their communities, sensitive to the well-being of employees, and yielding a fair return to shareholders.

ADDRESS   P. O. Box 270
Hartford, CT 06141-0270

INDUSTRY CATEGORY   Utility

CORPORATE DESCRIPTION

Northeast Utilities is the parent company of the NU system (collectively referred to as NU). NU is among the 20 largest electric utilities in the country and the largest in New England, serving about 1.7 million customers in Connecticut, New Hampshire, and western Massachusetts.

SIZE REVENUES $3,629,093,000 as of 1993

NUMBER OF EMPLOYEES   9,300 as of 1994

SOURCES   *1992 Annual Report*, company representative

COMPANY | *Northern States Power Company*

STATEMENT | **NSP**
Our commitment to our customers is to be:

| **Your Energy Partner of Choice**

By exhibiting this commitment, NSP will be the leader in growth and profitability in the expanding markets where the Company competes.

As employees of NSP, we will increase the value provided to our customers by surrounding them with options from the NSP portfolio of energy products and services. We will continuously improve the ways we benefit our shareholders, customers, the communities we serve and each other.

ADDRESS   414 Nicollet Mall
Minneapolis, MN 55401

INDUSTRY CATEGORY   Utility

CORPORATE DESCRIPTION
Northern States Power Company (NSP), with headquarters in Minneapolis, serves customers in Minnesota, Wisconsin, North Dakota, South Dakota, and Michigan's Upper Peninsula.

SIZE REVENUES $2,404,000,000 as of 1993

NUMBER OF EMPLOYEES   7,362 as of 1993

SOURCES   *1993 Annual Report;* "The Fortune Service 500," *Fortune* 129, no. 11 (May 30, 1994)

COMPANY | *Northwestern Mutual Life*

STATEMENT | **The Northwestern Mutual Way**

The ambition of The Northwestern has been less to be large than to be safe; its aim is to rank first in benefits to policyowners rather than first in size. Valuing quality above quantity, it has preferred to secure its business under certain salutary restrictions and limitations rather than to write a much larger business at the possible sacrifice of those valuable points which have made The Northwestern pre-eminently the policyowner's Company.

Executive Committee, 1888

ADDRESS 720 E. Wisconsin Ave.
Milwaukee, WI 53202

INDUSTRY CATEGORY Insurance

CORPORATE DESCRIPTION
Northwestern Mutual offers life insurance, disability income, and annuities for the protection of human life value.

SIZE REVENUES $46,116,900,000 (assets) as of June 30, 1994

NUMBER OF EMPLOYEES 3,304 as of June 30, 1994

SOURCE Company representative

MISSION STATEMENT

Providing reliable natural gas services to customers in Oklahoma.

VISION STATEMENT

We will be a recognized model of excellence, challenging traditional boundaries, seizing opportunities, setting the standard to become a renowned provider of energy and innovative products and services.

CORE VALUES OF OKLAHOMA NATURAL GAS COMPANY

ETHICS

Our actions are founded on trust, honesty, and integrity through open communications and adherence to the highest standards of business ethics.

QUALITY

Our commitment to quality is driven by continuous improvement and our quest for excellence.

LOYALTY

We acknowledge the dignity and worth of each employee and the necessity for a workplace environment that provides opportunities and rewards for teamwork, innovation, and loyalty.

VALUE

We are committed to maximizing value for all investors, customers, employees, and the public, recognizing their concern for optimum development and utilization of our resources.

| **SERVICE**

We will provide responsive flexible service while enthusiastically embracing our commitment to improving quality of life and preserving the environment.

ADDRESS   100 W. Fifth St.
Tulsa, OK 74103-0871

INDUSTRY CATEGORY   Utility

CORPORATE DESCRIPTION

Oklahoma Natural Gas Company provides natural gas to customers in Oklahoma. It is a division of ONEOK Inc., a diversified energy company headquartered in Tulsa, Oklahoma. It is primarily a natural gas company with three divisions and 15 subsidiaries.

Oklahoma Natural Gas Company division and ONG Transmission Company division provide natural gas utility services to three-quarters of Oklahoma. These divisions purchase, gather, compress, transport, distribute, sell and store natural gas. They also lease pipeline capacity and provide the link for interstate gas transportation. Oklahoma Natural has been in existence since 1908.
[Author's note: Statistics provided are for ONEOK Inc.]

SIZE REVENUES $789,100,000 as of 1993

NUMBER OF EMPLOYEES   2,208 as of 1993

SOURCES   *1993 Annual Report*, company representative

COMPANY | *Old Kent Financial Corporation*

STATEMENT | Old Kent Financial Corporation
Philosophy of the Corporation

Our corporate mission and culture statement reflect our long-standing commitment to shareholders, customers, employees and the communities we serve. Key tenets of the Corporation's business philosophy are—to maximize the value of shareholders' investment, to meet the needs of customers with quality products and services, to provide a meaningful and challenging work environment for our employees, and to serve communities as a good citizen.

Corporate Mission

Increase shareholder value as a high performing independent regional bank holding company serving select communities with quality products and services.

Corporate Culture

The management of Old Kent has the ultimate responsibility for achieving profit levels which assure the quality of the balance sheet and the continuation of the Corporation, for the benefit of our shareholders, communities we serve and our employees.

Old Kent's purpose is to understand and fulfill the needs of our customer groups resulting in long-term, multiple-service client relationships. This customer-driven purpose requires that we earn and retain the respect, confidence and loyalty of our customers by serving them so that they will benefit from their association with us.

ADDRESS One Vandenberg Center
Grand Rapids, MI 49503

INDUSTRY CATEGORY Banking

CORPORATE DESCRIPTION

Old Kent Financial Corporation is a bank holding company head-quartered in Grand Rapids, Michigan, with total assets of $10 billion. Old Kent is in the business of commercial banking and related services through its 16 banking subsidiaries and five non-banking subsidiaries. Old Kent's principal markets for financial services are communities within Michigan and Illinois, where its 228 banking offices are located.

SIZE REVENUES $127,902,000 (net income) as of 1993

NUMBER OF EMPLOYEES   4,745 as of 1993

SOURCE   *1993 Annual Report*

◆ ◆ ◆ ◆ ◆ ◆ ◆

COMPANY | *Olin Corporation*

STATEMENT | OLIN STRATEGY

Olin's fundamental strategy is to build and maintain market leadership positions for businesses that we are in and know well. This will be achieved by satisfying our customers, and by focusing our resources, human and capital, in areas where we have an acceptable competitive position. We will concentrate on continuous operational improvement to achieve excellence in our businesses and will seek only limited diversification that builds on our strengths.

While we expect to double sales over a ten year period, our primary emphasis will be on market leadership and profitability, which will result from our commitments to total quality, continual operational improvement, ensuring customer satisfaction and achieving commensurate financial rewards. All of this requires a high degree of management discipline.

Achieving effectiveness requires being the low cost producer and demonstrating an ability to outperform economic business cycles.

Division Presidents will view their responsibilities on a global basis, have the primary leadership role, and be fully empowered to execute business plans that have gained the concurrence of the corporation's senior executive management. The empowerment of Division Presidents requires accountability for executing plans successfully and achieving projected results.

As a company, Olin will represent more value than the sum of our individual businesses. The Executive Office will be responsible for maintaining the mix of businesses, the organization, and the policy direction that will ensure superior value added.

To effectively execute this corporate strategy, we will primarily rely on open and frequent communications. Formal controls will be used only to the extent absolutely necessary. In addition, the Corporate Center's activities will be limited to those functions required of a publicly held company and high value added services.

A total commitment to quality and a renewed emphasis on operational effectiveness, while staying with our strengths, will provide improved quality of earnings and share value.

ADDRESS   120 Long Ridge Rd.
P. O. Box 1355
Stamford, CT 06904-1355

INDUSTRY CATEGORY   Chemicals

CORPORATE DESCRIPTION
Olin Corporation is concentrated primarily in chemicals, metals, defense-related products and services, and ammunition.

SIZE REVENUES $2,423,000,000 as of 1993

NUMBER OF EMPLOYEES 12,400 as of 1993

SOURCE *1993 Annual Report*

◆ ◆ ◆ ◆ ◆ ◆ ◆

COMPANY | *Oneida Ltd.*

STATEMENT | ONEIDA LTD. MISSION STATEMENT:
"To profitably and ethically satisfy our customers' needs in a manner that enhances the welfare of our stockholders, our employees and the communities in which we reside."

ADDRESS Kenwood Station
Oneida, NY 13421

INDUSTRY CATEGORY Manufacturing

CORPORATE DESCRIPTION
A manufacturer and marketer of two diversified product groups—tableware for the consumer and foodservice markets, and industrial wire for original equipment manufacturers.

SIZE REVENUES $455,200,000 as of January 29, 1994

NUMBER OF EMPLOYEES   5,400 as of November, 1994

SOURCE   Company representative

◆　◆　◆　◆　◆　◆　◆

COMPANY │ *Oryx Energy Corporation*

STATEMENT │ **Mission Statement**
Oryx Energy is one of the largest independent oil and gas
companies in the world. Our mission is to create value for our
shareholders.

ADDRESS   13155 Noel Rd.
Dallas, TX 75240

INDUSTRY CATEGORY   Oil and Gas

CORPORATE DESCRIPTION
Oryx Energy is an independent oil and gas company.

SIZE REVENUES $1,054,000,000 as of 1993

NUMBER OF EMPLOYEES   1,500 as of 1993

SOURCE   *1993 Annual Report*

COMPANY | *Owens & Minor*

STATEMENT | **Our Mission...**

To provide our customers and suppliers with the most responsive, efficient and cost-effective distribution system for the delivery of healthcare products and services in the markets we serve; to earn a return on our invested capital consistent with being an industry leader; and to manage our business with the highest ethical standards in a socially responsible manner with particular emphasis on the welfare of our teammates and the communities we serve.

ADDRESS 4800 Cox Rd.
P. O. Box 27626
Richmond, VA 23261-7626

INDUSTRY CATEGORY Medical Products and Services

CORPORATE DESCRIPTION

Owens & Minor is the nation's second largest medical/surgical supply distributor. The company strives to reduce costs in the healthcare delivery system by adding efficiency to the supply chain through improved linkage between healthcare providers and manufacturers of medical/surgical supplies. Stockless, just-in-time, materials management, information flow, electronic data interchange (EDI) and logistics programs are part of Owens & Minor's array of customer services, in conjunction with the delivery of its 100,000+ items product offering.

SIZE REVENUES $1,396,971,000 as of 1993

NUMBER OF EMPLOYEES 3,000 as of 1994

SOURCES 1993 *Annual Report*; company representative

COMPANY | *PacifiCorp*

STATEMENT | **MISSION**

The mission statement explains our reason for being in business, our key constituents, and the overall way in which we choose to conduct our business:

PacifiCorp's mission is to help our customers prosper in our economic system by satisfying their electric energy wants and needs with electricity, energy efficiency and other related value-added products and services. PacifiCorp can only do this by maintaining competitive prices and quality service for its customers, creating a favorable work environment for its employees, being a responsible steward of the natural environment, and in the end growing value for its shareholders.

ADDRESS   700 N.E. Multnomah St.
Portland, OR 97232-4116

INDUSTRY CATEGORY   Utility

CORPORATE DESCRIPTION

As the third largest electric utility company west of the Rocky Mountains, PacifiCorp serves 1.3 million customers through Pacific Power and Utah Power. PacifiCorp also holds a major telecommunications utility. Pacific Telecom, an 87 percent-owned subsidiary, is one of the nation's largest nonBell telephone companies

SIZE REVENUES $3,412,000,000 as of 1993

Number of Employees   13,635 as of 1993

SOURCES   *1993 Annual Report;* "The Fortune Service 500," *Fortune* 129, no. 11 (May 30, 1994)

COMPANY | *Penney (J. C. Penney Company, Inc.)*

STATEMENT | **THE PENNEY IDEA**

To serve the public, as nearly as we can, to its complete satisfaction.

❖ ❖ ❖ ❖

To expect for the service we render a fair remuneration and not all the profit the traffic will bear.

❖ ❖ ❖ ❖

To do all in our power to pack the customer's dollar full of value, quality and satisfaction.

❖ ❖ ❖ ❖

To continue to train ourselves and our associates so that the service we give will be more and more intelligently performed.

❖ ❖ ❖ ❖

To improve constantly the human factor in our business.

❖ ❖ ❖ ❖

To reward men and women in our organization through participation in what the business produces.

❖ ❖ ❖ ❖

To test our every policy, method and act in this wise: "Does it square with what is right and just?"

Adopted 1913

ADDRESS   P. O. Box 10001
Dallas, TX 75301-8105

INDUSTRY CATEGORY   Retail

CORPORATE DESCRIPTION

J. C. Penney is 5th among the 50 largest retailers, according to Fortune magazine. J. C. Penney is a national department store, the largest department store retailer in the United States.

SIZE REVENUES $19,578,000,000 as of January 1994

NUMBER OF EMPLOYEES   193,000 as of January 1994

SOURCE   *1993 Annual Report*

◆ ◆ ◆ ◆ ◆ ◆ ◆

COMPANY | *Pennsylvania Power & Light Company*

STATEMENT

[Author's note: This entry for Pennsylvania Power & Light Company is unusually lengthy because it includes:
1) The updated, current versions of the company's Vision, Values, and Principles,
2) The earlier versions of the company's Vision, Values, Mission, and Philosophy (developed in the 1980s) that the current versions replace.

Please see the case history on PP&L in Part I, which includes an interview with James Marsh, director of corporate communications at PP&L. Mr. Marsh explains how and why the versions differ, as well as the process involved in creating a new set of statements. The case history includes the valuable "definition of terms" (from the earlier versions), which explain the meaning of a Vision, Values, Mission, and Business Philosophy statement. The case history also reflects the company's significant commitment to expressing and communicating such statements that clarify the company's direction and focus.

The two sets of statements are reprinted with the expressed permission of PP&L.]

(Current Version)

OUR VISION

PP&L—People Leading, Growing and Winning in the Changing Electric Energy Markets

Our vision is a statement of where we are going. To get there, we will have to transform our company by building on our solid reputation and acquiring new skills. Supporting this new vision are the three cornerstones of competitive performance, creating change and a commitment to excellence.

First, we are performance-driven. Our financial strength is a result of our commitment to continuous improvement and a commitment by all of us to perform to our full potential. We are accountable for personal and organizational success.

Second, we embrace change. Everyone must be willing to fundamentally challenge our existing ways of doing business. Everyone is encouraged to contribute new and better ideas for improved performance in every area of our business. We will be pioneers in the new electricity marketplace—out front leading the market through innovation.

COMPANY | *Melaleuca, Inc.*

STATEMENT | **Corporate Mission Statement**

"To enhance the lives of those we touch by helping people reach their goals."

CORPORATE DESCRIPTION

Melaleuca, Inc. is a consumer direct marketing company which offers over 80 nutritional, pharmaceutical, personal care and household care

Finally, we strive for excellence in all areas. This is a common personal goal shared by all of us. Our commitment to excellence unifies and strengthens us. It differentiates us from other organizations.

With more companies competing for our customers, we will have to reaffirm our commitment to our guiding values and commit to the CPIP principles that will help us achieve our vision.

Our success in a competitive environment hinges on our commitment to the values that will help us achieve our vision.

OUR VALUES

While our vision provides direction and our principles identify the behaviors that will help us succeed in the future, we are committed to certain guiding values that continue to govern the way we do business:

Integrity—We are honest, open and fair. Respect for individuals is not to be compromised.

products to homes across the U. S. and Canada. As of 1993, the company had annual sales of $206,828,000 and 953 employees.

ADDRESS   3910 S. Yellowstone Hwy.
Idaho Falls, ID 83402

SOURCE   Company representative

Safety—We create a culture that promotes the safety and well-being of employees and the public.

Diversity—We seek a diverse work force at all levels of the organization, as well as a variety of experience and ideas. Differing points of view and opinions will be sought and valued.

Environmental Commitment—We operate our facilities and serve our customers in a manner that protects the environment for present and future generations.

OUR PRINCIPLES

The following eight key principles of the CPIP program are integral to the successful implementation of our vision:

1. Serving our customers.
2. Striving to meet customer, employee and shareowner expectations by being a cost-competitive producer.
3. Measuring and assessing performance constantly.
4. Ensuring that all employees understand and support strategic and operational plans.
5. Leaders role modeling the behavior they expect from others.
6. Creating a climate of trust.
7. Empowering people to think and act.
8. Creating a high level of teamwork throughout the organization.

❖ ❖ ❖

(Older Version—see Author's note, page 429)

Our Vision

PP&L will be the energy supplier of choice.

Our Values

PP&L stands for integrity, customer satisfaction, financial strength, excellence, employee fulfillment, equal opportunity, teamwork, safety, environmental commitment and public service commitment.

Integrity

As stated in our "Standards of Integrity," we are an organization that is here to serve people efficiently in ways that are decent and honorable. Integrity is essential to pursue our vision and to ensure that all other values are meaningful.

Integrity means:

- living up to our responsibilities, meeting our obligations, fulfilling our commitments;
- maintaining our credibility by open, accurate and timely communications with customers, employees, regulators, investors and all others affected by our business;
- instilling confidence in all who deal with the company that PP&L people can be depended upon to act with highest moral and ethical standards. Unethical behavior to accomplish a desired end result is not acceptable.

Customer Satisfaction

Satisfied customers are the lifeblood of our business. Customers are not only those who purchase our service, but also our fellow employees who rely on each other for business-related services. All are entitled to have their needs and expectations realized. Customer satisfaction means:

- exceeding customer expectations;
- treating them with respect in an open and forthright manner;
- adding value to our customer services;
- putting ourselves in their place, asking how we can provide better service, and then improving our performance to provide that service;
- seeking continual feedback on how well we are meeting customer expectations.

Financial Strength

PP&L can successfully accomplish its mission only if it has the financial resources to do so. Financial strength results from:

✦ applying sound judgment to all expenditures to assure that full value is obtained for every dollar spent;

✦ setting financial objectives that increase shareowner value and implementing thoughtful business plans to achieve those objectives;

✦ providing superior service—on time, every time.

Excellence

We set high standards in all aspects of our business, measure our performance against those standards and focus on continuous improvement. Commitment to excellence means:

✦ satisfying ourselves that excellent performance is more than mere adherence to rules, regulations and requirements;

✦ assessing ourselves, identifying opportunities to improve our performance;

✦ admitting our mistakes and learning from them to do better the next time;

✦ going the "extra mile" to improve performance;

✦ setting challenging goals and embracing the concept of rising expectations. Rising expectations recognizes that today's challenging goals will evolve into tomorrow's standards of performance.

Employee Fulfillment

A work force that is productive, well-trained, properly equipped and motivated is an essential element to success. Employee fulfillment means:

✦ providing a work environment that encourages all employees to fully utilize their skills to effectively meet our mission;

✦ valuing each employee's contribution to achieving objectives;

✦ being aware of, and responsive to, the needs and values of employees;

✦ committing ourselves to sound safety, health, compensation and communications practices.

Equal Opportunity and Affirmative Action

An integral part of our commitment to people is to take positive actions to assist each PP&L person to become the best that he or she can be. To accomplish this, we must open our doors to every qualified person and remove all barriers to their development.

Equal Opportunity/Affirmative Action means:

❖ taking a positive stand against discrimination of any sort;

❖ ensuring that no person is excluded from full participation in our company and its activities due to race, color, religion, sex, age, national origin or handicap;

❖ seeking qualified, motivated, enthusiastic candidates for job openings; welcoming them as part of the PP&L team, and taking active steps to improve their capabilities.

Teamwork

Change is an inevitable part of our business life. Identifying, understanding and shaping change to the benefit of our company requires creative thinking and innovation from each employee. As part of our problem solving and decision-making process, we encourage a climate which is open and supportive of suggesting and trying out new approaches or ideas. Teamwork means:

❖ employee participation, engaging employees at all levels in molding the future of the company;

❖ reaching out, soliciting input from those who may be affected by what we do and how we do it;

❖ encouraging teamwork among employees and cooperation among work groups to achieve our common goals and objectives more effectively.

Safety

Maintaining a work environment that promotes the safety and well being of employees and the public is a top priority at PP&L. No job is so important, or so urgent, that safety precautions can be bypassed.

Safety means:

❖ providing tools, equipment and training to enable PP&L people to carry out their responsibilities safely and productively;

❖ maintaining a safety awareness among PP&L people for themselves, their co-workers and the public;

❖ searching for new initiatives to improve safety performance.

Environmental Commitment

PP&L will serve its customers in a manner that protects the environment for present and future generations. Environmental Commitment means:

❖ being alert to the environmental voices of customers, employees and the general public;

❖ demonstrating leadership in sound environmental management;

❖ promoting open and honest communication about environmental impacts of, and on, our operations;

❖ using our expertise to assist in resolving public environmental issues.

Public Service Commitment

PP&L is an integral part of the economic, political, and social structure of Central Eastern Pennsylvania. Our success depends upon the vitality of our service area. PP&L people participate in community activities that contribute to enhancing the quality of life in the area we serve. Community Involvement means:

❖ being a responsible and responsive corporate citizen;

❖ caring about the cultural and civic values of the communities we serve, and operating our business in harmony with those values;

❖ sharing our knowledge and experience to enhance economic prosperity and quality of life.

PP&L's Vision and Values will have maximum benefit when communicated, understood and practiced throughout the organization. Our *Vision and Values* should become an ongoing topic for discussion among all employees; they are the foundation for development of vision and values for work groups throughout the company. Our *Vision and Values* will require periodic review and modification to reflect changing conditions or circumstances.

Our Mission

To meet our customers' ongoing needs for economical and reliable electric service in ways that merit the trust and confidence of our publics.

Our Business Philosophy

PP&L will strive to accomplish its mission in conformance with our Standards of Integrity and within the framework of the following philosophy and policies:

❖ We will be an institution that is humane, responsible and contributive to the betterment of society, with special emphasis on helping to develop both economic prosperity and a better quality-of-life in our service area. We will not compromise safety, public health or environmental quality in carrying out our mission.

❖ We will maintain an open and full disclosure policy with customers, employees, investors, and others affected by our business.

❖ We will seek public input in the development and implementation of plans to meet our commitment to provide economical and reliable electric service. We will inform the public about our progress and about probable effects of our plans and actions.

❖ We will search for new ideas and perspectives so as to anticipate and effectively respond to change.

❖ We will support the development and application of sound governmental policies that we believe to be in the best interests of our publics.

❖ We will create and maintain a work environment that attracts and retains capable people, encourages self-development and enables them to take pride and satisfaction in their work.

❖ We will support improved coordination among interconnected utilities in the planning and operation of generation and bulk power transmission facilities.

❖ We will strive to earn a fair return on the capital provided by investors, maintain a sound credit standing and have the financial strength required to raise needed capital at reasonable costs.

❖ We recognize our responsibility to be good stewards of the resources entrusted to us. We will utilize those resources efficiently and effectively to carry out our mission. We will promote the wise use of electricity and provide excellent customer service.

❖ We will constantly look for methods to improve the operating efficiency of the electric supply system, search out cost-effective programs to improve continuity of service and develop ways to minimize adverse impacts of unforeseen circumstances.

❖ We will pursue a climate of excellence and intend to be a well-run, responsive, cost-effective company. We will measure our performance by regularly comparing it to the best that others achieve under similar conditions.

ADDRESS   2 N. 9th St.
Allentown, PA 18103

INDUSTRY CATEGORY   Utility

CORPORATE DESCRIPTION

Pennsylvania Power & Light Co. headquartered in Allentown, PA, provides electric service to approximately 1.2 million homes and businesses throughout a 10,000-square-mile area in 29 counties of Central Eastern Pennsylvania.

SIZE REVENUES $2,727,002,000 as of 1993

NUMBER OF EMPLOYEES   7,765 as of 1993

SOURCE   *1993 Annual Report*

◆ ◆ ◆ ◆ ◆ ◆ ◆

COMPANY | *PepsiCo, Inc.*

STATEMENT | **(Objective and Strategy)**

Our overriding objective is to maximize shareholder value. Our strategy is to concentrate our resources on growing our businesses, both through internal growth and carefully selected acquisitions within these businesses. The corporation's success reflects our continuing commitment to growth and a focus on those businesses where we can drive our own growth and create opportunities.

| **(Values)**

Results—PepsiCo people are recognized and rewarded for achieving results. To create shareholder value, we must perform brilliantly on millions of consumer transactions each day.

Integrity—At PepsiCo, integrity means more than corporate honesty. It takes openness and trust to run a huge flexible corporation. Warmth and good humor help, too.

People—In the end, it's always the special efforts of people that make great things happen. We value our employees, customers, business partners, franchisees, suppliers and shareholders. We know without them there would be no PepsiCo.

ADDRESS   700 Anderson Hill Rd.
Purchase, NY 10577-1444

INDUSTRY CATEGORY   Food/Beverage

CORPORATE DESCRIPTION
PepsiCo operates on a worldwide basis within three industry segments: beverages, snack foods, and restaurants. The beverage segment markets Pepsi, Diet Pepsi, Mountain Dew and other brands worldwide and 7UP outside the U. S. The snack food segment manufactures and markets snack chips worldwide, with Frito-Lay representing the domestic business. The restaurant segment includes operations of the worldwide Pizza Hut, Taco Bell, and KFC (Kentucky Fried Chicken) chains.

SIZE REVENUES $25,021,000,000 as of 1993

NUMBER OF EMPLOYEES   423,000 as of 1993

SOURCE   *1993 Annual Report*

COMPANY | *Perini Corporation*

STATEMENT

[From the "President's Message"]

Perini Corporation's mission in our second century is to be the best in our business.

We believe we must:

❖ Strive to meet or exceed the expectations of our clients;

❖ Foster a professional environment in which Perini employees, subcontractors and suppliers work together in partnership with our clients to perform quality work;

❖ Earn an equitable financial return for our shareholders;

❖ Be responsible citizens, concerned for the safety of our employees and the public, and responsive to the needs of the communities in which we live and work;

❖ Employ a highly motivated, competent and diverse management team and employee group who strive to continuously improve their job performance;

❖ Earn the respect, confidence and good will of our clients, shareholders, employees, subcontractors and suppliers, and build upon our 100-year tradition of integrity and excellence.

ADDRESS 73 Mt. Wayte Ave.
Framingham, MA 01701

INDUSTRY CATEGORY Construction

CORPORATE DESCRIPTION

Perini Corporation, headquartered in Framingham, Massachusetts, is engaged in two principal businesses: Construction and Real Estate Development.

Perini provides general contracting, both building and heavy, and construction management services to private clients and public agencies throughout the United States and in selected overseas locations.

Real estate development operations are conducted by Perini Land & Development Company, a wholly-owned subsidiary with offices in Arizona, California, Florida, Georgia and Massachusetts.

SIZE REVENUES $1,100,116,000 as of 1993

NUMBER OF EMPLOYEES   1000+ as of 1994

SOURCES   *1993 Annual Report*, company representative

◆   ◆   ◆   ◆   ◆   ◆   ◆

COMPANY | *Pet Incorporated*

STATEMENT | **MISSION STATEMENT**

The Mission of Pet is to continuously improve all facets of our organization and by 1996 be recognized as one of the four best companies in the packaged foods industry.

PET STRATEGIES

Provide imaginative, category-leading marketing for all our brands

Accelerate business-building initiatives domestically, focusing on Mexican, Italian and Van de Kamp's

Achieve operational excellence in manufacturing, distribution, purchasing and R&D

Selectively build new growth opportunities in mature/declining brands

Achieve worldwide Mexican food leadership with Old El Paso

Establish Pet as the innovation leader in Italian foods in North America with Progresso/Primo

Achieve significant financial flexibility to provide for future growth of business

PET VALUES

Ethics and compliance with all applicable laws

Consumer and customer driven in the development and delivery of all products and services

Good citizenship in all the communities where we have operations

Company-wide continuous improvement activities using a team approach

The development and training of our employees

An environment which supports the creativity and initiative of all our employees

Equal opportunities for all employees

Fulfillment of our commitment—what we say we do, we *do* do

ADDRESS   P. O. Box 392
                 St. Louis, MO 63166-0392

INDUSTRY CATEGORY   Food/Beverage

CORPORATE DESCRIPTION
Founded in 1885, Pet Incorporated is a leading packaged food company producing a diverse range of products under many well-known brand names.

SIZE REVENUES $1,581,600,000 as of 1994

NUMBER OF EMPLOYEES   5,739 as of June 30, 1994

SOURCE   *1994 Annual Report*

COMPANY | *Pillsbury (The Pillsbury Company)*

STATEMENT | **MISSION STATEMENT**
BEST FOOD COMPANY

The Pillsbury Company will be known by its trade customers, consumers, shareholders, employees and communities as the Best Food Company in the world.

We will achieve Best Food Company status through a dedication to and relentless pursuit of the following strategic principles:

BUILD LEADING BRANDS

#1 or #2 brand in every category in which we compete

WIN IN THE MARKETPLACE

Focus on consumers, trade customers and the competition, while building volume and share

BUILD SHAREHOLDER VALUE

Superior financial performance—profit, cash flow, return on assets and strategic allocation of resources

DEVELOP PEOPLE

Best people with the right skills and a passion for our brands

ADDRESS   200 S. 6th St.
Minneapolis, MN 55402

INDUSTRY CATEGORY   Food/Beverage

CORPORATE DESCRIPTION
Started in 1869 as a Minneapolis-based flour miller, Pillsbury has evolved into a highly regarded food company with annual sales of approximately $4 billion and about 18,000 employees worldwide. The company still markets flour for home, retail and institutional use, and provides a wide range of value-added food products: fresh,

frozen, and canned vegetables; side dishes; baking mixes; prepared dough products; ice cream; frozen yogurt; frozen pizza and pizza snacks; pet food and others.

In 1989 Pillsbury became part of U.K.-based Grand Metropolitan PLC.

SIZE REVENUES $4,000,000,000 as of June, 1994

NUMBER OF EMPLOYEES   18,000 as of June, 1994

SOURCE   "Pillsbury Fact Sheet" company publication (June, 1994)

◆ ◆ ◆ ◆ ◆ ◆ ◆

COMPANY | *Pioneer Hi-Bred International, Inc.*

STATEMENT | **Mission Statement**

❖ Our mission is to provide products and services which increase the efficiency and profitability of the world's farmers.
❖ Our core business is the broad application of the science of genetics.
❖ We will ensure the growth of our core business and develop new opportunities which enhance the core business.

ADDRESS   700 Capital Square
400 Locust St.
Des Moines, IA 50309

INDUSTRY CATEGORY   Agriculture

CORPORATE DESCRIPTION

Pioneer Hi-Bred's business is the broad application of the science of genetics. Pioneer was founded in 1926 to apply newly discovered genetic techniques to hybridize corn. Today, the Company develops, produces, and markets hybrids of corn, sorghum, and sunflower, and varieties of soybean, alfalfa, wheat, canola, and vegetables.

SIZE REVENUES $1,343,437,000 as of 1993

NUMBER OF EMPLOYEES   4,807 as of 1993

SOURCES   *1992 Annual Reports*; *1993 Annual Report*

◆ ◆ ◆ ◆ ◆ ◆ ◆

COMPANY | *Ply Gem Industries, Inc.*

STATEMENT

Our goal is to become the supplier of choice to the home improvement industry. By supplying top quality products, delivering excellent customer service and working in partnership with our customers to satisfy their needs, we aim to be the best. As we see it, that's the best way we can properly serve the long-term interests of all our constituents: customers, suppliers, employees and stockholders.

ADDRESS   777 Third Ave.
New York, NY 10017

INDUSTRY CATEGORY   Construction

CORPORATE DESCRIPTION
Ply Gem is a national manufacturer and distributor of specialty products for the home improvement industry. The company was founded in 1943 and is headquartered in New York City. Ply Gem's 11 independent operating companies employ over 4,000 people in more than 50 locations throughout the United States and Canada.

SIZE REVENUES $723,000,000 as of 1993

NUMBER OF EMPLOYEES   4,000 as of 1993

SOURCES   *1992 Annual Report*; "The Fortune 500," *Fortune* 129, no. 8 (April 8, 1994)

◆ ◆ ◆ ◆ ◆ ◆ ◆

COMPANY | *Premark International, Inc.*

STATEMENT | **MISSION STATEMENTS**
Premark International
FEG
Wilsonart
Tupperware
Precor
West Bend
Hartco
Florida Tile
PREMARK INTERNATIONAL, INC.
To be recognized by our customers as a provider of outstanding service and leadership, thereby adding value to the corporation, its shareholders, and employees.

FOOD EQUIPMENT GROUP (FEG)

FEG's mission is to achieve global recognition as the preeminent supplier and servicer to the food service industry by:

◆ supplying products that exceed each customer's quality expectations,

◆ supporting its customers with services unparalleled in the industry, and

◆ achieving adequate levels of profitability through continuous improvement of products, facilities and human resources.

WILSONART

Become a "World Class Company" by achieving total customer satisfaction.
—Perfect Quality
—Perfect Delivery
—Perfect Service

TUPPERWARE

To design and manufacture high quality, high value-added products, primarily in plastic housewares, and to market and distribute those products worldwide through a direct selling approach, by ensuring outstanding customer satisfaction while providing an acceptable profit and return on net assets.

The Company is committed to implement alternative selling methods, compatible with our distribution system, to satisfy those consumers who cannot or will not attend a Tupperware party, and to enhance the covenantal relationship with our field sales force by continuing to offer unlimited professional and personal growth opportunities to all those who so desire.

PRECOR

Our mission is to continually improve our products and services in order to exceed our customers' needs and expectations, allowing us to lead the world in the design and manufacture of advanced technology fitness equipment.

WEST BEND

At The West Bend Company, customers are the reason we exist. Our mission is to provide products and services that exceed our customers' expectations. We are committed to Total Quality/ Just-in-Time operating philosophies and implementing change to achieve this goal. To this end, we will:

- Empower People
- Continuously Improve
- Provide Educational Opportunities
- Eliminate Waste
- Create Partnerships with our Customers, both internal and external, as well as our suppliers

HARTCO

Grow Hartco through superior product quality and customer service, achieve satisfactory earnings and cash flow for the corporation, and provide desirable working conditions and careers for employees.

FLORIDA TILE

Mission

We are dedicated to leadership in the ceramic tile industry by supplying the highest quality products and services at competitive prices.

Vision

How we accomplish our mission is as important as the mission itself. Fundamental to the success of the company are these basic values:

- Customers: Our customers must be the focus of everything we do and exceeding their expectations is our goal.
- People: We will attain leadership by cultivating a culture that values all employees and derives strength from developing their talents and empowering them to create change in favor of customers.
- Profitability: The survival of our company depends on profitability. It is the ultimate measure of how efficiently we exceed our customers expectations. We are committed to

increasing stockholder value and sharing the prosperity of
Florida Tile with all employees.

ADDRESS   1717 Deerfield Rd.
Deerfield, IL 60015

INDUSTRY CATEGORY   Manufacturing

CORPORATE DESCRIPTION
Premark International, Inc. manufactures and markets consumer
and commercial products under such leading brand names as Tupperware, Hobart, Wilsonart, West Bend, Florida Tile, Vulcan, Foster, Hartco, and Precor. Premark is international in scope.

SIZE REVENUES $3,097,300,000 as of 1993

NUMBER OF EMPLOYEES   24,000 as of 1993

SOURCE   *1993 Annual Report*

♦ ♦ ♦ ♦ ♦ ♦ ♦

COMPANY | *Principal Financial Group*

STATEMENT | **MISSION**
What we do
To help individuals, groups and businesses meet their
financial goals by providing high quality insurance and
financial services.

VISION

Where we want to be

To become the financial services company of choice for individuals, groups, businesses and their employees, and communities around the world.

CORE VALUES

These four values are the soul of our company...our culture. They define how we conduct ourselves, shape our business approach and form our unique perspective on the world. These basic values, and the points that follow each one, comprise what is necessary for our success.

Customer Service

Quality

Strength

Integrity

CUSTOMER SERVICE

❖ **Service**—Our reason for existence is to provide excellent service to customers. We believe excellent service is defined by the customer.

❖ **Mutuality**—We have no stockholders; we operate on behalf of our customers. Mutuality provides a strong focus on customers and enables us to concentrate on the long-term view.

❖ **Financial Stability**—Maintaining and improving our financial soundness is a fundamental part of serving customers well. Financial stability gives The Principal® flexibility. In short, it prepares us for good times and bad.

❖ **Marketing**—We will know our customer markets well, understand and meet a variety of their financial needs.

❖ **Cost**—Our commitment to customers includes offering the lowest possible cost for high quality service. We emphasize both expense control and growth in numbers of customers to reduce the cost per customer.

❖ **Management**—We work toward continuous improvement in our operations, which over time, has a large positive impact.

❖ **Products and Services**—We find out what customers need and then build quality products and services to meet their needs. We continually seek to improve and enhance existing products and services to meet customers' changing needs.

❖ **Corporate Identity**—Our identity and image distinguishes us from the competition. We strive to increase recognition of The Principal Financial Group and improve our quality reputation as a financially sound, customer-oriented company.

STRENGTH

❖ **Human Resources**—We are only as strong as our people. The Principal is committed to giving employees the training, tools, opportunities and rewards, along with a stimulating work environment, to do their jobs well. We seek diversity to draw excellence from all available sources.

❖ **Growth and Profit**—We strive to balance orderly growth with adequate profits. Growth enables us to provide economies of scale; in other words we can provide more for less. Profit allows us to keep our promises to customers, continue growth and provide new services.

❖ **Asset Management**—We seek above average, long-range rates of return from our investments. In managing our assets (what we own), we consider our own liabilities (what we owe) and the level of risk our customers desire.

❖ **Diversification**—as the economy changes and as customer needs change, our various businesses may grow and decline over time. We diversify into a number of businesses so that the decline of any one business doesn't have an overwhelming impact on the entire company and our customers.

❖ **Decentralization**—The Principal will continue to offer products and services through separate business units. Our business units are empowered to conduct their ongoing businesses and make decisions regarding their operations, customer service and products and service offerings. This autonomy brings success to the whole company because the business units can be flexible and efficient in responding to customers' needs. However, communication and coordination through a central company management group is crucial. This central management group will be the focus of decisions regarding the businesses we are in and the allocation of resources. The group will also review all business plans.

✦ **Globalization**—We are committed to becoming a global financial services organization.

INTEGRITY

✦ **Ethics**—We operate in an ethical and legal manner. We are dedicated to being honest and straightforward in our dealings with customers, the public and each other.

✦ **Social Responsibility**—The Principal is a responsible member of the communities in which it operates. We do our best to support society, the global community, the economy, the insurance and financial services industries and the nations, states and local communities where our employees and customers work and live.

ADDRESS   711 High St.
Des Moines, IA 50392

INDUSTRY CATEGORY   Insurance

CORPORATE DESCRIPTION
The Principal Financial Group is a diversified family of financial companies offering a full range of insurance and financial products and services for businesses, groups and individuals.

SIZE REVENUES $12,370,000,000 as of December 31, 1993

NUMBER OF EMPLOYEES   14,275 as of December 31, 1993

SOURCE   *1993 Annual Report*

◆ ◆ ◆ ◆ ◆ ◆ ◆

COMPANY | *Promus Companies Incorporated, The*

STATEMENT | Our Vision
Our vision is to provide the best experience to our casino entertainment and hotel customers by having the best people trained, empowered and pledged to excellence, delivering the best service, quality and value to every customer, every time...guaranteed.

ADDRESS   1023 Cherry Rd.
Memphis, TN 38117-5423

INDUSTRY CATEGORY   Hotel, Hospitality, and Related

CORPORATION DESCRIPTION
The Promus Companies Incorporated is the service, quality and value leader in the casino entertainment and hotel industries. Dedicated to providing the best experience to its customers—100% guaranteed at Harrah's Casinos, and Embassy Suites, Hampton Inn, and Homewood Suites hotels.

SIZE REVENUES $1,200,000,000 as of 1993

NUMBER OF EMPLOYEES   27,000 as of 1993

SOURCE   Company representative

◆ ◆ ◆ ◆ ◆ ◆ ◆

COMPANY | *Protective Life Corporation*

STATEMENT | **PROTECTIVE LIFE'S MISSION AND VALUES**

Protective Life Corporation provides financial security through life and health insurance and investment products. Our vision is to enhance the quality of life of our customers, our stockholders, and our people.

We hold to three preeminent values—quality, serving people, and growth—which by tradition and choice transcend all others. They are the foundation of our aspirations, our plans, our best energies, and our life together in this Company.

QUALITY

The heart of quality is integrity. Quality is the cornerstone on which all our activity rests—quality products, services, people, and investments. We strive for superior quality and continuous quality improvement in everything we do.

SERVING PEOPLE

Serving people is vital. We find our ultimate reward in the service and support of three groups:

Customers: Our customers come first. We prosper only to the extent that we create long-term relationships with satisfied customers. We do so in discerning their needs and responding to them; in providing high value, distinctive products; in prudent investment of policyholder funds; in systems, information, and counsel which help our customers solve problems; and in prompt, accurate, innovative, and courteous service which is the best in the business.

Stockholders: Our stockholders provide the equity essential for our success. We are stewards of their investment and must return a profit to them. Profit is essential for implementing our commitment to quality, serving people, and growth. It is a critical measurement of our performance. Our objective is to rank at the top of the industry in long-range earnings growth and return on equity.

Protective People: The accomplishment of our mission depends on all Protective people working together. We want our people to enjoy their work and take pride in Protective Life, its mission and values. We are committed to opportunity and training for all to help us fulfill our potential; open, candid communication; the input, initiative, and empowerment of all our people; the encouragement of one another; and creating a place where a zeal to serve our customers, stockholders, and each other permeates the Company.

GROWTH

We are dedicated to long-term growth in sales, revenues, and profit, not only for our stockholders but also for personal growth and development of Protective people. We achieve growth through resourceful marketing, superior service, and acquisitions. Growth is critical for improving quality and serving people. It is essential to maintaining a position of strength in our marketplace and attracting and retaining high caliber people.

ADDRESS   P. O. Box 2606
Birmingham, AL 35202

INDUSTRY CATEGORY   Insurance

CORPORATE DESCRIPTION

Protective Life Corporation provides financial services through the production, distribution, and administration of insurance and investment products. It has five marketing divisions: Agency, Group, Guaranteed Investment Contracts, Financial Institutions, and Investment Products.

Founded in 1907, the Company's principal operating subsidiary is Protective Life Insurance Company (Protective Life).

SIZE REVENUES $759,637,000 as of 1993

NUMBER OF EMPLOYEES   1,079 as of November 15, 1994

SOURCE   *1993 Annual Report*

◆   ◆   ◆   ◆   ◆   ◆   ◆

COMPANY | *PSICOR, Inc.*

STATEMENT | MISSION STATEMENT

PSICOR, Inc. is committed to:

❖ Deliver quality services and technology to hospitals and physicians.

❖ Provide client hospitals with cost-effective services.

❖ Maintain a safe environment for employees which promotes self-actualization and professionalism.

❖ Optimize the fair return on stockholder's investment.

ADDRESS   16818 Via Del Campo Ct.
San Diego, CA 92127-1799

INDUSTRY CATEGORY   Medical Products and Services

CORPORATE DESCRIPTION

PSICOR, Inc., founded in 1968, is the nation's leading provider of cardiovascular technology and services. The company supplies over 400 hospitals with advanced life-sustaining equipment, skilled technicians, disposable supplies, and expert resource management on a cost-effective contract basis.

SIZE REVENUES $76,918,000 as of 1993

NUMBER OF EMPLOYEES   537 as of 1993

SOURCE   Company representative; Financial Report

◆   ◆   ◆   ◆   ◆   ◆   ◆

COMPANY | *Public Service Enterprise Group Incorporated*

STATEMENT | PSEG vision

WORKING TOGETHER TO SET THE STANDARD OF EXCELLENCE IN DELIVERING ENERGY SERVICES TO CUSTOMERS

We believe the vision is further defined when it is explained in terms of how we would want our key constituencies to view us in the future.

CUSTOMERS

We know our customers and take care of their individual problems as if they were our own.

EMPLOYEES

Employees enjoy working here because the work we do is very important and we do it better than anyone else.

INVESTORS & FINANCIAL COMMUNITY

When thinking of energy services companies, any group of investors would put PSEG at the top of their list of well-run, high quality companies.

GENERAL PUBLIC & OPINION LEADERS

PSEG adds more value in solving important public policy issues than any other energy services company.

Achieving the vision would result in PSEG being known as a company that is:

- ❖ EFFICIENT
- ❖ RESPONSIVE
- ❖ CARING
- ❖ INNOVATIVE

ADDRESS   P. O. Box 570
Newark, NJ 07101

INDUSTRY CATEGORY   Utility

CORPORATE DESCRIPTION

Public Service Enterprise Group Incorporated is a diversified public utility holding company. Public Service Electric and Gas Company (PSE&G), the principal subsidiary of Enterprise, is a regulated utility providing electric and gas service to more than two million customers and more than five and a half million residents of New Jersey. It is the state's largest utility and one of America's largest combined electric and gas companies.

SIZE REVENUES $5,705,559,000 as of 1993

NUMBER OF EMPLOYEES   12,027 as of December 31, 1993

SOURCE   *1993 Annual Report*

COMPANY | *Rainbow Technologies*

STATEMENT | **MISSION**
Rainbow is committed to providing high quality products and services through a relationship of excellence with customers, employees, shareholders and suppliers.

| **VISION**
Rainbow is committed to being the leading worldwide provider of products and services to protect and/or distribute intellectual property.

ADDRESS   9292 Jeronimo Rd.
Irvine, CA 92718

INDUSTRY CATEGORY   High Technology

CORPORATE DESCRIPTION
Rainbow produces computer software and hardware systems to prevent illegal use of software.

SIZE REVENUES $35,118,000 as of 1993

NUMBER OF EMPLOYEES Not available

SOURCE   *1993 Annual Report*

COMPANY | *Raytheon Aircraft Company*

STATEMENT | **The Beechcraft Vision**

To be the world standard for quality and performance in general aviation, related products, and services.

| **The Beechcraft Mission**

To build and sell the best aircraft and aerospace products in their class, through continuous quality improvement, effective use of resources, and the full involvement and contribution of Beech employees, in order to increase market-share, customer satisfaction and profitability.

ADDRESS   P. O. Box 85
9709 E.Central
Wichita, KS 67206

INDUSTRY CATEGORY   Aerospace

CORPORATE DESCRIPTION

Raytheon Aircraft Company is one of the world's leading manufacturers of business aircraft and dual use aircraft for the military. With headquarters and major facilities in Wichita, Kansas, and major manufacturing operations in Andover and Salina, Kansas, Little Rock, Arkansas, and the United Kingdom, the company offers the broadest and strongest product lines in business aviation.

The Raytheon Aircraft Company was formed following the combination of Beech Aircraft Corporation, founded in 1932 and one of the world's oldest, most prestigious aviation companies, and Raytheon Corporate Jets, manufacturer of the Hawker line of business aircraft. Together, the two entities have produced more than 51,000 airplanes.

SIZE REVENUES $1,700,000,000 as of 1994

NUMBER OF EMPLOYEES   10,690 (worldwide) as of 1994

SOURCE   Company representative

◆ ◆ ◆ ◆ ◆ ◆ ◆

COMPANY | *Research Industries Corporation*

STATEMENT | **Corporate Mission Statement**
To provide cardiovascular & other specialty surgeons with innovative, low-priced disposable products that are cost-effective & improve therapeutic outcomes—thereby providing challenging employment opportunities while enhancing long-term shareholder value.

ADDRESS   6864 S. 300 West
Midvale, UT 84047

INDUSTRY CATEGORY   Pharmaceutical/Biotechnology

CORPORATE DESCRIPTION
The Company develops, manufactures and sells disposable medical products and specialty pharmaceuticals to hospitals, distributors and other medical related facilities.

SIZE REVENUES $27,499,000 as of 1994

NUMBER OF EMPLOYEES   200 as of 1994

SOURCES   *1994 Annual Report*; company representative

COMPANY | *Reynolds Metals Company*

STATEMENT | OUR VISION

We, the men and women of Reynolds Metals Company, are dedicated to being the premier supplier and recycler of aluminum and other products in the global markets we serve.

| OUR MISSION

Working together, our mission is to provide our customers with uncompromising quality, innovation and continuous improvement, which will result in the profitable growth and financial strength of our company.

| OUR VALUES

Exceed customer expectations
Employee empowerment
Continuous improvement
Stockholder satisfaction
Supplier involvement
Social responsibility
We are committed to the success of our customers, employees, stockholders, suppliers, and the communities in which we operate.

ADDRESS   6601 W. Broad St.
Richmond, VA 23230

INDUSTRY CATEGORY   Manufacturing

CORPORATE DESCRIPTION

Founded in 1919, Reynolds Metals Company is the second largest aluminum company in the United States and the third largest in the world.

SIZE REVENUES $5,294,200,000 as of 1993

NUMBER OF EMPLOYEES 29,000 (worldwide) as of 1993

SOURCE *1993 Annual Report*

◆ ◆ ◆ ◆ ◆ ◆ ◆

COMPANY | *Rhône-Poulenc Rorer Inc.*

STATEMENT | THE RHÔNE-POULENC RORER MISSION

Our Mission is to become the BEST pharmaceutical company in the world by dedicating our resources, our talents and our energies to help improve human health and the quality of life of people throughout the world.

COMPANY | *Monterey Homes*

STATEMENT | MISSION STATEMENT

The true essence of quality home building is achieved by the combination of selecting prime locations, creating innovative architectural design, implementing fine craftsmanship and offering a superb warranty program with first-class customer service. The result of this accomplishment is the exceptional living environments we build—in our homes and the surrounding community.

BEING THE BEST MEANS:

❖ Being the BEST at satisfying the needs of everyone we serve: patients, healthcare professionals, employees, communities, governments and shareholders;

❖ Being BETTER AND FASTER than our competitors at discovering and bringing to market important new medicines in selected therapeutic areas;

❖ Operating with the HIGHEST professional and ethical standards in all our activities, building on the Rhône-Poulenc and Rorer heritage of integrity;

❖ Being seen as the BEST place to work, attracting and retaining talented people at all levels by creating an environment that encourages them to develop their potential to the full;

❖ Generating consistently Better results than our competitors, through innovation and a total commitment to quality in everything we do.

CORPORATE DESCRIPTION

Monterey Homes is a dynamic home building and real estate development company, listed as one of the top 100 privately-held companies in Arizona.

ADDRESS   6263 N. Scottsdale Rd., Ste. 220
Scottsdale, AZ 85250

SOURCE   Company representative

Satisfying the needs of our customers

We will strive for the highest quality and continuous improvement in our products and services for all our customers, external and internal, maintaining the highest standards of integrity in all our relationships.

Global communication and collaboration

We will be a global company, fostering open communication, receptivity to new ideas and (worldwide) collaboration on strategies that support the growth and success of the company.

Being entrepreneurial and acting quickly

We will be entrepreneurial, working with a great sense of urgency, encouraging teamwork and quick decision-making, rewarding innovation and results at every level of the organization.

Treating each other fairly and valuing diversity

We will treat each other fairly, with trust and respect, valuing cultural and individual differences so that our company is strengthened by our diversity.

Caring for our communities and the environment

We will be good neighbors, working to improve the safety of the environment and the vitality of our communities and our workplace.

When we operate according to these principles, Rhône-Poulenc Rorer will grow and prosper as a company and so will we as individuals.

ADDRESS   500 Arcola Rd.
P. O. Box 1200
Collegeville, PA 19426-0107

INDUSTRY CATEGORY   Pharmaceutical/Biotechnology

CORPORATE DESCRIPTION
Rhône-Poulenc Rorer Inc. is a global pharmaceutical company dedicated to the discovery, development, manufacturing, and marketing of human pharmaceuticals.

SIZE REVENUES $4,019,400,000 as of 1993

NUMBER OF EMPLOYEES   22,000 as of 1993

SOURCE   *1993 Annual Report*

◆　◆　◆　◆　◆　◆　◆

COMPANY | *Rich Products Corporation*

STATEMENT | **Our Philosophy Statement**
Our Mission
Rich Products Corporation is a dynamic growth-oriented company on a World Class Mission to set new standards of excellence in customer satisfaction and achieve new levels of competitive success in every category of business in which we operate.
Our Strategy
We will achieve our World Class Mission by working together as a team in a total quality effort to:

❖ **Impress Our Customers**
  Provide exceptional service to our external and internal customers the first time and every time.

❧ **Improve, Improve, Improve!**
Continuously improve the quality and value of the goods
we produce and services we provide.

❧ **Empower People**
Unleash the talents of all our associates by creating an
environment that is safe, that recognizes and rewards their
achievements, and encourages their participation and
growth.

❧ **Work Smarter**
Drive out all waste of time, effort and material—all the
barriers and extra steps that keep us from doing our jobs
right.

❧ **Do The Right Thing!**
Maintain the highest standards of integrity and ethical conduct and behave as good citizens in our communities.

ADDRESS   One W. Ferry St.
P. O. Box 245
Buffalo, NY 14240

INDUSTRY CATEGORY   Food/Beverage

CORPORATE DESCRIPTION
Rich Products Corporation is the nation's largest family-owned
frozen food manufacturer supplying the bakery, food service and
retail food industry with non-dairy, bakery, and specialty food items.

SIZE REVENUES $990,000,000 as of 1993

NUMBER OF EMPLOYEES   6,500 as of 1994

SOURCES   "Rich's Magazine" company publication
(November, 1992); company representative

COMPANY | *Roadway Services, Inc.*

STATEMENT | **Mission Statement**

Roadway Services, Inc., through its operating companies, is in the business of satisfying customers by meeting their requirements for value added transportation and logistics services, thereby creating value for our shareholders.

❖ We will be quality driven and customer focused in pursuit of this mission. We will be the best there is at the art and science of satisfying the customer.

❖ We will be efficient in the use of human and other resources.

❖ We will provide our people with a challenging and satisfying work experience.

❖ We will conduct our affairs with integrity as a responsible corporate citizen.

ADDRESS   P. O. Box 88
1077 Gorge Blvd.
Akron, OH 44309-0088

INDUSTRY CATEGORY   Transportation

CORPORATE DESCRIPTION

Roadway Services, Inc. is a holding company engaged through its operating companies in the transportation and logistics businesses. Its operating companies are: Roadway Express, Inc.; Roadway Package System, Inc.; Roadway Global Air, Inc.; Viking Freight, Inc.; Spartan Express, Inc.; Coles Express, Inc.; Central Freight Lines Inc.; Roberts Transportation Services, Inc.; and Roadway Logistics Systems, Inc.

SIZE REVENUES $4,155,940,000 as of 1993

NUMBER OF EMPLOYEES   46,600 as of 1993

SOURCE   *1993 Annual Report,* Form 10-K (December 31, 1993)

◆ ◆ ◆ ◆ ◆ ◆ ◆

COMPANY | *Rockwell International Corporation*

STATEMENT | **The Rockwell Credo: What We Believe**

We believe maximizing the satisfaction of our customers is our most important concern as a means of warranting their continued loyalty.

We believe in providing superior value to customers through high-quality, technologically-advanced, fairly-priced products and customer service, designed to meet customer needs better than all alternatives.

We believe Rockwell people are our most important assets, making the critical difference in how well Rockwell performs; and, through their work and effort, separating Rockwell from all competitors.

We believe we have an obligation for the well-being of the communities in which we live and work.

We believe excellence is the standard for all we do, achieved by encouraging and nourishing:

- ◆ Respect for the individual
- ◆ Honest, open communication
- ◆ Individual development and satisfaction
- ◆ A sense of ownership and responsibility for Rockwell's success
- ◆ Participation, cooperation and teamwork
- ◆ Creativity, innovation and initiative

- Prudent risk-taking
- Recognition and rewards for achievement

We believe success is realized by:

- Achieving leadership in the markets we serve
- Focusing our resources and energy on global markets where our technology, knowledge, capabilities and understanding of customers combine to provide the opportunity for leadership
- Maintaining the highest standards of ethics and integrity in every action we take, in everything we do

We believe the ultimate measure of our success is the ability to provide a superior value to our shareowners, balancing near-term and long-term objectives to achieve both competitive return on investment, and consistent increased market value.

ADDRESS   2201 Seal Beach Blvd.
P. O. Box 4250
Seal Beach, CA 90740-8250

INDUSTRY CATEGORY   Electronics

CORPORATE DESCRIPTION
Rockwell is a high technology, diversified company with leadership market positions in automation, avionics, defense, electronics, telecommunications, aerospace, automotive components, and graphic systems, with annual sales of $11 billion.

SIZE REVENUES $10,840,000,000 as of 1993

NUMBER OF EMPLOYEES   77,028 as of 1993

SOURCE   *1993 Annual Report*

COMPANY | *Rollins Inc.*

STATEMENT | MISSION OF EXCELLENCE

Our Mission is to be the Nation's Best Service Company. We will accomplish this goal by delivering the finest quality services and value to our customers, while being environmentally responsible. This will provide opportunities and security for employees, as well as maximize long-term financial performance for stockholders.

ADDRESS 2170 Piedmont Rd., N.E.
Atlanta, GA 30324

INDUSTRY CATEGORY Diversified

CORPORATE DESCRIPTION

Rollins, Inc. owns and operates Orkin Exterminating Company, Inc. and Rollins Protective Services. Orkin is the world's largest termite and pest control company, and also provides plantscaping and lawn care services. Rollins Protective Services is a leader in electronic security systems.

SIZE REVENUES $575,802,000 as of 1993

NUMBER OF EMPLOYEES Not available

SOURCE *1993 Annual Report*

STATEMENT | Philosophy

Rubbermaid's philosophy is based upon these fundamental beliefs:

We believe that partnerships with our customers, suppliers, communities, governments, shareholders, and Rubbermaid associates are the most effective and efficient means of continuously improving the value we create for our consumers.

We believe that value is a carefully balanced and consumer-defined combination of quality, price, timeliness, service, and innovation. We believe these value attributes are based on a solid foundation of innovation which is the main driver of Rubbermaid's Continuous Value Improvement Process.

We believe that internal partnerships, meaningful teamwork, and ongoing learning will instill in every Rubbermaid associate the skills, the understanding, and the desire to achieve continuous improvement in every link of our value chain.

We believe in partnerships which strive for:

❖ A relationship of mutual respect, recognition, and reward for performance

❖ A commitment to a highest standards of integrity and ethical conduct

❖ A dedication to safety and protection of the environment, and

❖ A fair return on investment

We believe that through this partnership and teamwork philosophy, Rubbermaid will be greater than the sum of its parts.

We believe that the best way to create shareholder wealth

consistently and sustainably is to best satisfy the needs of consumers. We will excel when we make them happy. We will make them happy by delighting them with our value.
(Signed)

Wolfgang R. Schmitt
Co-Chairman of the Board
and Chief Executive Officer

Charles A. Carroll
President and Chief Operating Officer

(June 1994)

Management Principles

We believe our primary responsibility is to the consumers and customers who buy Rubbermaid's products and services. We will consistently delight them with our quality, innovation, and prompt and accurate service. We will use teamwork, benchmarking, and advanced technologies to compress time and improve our business processes. Every associate must contribute to continuously improving the value being created by the business. We will eliminate boundaries between our business partners as the best means of improving our total value chain.

We believe our partners are entitled to share in the economic benefits derived from Rubbermaid's development, production, sourcing, and marketing of products worldwide.

For our consumers, we will strive to:

- Be creatively responsive to their changing needs
- Consistently improve our value for them
- Stand behind our products and services, and
- Help protect and improve the environment

For our customers we will strive to:

- Work as partners with integrity and principled negotiation

❖ Invest aggressively in research, new products, capacity, and advanced technologies

❖ Offer on-trend products of exceptional design, fashion, quality, and utility

❖ Work together to reduce or eliminate non-value activities to improve productivity

❖ Provide mass customization and creative, aggressive marketing programs, and

❖ Understand and respond innovatively to their changing requirements

For our suppliers we will strive to:

❖ Foster mutually beneficial long-term strategic partnerships

❖ Consider all their attributes, not just price

❖ Utilize their capabilities to improve the total value chain

❖ Be objective and ethical in all our business dealings

For our associates, we will strive to:

❖ Have management lead by example

❖ Provide an environment which is positive, reality-based, and reinforces initiative

❖ Encourage experimentation, attentive listening, and risk taking

❖ Nurture diversity and variety of thought

❖ Offer a continuous learning environment

❖ Empower associates to the fullest extent with accountability

❖ Offer equal opportunity for career growth and advancement

❖ Provide rewards and opportunities which recognize associate contributions

❖ Develop a global view of customers, consumers, vendors, and opportunities

For our communities and governments, we will strive to:

❖ Support the economy and general welfare

❖ Conduct business in an ethical and responsible manner

- ✦ Encourage associates to participate actively in community affairs
- ✦ Communicate the many benefits of the free enterprise system, and
- ✦ Be a good corporate citizen

For our shareholders, we will strive to:

- ✦ Provide an attractive and consistent return on investment
- ✦ Continuously improve our people, products, processes, plans, and programs
- ✦ Optimize and utilize the full resources of Rubbermaid
- ✦ Provide superior management with depth and continuity
- ✦ Provide leadership which is proactive and demands excellence
- ✦ Balance our incremental and leap growth strategies
- ✦ Communicate financial performance effectively on a timely basis

For all our stakeholders, we will strive to:

- ✦ Ensure that every Rubbermaid associate acts with high integrity and observes our shared ethical standards

Vision and Mission

Rubbermaid's vision is to grow as a leading global business by creating the best value solutions as defined by our customers and consumers.

Our mission is to be the leading marketer under our global umbrella brands of products and services which are responsive to consumer needs and trends and make life more productive and enjoyable. We will achieve this mission by creating the best value for the consumer, commercial, and industrial markets.

We will think, plan, and manage strategically to execute a balanced combination of the following Incremental and Leap Avenues of Growth.

Incremental Avenues of Growth

❖ *Continuous Value Improvement*—Make today's products a better value

❖ *Market Penetration*—Creatively sell more current products and enter emerging distribution channels

❖ *Product Enhancement*—Upgrade and revitalize our current product designs and features

❖ *Product Line Extensions*—Expand our current product lines

❖ *Licensing*—Leverage our strengths and those of strategic partners

❖ *New Products*—Add new product lines to strengthen current market positions

Leap Avenues of Growth

❖ *New Markets*—Enter new core businesses where our strengths can create leadership value positions

❖ *New Technology*—Aggressively apply new materials and processes to create innovative new products

❖ *Global Expansion*—Think and compete internationally

❖ *Service*—Make our products easy to buy, easy to handle, and easy to sell

❖ *Acquisitions*—Acquire selected complementary businesses

❖ *Joint Ventures and Alliances*—Capitalize upon synergistic expertise

Incremental and Leap Avenues of Growth

❖ *Rubbermaid Resources*—Share all of Rubbermaid's unmatchable resources to leverage the technology and knowledge existing within the Company for growth and global competitiveness.

Objectives

Associate Objectives Are To:

❖ Stress open and frequent communications

❖ Invest consistently in growing our capabilities

- Train associates to achieve Continuous Value Improvement and Creative Innovation goals
- Create a global competitive capability
- Recognize, reinforce and reward teamwork, results and excellence

Growth Objectives Are To:

- Double sales every five years
- Maintain 33% of yearly sales from new products introduced in the previous five-year period
- Enter a new market every 12 to 18 months
- Attain more than 30 percent of sales outside the United States by the year 2000
- Create leading destination brands worldwide

COMPANY | *National Register Inc.*

STATEMENT | **National Register Inc.**
Mission Statement

National Register is dedicated to discerning, solving, and supporting the needs of our clients in the areas of mailing, and shipping in the order fulfillment process. We are devoted to the use of technology to improve efficiencies in shipping and mailing through providing carrier management systems that link with the rest of the organization. We are committed to providing our clients with the highest level of quality service, support, and ideas carried out in a continuing atmosphere of excellence.

Profit Objectives Are To:

❖ Double earnings per share every five years

❖ Achieve a 13.5% return on assets employed

❖ Improve our value position by $335 million by 1998·
Utilize profits for people and productivity improvement,
growth, and dividends

Leadership Objectives Are To:

❖ Achieve and maintain the leading value position

❖ Create compelling competitive advantages in each marketing mix element

❖ Be proactive on environmental and safety issues

❖ Embrace the process of change and make it an integral
part of the corporate culture

CORPORATE DESCRIPTION

National Register Inc. has been providing shipping and mailing solutions since 1976. The Company's PC-based shipping and manifesting system is installed throughout the United States, Canada, and Mexico. NRI employs 31 people primarily at its offices in Lakewood, Colorado.

ADDRESS   6900 W. Jefferson Ave.
Lakewood, CO   80235-2310

SOURCE   Company representative

❧ Be recognized for excellence by customers, suppliers, the media, governments, communities, financial constituencies, and our associates

Technological Objectives Are To:

❧ Utilize the basic and applied research and technology capabilities of supplier partners

❧ Enhance our applied research capabilities

❧ Encourage experimentation and learning by all associates

❧ Use common global management information systems as a competitive advantage

Competency Objectives Are To:

❧ Recognize and strengthen the core competencies of:

— Corporate associates

— Division associates

— Centralized capabilities

— Business teams

— Project, process, partner, and self-directed teams

Shareholder Objectives Are To:

❧ Consistently create wealth on a sustainable long-term basis

❧ Deliver a superior 20% return on equity

❧ Communicate the Company's performance clearly and in a timely fashion

© 1994 Rubbermaid Incorporated

ADDRESS   1147 Akron Rd.
P. O. Box 6000
Wooster, OH 44691-6000

INDUSTRY CATEGORY   Consumer Goods and Services

CORPORATE DESCRIPTION
Rubbermaid produces plastic products for the consumer, institutional, office products, agricultural, and industrial markets.
(From the 1993 *Annual Report.*)

In 1994, Fortune magazine announced that Rubbermaid had been ranked the Most Admired Corporation in America by the 10,000 senior executives, outside directors, and financial analysts who participated in the publication's 12th annual Corporate Reputations Survey.

SIZE REVENUES $1,960,207,000 as of 1993

NUMBER OF EMPLOYEES   11,978 as of 1993

SOURCES   1993 *Annual Report;* "Rubbermaid® Philosophy, Management Principles, Vision & Mission, Objectives" company publication (June, 1994)

◆ ◆ ◆ ◆ ◆ ◆ ◆

COMPANY │ *Ryder System, Inc.*

STATEMENT │ **Ryder's Vision Statement**
Ryder will serve its customers with the best value in logistics and transportation solutions around the world or around the corner.

ADDRESS   3600 N.W. 82 Ave.
Miami, FL 33166

INDUSTRY CATEGORY   Transportation

CORPORATE DESCRIPTION
Ryder System is an international company which provides highway transportation services throughout the United States and in Canada, Puerto Rico, the United Kingdom, Germany and Poland.

SIZE REVENUES $4,217,030,000 as of 1993

NUMBER OF EMPLOYEES   39,235 as of June 30, 1994

SOURCE   *1993 Annual Report*

◆ ◆ ◆ ◆ ◆ ◆ ◆

COMPANY | *Rykoff-Sexton, Inc.*

STATEMENT | **MISSION STATEMENT**
◈ Be the leader in our industry by providing the finest people, products and services.
◈ Assist our customers to be successful by building long-term business relationships through our people, proven quality products, demonstrated integrity and superior service.
◈ Have a business environment, based on sincerity of purpose, for all of our people that provides opportunity for growth and advancement as a reward for excellence and individual accomplishments.
◈ Achieve for our shareholders a premium return on investment through optimal utilization of capital and human resources.

❖ Continue our tradition: All who come here to trade fairly, whether to buy or to sell, are always welcome.

ADDRESS   761 Terminal St.
Los Angeles, CA 90021

INDUSTRY CATEGORY   Food/Beverage

CORPORATE DESCRIPTION
Established in 1911, Rykoff-Sexton, Inc. is a leading manufacturer and distributor of high quality foods and related non-food products and services for the foodservice industry throughout the United States.

The Company's products and services are sold wherever food is prepared and consumed away from home. Customers include restaurants, industrial cafeterias, health care facilities, schools and colleges, hotels, airlines, membership warehouse stores and other segments of the travel and leisure markets.

SIZE REVENUES $1,524,672,000 (net sales) as of 1994

NUMBER OF EMPLOYEES   Not available

SOURCE   *1994 Annual Report*

COMPANY | *Safety-Kleen Corporation*

STATEMENT | Corporate Mission

"To maximize the value of the Company's unique marketing, distribution, and recycling capabilities by becoming the world's leading specialty reclaimer of hazardous and quasi-hazardous automotive and industrial fluids, with primary emphasis placed on serving the needs of the small quantity generator of these fluids."

ADDRESS | 1000 Randall Rd
Elgin, IL 60123

INDUSTRY CATEGORY Industrial, Specialized

CORPORATE DESCRIPTION
Safety-Kleen is the world's largest recycler of automotive and industrial hazardous and non-hazardous fluids. The Company provides safe and environmentally responsible services that are targeted primarily at small quantity generators of such fluids. The Company collects, processes and recovers contaminated fluids for reuse, or use in another manner that is in harmony with the environment.
[*Author's note:* Safety-Kleen provided the following statement]
"The mission statement was issued in 1987 when the company was almost exclusively a parts cleaner service company. The company's mission statement became the strategic focal point for subsequent action. Five years later, in 1992, Safety-Kleen achieved its stated mission. Our company has continued to build on this position in succeeding years."

SIZE REVENUES $795,508,000 as of 1993

NUMBER OF EMPLOYEES 6,600 as of 1993

SOURCE 1993 *Annual Report*

COMPANY | *San Francisco Federal Savings (SFFed Corp.)*

STATEMENT | **A Unique Factor: Our Mission Statement**

The key to success for businesses whose products and services are similar, is to be *different* from the others. To create that distinguishing characteristic, that unique factor that makes the statement, "We are a step ahead. We are leaders in our industry."

While products, services, pricing and promotion are all important elements, our future success depends on identifying and living up to the unique promises our Mission Statement outlines below:

"San Francisco Federal is committed to being a high performance regional financial company offering real estate financing, retail deposit services, and related products. We are dedicated to providing superior service and quality products to meet the financial needs of our customers, now and in the future.

"Our success, as judged by our customers, employees and shareholders, will be measured by our profits, quality of service, standards of business ethics, innovation, and contributions to the communities we serve."

We believe that strict adherence to the spirit contained in this statement will set us apart from our competition.

This Mission Statement tells people who we are and what we stand for. It creates a unique place for San Francisco Federal in the minds of the public. In short, at San Francisco Federal:

"Nobody does it better"

This positioning statement is more than a slogan. For us, it's a commitment to our customers. It means we will do our jobs well. It means we will respect our customers as individuals and treat them in a manner we would like to be treated. It means customers can look to us for financial expertise and an uncompromising attitude of personal performance.

ADDRESS 88 Kearny St.
San Francisco, CA 94108-5591

INDUSTRY CATEGORY Banking

CORPORATE DESCRIPTION
SFFed Corp. is the holding company for San Francisco Federal Savings and Loan Association, a federally chartered FDIC-insured institution with $3.4 billion in assets (as of 1993). The Association has 35 savings branches and 16 loan centers located throughout Northern and Central California.

SIZE REVENUES $9,894,000 (net income) as of 1993

NUMBER OF EMPLOYEES 577 as of 1993

SOURCE *1993 Annual Report*

♦ ♦ ♦ ♦ ♦ ♦ ♦

COMPANY | *Sanwa Bank*

STATEMENT | **Sanwa Bank California**
VISION STATEMENT
"THE BEST QUALITY BANK IN THE U. S."
Sanwa Bank California intends to become the best quality bank in the U. S.:
- To embody the highest standards of quality
- To be a firm our peers want to emulate
- To have employees proud to be a "SanwaBanker"
- To have the public express "I want a Sanwa...[relationship]"

- To have our shareholder pleased with its investment
- To demonstrate superior management practices

While this won't be achieved easily or quickly, it reflects the breadth of the strides we intend and the depth of our commitment to completing those strides. We won't be an "also ran" in what we do and therefore cannot do everything. We can be the best at providing relationship-oriented financial services primarily among small- to medium-size commercial and retail customers in selected markets.

We'll be measured by common standards of profitability, efficiency and loan quality, and surpass peers on these measures. We will achieve distinction through the QUALITY of our organization and the services provided, the UNIQUENESS of our approach to meeting financial needs and the TEAMWORK which binds our diverse staff to this common purpose.

QUALITY

Everything we do will portray an image of high quality. Sanwa won't be significantly bigger until we're better. We'll focus on building strength in markets where we are now represented by:

- Improving sustainable profits while maintaining our relative market presence
- Concentrating on markets where we have competence
- Leveraging our international affiliations to become known in the Western U. S. as the bank to use if you want to do business in or from the Pacific Rim
- Either strengthening or exiting areas of weakness

The heart of our quality will be our people and the professional manner in which they represent the Bank in serving customers and colleagues. To support this:

- We will invest in the development of our people to assure they are top quality
- Excellence of conduct, performance and business production will be encouraged, expected and rewarded

◈ Creativity will be encouraged

◈ Individual performance which reflects poorly on the Bank or inhibits Bank performance will not be accepted

Investment in technology will be made to enable us to excel at managing the information which is vital to our business success and underpins quality customer service.

UNIQUENESS

We will not be limited by perceptions of what is traditional in banking. We will:

◈ Chart innovative—even revolutionary—paths to success

◈ Strive to be perceived as unique in the ways we do business

Our vision will not be limited by declaring that we are a retail bank or a commercial bank. We envision:

◈ Being a major regional bank that stays close to and responsive to its customers

◈ Being community bank–oriented in our style and quality of service, combined with the strength of one of the largest banks in the world

◈ Actively supporting the communities we serve

TEAMWORK

We benefit from a diversity of talents and viewpoints. This diversity will be unified to build strength upon strength. Open communication, sharing of ideas, and mutual support will be hallmarks of our management style.

While our Parent provides us with the pride of worldwide strength, the Sanwa Team is self-sufficient and our success will be self-determined.

ADDRESS   601 S. Figueroa St.
Los Angeles, CA 90017

INDUSTRY CATEGORY   Banking

CORPORATE DESCRIPTION

Sanwa Bank California is the largest overseas subsidiary of The Sanwa Bank, Limited. With $7.3 billion in assets, Sanwa Bank is the sixth largest and one of the best capitalized banks in the state. Sanwa offers both quality service and strength for businesses and consumers in over 100 communities from Sacramento to San Diego.

SIZE REVENUES $7,500,000,000 (assets) as of 1993

NUMBER OF EMPLOYEES   3,023 (full and part time) as of 1993

SOURCES   *1993 Annual Report*; company representative

◆　◆　◆　◆　◆　◆　◆

COMPANY | *SAS Institute Inc.*

STATEMENT | Our Mission and Philosophy

SAS Institute develops and maintains the SAS System for Information Delivery, the world's leading integrated system of hardware-independent software, as well as other software products. Our primary goal is to help the organizations we serve—in business, industry, education, and government— become the beneficiaries of advanced technology by providing software and services to help them meet their organizational goals. To this end, we are dedicated to:

❖ providing the most capable and reliable software in the industry

❖ devoting a significant portion of our human and financial resources to research and development

❖ establishing an uncommon commitment to customer service and support through a continuous dialogue with our worldwide community of users

❖ attracting and retaining the most talented people in the industry by providing the highest quality work environment where productivity, creativity, and personal and professional growth can flourish.

ADDRESS   SAS Campus Dr.
Cary, NC 27513

INDUSTRY CATEGORY   High Technology

CORPORATE DESCRIPTION

Incorporated in 1976, SAS Institute is one of the world's largest independent software companies. The Institute is devoted to the development, support and maintenance of its software and related services. The Institute's flagship product—the SAS® System—is an integrated suite of software for enterprise-wide information delivery.

SIZE REVENUES $420,300,000 (gross, worldwide) as of 1993

NUMBER OF EMPLOYEES   3,200 (worldwide) as of 1994

SOURCE   *1993 Annual Report*; "SAS Institute Inc. Company Backgrounder"

COMPANY | *Savannah Foods & Industries, Inc.*

STATEMENT | **SAVANNAH FOODS' VISION STATEMENT**
Savannah Foods' vision is to strive for excellence in products, service, and profitability through honesty, integrity, respect for the individual and concern for those we serve.

ADDRESS   2 E. Bryan St.
P. O. Box 339
Savannah, GA 31402-0339

INDUSTRY CATEGORY   Food/Beverage

CORPORATE DESCRIPTION
Savannah Foods & Industries, Inc., one of the nation's largest refined cane and beet sugar producers, markets products primarily in the eastern half of the United States under the labels Dixie Crystals®, Evercane®, Colonial®, and Pioneer®, as well as private and control labels.

Savannah Foods operates cane sugar refineries in Georgia, Florida, and Louisiana, four sugar beet processing plants in Michigan, a sugar beet processing plant in Ohio, and a raw sugar mill in Louisiana.

SIZE REVENUES $1,123,000,000 as of 1993

NUMBER OF EMPLOYEES   2,244 as of 1993

SOURCES   *1992 Annual Report;* "The Fortune 500," *Fortune* 129, no. 8 (April 8, 1994); company representative

COMPANY | *Schwab (The Charles Schwab Corporation)*

STATEMENT | **The Mission Statement For Our Company**

Our mission as a company is to serve the needs of investors. We have all kinds of customers: individuals, professional money managers, companies and their employees. We know our customers have many different needs in meeting their own financial goals. We will focus our resources on the financial services that best meet our customers' needs, whether they are transactional, informational, custodial services, or something new. We will strive to deliver to our customers:

❧ High quality, reliable, ethical products and services at a fair price,

❧ Superior service from the best team of trained, motivated and ethical employees, supported by the best technology,

❧ A strong company, financially viable under any circumstance.

ADDRESS 101 Montgomery St.
San Francisco, CA 94104

INDUSTRY CATEGORY Financial Investment services

CORPORATE DESCRIPTION

The Charles Schwab Corporation provides financial services for more than 2 million investors with $66 billion in assets.

SIZE REVENUES $965,000,000 as of 1993

NUMBER OF EMPLOYEES 6,500 as of 1993

SOURCES *1992 Annual Report*; "The Fortune Service 500," *Fortune* 129, no. 11 (May 30, 1994)

COMPANY | *Scripps (The E. W. Scripps Company)*

STATEMENT | **Mission**

The Company aims at excellence in the products and services it produces and responsible service to the communities in which it operates. Its purpose is to engage in successful, growing enterprises in the fields of information and entertainment. The Company intends to expand, to develop and acquire new products and services and to pursue new market opportunities. Its focus shall be long-term growth for the benefit of its stockholders and employees.

ADDRESS   P. O. Box 5380
Cincinnati, OH 45201

INDUSTRY CATEGORY   Media/Printing/Publishing

CORPORATE DESCRIPTION

The E. W. Scripps Company is a diversified media company that operates 19 daily newspapers with aggregate circulation of 1.3 million daily and 1.4 million Sunday, 9 television stations, and cable television systems in 10 states with 718,000 basic subscribers. Through its emerging entertainment division, the Company operates 2 television production companies, a 24-hour cable channel (The Home & Garden Television Network), and United Media, a worldwide syndicator and licensor of newspaper features and comics.

SIZE REVENUES $1,205,771,000 as of 1993

NUMBER OF EMPLOYEES   7,900 as of December 31, 1993

SOURCE   *1993 Annual Report*

COMPANY | *Sensormatic*

STATEMENT | **Mission Statement**

Our mission is to strengthen our position as the world leader in the design, production, marketing, sales, and servicing of electronic loss prevention systems for the retail industry. It is also our mission to become a leading worldwide provider of electronic loss prevention and asset control systems for the commercial and industrial marketplace and a significant supplier of electronic loss prevention systems to government agencies. Our mission will be achieved by providing superior customer service and unique, high quality products which will enhance customer productivity and profitability. Our products will be designed and manufactured at the lowest cost, consistent with our customers' needs and requirements.

We will accomplish this mission while attaining superior profitability which will fund our continued rapid growth.

We are committed to maintain the Sensormatic culture of dedicated, spirited and ethical performance while fulfilling our responsibilities to:

❖ Serve our <u>customers</u> well, driven by the need to stay close to, anticipate, listen and respond to their changing requirements while providing products and services of superior quality.

❖ Serve our <u>shareholders</u> by preserving and building the value of the shareholders' investment.

❖ Serve our <u>employees</u> by creating an environment where they can contribute, learn, grow and advance based on merit.

❖ Serve the business, social and cultural needs of the <u>communities</u> in which we operate.

ADDRESS   500 N.W. 12th Ave.
Deerfield Beach, FL 33442-1795

INDUSTRY CATEGORY   Electronics

CORPORATE DESCRIPTION
Sensormatic is a fully integrated market-driven company which develops, manufactures, sells, and services electronic loss prevention and asset control systems on a worldwide basis to the retail and industrial marketplace, as well as government agencies.

SIZE REVENUES $656,000,000 as of June 30, 1994

NUMBER OF EMPLOYEES   5,000 as of June 30, 1994

SOURCE   Company representative

◆ ◆ ◆ ◆ ◆ ◆ ◆

COMPANY | *Shaklee U. S., Inc.*

STATEMENT | **Mission Statement**
Shaklee Multi-Level Marketing
Companies, Worldwide

We are deeply committed to being the best Multi-level Direct Selling Company in the world. We feel strongly that our success is due to our passion for sharing the Shaklee Opportunity. Specifically:

❖ We offer the most attractive earning and lifestyle opportunity that has, at its core, the pride of a career with a conscience.

❖ We proudly manufacture and distribute exciting-to-talk-about products that are backed by scientific integrity and are in harmony with nature and good health.

❖ We stay true to the ethics of our unique and highly valued philosophy of the Golden Rule.

❖ We do whatever it takes to ensure superior Customer Service.

❖ We foster a culture of excellence and fun, highly supportive of employee growth and development.

All of this results in a growing number of distributors worldwide, creating financial success for our field, our employees, and our companies.

ADDRESS   444 Market St.
San Francisco, CA 94111

INDUSTRY CATEGORY   Consumer Goods and Services

CORPORATE DESCRIPTION

Shaklee Corporation, founded in 1956, is a consumer products company with two main operating divisions, multilevel marketing under the Shaklee name and direct mail products sold through Bear Creek Corporation.

Shaklee Corporation manufactures and distributes products through multilevel operations in the U. S., Canada, Mexico, Taiwan and Malaysia. As one of the oldest and most respected multilevel marketers, Shaklee product lines include nutritional supplements, personal care and household products as well as home water treatment products. Not available in stores, products are sold directly to consumers by a network of independent distributors.

SIZE REVENUES $459,000,000 as of 1993

NUMBER OF EMPLOYEES   700 (at corporate office) as of 1994

SOURCE   Company representative

COMPANY | *Shell Chemical Company*

STATEMENT | **SHELL Chemical Company's Mission Statement**

Shell Chemical Company's mission is to be a leading chemical company by:

❥ Growing with our customers as their preferred supplier.

❥ Utilizing and building the skills and creativity of our people.

❥ Building on our strengths in markets, technology and feedstocks.

ADDRESS   One Shell Plaza
P. O. Box 2463
Houston, TX 77252

INDUSTRY CATEGORY   Oil and Gas

CORPORATE DESCRIPTION
Shell Chemical Company is a fully integrated manufacturer and supplier of basic industrial chemicals and performance products.

SIZE REVENUES $3,598,000,000 as of 1993

NUMBER OF EMPLOYEES   5,500 as of 1993

SOURCE   Company representative

STATEMENT | **THE NEW SKYWEST AIRLINES VISION**

Working together to be the airline of choice

DEFINING STATEMENTS

1. *Guiding principles...A Preferred Airline*

A. Achieve the highest quality; we provide honest, courteous, professional service that exceeds customer expectations.

B. Safe, reliable, and on time; Every flight operates as scheduled.

C. Frequency and convenience; we provide well timed flights to meet the needs of both connecting and local passengers.

2. *Guiding principle...A Preferred Employer*

A. Job satisfaction; we maintain a work environment characterized by meaningful challenge, positive expectation and rewards which are consistent with performance.

B. Involved, empowered employees; our employees are involved in decisions which affect their job duties and work environment, as well as being supported and properly equipped to identify and achieve customer satisfaction.

C. Developing people; we assist our employees with career development including education, training and advancement opportunity consistent with the Company's needs and the employee's interest and ability.

3. *Guiding principle...A Preferred Investment*

A. Cost efficient airline; our overall cost of providing quality service is among the lowest in the industry.

B. Recognizing opportunity; we foster innovation in discovering better ways to maximize our existing opportunities and recognize, create and seize new opportunities in the Airline industry.

C. Optimum utilization of assets; we make the best possible use of all resources.

ADDRESS   444 S. River Rd.
St. George, UT 84770

INDUSTRY CATEGORY   Transportation

CORPORATE DESCRIPTION
SkyWest Airlines, a large regional airline operating as a Delta Connection carrier, offers scheduled passenger and cargo air services to 42 cities in nine western states and completes over 500 flights daily.

SkyWest, Inc. is the holding company for SkyWest Airlines. Revenue and Employee statistics listed here are for SkyWest Inc.

SIZE REVENUES $187,993,000 as of 1993

NUMBER OF EMPLOYEES   1,600 as of 1994

SOURCES   *1994 Annual Report*; company representative

◆ ◆ ◆ ◆ ◆ ◆ ◆

COMPANY | *Sonoco Products Company*

STATEMENT | **Mission Statement:**
Sonoco will be a customer-focused, global packaging leader, recognized for superior quality and high-performance results. Integrity and a commitment to excellence will be the hallmark of our culture.

| **Strategy Statement:**
We will achieve this mission by satisfying customers, creating value through the consistent delivery of products and services which clearly meet the present and future needs of our customers worldwide.

Primary Goals:

Safety: We will maintain a safe, injury-free work place.

Customer Satisfaction: We will understand the present and future requirements and expectations of our customers and provide value that meets or exceeds these expectations.

Shareholder Value: We will improve shareholder value by growing after-tax earnings 10%–15% or more annually, and increase dividends as the Company grows.

Market Leadership: We will be a leading supplier in all markets served.

Technology Leadership: We will be recognized for technology leadership in the markets we serve and use our technology to consistently maintain competitive advantage.

Integrity: We will be characterized by the trust and confidence we share with our customers, our employees, our shareholders, our communities and our suppliers.

COMPANY | *Nypro Inc.*

STATEMENT | **Our Mission:**

To be the best in the world in precision plastics injection molding...creating value for our customers, employees, and communities.

CORPORATE DESCRIPTION

Nypro Inc. and certain of its subsidiaries and affiliates manufacture custom injection molded components and assemble various products. In addition, a subsidiary of the Company designs, builds, and markets ro-

Organizational Effectiveness: We will be well managed and maintain a highly motivated, qualified workforce, providing all employees with continuous training and the guidance, resources, support, recognition and rewards to accomplish continuous improvement.

Environmental Stewardship: We will take seriously our responsibility to protect the environment in which we work and live, and will conduct our business in accordance with all legal requirements and ethical responsibilities, using scientific knowledge, technical innovation and sound environmental management practices.

Cost Effectiveness: We will always be committed to cost effectiveness and to continuous cost reduction in all areas of our business.

bots and material handling systems for use within the plastics injection molding industry. 1994 sales including joint ventures approached $200 million. Net profits were $10,826,000. Nypro has over 2,000 employees.

ADDRESS   101 Union St.
                 Clinton, MA 01510

SOURCE   *1994 Annual Report*

Supporting Principles:

Participation: We will nurture an atmosphere of teamwork, built around loyal, dedicated employees who are given the opportunity to participate in the decision-making process related to their jobs, and who are equipped with the training, resources and authority to act.

Creativity: We will foster an environment of creativity, innovation and personal ownership, taking well-calculated risks to continuously improve existing businesses and to generate new products and services.

Continuous Improvement: Every employee will be involved in the never-ending improvement of our products, services and processes.

Fact-Based Decision-Making: We will base our decisions on facts and not opinions.

Cross-Functional Linkage: We will allocate, align and monitor staff resources and line operating personnel, based on customer-driven priorities, to work as a team towards solving problems and improving processes, products and services.

Process Management: We will view our jobs as value-adding processes and adopt the approach of process improvement, using analytical measurement and statistical techniques.

Internal/External Customers: We will focus on meeting the needs of our internal and external customers; both are essential and inseparable.

ADDRESS   P. O. Box 160
N. Second St.
Hartsville, SC 29550-0160

INDUSTRY CATEGORY   Manufacturing

CORPORATE DESCRIPTION
Sonoco is a major packaging manufacturer serving a wide variety of consumer and industrial markets with containers and carriers made

from paper, plastic, metal and wood. Sonoco has a high degree of vertical integration, producing most of its adhesives, paperboard and paper converting machinery.

SIZE REVENUES $1,947,000,000 as of 1993

NUMBER OF EMPLOYEES   17,000 (worldwide) as of 1993

SOURCES   *1992 Annual Report*, "The Fortune 500," *Fortune* 129, no. 8 (April 8, 1994)

◆ ◆ ◆ ◆ ◆ ◆ ◆

COMPANY | *Southern California Edison Company*

STATEMENT | Vision and Values
Our Vision

We will be a great company that provides business and regional leadership.

Business Leadership: We will set the national standard of performance among utilities. We will provide our customers cost-competitive, reliable electricity; energy-saving services; and creative solutions to their energy needs.

Regional Leadership: We will anticipate and address the challenges of economic competitiveness and environment quality facing our customers and communities. As a public utility, we are committed to helping Southern California prosper as an excellent place to live and do business.

Challenge:

We will challenge ourselves to continuously improve our performance and constantly renew our understanding of our changing business.

Candor:

We will conduct ourselves with honesty, openness and integrity in all our relationships.

Commitment:

We will achieve:

- Value for our customers
- Leadership for our community and environment
- Excellence as a team
- Shared purpose with regulators, and
- Value for our shareholders

ADDRESS   P. O. Box 800
8631 Rush St.
Rosemead, CA 91770

INDUSTRY CATEGORY   Utility

CORPORATE DESCRIPTION

Southern California Edison Company is the nation's second-largest electric utility, providing service to customers in Central and Southern California.

SIZE REVENUES $7,800,000,000 as of 1993

NUMBER OF EMPLOYEES   17,000 as of 1993

SOURCE   *1993 Annual Report*

OUR BUSINESS IS CUSTOMER SATISFACTION

CORE VALUES

The Southern Company is committed to the highest ethical standards. We pledge integrity, trust, and candor in our business relationships. Through our actions, we will be worthy of public confidence—both as individuals and as a company.

CUSTOMER COMMITMENT

Our commitment to our customers will be marked by quality, value, dependability, and technical excellence. We intend to guarantee the highest level of customer satisfaction with world-class service that makes our company the competitive choice. Through research and listening, we will thoroughly understand our customers' needs, and we will meet their expectations.

EMPLOYEE ACHIEVEMENT

We will encourage employees to be innovative, aggressive team players—taking personal responsibility to better satisfy customers, solve problems, and improve business results. For their initiative and accomplishments, employees will earn recognition, professional satisfaction, and financial reward.

The Southern Company respects the dignity of each employee and emphasizes strongly the importance of a safe work place. The company is committed to providing opportunities for individual fulfillment and professional development.

BUSINESS DIMENSIONS

The Southern Company will continue to be a leading supplier of energy and energy services. We will be market-driven—the needs of our customers will be the driving force in all our decisions. Our business units will maximize the efficiencies and economies available to them as part of The

Southern Company. We will prudently expand electric sales in traditional markets and compete in the independent power business. We will make sound acquisitions related to our energy businesses.

We will provide for the future energy needs of our customers by building and owning new power supply facilities, supplemented by purchases from others as appropriate. We will build and maintain our electric system to the highest practical standards of quality.

As a company that takes actions based on the needs of its markets, we will expand our sales "beyond the meter"—offering a range of energy products and related services. We will explore all avenues to profitably increase our revenues.

As the regulation of our business changes, we will work to balance and protect the interests of our customers and shareholders. Where competition is permitted, we will aggressively pursue sustainable, profitable market share. We will succeed in a more competitive environment by developing the necessary cost structures, product quality, skills, and culture.

We will build relationships with our regulators that are based on mutual trust and respect and that permit innovative approaches to the pricing and marketing of our products.

We will establish partnerships with other businesses that will allow us to offer our customers technologies to improve energy efficiency.

INVESTOR VALUE

The Southern Company will seek to provide investors with long-term appreciation and dividend growth—consistently delivering returns on investment that are in the upper range as compared with similar companies. Growth in earnings will come by achieving our allowed rates of return and by profitably participating in free-market activities. We will become a premier investment through gains derived from new activities and by sharing with customers and stockholders the productivity improvements in our traditional business.

BUSINESS EXCELLENCE

Throughout The Southern Company, we will encourage innovation, reward initiative, build teamwork, and focus on business results. We will minimize the number of management layers between the top and the front lines, creating broader spans of control and improved communication. Decision making will be pushed downward, and employees will be given greater individual responsibility, authority, and accountability. They will be expected to make decisions as if the business were their own.

Employees will be appropriately informed and trained in vital aspects of the business so that they fully understand the consequences of their actions and decisions. We will develop leaders from within our ranks and provide career opportunities throughout the company.

Our communications will be honest, open, timely, and widely shared.

COMMUNITY ENHANCEMENT

The Southern Company will enhance the standard of living, the quality of life, and the economic success of the communities we serve. As a corporate citizen, we will improve the welfare of our communities and encourage broad community involvement by our employees.

ENVIRONMENTAL COMMITMENT

We affirm the importance of protecting the environment and making wise use of our natural resources. We will set and achieve environmental goals that are in concert with other goals needed to further the well-being of society.

ADDRESS   64 Perimeter Center E.
Atlanta, GA 30346-6401

INDUSTRY CATEGORY   Utility

CORPORATE DESCRIPTION

The Southern Company is the parent firm of one of the nation's largest investor-owned electric utility groups. The company includes five utilities—Alabama Power, Georgia Power, Gulf Power, Mississippi Power, and Savannah Electric—as well as Southern Company Services, Southern Electric International, and Southern Nuclear.

The Southern Company supplies energy to customers in most of Alabama and Georgia, the panhandle of Florida, and Southeastern Mississippi. The company's 255 generating units have a total capacity of 29.5 million kilowatts. Some 26,000 miles of transmission lines and 130,000 miles of distribution lines carry electricity across the 120,000-square-mile service area.

SIZE REVENUES $8,489,146,000 as of 1993

NUMBER OF EMPLOYEES   28,743 as of year-end 1993

SOURCE   *1993 Annual Report*

COMPANY | *Southern Pacific Rail Corporation*

STATEMENT | **MISSION STATEMENT**

Southern Pacific Lines' mission is to anticipate and satisfy the requirements of its customers for highly responsive and cost-effective transportation and distribution services.

ADDRESS   One Market Plaza, Room 950
San Francisco, CA 94105

INDUSTRY CATEGORY   Transportation

CORPORATE DESCRIPTION

Southern Pacific Rail Corporation, through the integrated railroad network of its principal subsidiaries, transports freight in the Western and Southwestern United States. The Company's five main routes cover 15 states over approximately 15,000 miles of track.

Its rail lines serve most West Coast ports and large Western population centers; connect with Eastern railroads at all major gateways; and reach the principal Gulf Coast ports south from Chicago and east from the Los Angeles Basin. SP also has six gateways into Mexico, more than any other U. S. railroad.

The Company is the leading U. S. rail carrier of containerized freight, and its Intermodal Container Transfer Facility in Southern California is the nation's largest international container yard.

SIZE REVENUES $2,900,000,000 as of 1993

NUMBER OF EMPLOYEES   18,982 as of 1993

SOURCE   *1993 Annual Report*

COMPANY | *SouthTrust Corporation*

STATEMENT | **SOUTHTRUST CORPORATION**
MISSION STATEMENT

As a high-performing Southeastern regional bank holding company, our mission is to offer banking and specialized financial services to customers found in select geographic markets and market segments. To attain a superior return for our shareholders through quality earnings growth, we will distinguish ourselves by our excellence in—

- Customer Service
- Employee and Team Performance
- Risk Management
- Local Leadership
- Business Ethics and
- Community Involvement

ADDRESS   P. O. Box 2554
Birmingham, AL 35290

INDUSTRY CATEGORY   Banking

CORPORATE DESCRIPTION
SouthTrust Corporation, a multibank holding company with headquarters in Birmingham, Alabama, currently owns 40 banks and several bank-related affiliates in Alabama, Florida, Georgia, North Carolina, South Carolina, and Tennessee. The banks serve their customers from 400 offices located throughout the six-state area.

SIZE REVENUES $150,535,000 (net income) as of 1993

NUMBER OF EMPLOYEES   7,243 as of June, 1994

SOURCE   *1993 Annual Report*

COMPANY | *Southwest Airlines Co.*

STATEMENT | **The Mission Of Southwest Airlines**

The mission of Southwest Airlines is dedication to the highest quality of Customer Service delivered with a sense of warmth, friendliness, individual pride, and Company Spirit.

To Our Employees

We are committed to provide our employees a stable work environment with equal opportunity for learning and personal growth. Creativity and innovation are encouraged for improving the effectiveness of Southwest Airlines. Above all, employees will be provided the same concern, respect, and caring attitude within the organization that they are expected to share externally with every Southwest Customer. (January 1988)

ADDRESS   P. O. Box 36611
Dallas, TX 75235-1611

INDUSTRY CATEGORY   Transportation

CORPORATE DESCRIPTION

Southwest Airlines Co. is the nation's low fare, high Customer Satisfaction airline. It primarily serves shorthaul city pairs, providing single class air transportation, which targets the business commuter as well as leisure travelers. The Company, incorporated in Texas, commenced Customer Service on June 18, 1971 with three Boeing 737 aircraft serving three Texas cities—Dallas, Houston, and San Antonio. At yearend 1993, Southwest, together with newly acquired Morris Air, operated 178 Boeing 737 aircraft and provided service to 52 airports in 51 cities principally in the midwestern, southwestern, and western regions of the United States.

SIZE REVENUES $2,296,673,000 as of 1993

NUMBER OF EMPLOYEES   16,000 as of 1994

SOURCES   *1993 Annual Report*; company representative

◆ ◆ ◆ ◆ ◆ ◆ ◆

COMPANY │ *SpaceLabs Medical, Inc.*

STATEMENT │ SpaceLabs Medical

In business, success is best attained when there is commonality of purpose. SpaceLabs Medical is committed to accomplishing our mission guided by a framework of shared principles.

MISSION STATEMENT

SpaceLabs Medical's mission is to be the leading worldwide provider of quality, cost-effective systems that gather, analyze, and present clinical information beneficial to the delivery of healthcare.

CORPORATE VALUES

Respect for individuals and development of their potential
Excellence in product quality and customer service
The importance of innovation
The spirit of persistence and entrepreneurism
The power of teamwork
The importance of ethical behavior
Sound financial performance
The urgency of today and the promise of the future

OPERATING PHILOSOPHY

Understand and support SpaceLabs Medical's mission, priorities, and Corporate Values
Set clear objectives, plan well, prioritize, measure progress, reassess as needed

Practice systematic and continuous improvement to be the best at what we do

Align personal career objectives with the long-term needs of the corporation

Accept responsibility, admit mistakes, learn, and improve as a result

Manage financial resources in the best interest of the corporation

Reduce politics, bureaucracy, and gamesmanship

Emphasize fundamentals—keep it simple

Have fun

Our commitment to these principles will promote understanding, trust, and respect in the Organization as we pursue our business objectives.

(Signed)
Carl A. Lombardi
Chairman and Chief Executive Officer

ADDRESS   15220 N.E. 40th St.
P. O. Box 97013
Redmond, WA 98073-9713

INDUSTRY CATEGORY   Medical Products and Services

CORPORATE DESCRIPTION
SpaceLabs Medical is a leading worldwide supplier of patient monitoring equipment and clinical information systems.

SIZE REVENUES $248,659,000 as of 1993

NUMBER OF EMPLOYEES   1,575 as of February 18, 1994

SOURCE   *1993 Annual Report*

COMPANY | *SPX Corporation*

STATEMENT | **Statement of Mission and Driving Forces**

SPX Corporation's mission is to build long-term stakeholder value through global market leadership in specialty service tools and original equipment components for the motor vehicle industry.

In the global specialty service tool and equipment market, SPX is the world leader. The driving force behind this worldwide market leadership is the company's close partnership with its original equipment and aftermarket customers, and its unique ability to anticipate and meet customer needs.

SPX is also a leader in the global market for proprietary original equipment components. The driving force behind the company's leadership in this market is its design, production and technology capabilities, market position, and its differentiated quality products and services.

SPX intends to be the leader in each of the product/market sectors it serves and will provide its business units with the resources required for building value when:

- There is an acceptable contribution to building long-term value.
- The unit has a high probability of sustained growth in earnings and cash flow.
- There is a clear synergy or match between the investment and the company's strategic domestic and international markets.
- The unit has a strategic commitment to total quality, people empowerment, teamwork and continuous improvement.

The priority for new business opportunities for SPX units serving the specialty service tool product/market sector shall be to focus on identifying and meeting the new and emerging needs of key customer groups.

For SPX units serving the market for original equipment components and systems, the priority for new business opportunities shall be to focus on developing new markets, including customers and geographic regions, for the same or similar products and services.

Moving forward, SPX will consider value building opportunities that complement existing businesses and build on their strengths. SPX will also provide guidance and resources to assist its business units to identify their future strategies, providing human, material and informational resources as appropriate.

Values and Beliefs

Value building results from excellent customer service and continuous improvement. Ultimately, value is measured by:

- Exceptional customer satisfaction;
- Returns to the shareholders in excess of the company's cost of capital;
- The teamwork, motivation and commitment of SPX people;
- Quality commitment and long-term relationships with key suppliers; and
- The company's reputation as a fair and responsible corporate citizen.

We are committed to total quality in everything we do as evidenced by:

- Teamwork within and across all functional areas of the company;
- External and internal customer satisfaction;
- Focus on quality training, planning, and elimination of waste in all processes, products and services;
- Continuous improvement targets and monitoring for all processes, products and services; and

❖ Long-term customer and supplier cooperative partnerships.

**SPX people are the single most important element behind
successful implementation of our mission and strategies.
We therefore will provide an environment which:**

❖ Attracts and retains action oriented, creative, high
achieving people;

❖ Presents opportunities for personal development, satisfaction and teamwork, in an atmosphere characterized by
open communication and involvement;

❖ Provides recognition for excellence through innovation
and prudent risk taking; and

❖ Is founded upon teamwork, mutual respect, trust and
strict standards of legal and ethical conduct.

ADDRESS   700 Terrace Point Dr.
P. O. Box 3301
Muskegon, MI 49443-3301

INDUSTRY CATEGORY   Transportation

CORPORATE DESCRIPTION

SPX Corporation is a world leader in the design, manufacture, and
marketing of specialty service tools and original equipment components for the global motor vehicle industry. A Fortune 500 company,
SPX is headquartered in Muskegon, Michigan, where it was founded in 1911. The company has divisions and subsidiaries in 14 nations,
and employs nearly 8,600 people worldwide.

SIZE REVENUES $756,145,000 as of 1993

NUMBER OF EMPLOYEES   8,600 as of 1993

SOURCES   *1993 Annual Report;* "SPX Corporation Mission
Values Beliefs" company publication (March 15, 1994)

COMPANY | *St. Paul Bancorp, Inc.*

STATEMENT | **OUR MISSION**

At St. Paul Bancorp, Inc. our mission is to provide quality, innovative, and competitive consumer financial products and services to our customers and the communities we serve. We believe that our success is rooted in sound business practices coupled with respect and responsiveness to our customers, stockholders, employees and communities.

In support of this, we are committed to:

—Understand and respond to the financial needs of our customers and provide them with a variety of financial products to help realize their life's visions and dreams;

—Provide our stockholders with maximum value achieved through a steady focus on profitability and financial strength principally through the investment of our customers' deposits in quality real estate mortgages;

—Provide an equal opportunity for all employees to contribute to the bank in an environment which links pay and advancement to performance and accomplishments;

—Maintain an active partnership with our neighborhoods, characterized by a sensitivity to their housing, credit and savings needs, and the understanding that contributing to the community's well-being is vital to our future.

ADDRESS   6700 W. North Ave.
Chicago, IL 60635

INDUSTRY CATEGORY   Banking

CORPORATE DESCRIPTION

St. Paul Bancorp, Inc., is the holding company for St. Paul Federal Bank For Savings, the largest independent Illinois-based thrift.

Founded in 1889, St. Paul Federal offers a complete range of checking, savings, mortgage and consumer loan products and services through 52 offices in metropolitan Chicago.

SIZE REVENUES $41,387,000 (net income) as of 1993

NUMBER OF EMPLOYEES   1,046 (full-time equivalent) as of December 31, 1993

SOURCE   *1993 Annual Report*

◆　◆　◆　◆　◆　◆　◆

COMPANY | *Sta-Rite Industries*

STATEMENT | **STA-RITE MISSION STATEMENT**
Sta-Rite will be a leading innovative provider of water moving and improving equipment to the world. We will act aggressively to profitably grow our business, satisfy our customers and responsively meet the needs of our employees and the communities in which we do business.
(Water Systems Group Vision)

| **OUR VISION**
Profitably grow in the defined markets by increasing market share, introducing new products, and acquiring complementary product lines. It is our goal to be a global leader in our defined markets. We will be market-driven focusing on the following areas:
PRODUCT PERFORMANCE
CUSTOMER SERVICE

TECHNICAL SUPPORT/SERVICE

We will gain competitive advantage by building on existing strengths and developing new competencies. We will be the best-cost manufacturer.

ADDRESS   293 Wright St.
Delavan, WI 53115

INDUSTRY CATEGORY   Manufacturing

CORPORATE DESCRIPTION
Sta-Rite, headquartered in Delavan, Wisconsin, is a leading worldwide manufacturer of pumps and water processing equipment serving agricultural, residential and industrial markets. Its products are sold in 110 countries.

SIZE REVENUES $228,000,000 as of 1993

NUMBER OF EMPLOYEES   1,600 (worldwide) as of November, 1994

SOURCE   Company representative

STATEMENT | **the Mission**

A Commitment to Excellence

Standard Register's Forms Division serves the information and transactional needs of business with superior quality printed and associated products and services at a fair price.

We are a people-oriented, customer-focused organization:

—Committed to providing exceptional service to our customers.

—Committed to sustaining growth over the long term.

—Committed to showing appreciation to our dedicated employees.

—Committed to encouraging a free flow of information and an open style of management with emphasis on the team concept.

—Committed to contributing to the communities in which we operate.

—Committed to supporting and expanding on environmentally acceptable programs.

—Committed to providing an acceptable return for our corporate shareholders.

the Vision

Customer Driven Quality

Standard Register's vision is to be a customer-driven organization whose primary direction is to serve the information and transactional needs of business, focused on key market segments.

It is our purpose to increase revenues and profits by providing high quality, value-desired products and services through innovation and technological development.

Key to the achievement of the Company's growth plans and strategies is the Standard Register employee, who through his or her daily commitment to quality work and customer service, makes our vision a reality.

ADDRESS   600 Albany St.
Dayton, OH 45408

INDUSTRY CATEGORY   Business Products

CORPORATE DESCRIPTION
Standard Register serves the information and transaction needs of its customers as a leading provider of business forms, pressure sensitive labels, business equipment and systems, direct mail marketing materials and materials management software.

SIZE REVENUES $722,120,000 as of 1993

NUMBER OF EMPLOYEES   5,769 as of 1993

SOURCE   *1993 Annual Report*

COMPANY | *State Auto Insurance Companies*

STATEMENT | MISSION STATEMENT

Your Company's mission is to excel by providing a strong and stable insurance market and overwhelming service to its customers, both policyholders and agents.

We believe that regardless of the insurance industry cycles, responsible pricing and underwriting will bring about profit, consistent growth and opportunities for shareholders, agents, employees and policyholders.

ADDRESS   518 E. Broad St.
Columbus, OH 43216

INDUSTRY CATEGORY   Insurance

CORPORATE DESCRIPTION

State Auto Financial Corporation is a holding company located in Columbus, Ohio. The Company and its subsidiaries are affiliated with State Automobile Mutual Insurance Company, which owns 68% of the Company's common shares.

State Auto Property and Casualty (P&C) Insurance Company produces more than 99% of the revenues of State Auto Financial. Stateco Inc., a premium finance subsidiary, produces nominal revenues, and State Auto National Insurance Company, a specialty insurer, is a new company that began insurance operations in 1992. State Auto Life Insurance Company has no effect on State Auto Financial's earnings.

SIZE REVENUES $189,705,000 as of December 31, 1993

NUMBER OF EMPLOYEES   1,325 as of June 30, 1994

SOURCE   *1993 Annual Report*

COMPANY | *Stride Rite Corporation, Inc.*

STATEMENT | <u>The</u> <u>Values</u> <u>and</u> <u>Practices</u> <u>of</u>
<u>The</u> <u>Stride</u> <u>Rite</u> <u>Corporation</u>

The Stride Rite we will create builds on the foundation we have inherited, affirms the best of our Company's traditions and makes our policies and practices consistent with our principles.

Our goal is to sustain responsible financial success by achieving superior profitability. To accomplish this, we will build a Company where associates are proud and committed, and where all have an opportunity to contribute, learn, grow and advance based on merit. Associates will be respected, treated fairly, heard, involved and challenged. Above all, we want satisfaction from accomplishments, balanced personal and professional lives, to support the community, and to have fun in our endeavors.

We will make these goals a reality by being committed to new behaviors such as:

❧ <u>Diversity</u>: Valuing a diverse workforce and diversity in experience and perspectives. Diversity will be valued and honesty rewarded.

❧ <u>Recognition</u>: Recognizing individual and team contributions to our success. Recognition will be given to all who contribute—those who create and innovate as well as those who support the day-to-day business requirements.

❧ <u>Ethical</u> <u>Management</u> <u>Practices</u>: Behaving in a manner consistent with the Company's high standards for business ethics, enforced throughout the Corporation.

❧ <u>Communication</u>: Clarity regarding Company, divisional and individual goals. Associates will know what is expected and will receive ongoing communication that is timely, open, direct and honest.

❧ <u>Empowerment</u>: Increasing the authority and responsibility of those closest to our products and customers. By empowering associates and building trust, we will encourage and unleash the full capabilities of our people.

❖ Risk Taking: Encouraging and properly recognizing calculated risk-taking, regardless of the results. Openness to change will stimulate and support creative ideas and solutions.

❖ Customer Service: Striving for excellence with internal and external customers.

❖ Career Opportunities: Providing opportunities for career growth, where advancement within the Company becomes the normal practice, not the exception.

❖ Strategic Decision Making: Anticipating and supporting change by making decisions based on long-term strategies.

COMPANY | *Shepard Poorman Communications Corporation*

STATEMENT | **Shepard Poorman Mission and Philosophy**

♦ Shepard Poorman Communications Corporation is a high-quality print communications company which serves the graphic arts needs of American business and industry and achieves above average profits and growth for our ESOP stockholders. Shepard Poorman will seek and achieve a leadership position in its industry and is devoted to quality, dedicated to staff member and customer development and committed to the investment in and optimal utilization of modern technology.

♦ We will anticipate and fulfill the needs of our customers. We will deliver defect-free products and services on time to our clients and fellow staff members. We expect each person to do the job right the first time, in accordance with the job requirements.

❧ <u>Continual</u> <u>Improvement</u>: Constantly striving for excellence and high standards by challenging old methods and offering creative solutions.

❧ <u>Having</u> <u>Fun</u>: While we work very hard to achieve our goals, we must not lose sight of a very important element in our lives—having fun!

By committing to these new behaviors and showing support and trust toward all members of The Stride Rite Team, we will achieve our overall goal of commercial success.

ADDRESS   5 Cambridge Center
Cambridge, MA 02142

♦ We will anticipate and recognize competitive, technological and environmental changes to satisfy our customer's needs. We will meet these challenges with competitive urgency and a results-oriented willingness to innovate and lead.

♦ We will comply with all existing laws and be guided by high ethical standards in our relationships with customers, suppliers and fellow staff members, resulting in fair and competitive service, pricing and products.

♦ Decisions will be based on facts, be reached objectively and implemented promptly.

♦ We will work as a team of individual business persons for the accomplishment of common goals.

♦ We encourage and foster open lines of communication, without fear of reprisal. The freedom to speak one's mind on any subject concerning the company's welfare is a vital ingredient to our success.

INDUSTRY CATEGORY   Consumer Goods and Services

CORPORATE DESCRIPTION

The Stride Rite Corporation is the leading marketer of high quality children's footwear in the United States and is a major marketer of athletic and casual footwear for children and adults.

The Company manufactures products in its own facilities in the United States and Puerto Rico and imports products from abroad.

The Company markets children's footwear under the trademarks STRIDE RITE® and KEDS®. Boating shoes and outdoor recreational and casual footwear are marketed under the Company's SPERRY TOP-SIDER® trademark. Additionally, casual and athletic footwear is marketed under the Company's KEDS®, PRO-Keds® and GRASSHOPPERS® trademarks.

♦ We respect the contribution of each staff member and encourage development of their God-given abilities. We will provide a positive, safe and healthy environment. It is each staff member's innovation, dedication and loyalty that will enable our company to prosper and provide economic security for all.

♦ We believe in the American free enterprise system and accept responsibility to further its greatness. We actively pledge our corporate and personal participation and support to our community and society as a whole.

♦ We are a profit-oriented company dedicated to growth which provides the highest possible return on investment. We are committed to sharing and reinvesting our profits so that our staff members will be able to earn a standard of living commensurate with their performance and contribution to company profits.

The Company sells its products nationwide to independent retail shoe stores, department stores, sporting goods stores, and marinas. The Company also markets its products directly to consumers by selling children's footwear through 135 of its own Stride Rite Bootery stores and in 52 leased departments within leading department stores. Products of the Company's brands are also sold directly to consumers in two manufacturers' outlet stores.

SIZE REVENUES $582,868,000 (net sales) as of 1993

NUMBER OF EMPLOYEES   3,300 as of 1993

SOURCE   *1993 Annual Report*

CORPORATE DESCRIPTION
Shepard Poorman Communications Corporation is a high-quality print communications company which serves the graphic arts needs of American business and industry.

In fiscal 1993, the Company had sales of $42.9 million and nearly 500 employees.

ADDRESS   P. O. Box 68110
Indianapolis, IN 46268

SOURCES   *1993 Annual Report*, company representative

COMPANY | *Stroh Brewery Company, The*

STATEMENT | **VISION**

Our vision of The Stroh Brewery Company is one of a growing and prospering company with a dynamic and motivated organization providing our shareholders with a reasonable return on their investment.

| **MISSION**

To achieve this vision, our mission is to produce, distribute, and market a variety of high-quality beers in a manner that meets or exceeds the expectations of our customers.

ADDRESS   100 River Pl.
Detroit, MI 48207-4291

INDUSTRY CATEGORY   Food/Beverage

CORPORATE DESCRIPTION

The Stroh Brewery Company is a producer of high-quality alcoholic and non-alcoholic beverage products sold globally.

SIZE REVENUES   Not available (privately held)

NUMBER OF EMPLOYEES   Not available

SOURCE   Company representative

COMPANY | *Sun Company, Inc.*

STATEMENT | **Our purpose:**

To be a source of excellence for our customers; to provide a challenging professional experience for our employees; to be a rewarding investment for our shareholders; to be a respected citizen of community and country.

Our values:

Sun Company is committed to:

Profitable Growth—Seeking sustainable, profitable growth through relentless pursuit of our vision, simplicity of style, speed of action, innovation and leadership in all of our chosen business activities.

Positive Change—Embracing and capitalizing on change, recognizing that every employee must be empowered to stimulate continuous improvement in all aspects of our business.

Enthusiastic Customers—Enhancing our reputation as a company that customers can rely on to deliver products so excellent in their quality, and service so outstanding in its responsiveness, that Sun will be recognized for leadership in the marketplace.

Involved Employees—Striving for a workplace where opportunity, openness, enthusiasm, diversity, teamwork, accountability and a sense of purpose combine to provide a rewarding professional experience that promotes fairness, dignity and respect for all employees.

Confident Shareholders—Managing all parts of our business in a manner that builds value into the investment of all shareholders, confirming their confidence in participating in the ownership of this company.

Responsible Citizenship—Conducting our business with the highest standards of ethics, adherence to the law, and "doing what's right"—thereby continuing Sun's legacy of encouraging a healthy and safe workplace, responsible government, a highly competitive free enterprise system, environmental excellence and community enrichment.

ADDRESS   Ten Penn Center
1801 Market St., 27th Floor
Philadelphia, PA 19103-1699

INDUSTRY CATEGORY   Oil and Gas

CORPORATE DESCRIPTION
Sun operates six domestic refineries and markets gasoline under the Sunoco brand in 18 states from Maine to Indiana and the District of Columbia. Sun also markets under the Atlantic brand in Pennsylvania and New York State. It is converting Atlantic gasoline outlets to Sunoco. Sun sells lubricants and petrochemicals world wide, operates domestic pipelines and terminals and produces crude oil and natural gas internationally. Sun is 55 percent owner of Suncor, a fully integrated Canadian oil company.

SIZE REVENUES $9,180,000,000 as of 1993

NUMBER OF EMPLOYEES   14,547 as of 1993

SOURCE   *1993 Annual Report*

COMPANY | *Sundstrand Corporation*

STATEMENT | **SUNDSTRAND CORPORATION COMMITMENTS**

Mission

❖ To satisfy the needs of selected worldwide aerospace and industrial markets by developing and manufacturing high quality, proprietary, technology-based components and subsystems and by achieving customer satisfaction.

❖ To serve market segments where we can either be a market leader or have a strategy to become one while achieving returns that reward shareholders and employees and permit the business to grow and prosper.

Goals

❖ To provide superior rewards to investors by achieving returns on equity among the top quartile of Fortune 500 manufacturing companies.

❖ To anticipate and fully satisfy customer needs by providing superior products utilizing appropriate advanced technology and customer service.

❖ To recognize that every member of the Sundstrand team is a valued individual and important contributor.

❖ To be a responsible Corporate citizen by being an active participant and a positive contributor both in the local community and at the national level.

❖ To team with strong business partners with similar philosophies and objectives.

Beliefs

❖ Continuously improving the way we do our jobs, managing our businesses and serving our customers.

❖ Having a genuine concern for cost while fulfilling all commitments and providing total value to our customers.

❖ Maintaining the highest level of integrity and trust in all our relationships, reflecting respect and fairness in all our actions.

❖ Adhering strictly to our Code of Business Conduct and Ethics.

❖ Managing our businesses aggressively yet prudently.

❖ Encouraging the personal and professional growth of each member of the Sundstrand team.

❖ Developing a sense of ownership and belonging in each team member through effective two-way communications.

❖ Fostering innovation in all business and technical activity by recognizing and rewarding superior contribution.

❖ Developing and maintaining relationships rather than just executing transactions.

❖ Providing superior quality in all things. This is our most important belief.

ADDRESS   4949 Harrison Ave.
P. O. Box 7003
Rockford, IL 61125-7003

INDUSTRY CATEGORY   Aerospace

CORPORATE DESCRIPTION
Sundstrand Corporation is a market leader in the design, manufacture, and sale of a variety of proprietary technology-based components and subsystems requiring significant research, development engineering, and processing expertise. The business segments of the Corporation are: Industrial and Aerospace.

SIZE REVENUES $1,383,000,000 as of 1993

NUMBER OF EMPLOYEES   9,300 as of 1993

SOURCES   *1992 Annual Report;* "The Fortune 500," *Fortune* 129, no. 8 (April 8, 1994)

STATEMENT

[*Author's note:* Sysco stresses that the following is not their mission statement, but is instead their philosophy of doing business.]

THE SYSCO PHILOSOPHY

The scale and scope of its operations are such that SYSCO can:

- Provide high levels of customer service;
- Buy in quantity on favorable terms;
- Retain professional marketing and merchandising personnel who possess a wide knowledge of the many different supply markets;
- Accumulate broad experience which enables the company to work with manufacturers, processors and customers to reduce operating costs;
- Assure quality and consistency of products produced in thousands of locations;
- Maintain minimum levels of inventory while supporting customers' needs;
- Consolidate expenses for promotions and advertising;
- Test new merchandising and marketing methods on a pilot basis;
- Provide sales aids and training tools to enable marketing associates to represent the SYSCO product line effectively; and therefore;
- Undergird the success of SYSCO's customers.

Meanwhile, SYSCO's corporate structure ensures that the entrepreneurial spirit and drive is as strong in the parent company as in each of its subsidiary companies.

That spirit—a combination of personal interest, drive, creativity and determination to benefit customers—is the guiding philosophy of SYSCO Corporation, the key to its past success and to continued growth.

ADDRESS   1390 Enclave Pkwy.
Houston, TX 77077-2099

INDUSTRY CATEGORY   Food/Beverage

CORPORATE DESCRIPTION
SYSCO is the largest marketer and distributor of foodservice products in America. Operating from distribution facilities nationwide, the company serves more than 150 of the largest cities in the continental United States and the Pacific Coast region of Canada. Products and services are provided to approximately 245,000 restaurants, hotels, schools, hospitals, nursing homes and other institutions.

SIZE REVENUES $10,942,499,000 as of 1994

NUMBER OF EMPLOYEES   26,200 as of July 2, 1994

SOURCES   *1994 Annual Report*, company representative

◆   ◆   ◆   ◆   ◆   ◆   ◆

COMPANY | *TCF Financial Corporation*

STATEMENT | TCF's PHILOSOPHY OF COMMUNITY BANKING
❖ TCF believes in community banking. TCF serves individuals and small to medium-sized businesses in its market areas. We believe that community banking is the most consistently profitable type of banking.
❖ TCF believes that community banking operates best with separate geographic banking charters, with local management and boards of directors.

❧ **TCF** emphasizes funding of its assets with retail core deposits generated in its branches. TCF does not use brokered deposits and believes borrowings should be kept to a minimum. Core deposits are cheaper and more dependable than wholesale borrowings.

❧ **TCF** emphasizes checking and savings deposits due to their low interest cost and high fee income.

❧ **TCF** believes interest rate risk should be minimized. Interest rate speculations are too risky and do not generate consistent profits.

❧ **TCF** is primarily a secured local lender and always emphasizes credit quality over asset growth. The costs of poor credit far outweigh the benefits of unwise asset growth.

❧ **TCF** believes it is essential to be well-capitalized with a strong balance sheet. Capital is the cushion against poor economic times and errors in credit judgment.

❧ **TCF** is very expense control oriented, operating on a profit center budgeting system. A profitable community bank must be a low-cost provider of services.

❧ **TCF** is very sales oriented and believes in incentives and commissions.

❧ **TCF** emphasizes the generation of fee income and operates lines of business accordingly. Fee income requires less capital and helps reduce the cost of business.

❧ **TCF** operates like a partnership, organized by function with profit center goals and objectives. We know which products are profitable and which are not.

❧ **TCF** places a high priority on the development of technology to enhance productivity, customer service and new products. Properly applied technology reduces costs and enhances service.

❧ **TCF** is committed to providing extra services through longer hours, convenient access, innovative products and good customer relations. Many of our customers bank with us because we are convenient.

❖ **TCF** encourages open employee communications. TCF promotes from within whenever possible and places the highest priority on honesty, integrity and ethical behavior.

❖ **TCF** believes in community participation, both financially and through volunteerism.

❖ **TCF** practices affirmative action and does not discriminate against anyone in employment or the extension of credit. As a result of TCF's community banking philosophy, we market to all the customers in our communities, with a special emphasis on low- and moderate-income people. Our management and boards of directors take our Community Reinvestment Act responsibilities seriously.

ADDRESS   801 Marquette Ave.
Minneapolis, MN 55402

INDUSTRY CATEGORY   Banking

CORPORATE DESCRIPTION
TCF Financial Corporation is a stock savings bank holding company with $5 billion in assets and 182 retail offices at June 30, 1994. TCF Bank operates primarily in Minnesota, Illinois, Wisconsin and Michigan. TCF affiliates include mortgage banking, title insurance, annuity, mutual fund, and consumer finance companies.

SIZE REVENUES $37,971,000 (net income) as of 1993

NUMBER OF EMPLOYEES   3,625 as of August 17, 1994

SOURCE   Company representative

COMPANY | *Texas Industries, Inc.*

STATEMENT | **OUR MISSION:**
We will be the most efficient, high value supplier of cement and aggregate products and will provide superior service in the markets we serve. We will continue to grow in our industry through innovation and geographic diversification.

ADDRESS   7610 Stemmons Freeway
Dallas, TX 75247

INDUSTRY CATEGORY   Construction

CORPORATE DESCRIPTION
Texas Industries, Inc. is a leading producer of steel and construction materials, including cement, aggregates, and concrete. Chaparral Steel Company, an 81-percent-owned subsidiary of TXI, produces a broad range of carbon steel products and distributes them to markets in North America, Europe and Asia. TXI's cement, aggregate and concrete products operations are concentrated in Texas and Louisiana. The Company is the largest producer of cement in Texas.

SIZE REVENUES $707,147,000 as of 1994

NUMBER OF EMPLOYEES   2,700 as of 1994

SOURCE   *1994 Annual Report*

COMPANY | *Times Mirror Company*

STATEMENT | **TIMES MIRROR MISSION STATEMENT**

Our mission is to be the information partner of choice in each market we serve—helping people gain the knowledge they need to work, live and govern themselves.

Values

In accomplishing this mission, we are guided by an abiding set of values:

Adhering to the highest standards of ethics and integrity.

Exceeding our customers' expectations for editorial excellence, product quality and service.

Fostering a creative working environment with development, openness, challenge, accountability, diversity, teamwork and respect for every colleague.

Actively contributing to the social, cultural and environmental well-being of the communities we serve.

Operating Goals

We strive to make Times Mirror an attractive investment by:

Providing superior total shareholder returns and dividend growth.

Adopting the best operating practices as judged by world standards of excellence.

Managing risk through business diversity and financial flexibility.

Making our wide array of information resources available in all desirable forms, including traditional and electronic.

ADDRESS   Times Mirror Square
Los Angeles, CA 90053

INDUSTRY CATEGORY   Media/Printing/Publishing

CORPORATE DESCRIPTION

Times Mirror is a diversified media and information company. Its holdings include newspapers and magazines; information and educational products and services for professional markets; and cable television systems in 13 states.

The company publishes the Los Angeles Times, Newsday and New York Newsday, the Baltimore Sun newspapers, The Hartford Courant, The Morning Call, The (Stamford) Advocate and Greenwich Time.

Book publishing includes Matthew Bender law books, Mosby-Year Book medical books, journals and college texts; Wm C. Brown Communications, Inc., science, mathematics and social science textbooks and products; Richard D. Irwin business and economics textbooks; and CRC Press scientific and technical books. Jeppesen Sanderson produces aeronautical charts and pilot training materials. Learning International, Zenger-Miller, Inc. and Kaset International are in the professional training field. The company also publishes Abrams art and illustrated works.

Times Mirror Magazines publishes nine special-interest magazines, two trade magazines and has a custom publishing division.

SIZE REVENUES $3,714,158,000 as of 1993

NUMBER OF EMPLOYEES   26,936 as of 1993

SOURCE   *1993 Annual Report*

COMPANY | *TOOTSIE ROLL INDUSTRIES, INC.*

STATEMENT | **Corporate Principles**

We believe that the differences among companies are caused by the differences among their people, and therefore we strive to attract and retain the best people available for the job.

We believe that an open, family atmosphere at work combined with professional management fosters cooperation and enables each individual to maximize his or her contribution to the company and realize the corresponding rewards.

We do not jeopardize long-term growth for immediate, short-term results.

We view our well known brands as prized assets to be aggressively advertised and promoted to each new generation of consumers in the United States and selected foreign markets.

We run a trim operation and continually strive to eliminate waste, minimize cost and seek performance improvements.

We invest in the latest and most productive equipment to deliver the best quality product to our customers at the lowest cost.

We seek to vertically integrate operations to the greatest practical extent.

We maintain a conservative financial posture in the employment and management of our assets.

ADDRESS   7401 S. Cicero Ave.
Chicago, IL 60629

INDUSTRY CATEGORY   Food/Beverage

CORPORATE DESCRIPTION

Tootsie Roll Industries, Inc. has been engaged in the manufacture and sale of candy since 1896. The Company's products are primarily sold under the familiar brand names Tootsie Roll, Tootsie Roll Pops,

Child's Play, Charms, Blow Pop, Blue Razz, Cella's, Mason Dots, Mason Crows, Junior Mints, Charleston Chew, Sugar Daddy and Sugar Babies.

SIZE REVENUES $259,593,000 (net sales) as of 1993

NUMBER OF EMPLOYEES   1,300 as of 1994

SOURCE   *1993 Annual Report*; company representative

◆ ◆ ◆ ◆ ◆ ◆ ◆

COMPANY | *Total System Services, Inc.*

STATEMENT | **TSYS® MISSION STATEMENT**
To Exceed the Expectation of Our Customers through the Delivery of Superior Service and Continuous Quality Improvement that Rewards Our Employees and Enhances the Value of Our Shareholders' Investment.

ADDRESS   1000 Fifth Ave.
P. O. Box 120
Columbus, GA 31902

INDUSTRY CATEGORY   Business Services

CORPORATE DESCRIPTION
Total System Services, Inc.SM (TSYS®) is a bankcard and private label card processing company based in Columbus, Georgia, which provides card-issuing institutions with a comprehensive on-line system of data processing services marketed as THE TOTAL SYSTEMSM. It

is an 80.8 percent-owned subsidiary of Synovus Financial Corp.®, a $5.6 billion multi-financial services company composed of TSYS, 31 banking affiliates in three states, and a full-service brokerage firm.

TSYS® is a federally registered service mark of Total System Services, Inc., and THE TOTAL SYSTEM^SM, and Total System Services, Inc.^SM, are service marks of Total System Services, Inc. Synovus Financial Corp.® is a federally registered service mark of Synovus Financial Corp.

SIZE REVENUES $152,074,000 as of 1993

NUMBER OF EMPLOYEES 1,587 as of 1993

SOURCE *1993 Annual Report*

◆ ◆ ◆ ◆ ◆ ◆ ◆

COMPANY | **Tribune Company**

STATEMENT | **Mission**
Tribune's mission is to develop leading sources of information and entertainment. We will continue to grow in major metropolitan markets, as well as through related businesses of national and international scope.

Strategies
Four strategies form the foundation of our actions:
- ◆ Emphasize local market growth
- ◆ Emphasize content creation and control
- ◆ Add targeting to efficient mass media
- ◆ Foster a development orientation

Values

We are guided by a strong set of values:
- ❖ Integrity
- ❖ Customer Satisfaction
- ❖ Innovation
- ❖ Employee Involvement
- ❖ Financial Strength
- ❖ Citizenship
- ❖ Diversity
- ❖ Teamwork

ADDRESS   435 N. Michigan Ave.
Chicago, IL 60611

INDUSTRY CATEGORY   Media/Printing/Publishing

CORPORATE DESCRIPTION
Tribune is a leading information and entertainment company with businesses in 13 of the nation's largest metropolitan markets. Through the Company's print and broadcast media, it can reach more than half of U. S. households daily. Tribune publishes six daily newspapers, as well as books and information in print and digital formats. Tribune also provides editorial and advertising services to client newspapers and electronic media. Tribune's broadcasting and entertainment business operates eight independent television stations and six radio stations, produces and syndicates television and radio programming, and owns a major-league baseball team. In addition to its media business, the Company has an ownership interest in one of Canada's largest newsprint manufacturers.

SIZE REVENUES $1,952,510,000 as of 1993

NUMBER OF EMPLOYEES   9,900 as of 1993

SOURCES   *1993 Annual Report*; company releases

COMPANY | *TRINOVA Corporation*

STATEMENT | **OUR MISSION**

TRINOVA is a world leader in the manufacture and distribution of engineered components and systems for industry. Our mission is to create economic value for our shareholders through superior growth and profitability.

To accomplish our mission, we will develop strategies that create sustainable competitive advantage; and we will build an organization fully capable of implementing these strategies.

Our success will not be a matter of chance, but of commitment to the core values that distinguish us:

Customer Orientation. We listen to our customers and respond to their needs.

Quality. We provide quality in everything we do.

Technology. We invest in technology to enhance our productivity and effectiveness.

Innovation. We take personal initiative for constructive change.

Integrity. We conduct ourselves ethically, respect the dignity of the individual and are responsible community citizens.

Teamwork. We work as a team across functions, businesses and cultures.

We are the force for fulfilling TRINOVA's mission and achieving its goals. By personalizing these core values and by working hard, we will win and we will all share in our success.

ADDRESS 3000 Strayer
P. O. Box 50
Maumee, OH 43537-0050

INDUSTRY CATEGORY Manufacturing

CORPORATE DESCRIPTION

TRINOVA is a world leader in the manufacture and distribution of engineered components and systems for industry. Their two operating companies, Aeroquip and Vickers, supply products for worldwide markets in three areas—industrial, aerospace & defense, and automotive. Sales are direct to customers through their sales personnel, or indirect through independent distributors.

SIZE REVENUES $1,643,800,000 as of 1993

NUMBER OF EMPLOYEES   15,012 as of 1993

SOURCE   *1993 Annual Report*

COMPANY | *TRW Inc.*

STATEMENT | **TRW Mission & Values**
Mission

TRW is a global company focused on providing superior products and services to customers in the space and defense, automotive, and information systems markets. Our mission is to achieve leadership positions in these markets by serving the needs of our customers in innovative ways—by being the best in everything we do. We will create value for our shareholders by balancing short-term performance and long-term financial strength.

Values

Customers

Customer satisfaction is essential. We will deliver superior value to our customers through quality, reliability and technology. We grow and prosper by serving the needs of our customers better than our competitors, while effectively controlling costs.

People

The men and women of TRW make our success possible. We encourage the involvement and reward the contribution of each employee. We value open and honest communications. We create a workplace where every employee can share a sense of ownership for TRW's success. We provide equal opportunity in our employment and promotion practices.

COMPANY | *SkyNet Worldwide Courier*

STATEMENT | **MISSION STATEMENT**

The SKYNET WORLDWIDE COURIER NETWORK sets the standard for international delivery & distribution services by consistently exceeding customer expectations.

SKYNET delivers customer satisfaction by:
- Integrating all aspects of the transportation process
- Personalizing service worldwide
- Investing in quality people & technology
- Innovating & adapting to meet customer's unique & changing requirements.

Quality
Quality is important in everything we do. Quality is everyone's responsibility and is achieved through continuous improvement. We routinely seek ways to do things better.

Integrity
We pursue our business interests worldwide in a socially responsible manner. We conduct our businesses in accordance with the highest standards of legal and ethical conduct. We encourage every TRW employee to participate in and support community activities.

ADDRESS   1900 Richmond Rd.
Cleveland, OH 44124

CORPORATE DESCRIPTION
SkyNet Worldwide Courier is an international courier company providing expedited delivery of documents and shipments under 70 pounds to 168 countries. In addition to international courier, SkyNet offers a private postal service for persons living abroad by offering a U. S. address in which they can receive correspondence, magazine subscriptions and catalog merchandise. In 1994 the Company had sales of $9.0 million and 87 employees.

ADDRESS   4405 N.W. 73rd Ave.
Miami, FL 33166

SOURCE   Company representative

INDUSTRY CATEGORY   Diversified

CORPORATE DESCRIPTION
TRW Inc. manufactures automotive systems, including occupant restraints, steering systems and engine components; spacecraft, electronics and defense systems; and commercial information systems.

SIZE REVENUES $7,900,000,000 as of 1993

NUMBER OF EMPLOYEES   60,000 as of 1993

SOURCE   *1993 Annual Report*

◆   ◆   ◆   ◆   ◆   ◆   ◆

COMPANY | *Tultex Corporation*

STATEMENT | **Tultex...Our Values**
Trust...Integrity...Respect

| **Tultex...Our Vision**
To be the world's best apparel company
Our Mission is to provide superior returns to our Stakeholders (our Shareholders, Employees, Customers and the Communities where our people work and live).
Our Vision for these Stakeholders, toward which we will continually strive, is as follows:
SHAREHOLDERS
Shareholders would see their investment appreciate by at least 15 percent per year (a 15 percent Return on Equity).

EMPLOYEES

Employees would receive compensation that is above industry average in return for working together as an effective team. It is through teamwork that we will achieve the industry's lowest cost with the best quality and best customer service. All Tultex people would have the opportunity to participate directly in the profits, ownership and decisions of the business.

We will create, through the contributions of each of us, a quality of worklife that is recognized by the caring, openness and understanding of each other. We will create an environment that fosters the building of trust, integrity and respect among all of our employees. Work should be challenging, satisfying and rewarding. We will create a company attitude that encourages, recognizes and rewards excellence and team performance.

CUSTOMERS

Customers will receive high quality and high value products from Tultex—with service and support better than anyone else in the business. We will establish among each other a sincere feeling of pride...in our products, our quality, our service and pride in each other and this pride will be obvious to our customers. Through building partnerships, all of us will constantly focus on delighting our customers.

COMMUNITIES

Communities of Tultex people will be made significantly better by the presence of our company as a major employer.

ADDRESS   P. O. Box 5191
Martinsville, VA 24115

INDUSTRY CATEGORY   Consumer Goods and Services

CORPORATE DESCRIPTION

Tultex Corporation is a vertically integrated marketer and manufacturer of quality activewear and licensed sports apparel. The company is headquartered in Martinsville, Virginia.

Tultex offers a wide range of activewear apparel products under the Tultex®, Discus Athletic®, Brittania®, and Logo7® and Logo Athletic® brand names, as well as numerous private label brands for various customers. Tultex products can be found with the Levi Strauss, Nike, Gitano and Pro Spirit label.

SIZE REVENUES　$533,611,000 (net sales) as of January 1, 1994

NUMBER OF EMPLOYEES　7,513 as of January 1, 1994

SOURCE　*1993 Annual Report*

◆　◆　◆　◆　◆　◆　◆

COMPANY | *Turner (The Turner Corporation)*

STATEMENT | **Mission Statement**

Turner will be the recognized leader in providing building construction services, both nationally and in every location in which Turner operates. We will achieve this by consistently exceeding our commitments to and the expectations of clients, design professionals, subcontractors and vendors, and the community at large. These services will be delivered by team-oriented, responsive, innovative, reliable, ethical and skilled staff who participate in a world-class training and development program and benefit from a career employment opportunity.

ADDRESS   375 Hudson St.
New York, NY 10014

INDUSTRY CATEGORY   Construction

CORPORATE DESCRIPTION
The Turner Corporation, through Turner Construction Company and other construction subsidiaries, is the nation's leading builder. Turner provides a complete range of construction and program management services in all segments of the non-residential building market. With more than sixty percent of Turner's business coming from repeat clients, we are a recognized industry leader in providing quality service in diverse markets. Turner, operating through more than 34 offices, has construction projects underway throughout the United States and abroad. During 1993, The Turner Corporation completed $2.8 billion of construction.

SIZE REVENUES $2,800,000,000 as of 1993

NUMBER OF EMPLOYEES   2,400 as of 1993

SOURCE   *1993 Annual Report*

COMPANY | *Union Carbide*

STATEMENT | CORPORATE MISSION

❖ To grow the value of the Corporation by successfully pursuing strategies that capitalize on our business strengths in chemicals and polymers;

❖ To successfully execute wealth creation strategies that consistently deliver value to all stakeholders over the course of the business cycle.

| CORPORATE VISION

❖ Union Carbide is a leading global chemical company, focused on being the low cost and preferred supplier of chemicals and polymers in the industry segments in which we participate. We have the best olefins chain petrochemicals businesses, augmented by a related portfolio of high quality, focused performance product businesses.

❖ Our leadership is measured by our technology and cost positions, customer satisfaction, product performance, people excellence, earnings performance, and investor returns.

| CORPORATE VALUES

❖ Safety and Environmental Excellence
❖ Customer Focus
❖ Technology Leadership
❖ People Excellence
❖ Simplicity and Focus

ADDRESS   39 Old Ridgebury Rd.
Danbury, CT 06817-0001

INDUSTRY CATEGORY   Chemicals

CORPORATE DESCRIPTION

Union Carbide is a basic chemicals company with many of the industry's most advanced process technologies and some of the most efficient large-scale chemical production facilities found anywhere in the world.

SIZE REVENUES $4,640,000,000 as of 1993

NUMBER OF EMPLOYEES   13,051 as of 1993

SOURCE   *1993 Annual Report*

◆   ◆   ◆   ◆   ◆   ◆   ◆

COMPANY | *Union Electric*

STATEMENT | Statement of Policy

We are a business enterprise—dependent for success on the high quality and fair price of our service; on the skill, courtesy, and loyalty of our employees; on the confidence of our investors; and on the ability of our management to forecast and provide for the energy requirements of our area.

In the conduct of our business, we will render service of the highest quality to our customers—promptly, courteously, and efficiently—at the lowest prices consistent with paying fair wages and affording job satisfaction and security to our employees; providing modern facilities for our customers' expanding needs for energy service; and paying a fair return to our investors who have provided the funds to make such service possible.

As a private enterprise entrusted with an essential public service, we recognize our civic responsibility in the communities we serve. We shall strive to advance the growth and welfare of these communities and shall participate in civic activities which fulfill that goal...for we believe this is both good citizenship and good business.

ADDRESS   P. O. Box 149
St. Louis, MO 63166

INDUSTRY CATEGORY   Utility

CORPORATE DESCRIPTION
Union Electric is a utility company, primarily engaged in providing energy to 1.2 million customers in the strategic center of America—a 24,500 square-mile area in Missouri and Illinois.

SIZE REVENUES $2,066,004,000 as of December 31, 1993

NUMBER OF EMPLOYEES   6,400 as of December 31, 1993

SOURCES   *1992 Annual Report;* "The Fortune Service 500," *Fortune* 129, no. 11 (May 30, 1994); company representative

COMPANY | *Unisys Corporation*

STATEMENT | **Our Corporate Mission.**
We build long-term relationships with clients, helping them creatively use information and apply technology to improve service to their customers, enhance their competitive position in the marketplace, and increase their profitability.

ADDRESS   P. O. Box 500
Blue Bell, PA 19424-0001

INDUSTRY CATEGORY   Business Services

CORPORATE DESCRIPTION
Unisys is one of the largest providers of information services, technology, and software in the world. The Company does business in some 100 countries. About 80 percent of its revenue is derived from commercial information systems and services, with the remainder coming from electronic systems and services for the defense market. Slightly more than one-half of their revenue is from business in the United States.

Unisys specializes in providing business-critical solutions, based on open information networks, for organizations that operate in transaction-intensive environments. These organizations include financial services companies, airlines, telephone companies, government agencies, and other commercial enterprises. The Company's solutions are used by 41 of the world's 50 largest banks, 140 airlines worldwide, 35 of the world's largest telecommunications companies, and more than 1,600 government agencies worldwide.

SIZE REVENUES $7,742,500,000 as of 1993

NUMBER OF EMPLOYEES   49,000 as of 1993

SOURCE   *1993 Annual Report*

♦ ♦ ♦ ♦ ♦ ♦ ♦

COMPANY | **United Dominion Industries**

STATEMENT | **Mission**
Provide superior manufactured products, engineering and construction services through engineering-driven, market-leader businesses which serve construction and industrial markets worldwide.

ADDRESS   2300 One First Union Center
301 S. College St.
Charlotte, NC 28202-6039

INDUSTRY CATEGORY   Diversified

CORPORATE DESCRIPTION
A community of companies, United Dominion Industries is a worldwide manufacturing, engineering and construction enterprise built on more than a century of serving a wide range of construction markets and providing superior, value-added products for industrial and commercial markets.

SIZE REVENUES $2,000,000,000 as of 1994

NUMBER OF EMPLOYEES   11,700 as of 1994

SOURCE   "Corporate Profile" company publication

COMPANY | *United Parcel Service*

STATEMENT | **CORPORATE MISSION and STRATEGY**

UPS Corporate Mission Statement:

Customers

Serve the ongoing package distribution needs of our customers worldwide and provide other services that enhance customer relationships and complement our position as the foremost provider of package distribution services, offering high quality and excellent value in every service.

People

Be a well-regarded employer that is mindful of the well-being of our people, allowing them to develop their individual capabilities in an impartial, challenging, rewarding, and cooperative environment and offering them the opportunity for career advancement.

Shareowners

Maintain a financially strong, manager-owned company earning a reasonable profit, providing long-term competitive returns to our shareholders.

Communities

Build on the legacy of our company's reputation as a responsible corporate citizen whose well-being is in the public interest and whose people are respected for their performance and integrity.

UPS Corporate Strategy Statement:

UPS will achieve worldwide leadership in package distribution by developing and delivering solutions that best meet our customers' distribution needs at competitive rates. To do so, we will build upon our extensive and efficient distribution network, the legacy and dedication of our people to operational and service excellence, and our commitment to anticipate and respond rapidly to changing market conditions and requirements.

ADDRESS   55 Glenlake Pkwy. N.E.
Atlanta, GA 30328

INDUSTRY CATEGORY   Package Delivery Service

CORPORATE DESCRIPTION
United Parcel Service is in the business of delivering parcels and documents worldwide.

SIZE REVENUES $17,800,000,000 as of 1993

NUMBER OF EMPLOYEES   303,000 as of 1993

SOURCE   *1993 Annual Report*

◆ ◆ ◆ ◆ ◆ ◆ ◆

COMPANY | *United States Fidelity and Guaranty Corporation*

STATEMENT | **Vision Statement**
We aspire to build a company with a strong character of integrity and ethical conduct dedicated to providing very competitive, innovative, high quality insurance products and services to our customers.

We will secure a leadership position in our served markets and earn a superior return for our shareowners by adhering to four fundamental precepts of strategy:

❖ Create a performance driven culture and work environment conducive to the development and growth of our employees which enables them to exercise competitively superior skills.

❖ Compete only in attractive markets and businesses where we have the financial capability and market opportunity to attain a leadership position and earn an acceptable return.

❖ Build market-driven, highly-focused businesses that provide value-added, differentiated products and services to our customers.

❖ Organize in a manner that best leverages people, capital, and technology.

ADDRESS   P. O. Box 1138
Baltimore, MD 21203-1138

INDUSTRY CATEGORY   Insurance

CORPORATE DESCRIPTION
USF&G Corporation, with assets of $14.3 billion (at year-end 1993), is composed of property/casualty and life insurance subsidiaries. The principal subsidiary is United States Fidelity and Guaranty Company (USF&G Insurance), one of the nation's largest property/casualty insurers, founded in 1896. Life insurance products are written through Fidelity and Guaranty Life Insurance Company, founded in 1959. USF&G provides a wide variety of quality commercial, personal, fidelity-surety, and reinsurance products targeted to meet the diverse insurance needs of its customers.

SIZE REVENUES $3,249,000,000 as of 1993

NUMBER OF EMPLOYEES   6,500 as of 1993 (year end)

SOURCE   *1993 Annual Report*

COMPANY | *United States Shoe Corporation, The*

STATEMENT | THE U. S. SHOE CORPORATION STRATEGY

BUILD DOMINANT BRANDS by aggressively developing and growing winning consumer brands in well-defined retail niches.

PROVIDE LEGENDARY CUSTOMER SERVICE by achieving significantly higher customer satisfaction than competitors. Respond to customer needs by bringing preferred products to market faster than competitors.

EMPOWER ASSOCIATES by establishing a highly energized, decentralized organization that aggressively shares expertise.

ACT WITH UNCOMPROMISING INTEGRITY in all our business endeavors.

ADDRESS   One Eastwood Dr.
Cincinnati, OH 45227-1197

INDUSTRY CATEGORY   Retail

CORPORATE DESCRIPTION
The United States Shoe Corporation is a specialty retailing company operating 2,468 retail stores, outlets and leased departments in three segments: women's apparel, optical and footwear. U. S. Shoe also manufactures, imports and wholesales prominent footwear brands, primarily for women.

SIZE REVENUES $2,650,700,000 as of 1992

NUMBER OF EMPLOYEES   38,000 as of 1993

SOURCES   *1992 Annual Report;* "The Fortune Service 500," *Fortune* 129, no. 11 (May 30, 1994)

Universal Foods will add value to customers' products worldwide by developing and delivering technically superior ingredients and ingredient systems for foods and other applications. Through dedication to our customers and employees, and commitment to continuous improvement and innovation, we will achieve superior quality, service and operating performance.

To drive above-average earnings growth, we must:

Shift to <u>HIGHER GROWTH</u> Opportunities

Develop new products internally.

Make acquisitions.

Adjust product mix in existing businesses.

Provide <u>BEST VALUE</u> as Perceived by the Customer

Deliver operations excellence.

Add value through responsiveness to customers.

Lead in product innovation.

Capitalize on core competencies.

Establish <u>MARKET LEVERAGE</u>

Build similar positions outside of the U. S.to achieve #1 or #2 position in U. S.non-volatile niche markets.

Operate <u>GLOBALLY</u>

Seek opportunities worldwide.

Leverage technology and product expertise.

<u>IMPROVE</u> Operating Margins

Target capital expenditures to boost efficiency.

Provide above-industry average spending on research and development.

Achieve low-cost operating structure.

<u>INVOLVE OUR PEOPLE</u>

Train people in skills that will allow them to make a difference in our business.

Foster teamwork and continuous improvement, The
Universal Way.

Create a work environment that fosters innovation.

Our Creed

Universal Foods Corporation is committed to conducting a
business enterprise which is of real and continuing value to
society. This requires bringing together, in an optimal manner,
shareholders, employees, suppliers, and civic resources so that
customers are well served, profits are fairly earned in the competitive marketplace, investors are rewarded, employees grow
in their careers, and the needs of communities are recognized
by appropriate commitment of corporate time and wealth.

ADDRESS   433 E. Michigan St.
Milwaukee, WI 53202

INDUSTRY CATEGORY   Food/Beverage

CORPORATE DESCRIPTION

Universal Food is an international manufacturer and marketer of
key ingredients, primarily for food processors. Key ingredients
include flavors and colors, yeast products and dehydrated vegetables. The Company's divisions maintain significant market shares in
their respective businesses through attention to product quality,
technological innovation and customer service.

SIZE REVENUES $891,566,000 as of 1993

NUMBER OF EMPLOYEES   4,000 as of August 1, 1994

SOURCES   *1993 Annual Report*, and company representative

COMPANY | *Unocal Corporation*

STATEMENT | **OUR MISSION**

Unocal produces and sells a broad array of essential energy resources, petroleum products, chemical fertilizers, and specialty minerals that help improve the quality of life for people around the world. Our primary mission is to maximize—ethically and responsibly—the total long-term returns to the owners of the company, our stockholders.

| **OUR VISION**

To be recognized leaders in creating value by identifying, developing, and producing crude oil, natural gas, and geothermal energy resources.

COMPANY | *Softub, Inc.*

STATEMENT | **SOFTUB Mission Statement**

We pledge to raise reliability, professionalism and customer satisfaction to the highest levels in the spa industry by providing innovative, versatile products and excellent customer service.

CORPORATE DESCRIPTION

Softub markets spa products.

ADDRESS   21100 Superior St.
Chatsworth, CA 91311

SOURCE   Company representative

To manufacture transport and market high-quality petroleum and chemical products safely and efficiently.

To combine the strengths of a large company with the speed and agility of a small business.

To achieve excellence in all staff functions, providing cost-effective, value-added services to company operations.

To be innovators, who find creative and cost-effective ways to produce new energy resources, develop needed technologies, and protect the environment.

OUR VALUES

Achieve continuous improvement in all of our business activities through teamwork, accountability, and sharing of ideas.

Meet our customers' requirements by providing quality products and services.

Act quickly to solve problems and seize opportunities.

Spend wisely and safeguard every company asset as if it were our own.

Create a work environment in which employees can develop their full potential.

Take appropriate business risks, encourage creativity and reward results.

Treat everyone fairly and with respect.

Communicate openly and honestly.

Meet the highest ethical standards in all of our business activities.

Maintain a safe and healthful workplace.

Protect the environment.

Obey the law and comply with all regulations.

Improve the quality of life in all the communities where we do business.

ADDRESS   1201 W. 5th St.
Los Angeles, CA 90051

INDUSTRY CATEGORY   Oil and Gas

CORPORATE DESCRIPTION
Unocal Corporation is the parent of Union Oil Company of California, a fully integrated, high-technology energy resources company whose worldwide operations comprise all aspects of energy production. Virtually all operations are conducted by Union Oil Company of California, which does business as Unocal.

SIZE REVENUES $8,344,000,000 as of 1993

NUMBER OF EMPLOYEES   13,613 as of 1993

SOURCE   *1993 Annual Report*

♦   ♦   ♦   ♦   ♦   ♦   ♦

COMPANY | *UNUM Corporation*

STATEMENT | **Our Mission is:**
To relieve clients of insurable financial risk.
　We protect clients from financial hardships that result from retirement, death, sickness and from disability or other casualty events.

| **Vision**
We will achieve leadership in our businesses. Leadership does not necessarily mean a dominant market share.
Rather, we will achieve leadership in areas which are meaningful and important to our business and the market, e.g., profitability, quality, reputation.

We will focus our business on specialty, risk-relieving products for which we can establish and sustain profitable positions. Development of these products will be driven by the needs of customers, in both domestic and international markets.

We will be a products-offered company:

❖ Developing products which meet customer needs and leveraging our expertise and strengths. Our product development efforts will focus on providing the right solution.

❖ Seeking market segments which are appropriate for our products.

❖ Delivering our products in a high-quality and efficient manner utilizing existing and new channels.

Our products will be perceived by customers as representing superior value in quality and price, and will consist of a total offering including risk, service, delivery and reliability.

We will be known for:

❖ Superior knowledge, expertise and risk management

❖ Quality service

❖ Being responsive to the needs of customers and intermediaries

❖ Being reliable, dependable and trustworthy

❖ Providing the right solutions to current and emerging needs

❖ Implementing good ideas well

We will be a well-managed company:

❖ Consistently-growing profits, an efficient cost structure, leadership returns and financially sound

❖ Anticipating, shaping and effectively responding to relevant external forces and events

❖ Making decisions in the best long-term interests of our stakeholders

❖ Planning well; making clear and sound business decisions

Values

We take pride in ourselves and the organization's leadership position:

- Acting with integrity and high ethical standards
- Achieving leadership in performance, the community and the industry
- Setting and meeting individual goals consistent with business goals, and owning our individual performance
- Being motivated and excited about the organization
- Believing in what we are doing
- Emphasizing the positives, celebrating our successes and strengths, and constantly striving to improve our performance
- Delivering results

We value and respect people:

- Dealing with each other as individuals, and treating each other as we would like to be treated
- Developing people to their fullest potential
- Working together in a common endeavor: recognizing each other as important elements to the success of the whole
- Having a common understanding of each other's role and how we fit with the corporate objectives
- Collaborating with each other and having a sense of team
- Recognizing and accepting differences among people, but sharing the same values

We value customers:

- Building long-term relationships with our customers and intermediaries
- Maintaining a strong orientation to service and the customer
- Delivering what we promise

We value communication:
- ❖ Communicating clearly, consistently and openly with everyone we deal with
- ❖ Building an environment which encourages open communication, participation, honesty and candor
- ❖ Listening

ADDRESS   2211 Congress St.
Portland, ME 04122

INDUSTRY CATEGORY   Insurance

CORPORATE DESCRIPTION
UNUM is a publicly held specialty insurance holding company that provides income protection through a range of disability, life, health, long term care and retirement income products and services.

SIZE REVENUES $299,900,000 (net income) as of 1993

NUMBER OF EMPLOYEES   7,000 as of 1993

SOURCE   *1993 Annual Report*

COMPANY | *UTILX Corporation*

STATEMENT

Our mission is what we focus and work on to achieve accomplishment now and forever.

Mission Statement

Our mission is to assist companies of the world in the installation and maintenance of a segment of their underground infrastructure. We will do this by providing UTILX services and products in a way that helps our customers achieve their goals and solve their problems. We will achieve success by making our customers successful.

In the process of providing the highest quality product and services to our customers, we will be admired and possibly held in awe by our competitors. This will occur because our technology will be the best in the world and because the people of UTILX, through their pride, commitment, teamwork and their ability to focus on doing what it takes to make our customers successful, will be absolutely unbeatable by our competition.

Through exceptional customer service and world class safety, quality and technology, our mission includes being the best in the entire world in what we do.

ADDRESS   22404 66th Ave. S.
Kent, WA 98064

INDUSTRY CATEGORY   Industrial, Specialized

CORPORATE DESCRIPTION

UTILX® Corporation provides services and products used in the replacement and renovation of underground utilities and related construction. The Company's FlowMole® and CableCure® divisions give UTILX a strategic advantage in solving the utility needs of the nation and the world. The FlowMole technology provides economic alternatives for the installation needs of electric, telephone, gas, water and sewer utilities while meeting the increasing demand for environmental remediation. CableCure dielectric enhancement technology restores water-damaged power and telephone cables at substantial savings compared to the cost of cable replacement. Domestically, UTILX provides its technology as a service, while internationally it supplies equipment, parts and training.

SIZE REVENUES $49,077,000 as of 1994

NUMBER OF EMPLOYEES   426 as of March 31, 1994

SOURCE   Company representative

◆　◆　◆　◆　◆　◆　◆

COMPANY | *Valassis Communications, Inc.*

STATEMENT | **Pledge To Shareholders**
As employees and fellow "owners" of Valassis Communications, we are committed to achieving maximum profits, short- and long-term growth, and an excellent return on your investment. We realize that next to our customers, our shareholders are the key to our success. Therefore, we promise to manage your investment like you would—by working hard and smart. We will constantly look for ways to improve our products and services, set and accomplish the highest objectives for ourselves and for our company, increase effficiencies through training and innovation, and conduct our business ethically and responsibly.

ADDRESS   36111 Schoolcraft Rd.
Westwood Office Park
Livonia, MI 48150

INDUSTRY CATEGORY   Media/Printing/Publishing

CORPORATE DESCRIPTION
Valassis Communications, Inc. is one of the world's largest publishers of printed sales promotion materials.

SIZE REVENUES $661,378,000 as of June 30, 1993

NUMBER OF EMPLOYEES   1,170 as of 1993

SOURCE   *1993 Annual Report*

◆ ◆ ◆ ◆ ◆ ◆ ◆

COMPANY | *Varlen Corporation*

STATEMENT | **THE VARLEN MISSION**
Varlen's primary objective is to increase the long-term value of its shareowners' investment. This will be achieved by building upon our employees' creativity and their commitment to serving customers better and more efficiently than our competitors do in the markets where Varlen chooses to compete.

Varlen will invest resources in selected industrial markets where it has, or can obtain, a leadership position; we will redeploy resources from markets where we cannot. We will continue to enhance our global presence. Varlen's engineered products for the niche markets in which it participates are characterized by differentiable process technology employed in their manufacture and/or superior performance attributes. Our dedication to continuous improvement will be unrelenting.

ADDRESS   55 Shuman Blvd.
P. O. Box 3089
Naperville, IL 60566-7089

INDUSTRY CATEGORY   Manufacturing

CORPORATE DESCRIPTION
The Company designs, manufactures, and markets a diverse range of products in its transportation products and laboratory and other products business segments. These products are marketed to the railroad, heavy duty truck and trailer and automotive industries, as well as to the life sciences research, petroleum, and consumer products industries.

SIZE REVENUES $291,908,000 (net sales) as of 1993

NUMBER OF EMPLOYEES   2,030 as of 1994

SOURCES   *1993 Annual Report;* company representative

COMPANY | *VF Corporation*

STATEMENT | **VF CORPORATION**
CODE OF BUSINESS CONDUCT
<u>**STATEMENT** **OF** **MISSION** **AND** **PURPOSE**</u>

VF is a diversified apparel company whose mission it is to provide above average shareholder returns by being the industry leader in marketing and servicing basic fashion apparel needs while maintaining conservative financial strategies.

The purpose of the Company is to manufacture and market products which offer superior real value to the customer and consumer compared to competition. In doing so, it is a cornerstone of our business philosophy to achieve a leadership position in every facet of our business and to judge our actions by the highest standards of excellence. We will restrict growth only by the stability and quality of profits and our ability to develop and market products offering superior value.

The Company intends to achieve profit levels sufficient to provide an attractive return to its shareholders and to provide adequate resources necessary to achieve corporate objectives.

The Company desires to provide stable employment in positions which will allow employees to develop personally and professionally. It is the Company's aim that our employees will derive satisfaction from achieving corporate objectives through superior performance in an organization environment characterized by competence, integrity, teamwork and fairness.

The conduct of business with employees, customers, consumers, suppliers, and all others shall be based on an honest, fair and equitable basis. It has been and will continue to be the Company's policy to obey the laws of each country and to honor our obligations to society by being an economic, intellectual, and social asset to each community and nation in which the Company operates.

ADDRESS   1047 N. Park Rd.
Wyomissing, PA 19610

INDUSTRY CATEGORY   Consumer Goods and Services

CORPORATE DESCRIPTION
VF Corporation is one of the world's largest publicly owned apparel companies and an international leader in the Jeanswear, Decorated Knitwear, Intimate Apparel, Playwear, and Specialty Apparel categories.

SIZE REVENUES $4,320,000,000 as of 1993

NUMBER OF EMPLOYEES   62,000 as of 1993

SOURCE   *1993 Annual Report,* "The Fortune 500," *Fortune* 129, no. 8 (April 8, 1994)

◆　◆　◆　◆　◆　◆　◆

COMPANY | *Vons (The Vons Companies, Inc.)*

STATEMENT | **The Vons Companies, Inc.**
Mission Statement & Visions
[Mission Statement]

Vons is a premier retailer of foods and related categories including products and services associated with drug stores. We respond to needs and preferences of a wide spectrum of customer segments with a dense and growing state-of-the-art store network employing several names and store types. All are merchandised, staffed and operated with highest integrity providing quality shopping experiences designed to create and keep customers. We are good corporate citizens of the communities in which we operate. We provide a rewarding work environment which attracts, develops and retains quality people. In this manner, we grow our business in volume, share and profits to maximize shareholder value.

[#1 Vision]

The Vons Companies is primarily an operator of supermarkets, super stores, and combination stores, all of which focus on food, drug store products and services, plus selected related categories. Special emphasis is placed on perishable product categories and departments. Our stores are merchandised, staffed and operated with an understanding of customer needs and preferences. This understanding enables us to operate our stores with sustainable competitive advantages.

[#2 Vision]

The Vons Companies is committed to being a growth company. We view opportunities for growth in the further development of our existing businesses, new store additions to our network and strategic acquisitions. We strive to be the share leader in our markets in order that we can most fully utilize our assets and our infrastructure.

[#3 Vision]

The Vons Companies is a customer driven company. We continuously identify value-added factors that create customer satisfaction. In response to our diverse customer base, we operate several separate state-of-the-art store chains each with different store types. Each is managed by a separate retail business unit organization that is served by a central umbrella of support services. This structure contains our non-customer operating costs and enables us to respond quickly to customers changing preferences so as to deliver a Quality Shopping Experience.

[#4 Vision]

Vons believes in involving its employees in managing the business. The Company respects all of its employees and provides them with good working conditions and "open door" policies. The Company fosters a "give a darn" attitude on the part of all employees to generate products and services of outstanding quality.

[#5 Vision]

The Vons Companies is a part of an industry that exists as the purchasing agent of its customers. Faithful to this purpose, we work with our suppliers in a constructive and participative manner to assure the lowest possible cost of product. Simultaneously, we diligently control expenses so as to provide customers with outstanding value from the goods and services we sell.

[#6 Vision]

The Vons Companies will operate from a position of financial strength by maintaining a solid yet flexible capital structure. We emphasize utilization of existing resources to maximize profitability.

[#7 Vision]

Vons has achieved technological leadership which it strives to maintain. We see technology as a vehicle by which to increase customer loyalty, enhance employee satisfaction and improve profitability.

[#8 Vision]

The Vons Companies is committed to being a good corporate citizen. We operate our business with the highest integrity.

[#9 Vision]

The Vons Companies is committed to maximizing shareholder value through consistent earnings per share growth. The Company operates its business for the long term.

ADDRESS   618 Michillinda Ave.
Arcadia, CA 91007-6300

INDUSTRY CATEGORY   Food/Beverage

CORPORATE DESCRIPTION
The Vons Companies, Inc. is the ninth largest supermarket chain in the nation and the market share leader in Southern California.

SIZE REVENUES $5,074,500,000 as of 1993

NUMBER OF EMPLOYEES   30,000 as of 1993

SOURCE   *1993 Annual Report*

◆   ◆   ◆   ◆   ◆   ◆   ◆

COMPANY │ *Vulcan Materials Company*

STATEMENT │ **MISSION**
VULCAN MATERIALS COMPANY is an international producer of industrial materials and commodities that are essential to the standard of living of advanced and developing societies.
OUR mission is to provide quality products and services that consistently meet our customers' expectations; to be responsible stewards with respect to the safety and environmental impact of our operations and products; and to earn superior returns for our shareholders.

WE recognize that success in all of our activities is related directly to the talents, dedication and performance of our employees throughout the Company.

GUIDING PRINCIPLES

INTEGRITY: We will work constantly to earn the respect and trust of all parties we interact with by acting fairly and honorably. We will observe high ethical standards and obey all laws and regulations.

EXCELLENCE: We are committed to excellence in all of our activities. We value innovation. We intend to maintain a position of leadership in each of our industries.

PEOPLE: We will maintain a high respect for people—for their dignity, their talents and their interests.

COMMITMENTS

Following are our most important commitments.
They embody goals that we strive to attain and values
that guide our conduct.

WE will strive to be the low cost producer in each of our industries and to be the standard-setter with regard to quality, service and technical support.

WE will respect the dignity of each of our employees and deal with them fairly. We will strive to maintain an environment that encourages them to develop their talents, exercise creativity and achieve superior performance. We will keep our compensation programs at fair and competitive levels. Employment and advancement will be based on qualifications, performance and organizational needs. We will maintain a firm commitment to employee health and safety.

WE will provide technical and educational assistance so that customers may use our products in an efficient, safe and environmentally proper manner. We will maintain a steadfast commitment to minimize any adverse impacts our activities have on the environments in which we operate. We will comply with all environmental laws and regulations.

WE will compete vigorously in each of our industries while maintaining a strict regard for compliance in all respects with the antitrust laws.

WE will be a good corporate citizen in each community in which we operate. We will support and take an active part in public and charitable projects.

WE will maintain a strong commitment to divisional autonomy consistent with high accountability and performance. Corporate and group staffs will be kept lean and highly competent so that their contributions will add value to divisional results without restricting the initiative and accountability of division managers. Corporate, group and divisional relationships will be marked by goodwill, teamwork and open communications.

WE are determined to achieve superior rates of return on the capital our shareholders have entrusted to us. We intend to rank in the top quartile of U. S. industrial companies as measured by profitability and growth in earnings. We will aggressively pursue profitable growth opportunities through extension of existing product lines, addition of new products, development of greenfield sites and business acquisitions.

ADDRESS   P. O. Box 530187
Birmingham, AL 35253-0187

INDUSTRY CATEGORY   Industrial, Specialized

CORPORATE DESCRIPTION
Vulcan is a producer of industrial materials and commodities with significant positions in two industries. It is the nation's foremost producer of construction aggregates and a leading chemicals manufacturer, producing a diversified line of chlorinated solvents and other industrial chemicals.

SIZE REVENUES $1,133,500,000 as of 1993

NUMBER OF EMPLOYEES   6,883 as of August 1, 1994

SOURCES   1993 *Annual Report*; company representative

◆   ◆   ◆   ◆   ◆   ◆   ◆

COMPANY | *Wackenhut Corporation, The*

STATEMENT | Corporate Vision:
By the year 2000, The Wackenhut Corporation will be recognized throughout the world as a uniquely diversified, superior performing and profitable protective and support services company.
Operating and Financial Goals
The Wackenhut Corporation will:
  ◈ Conduct all Corporate relationships according to the highest moral and ethical standards.
  ◈ Increase earnings per share and shareholder value on a continuing basis.
  ◈ Attract and retain a skilled work force, using only the highest standards in the recruitment and selection of personnel.
  ◈ Increase the productivity and professionalism of personnel at all levels within the organization, by emphasizing sound initial and ongoing training.
  ◈ Respect the dignity, rights and contributions of its employees.
  ◈ Maintain Return on Equity (ROE) at consistently high levels.

❖ Develop and retain a prestigious client base, including companies listed on the Fortune 500 and important agencies within federal, state and local governments.

❖ Seek long term relationships with our clients, based upon quality of service, not lowest price.

❖ Establish and maintain a mechanism for identifying and satisfying real customer needs through a total Corporate quality improvement program.

❖ Continue to improve the quality of Corporate services, to internal as well as external customers.

❖ Develop and achieve meaningful market share goals for each Business Unit.

❖ Continue to diversify into areas that will maximize profits and cash flow, and/or improve market penetration.

❖ Develop a balanced plan of short, medium and long-term interests while achieving sustained, profitable growth.

ADDRESS   1500 San Remo Ave.
Coral Gables, FL 33146

INDUSTRY CATEGORY   Business Services

CORPORATE DESCRIPTION

The Wackenhut Corporation is a diversified provider of security-related services to government, industrial, and business organizations worldwide. It is one of the world's largest security organizations, with offices in over 125 U. S. cities, and in over 50 other countries on six continents. Its uniformed security officers can be found protecting the assets of Fortune 500 companies, major industrial and government complexes, the business and professional communities, retail outlets, and residential neighborhoods. Its capabilities also include: investigations, fire and emergency services, facility management, training and educational services, prison/jail foodservice, and privatization of public services.

SIZE REVENUES $664,160,000 as of 1993

NUMBER OF EMPLOYEES   48,000 (worldwide) as of 1993

SOURCES   *1993 Annual Report;* company representative

◆ ◆ ◆ ◆ ◆ ◆ ◆

COMPANY | *Warner-Lambert Company*

STATEMENT | **OUR VISION**

OUR VISION at Warner-Lambert is to be the best by offering the most innovative, highest quality products to advance the health and well-being of people around the world. Toward this vision we will provide an environment where people can innovate and excel. To achieve this vision, we make these commitments to those whose lives we touch.

OUR CREED

To Our Customers

WE COMMIT OURSELVES to anticipating customer needs and responding first with superior products and services. We are committed to continued investment in the discovery of safe and valuable products to enhance people's lives.

To Our Colleagues

WE COMMIT OURSELVES to attracting and retaining excellent people, and providing them with an open and participative work environment, marked by equal opportunity for personal growth. Performance will be evaluated candidly, on the basis of fair and objective standards. Creativity, speed of action, and openness to change will be prized and rewarded. Colleagues will be treated with dignity and respect. They will have the shared responsibility for continuously improving the performance of the company and the quality of work life.

To Our Shareholders

WE COMMIT OURSELVES to providing fair and attractive economic returns to our shareholders. We are prepared to take prudent risks to achieve sustainable long-term corporate growth.

To Our Business Partners

WE COMMIT OURSELVES to dealing with our suppliers and other business partners fairly and equitably, recognizing our mutual interests.

To Society

WE COMMIT OURSELVES to being responsible corporate citizens, actively initiating and supporting efforts concerning the health of society and stewardship of the environment. We will work to improve the vitality of the worldwide communities in which we operate.

ABOVE ALL, our dealings with these constituencies will be conducted with the utmost integrity, adhering to the highest standards of ethical and just conduct.

ADDRESS   201 Tabor Rd.
Morris Plains, NJ 07950

INDUSTRY CATEGORY   Health Care

CORPORATE DESCRIPTION

Warner-Lambert is a leading worldwide company engaged in the research and development, manufacturing, and marketing of quality health care and consumer products. The company's prescription pharmaceutical business is focused on such major areas of medical need as cardiovascular disease, central nervous system disorders, women's health care, and infectious disease. Warner-Lambert also ranks as the world's leading supplier of empty hard-gelatin capsules for pharmaceutical use. The company's broad range of consumer products includes over-the-counter health care products, shaving and other personal care products, confectionery products, and home aquarium products. These products contribute to the health and well-being of people in more than 130 countries.

SIZE REVENUES $5,793,700,000 as of 1993

NUMBER OF EMPLOYEES   35,000 as of 1993

SOURCE   Company representative

◆　◆　◆　◆　◆　◆　◆

COMPANY | *Washington Gas*

STATEMENT | **OUR MISSION**

TO PROVIDE THE BEST ENERGY VALUE—A SUPERIOR PRODUCT AND QUALITY SERVICE AT A COMPETITIVE PRICE.

OUR BELIEFS

THE CUSTOMER IS THE KEY. **Customers have choices.** We compete with others to add and retain customers. To be the customer's choice, we must continuously and rapidly improve service and productivity. **We listen to our customers.** That is the only way we can identify and meet their changing needs and expectations. **We share community concerns.** We care about the quality of life in our communities and are committed to protecting the environment. We emphasize safety, encourage conservation, and promote efficient energy services at fair prices.

EMPLOYEES ARE THE **Company. Washington Gas is a team.** We must draw strength from diversity and work in partnership with each other and with our customers, communities, investors and suppliers. **We listen to each other.** By doing so, we can build an environment of openness and mutual respect where we can be our best and grow in our jobs. **We set high standards.** We must observe the highest ethical and professional standards in all that we do.

INVESTORS ARE ESSENTIAL. **The company must succeed financially.** We must earn competitive returns for our investors, since they provide the financial underpinning to meet customer, employee, and community needs.

ADDRESS   1100 H St. N.W.
            Washington, DC 20080

INDUSTRY CATEGORY   Utility

CORPORATE DESCRIPTION
Washington Gas and its distribution subsidiaries provide natural gas service to more than 700,000 customers in the growing Washington, D.C. metropolitan area and surrounding region.

Sales to residential and small commercial customers account for 86% of the company's revenues.

SIZE REVENUES $894,300,000 as of 1993

NUMBER OF EMPLOYEES   2,670 (utility and non-utility) as of 1993

SOURCE   *1993 Annual Report*

COMPANY | *Washington Mutual Savings Bank*

STATEMENT | **MISSION**

"Premier Consumer Financial Services Organization in the Northwest"

◇ Focus on Consumer Market
◇ Geographic Focus—Washington, Oregon, Idaho, and Contiguous States
◇ Offer Profitable Line of Loan, Deposit, Investment and Insurance Products
◇ Achieve Superior Long-term Return to Shareholders

ADDRESS 1201 3rd Ave. 12th floor
Seattle, WA 98101

INDUSTRY CATEGORY Banking

CORPORATE DESCRIPTION
Washington Mutual Savings Bank, founded in 1889, is the largest locally managed, independently owned financial institution in Washington.

SIZE REVENUES $179,676,000 (net income) as of December 31, 1993

NUMBER OF EMPLOYEES 4,700 as of December 31, 1993

SOURCE *1993 Annual Report*

COMPANY | *Weirton Steel Corporation*

STATEMENT | **Mission Statement**

Weirton Steel Corporation will lead the industry in satisfying customers with high quality products and services. We are committed to accomplishing this through highly trained and informed employee-owners who participate fully in the continuous process of improving performance, achieving the highest possible level of personal development.

| **VISION FOR SUCCESS**

WE ARE BOUND TOGETHER IN THESE COMMON BELIEFS AND VALUES

WE MUST...

FOR THE CUSTOMERS

❖ Have a total quality commitment to consistently meet the product, delivery and service expectations of all customers.

❖ Give customers increased value through processes that eliminate waste, minimize costs and enhance production efficiency.

FOR THE EMPLOYEE

❖ Reward teamwork, trust, honesty, openness and candor.

❖ Ensure a safe workplace.

❖ Recognize that people are the corporation and provide them with training and information that allows for continuous improvement.

❖ As employee-owners, obligate ourselves to provide a high level of performance and be accountable for our own actions.

❖ Respect the dignity, rights and contributions of others.

FOR THE COMPANY

❖ Continuously invest in new technology and equipment to ensure competitiveness and enhance stockholder value.

❖ Manage our financial and human resources for long-term profitability.

FOR THE COMMUNITY

❖ Commit to environmental responsibility.

❖ Fulfill our responsibility to enhance the quality of community life.

ADDRESS   400 Three Springs Dr.
Weirton, WV 26062-4989

INDUSTRY CATEGORY   Manufacturing

CORPORATE DESCRIPTION
Weirton Steel Corporation, a major integrated steel producer, was formed in 1982 for the purpose of acquiring the assets of the Weirton Steel Division of National Steel Corporation. The Company produces flat rolled carbon steels in sheet and strip form.

SIZE REVENUES $1,201,093,000 as of 1993

NUMBER OF EMPLOYEES   6,026 as of 1993

SOURCE   *1993 Annual Report*

COMPANY | *Wellman, Inc.*

STATEMENT | **WELLMAN, INC.**
THE FIBERS DIVISION

MISSION STATEMENT

The mission of the Wellman Fibers Division is to enhance the value of the company by achieving excellence in the production and marketing of high quality products. We will provide earnings, develop people, and produce value-added products, including those from recycled materials, to support the long term growth of the corporation.

ADDRESS 1040 Broad St., Ste. 302
Shrewsbury, NJ 07702
INDUSTRY CATEGORY Manufacturing

CORPORATE DESCRIPTION
Wellman, Inc., the nation's largest plastics recycler, manufactures and markets high-quality Fortrel® polyester textile fibers, recycled polyester and nylon staple fibers, PET and nylon resins, PET sheet and thermoformed packaging and various related products.

SIZE REVENUES $842,064,000 as of December 31, 1993

NUMBER OF EMPLOYEES 3,650 as of June 30, 1994

SOURCES *1993 Annual Report* and Form 10-K; Form 10-K and Quarterly Report (June, 1994)

COMPANY | *Wendy's International, Inc.*

STATEMENT | **WENDY's MISSION STATEMENT:**
Deliver Total Quality

| **WENDY's VISION STATEMENT:**
To Be The Customer's Restaurant Of Choice And The Employer Of Choice

ADDRESS   4288 W. Dublin Granville Rd.
Dublin, OH 43017

INDUSTRY CATEGORY   Food/Beverage

COMPANY | *Travelpro®*

STATEMENT | **CORPORATE MISSION STATEMENT**
To interact in the workplace as a cohesive team to fulfill employee aspirations, and to exceed customer expectations in every way, with an aim to achieve overall prosperity.

CORPORATE DESCRIPTION
Travelpro® is the innovator of vertical wheeled airline luggage. It ranked number 7 in the 1993 *Inc.* 500 list of fastest growing private companies. The company had 1993 revenues of $29 million, and it had 50 employees as of 1994.

ADDRESS   501 Fairway Dr.
Deerfield Beach, FL 33441

SOURCE   Company representative

CORPORATE DESCRIPTION

Wendy's International, Inc. is the third largest quick-service hamburger chain in the world with close to 4,200 restaurants worldwide, serving a wide variety of fresh, high-quality and nutritious products. Founded nearly 25 years ago, systemwide sales have grown to over $3.9 billion. The Wendy's system is made up of 1,224 company-operated and 2,944 franchised restaurants.

SIZE REVENUES $1,320,095,000 as of 1993

NUMBER OF EMPLOYEES   43,000 as of 1993

SOURCE   *1993 Annual Report*

◆ ◆ ◆ ◆ ◆ ◆ ◆

COMPANY | *Westin Hotels & Resorts*

STATEMENT | **WESTIN HOTELS & RESORTS**
NORTH AMERICA
<u>VISION</u>

Year after year, Westin and its people will be regarded as the best and most sought after hotel and resort management group in North America.

<u>MISSION</u>

In order to realize our Vision, our Mission must be to exceed the expectations of our customers, whom we define as guests, partners, and fellow employees.

We will accomplish this Mission by committing to our shared values and by achieving the highest levels of customer satisfaction, with extraordinary emphasis on the creation of value. In this way we will ensure that our profit, quality and growth goals are met.

ADDRESS   The Westin Building
2001 Sixth Ave.
Seattle, WA 98121

INDUSTRY CATEGORY   Hotel, Hospitality, and Related

CORPORATE DESCRIPTION
Westin Hotels & Resorts is the oldest hotel management company in North America.

SIZE REVENUES $1,100,000,000 as of 1994

NUMBER OF EMPLOYEES   35,000 as of 1994

SOURCE   Company representative

◆　◆　◆　◆　◆　◆　◆

COMPANY | *Weyerhaeuser*

STATEMENT
"A vision describes the desired future state of an organization. To be valid, a vision statement must endure and not change with every business cycle.

"By 'best,' I mean all our stakeholders—customers, employees, shareholders, communities—agree that we are the best and that we have evidence supporting their view."
—Jack Creighton, President

THE BEST FOREST PRODUCTS COMPANY IN THE WORLD

STRATEGIES

We shall achieve our vision by:

- Making Total Quality the Weyerhaeuser Way of doing business.
- Relentless pursuit of full customer satisfaction.
- Empowering Weyerhaeuser people.
- Leading the industry in forest management and manufacturing excellence.
- Producing superior returns for our shareholders.

| OUR VALUES

CUSTOMERS

We listen to our customers and improve our products and services to meet their present and future needs.

PEOPLE

Our success depends upon high-performing people working together in a safe and healthy workplace where diversity, development and teamwork are valued and recognized.

ACCOUNTABILITY

We expect superior performance and are accountable for our actions and results. Our leaders set clear goals and expectations, are supportive, and provide and seek frequent feedback.

CITIZENSHIP

We support the communities where we do business, hold ourselves to the highest standards of ethical conduct and environmental responsibility, and communicate openly with Weyerhaeuser people and the public.

FINANCIAL RESPONSIBILITY

We are prudent and effective in the use of the resources entrusted to us.

ACHIEVING THE VISION

"When this vision is attained, we will be more focused on our customers, our communities, our competition and our share-

holders. There will be more teaming, decisions will be made more quickly, and there will be a greater flow of information through all levels of the company. Perhaps the most striking thing will be that we'll have a more diverse work force."
—Charley Bingham, Executive vice president, timberlands, raw materials and external affairs

"My hope is that the vision and values touch every employee. I want employees to have a firm sense of where the company is going—and to share my confidence that we've begun a journey that will make us the Best Forest Products Company in the World."
—Jack Creighton, President

ADDRESS   Tacoma, WA 98477

INDUSTRY CATEGORY   Forest Products

CORPORATE DESCRIPTION

Weyerhaeuser is an international forest products company whose principal businesses are the growing and harvesting of trees; the manufacture, distribution and sale of forest products, including logs, wood chips, building products, pulp, paper and packaging products; real estate construction and development; and financial services. Weyerhaeuser is the world's largest private owner of merchantable softwood timber and the largest producer of softwood lumber and market pulp. Weyerhaeuser is the largest forest products exporter and among the largest exporters in the United States. It is also one of North America's largest producers of forest products and one of the largest recyclers of office wastepaper, newspaper and corrugated boxes.

SIZE REVENUES $9,544,792,000 as of 1993

NUMBER OF EMPLOYEES   37,000 as of 1993

SOURCES   *1993 Annual Report*; company representative

COMPANY | *Whirlpool Corporation*

STATEMENT | **WHIRLPOOL...REACHING WORLDWIDE TO BRING EXCELLENCE HOME**

Whirlpool, in its chosen lines of business, will grow with new opportunities and be the leader in an ever-changing global market. We will be driven by our commitment to continuous quality improvement and to exceeding in all of our customers' expectations. We will gain competitive advantage through this, and by building on our existing strengths and developing new competencies. We will be market-driven, efficient and profitable. Our success will make Whirlpool a company that worldwide customers, employees and other stakeholders can depend on.

ADDRESS   Administrative Center
2000 M-63
Benton Harbor, MI 49022-2692

INDUSTRY CATEGORY   Manufacturing

CORPORATE DESCRIPTION

Whirlpool Corporation is the world's leading manufacturer and marketer of major home appliances. The company manufactures in 11 countries and markets products in more than 120 countries under major brand names such as Whirlpool, KitchenAid, Roper, Estate, Bauknecht, Ignis, Laden and Inglis. Whirlpool is also the principal supplier to Sears, Roebuck and Co. of many major home appliances marketed under the Kenmore brand name.

SIZE REVENUES $7,533,000,000 as of 1993

NUMBER OF EMPLOYEES   39,590 as of 1993

SOURCE   *1993 Annual Report*

◆   ◆   ◆   ◆   ◆   ◆   ◆

COMPANY | *WICOR, Inc.*

STATEMENT | WICOR Vision

WICOR will be a recognized leader in our businesses, known for delivering the best possible value to our shareholders and customers. We will create economic value for shareholders by capitalizing on new developments in the deregulated natural gas industry and pursuing opportunities in the global marketplace through our manufacturing subsidiaries.

ADDRESS   626 E. Wisconsin Ave.
Milwaukee, WI 53202

INDUSTRY CATEGORY   Diversified

CORPORATE DESCRIPTION

WICOR, Inc. is a diversified company formed in 1980 to provide shareholders opportunities for financial return through investments in utility and non-utility businesses. WICOR operates three subsidiaries in two industries, natural gas distribution and manufacturing. Its subsidiaries are Wisconsin Gas Company, Sta-Rite Industries, Inc., and SHURflo Pump Manufacturing Co.

SIZE REVENUES $849,500,000 as of 1993

NUMBER OF EMPLOYEES   3,222 as of 1993

SOURCE   Company representative

◆ ◆ ◆ ◆ ◆ ◆ ◆

COMPANY | *Winnebago Industries, Inc.*

STATEMENT | **MISSION STATEMENT**

Winnebago Industries, Inc. is a profit-oriented company which manufactures and markets high-value, quality leisure products.

Secondary missions include financial management, brand licensing, OEM parts/sales and satellite courier services.

These activities do not exclude the possibility that Winnebago will participate in other endeavors, providing these endeavors are either synergistic to the primary and secondary missions defined above or represent activities that can be financially justified.

In all cases, the company will meet its defined missions through the proper and effective utilization of capital, processes and people.

ADDRESS   P. O. Box 152
605 W. Crystal Lake Rd.
Forest City, IA 50436

INDUSTRY CATEGORY   Motor Vehicles and Related

CORPORATE DESCRIPTION
Winnebago Industries, Inc., headquartered in Forest City, Iowa, is a leading United States manufacturer of motor homes, self-contained recreation vehicles used primarily in leisure travel and outdoor recreation activities. Motor home and van conversion sales represent more than 80 percent of the Company revenues.

Winnebago Industries also owns an 80 percent interest in Cycle-Sat, Inc., a telecommunications service firm that is a leading distributor of television and radio commercials using satellite, fiber optic and digital technologies.

SIZE REVENUES $452,116,000 as of 1994

NUMBER OF EMPLOYEES   3,100 as of November, 1994

SOURCE   Company representative

◆ ◆ ◆ ◆ ◆ ◆ ◆

COMPANY | *Wisconsin Dairies Cooperative*

STATEMENT | WISCONSIN DAIRIES' MISSION
The mission of Wisconsin Dairies Cooperative is to provide dairy farmers with a financially sound organization that efficiently assembles, processes and markets milk and related dairy products to customers in a manner that generates fair and equitable returns for past, present and future member-owners.

ADDRESS   P. O. Box 111
Baraboo, WI 53913

INDUSTRY CATEGORY   Food/Beverage

CORPORATE DESCRIPTION
Wisconsin Dairies Cooperative is a dairy cooperative serving member-owners.

SIZE REVENUES $548,289,000 as of March 31, 1994

NUMBER OF EMPLOYEES   946 as of 1994

SOURCE   *1994 Annual Report*

◆　◆　◆　◆　◆　◆　◆

COMPANY | *Wisconsin Energy Corporation*

STATEMENT | **Wisconsin Energy Corporation**
Mission and Goals Statement
Our Mission:
To be the premier provider of energy and energy related services in the North Central United States.
Our Goals:
❖ To establish a position as the low-cost provider of energy in the region.
❖ To focus on customer addition, retention and expansion through the development of value-added products and services.
❖ To grow through expansion of the area we serve, and through partnerships and alliances that complement our strengths.

ADDRESS   231 W. Michigan St.
P. O. Box 2046
Milwaukee, WI 53201

INDUSTRY CATEGORY   Utility

CORPORATE DESCRIPTION
Wisconsin Energy Corp. is a holding company with subsidiaries in utility and nonutility businesses. Its principal subsidiaries are Wisconsin Electric Power Co. and Wisconsin Natural Gas Co.

Wisconsin Electric is engaged principally in the generation, transmission, distribution and sale of electric energy in a territory of approximately 12,600 square miles in southeastern Wisconsin, the east central and northern portions of Wisconsin and the Upper Peninsula of Michigan. The operating area includes metropolitan Milwaukee and has an estimated population of more than 2 million.

Wisconsin Natural purchases gas from various supply areas, transports gas to Wisconsin through pipeline companies and then distributes and sells it in three areas in Wisconsin. The gas service territory has an estimated population of more than 1 million, mainly within the electric service area of Wisconsin Electric.

SIZE REVENUES $1,643,652,000 as of 1993

NUMBER OF EMPLOYEES   4,750 as of 1994

SOURCES   *1993 Annual Report*; company representative

OUR VISION

People Creating The World's Premier Energy Company

BEHIND THE WORDS OF THE VISION

A vision is a mental image of the company we want to be. It's intended to give all employees, as well as everyone else the company works with and serves, a consistent picture of the company we are creating.

"People"

All employees sharing a commitment to work together, and with customers and suppliers, to become the World's Premier Energy Company.

"Creating"

Employees immersing themselves in the excitement of continuously inventing and improving products and services in a world of ever-changing needs, expectations, and demands.

"World's Premier Energy Company"

An organization that, in the eyes of customers and all others creates best-value services and products for customers, constantly improves, and respects all people. Its employees share common beliefs, are committed to a common purpose and quality, and are highly skilled.

OUR MISSION

Provide Customers with the Best Value in Energy and Related Services

BEHIND THE WORDS OF THE MISSION

A mission describes the aim of our current business practices. It offers us direction.

"Provide Customers"

Employees working with customers, suppliers, and others to ensure that products and services exceed customers' expectations.

"Best Value"
What customers recognize as the most desirable combination of service, quality, reliability and price.
"Energy and Related Services"
Employees providing products primarily associated with electricity and natural gas, as well as expertise, assistance and programs associated with customers' energy use.

THE BELIEFS WE SHARE

To be the company we have described in our Vision, we need to create a new culture for ourselves—one that encourages and allows us to act in harmony with the following central beliefs.

It is important that each of us explore our understanding of these beliefs and decide whether we can share them with others in the company, because these beliefs will direct our company actions and decisions for the future.

❖ Our customers are the primary focus of our efforts.

❖ Our actions must always be rooted in honesty and integrity; we should always foster truth, faith in others, fairness and respect.

❖ Our learning through study, review, dialogue and experimentation benefits our customers, ourselves and our company.

❖ We must continuously work together to create and improve processes, and eliminate those that are no longer valuable.

❖ We cannot tolerate actions that crush people's self-esteem, aspirations, individuality or dignity.

❖ We must recognize that every employee adds value to the company; therefore, we must not allow job titles or positions to stand in the way of an employee's ability or willingness to contribute.

❖ We must acknowledge and use the experiences and insights brought to the company through people's diverse backgrounds, choices, life situations and perspectives, and ensure the freedom to express our diversity.

❖ We must be flexible as individuals and as a company.

❖ We must share information, ideas and knowledge freely, quickly, candidly and unencumbered by organizational structures or individuals.

❖ We must responsibly act as faithful stewards of the resources entrusted to us by others.

❖ Work should enrich and bring joy to every employee.

ADDRESS   700 North Adams
P. O. Box 19001
Green Bay, WI 54307-9001

INDUSTRY CATEGORY   Utility

CORPORATE DESCRIPTION
Wisconsin Public Service Corporation is an investor-owned electric and gas utility providing service to a 10,000 square mile area of Northeastern Wisconsin and an adjacent part of Upper Michigan.

SIZE REVENUES $680,632,000 as of 1993

NUMBER OF EMPLOYEES   2,562 as of May 28, 1994

SOURCES   *1993 Annual Report*; company representative

COMPANY | *WMX Technologies, Inc.*

STATEMENT

The mission of WMX Technologies, Inc. is to be the acknowledged worldwide leader in providing comprehensive environmental, waste management and related services of the highest quality to industry, government and consumers using state-of-the-art systems responsive to customer need, sound environmental policy and the highest standards of corporate citizenship.

In fulfilling this mission, we shall provide a rewarding work environment for our people, cooperate with all relevant government agencies, and promote a spirit of partnership with the communities and enterprises we serve as we strive to be a responsible neighbor, while increasing shareholder value.

ADDRESS   3003 Butterfield Rd.
Oak Brook, IL 60521-1100

COMPANY | *United Vision Group*

STATEMENT | MISSION STATEMENT

As a company and as individuals we will do our best to become a model company. We will achieve this by offering products of the highest quality at the right price with a standard of service that is rooted in our desire to serve others.

INDUSTRY CATEGORY   Diversified

CORPORATE DESCRIPTION

The WMX Technologies is a family of environmental services companies.

The WMX Technologies family of companies includes five subsidiaries: Waste Management, Inc., Chemical Waste Management, Inc., Wheelabrator Technologies, Inc., Rust International Inc. and Waste Management International plc.

These companies offer clear, comprehensive and lasting environmental solutions.

SIZE REVENUES $9,135,577,000 as of 1993

NUMBER OF EMPLOYEES   72,600 as of 1993

SOURCES   1993 *Annual Report;* "The Fortune Service 500," *Fortune* 129, no. 11 (May 30, 1994)

CORPORATE DESCRIPTION

United Vision Group is the parent company of three corporations that retail, manufacture, and import furniture, jewelry, and fresh cut flowers. United Vision Group had 1994 sales of $33 million and 310 employees.

ADDRESS   34 State St.
Ossining, NY 10562

SOURCE   Company representative

COMPANY | *York International*

STATEMENT | **Mission Statement**

Build on the York International tradition of innovative technology to become the worldwide leader of environmentally responsive heating, ventilation, air conditioning and refrigeration systems designed to improve the quality of life.

ADDRESS　　P. O. Box 1592-364B
York, PA 17405-1592

INDUSTRY CATEGORY　Manufacturing

CORPORATE DESCRIPTION

York International is the largest independent supplier of heating, ventilating, air conditioning and refrigeration products in the United States and a leading competitor worldwide. York designs, manufactures, sells and services heating, ventilation and air conditioning systems, and compressors for residential and commercial markets, gas compression equipment for industrial processing, industrial and commercial refrigeration equipment, and compressors for air conditioning and refrigeration applications.

SIZE REVENUES　$2,031,949,000 as of 1993

NUMBER OF EMPLOYEES　13,800 as of 1993

SOURCE　*1993 Annual Report*

A TAXING MISSION: THE MISSION OF THE INTERNAL REVENUE SERVICE

In real life, following close on the heels of the nation's top companies, is another organization dedicated to its own singular purpose: the U. S. Internal Revenue Service.

So it seems fitting to close this survey of corporate mission statements with the official mission of the I.R.S.

MISSION STATEMENT OF THE INTERNAL REVENUE SERVICE

The purpose of the Internal Revenue Service is to collect the proper amount of tax revenue at the least cost; serve the public by continually improving the quality of our products and services; and perform in a manner warranting the highest degree of public confidence in our integrity, efficiency, and fairness.

Source: *Guide to the Internal Revenue Service for Congressional Staff.* I.R.S. Publication #1273 (January, 1994).

A FINAL WORD

Many well-known companies are conspicuously absent from this book. You may have wondered why you didn't see certain familiar household names.

Hundreds of companies from the *Fortune* 2000 and *Forbes* 200 simply do not have mission statements. Of the 875 companies that responded to my first call-for-mission-statements mailing to 1,300 companies, more than half did not have one. I researched each of the four hundred twenty-five companies that did not respond. Roughly five percent actually had mission statements and only a handful of those were willing to be included in this book.

There are some verifiable reasons why some companies are absent from the list in this book. Many are in the process of rewriting their statements and would not grant me permission to reprint their old ones, as they did not reflect the companies' new direction or culture. And still others *do* have mission statements but would not allow me to reprint them—even though their statements are published in their annual reports.

The following is just a sample of the companies that, according to my research, do not have mission statements.

Aetna
Apple Computer
ARCO
Black & Decker
Borden
Campbell Soup Company
Chiquita Brands International
The Chubb Corporation
Colgate-Palmolive
Compaq Computer Corporation
Del Monte Foods
Dr. Pepper/Seven-Up Companies Inc.
DURACELL International Inc.

Eastman Kodak Company
Eli Lilly and Company
Ford Motor Company
The Great A. & P. Tea Company, Inc.
Harley-Davidson, Inc.
The Home Depot
Intel Corporation
International Paper
J. P. Morgan & Co. Incorporated
James River Corporation
John Hancock Mutual Life Insurance Company
Johnson & Johnson
Kelly Services
Mattel, Inc.
McDonald's Corporation
McGraw-Hill, Inc.
McKesson Corporation
Merrill Lynch
NAPA Genuine Parts Company
The New York Times Company
NYNEX Corporation
Pitney Bowes
The Quaker Oats Company
RJR Nabisco, Inc.
Safeway Inc.
Schering-Plough Corporation
Sears, Roebuck and Co.
Sherwin Williams
Toys "R" Us
The Travelers
Tyson Foods, Inc.
USX Corporation
Wal-Mart Stores, Inc.

The Walt Disney Company
Westinghouse Electric Corporation
Wm. Wrigley Jr. Company
Zenith Electronics Corporation

Of course, between the time I conducted my research and the release of this book, some companies on this list may have created mission statements. I welcome the opportunity to consider their statements, or any others that my research overlooked, for the next edition of *The Mission Statement Book*.

PART III

Advertising
Burnett (Leo Burnett Company, Inc.)

Aerospace
Raytheon Aircraft Company
Sundstrand Corporation

Agriculture
Cenex Inc
Pioneer Hi-Bred International, Inc.

Banking
Barnett Banks, Inc.
Bay View Capital Corporation (Bay View Federal Bank)
Centerbank
Centura Banks, Inc.
Chase Manhattan Corporation
Chemical Banking Corporation
Citicorp
Comerica Incorporated
Commercial Federal Corporation
Deposit Guaranty Corp
First American Corporation
First Bank System
First Financial Corporation
First Interstate Bancorp
First of America Bank Corporation
First Tennessee National Corporation
First Virginia Banks, Inc.
Firstar Corporation
Hibernia Corporation
Huntington Bancshares Incorporated
MBNA Corporation
Meridian Bancorp, Inc.
National City Corporation
Old Kent Financial Corporation
San Francisco Federal Savings (SFFed Corp.)

Sanwa Bank
SouthTrust Corporation
St. Paul Bancorp, Inc.
TCF Financial Corporation
Washington Mutual Savings Bank

Business Products
Deluxe Corporation
HON Industries
Miller (Herman Miller Inc.)
Standard Register Company, The

Business Services
Adia Personnel Services
Corporate Child Care Management Services
Ecolab Inc.
Johnson Controls, Inc.
Maritz Inc.
Total System Services, Inc.
Unisys Corporation
Wackenhut Corporation, The

Chemicals
Aristech Chemical Corporation
Betz Laboratories, Inc.
Cabot Corporation
Ciba-Geigy Corporation
Dow Chemical Company, The
Ethyl Corporation
Georgia Gulf
Grace (W. R. Grace & Co.)
Hanna (M. A. Hanna Company)
Hoechst Celanese Corporation
Lyondell Petrochemical Company
Nalco Chemical Company
Olin Corporation
Union Carbide

Computer Services
Computer Sciences Corporation

Construction
Butler Manufacturing Company
Caterpillar Inc.

Kaufman and Broad Home Corporation
Lafarge Corporation
Perini Corporation
Ply Gem Industries, Inc.
Texas Industries, Inc.
Turner (The Turner Corporation)

Consumer and Business Services
Borg-Warner Security Corporation

Consumer Goods and Services
Avon Products, Inc.
Blockbuster Entertainment Group
Clorox (The Clorox Company)
Gillette (The Gillette Company)
Johnson Wax (S. C. Johnson & Sons, Inc.)
Jostens, Inc.
Kellwood Company
Levi Strauss & Co.
Mary Kay Cosmetics, Inc.
Nike, Inc.
Rubbermaid Incorporated
Shaklee U. S., Inc.
Stride Rite Corporation, The
Tultex Corporation
VF Corporation

Diversified
Eastern Enterprises
GenCorp
General Electric Company
General Public Utilities Corporation
Rollins Inc.
TRW Inc.
United Dominion Industries
WICOR, Inc.
WMX Technologies, Inc.

Electronics
AMP Incorporated
Kent Electronics Corporation
Rockwell International Corporation
Sensormatic

Environmental Engineering
Geraghty & Miller, Inc.

Financial Investment Services
Advest, Inc.
Edwards (A. G. Edwards & Sons, Inc.)
First Financial Management Corporation
General Motors Acceptance Corporation (GMAC)
Household International, Inc.
MBIA Inc.
Schwab (The Charles Schwab Corporation)

Food/Beverage
Anheuser-Busch Companies, Inc.
Ben & Jerry's Homemade, Inc.
Bruno's, Inc.
Dreyer's Grand Ice Cream, Inc.
Flagstar Companies, Inc.
Fleming Companies, Inc.
General Mills, Inc.
Hershey Foods Corporation
Hormel Foods Corporation
International Dairy Queen, Inc.
Kellogg's (Kellogg Company)
Kroger (The Kroger Co.)
Mid-America Dairymen, Inc.
PepsiCo, Inc.
Pet Incorporated
Pillsbury (The Pillsbury Company)
Rich Products Corporation
Rykoff-Sexton, Inc.
Savannah Foods & Industries, Inc.
Stroh Brewery Company, The
Sysco Corporation
Tootsie Roll Industries, Inc.
Universal Foods Corporation
Vons (The Vons Companies, Inc.)
Wendy's International, Inc.
Wisconsin Dairies Cooperative

Forest Products
Weyerhaeuser

Health Care
Bard (C. R. Bard, Inc.)
Bausch & Lomb Incorporated
Columbia/HCA Healthcare Corp.
Continental Medical System
Warner-Lambert Company

High Technology
Applied Materials
Autodesk
Computervision Corporation
Conner Peripherals, Inc.
Cray Research, Inc.
Digi International Inc.
Hewlett-Packard Company
IBM (International Business Machines Corporation)
LSI Logic Corporation
Martin Marietta Corporation
Microsoft Corporation
National Semiconductor
Rainbow Technologies
SAS Institute Inc.

Hotel, Hospitality, and Related
International Game Technology
Marriott International, Inc.
Promus Companies Incorporated, The
Westin Hotels & Resorts

Industrial, Specialized
Alliant Techsystems Inc.
Allied Signal Inc.
Carpenter Technology Corporation
CBI Industries, Inc.
Ferro Corporation
Gates Rubber Company
Safety-Kleen Corporation
UTILX Corporation
Vulcan Materials Company

Insurance
American United Life Insurance Company

Ameritas Life Insurance Corp.
CNA Insurance Companies
CUNA Mutual Insurance Group
General American Life Insurance Company
Kansas City Life Insurance Company
Kemper Corporation
Keyport Life Insurance Company
Lincoln National Corporation
New England Mutual Life Insurance Company (The New England)
Northwestern Mutual Life
Principal Financial Group
Protective Life Corporation
State Auto Insurance Companies
United States Fidelity and Guaranty Corporation
UNUM Corporation

Manufacturing
AMETEK
Anthony Industries, Inc.
Armstrong World Industries, Inc.
Baldor Electric Company
Ball Corporation
Boise Cascade Corporation
Chemfab Corporation
Clark Equipment Company
Copperweld Corporation
Corning Incorporated
Duriron (The Duriron Company, Inc.)
Eaton Corporation
Federal-Mogul Corporation
Fuller (H. B. Fuller Company)
Harsco Corporation
Inland Container Corporation
Inland Steel Industries
Kaydon Corporation
Minnesota Mining and Manufacturing Company (3M)
Oneida Ltd.
Premark International, Inc.
Reynolds Metals Company
Sonoco Products Company
Sta-Rite Industries

TRINOVA Corporation
Varlen Corporation
Weirton Steel Corporation
Wellman, Inc.
Whirlpool Corporation
York International Corporation

Media/Printing/Publishing

Banta Corporation
Gannett Company, Inc.
Knight-Ridder, Inc.
Scripps (The E. W. Scripps Company)
Times Mirror Company
Tribune Company
Valassis Communications, Inc.

Medical Products and Services

Baxter Healthcare Corporation
Becton Dickinson and Company
Haemonetics Corporation
Medtronic, Inc.
Owens & Minor
PSICOR, Inc.
SpaceLabs Medical, Inc.

Motor Vehicles and Related

Chrysler Corporation
Coachmen Industries, Inc.
Cooper Tire & Rubber Company
Dana Corporation
Donnelly Corporation
General Motors Corporation
Goodyear Tire & Rubber Company
Winnebago Industries

Oil and Gas

Chevron Corporation
Diamond Shamrock, Inc.
Energen Corporation
Forest Oil Corporation
Maxus Energy Corporation
Mobil Corporation

Shell Chemical Company
Sun Company, Inc.
Unocal Corporation

Package Delivery Service
Airborne Express
United Parcel Service

Pharmaceutical/Biotechnology
ICN Pharmaceuticals, Inc.
Merck & Co., Inc.
Research Industries Corporation
Rhône-Poulenc Rorer Inc.

Retail
Ace Hardware Corporation
Best Products Co., Inc.
Federated Department Stores, Inc.
Gibson Greetings, Inc.
Lowe's Companies, Inc.
Meyer (Fred Meyer, Inc.)
Penney (J. C. Penney Company, Inc.)
United States Shoe Corporation, The

Security
American Protective Services, Inc.

Telecommunications
Ameritech
AT&T Corp.
Comptek Research, Inc.
MCI Communications Corporation

Transportation
AMR Corporation (American Airlines)
Burlington Northern Inc.
Chicago and North Western Transportation Co.
Consolidated Freightways, Inc.
Continental Airlines
CSX Corporation
Delta Air Lines, Inc.
Federal Express Corporation
Landstar Systems, Inc.

Norfolk Southern Corporation
Roadway Services, Inc.
Ryder System, Inc.
SkyWest Airlines, Inc.
Southern Pacific Rail Corporation
Southwest Airlines Co.
SPX Corporation

Utility
Atlanta Gas Light Company
CMS Energy
Duke Power Company
Entergy Corporation
FPL Group, Inc.
Houston Industries Incorporated
Illinois Power Company
Kansas City Power & Light Company
Montana Power Company
Niagara Mohawk Power Corp.
Northeast Utilities
Northern States Power Company
Oklahoma Natural Gas Company
PacifiCorp
Pennsylvania Power & Light Company
Public Service Enterprise Group Incorporated
Southern California Edison Company
Southern Company
Union Electric
Washington Gas
Wisconsin Energy Corporation
Wisconsin Public Service Corporation

General Motors Corporation—710,800 (average, worldwide)
PepsiCo, Inc.—423,000
AT&T Corp.—308,700
United Parcel Service—303,000
IBM (International Business Machines Corporation)—256,207
General Electric Company—222,000 (worldwide)
Penney (J. C. Penney Company, Inc.)—193,000
Kroger (The Kroger Co.)—190,000
Marriott International, Inc.—170,000
Columbia/HCA Healthcare Corp.—130,000
Chrysler Corporation—128,000
Flagstar Companies, Inc.—123,000
General Mills, Inc.—121,290
AMR Corporation (American Airlines)—118,422
Federal Express Corporation—103,900+ (worldwide)
Hewlett-Packard Company—96,200
Martin Marietta Corporation—92,000
Goodyear Tire & Rubber Company—90,384
Ciba-Geigy Corporation—87,480 (worldwide)
Borg-Warner Security Corporation—87,000
Minnesota Mining And Manufacturing Company (3M)—86,168
Allied Signal Inc.—86,400
Citicorp—81,500 (worldwide)
Rockwell International Corporation—77,028
WMX Technologies, Inc.—72,600
Delta Air Lines, Inc.—71,412
Ameritech—67,192
Federated Department Stores, Inc.—67,000+
Dow Chemical Company, The—65,400
VF Corporation—62,000
Mobil Corporation—61,900
Baxter Healthcare Corporation—60,400
TRW Inc.—60,000
Blockbuster Entertainment Group—55,000
Caterpillar Inc.—51,250
Johnson Controls, Inc.—50,100 (worldwide)
Eaton Corporation—50,000

Unisys Corporation—49,000

Wackenhut Corporation, The—48,000 (worldwide)

Chevron Corporation—47,576

Merck & Co., Inc.—47,100 (worldwide)

CSX Corporation—47,063

Roadway Services, Inc.—46,600

Anheuser-Busch Companies, Inc.—43,345

Continental Airlines—43,140

Wendy's International, Inc.—43,000

Chemical Banking Corporation—41,567

Whirlpool Corporation—39,590

Ryder System, Inc.—39,235

Corning Incorporated—39,200

Consolidated Freightways, Inc.—39,100

United States Shoe Corporation, The—38,000

Weyerhaeuser—37,000

Gannett Company, Inc.—36,500

Levi Strauss & Co.—36,400

MCI Communications Corporation—36,235

Dana Corporation—36,000

Lowe's Companies, Inc.—35,000

Warner-Lambert Company—35,000

Westin Hotels & Resorts—35,000

Grace (W. R. Grace & Co.)—34,000

Chase Manhattan Corporation—34,000

Gillette (The Gillette Company)—33,400

Burlington Northern Inc.—30,502

Avon Products, Inc.—30,000

Computer Sciences Corporation—30,000

Vons (The Vons Companies, Inc.)—30,000

Hoechst Celanese Corporation—29,900 (worldwide)

Norfolk Southern Corporation—29,304 (average)

Reynolds Metals Company—29,000 (worldwide)

Southern Company—28,743

First Interstate Bancorp—28,128

Bruno's, Inc.—27,000

Promus Companies Incorporated, The—27,000

Times Mirror Company—26,936

AMP Incorporated—26,900 (worldwide)

Sysco Corporation—26,200

Meyer (Fred Meyer, Inc.)—25,000

Premark International, Inc.—24,000

Fleming Companies, Inc.—23,000

National Semiconductor—22,300 (worldwide)

Rhône-Poulenc Rorer Inc.—22,000

Armstrong World Industries, Inc.—20,500

Knight-Ridder, Inc.—20,420 (worldwide)

National City Corporation—19,960

Becton Dickinson and Company—19,100

Southern Pacific Rail Corporation—18,982

Barnett Banks, Inc.—18,400

General Motors Acceptance Corporation (GMAC)—18,300

Duke Power Company—18,274

Pillsbury (The Pillsbury Company)—18,000

Deluxe Corporation—17,748

Boise Cascade Corporation—17,362

Household International, Inc.—17,300

Sonoco Products Company—17,000 (worldwide)

Southern California Edison Company—17,000

Inland Steel Industries—16,152

Kellogg's (Kellogg Company)—16,151

Southwest Airlines Co.—16,000+

Bausch & Lomb Incorporated—15,900 (worldwide)

Airborne Express—15,774

Kellwood Company—15,500 (worldwide)

Microsoft Corporation—15,257

TRINOVA Corporation—15,012

CNA Insurance Companies—15,000

Sun Company, Inc.—14,557

Federal-Mogul Corporation—14,400

Hershey Foods Corporation—14,300

Principal Financial Group—14,275

CBI Industries, Inc.—14,100

Continental Medical Systems, Inc.—14,000

Ball Corporation—13,954

York International Corporation—13,800

PacifiCorp—13,635

Unocal Corporation—13,613

First of America Bank Corporation—13,472

GenCorp—13,300 (worldwide)

Johnson Wax (S. C. Johnson & Sons, Inc.)—13,100+ (worldwide)

Union Carbide—13,051

American Protective Services, Inc.—13,000+

Harsco Corporation—12,900

FPL Group, Inc.—12,406

Olin Corporation—12,400

First Bank System—12,300

Public Service Enterprise Group Incorporated—12,027

Gates Rubber Company—12,000

Rubbermaid Incorporated—11,978

General Public Utilities Corporation—11,963

Entergy Corporation—11,914

Lincoln National Corporation—11,890

United Dominion Industries—11,700

Best Products Co., Inc.—11,500

First Financial Management Corporation—11,500

Comerica—11,424

Houston Industries Incorporated—11,350

Niagara Mohawk Power Corp.—11,295

Raytheon Aircraft Company—10,690 (worldwide)

Edwards (A. G. Edwards & Sons, Inc.)—10,206

Conner Peripherals, Inc.—10,000

Medtronic, Inc.—10,000 (approximately)

Tribune Company—9,900

CMS Energy—9,811

Hormel Foods Corporation—9,500

Northeast Utilities—9,300

Sundstrand Corporation—9,300

MBNA Corporation—9,221

Firstar Corporation—9,000

Nike, Inc.—9,000

SPX Corporation—8,600

Bard (C. R. Bard, Inc.)—8,450

Huntington Bancshares Incorporated—8,395

Jostens, Inc.—8,000

Scripps (The E. W. Scripps Company)—7,900

Pennsylvania Power & Light Company—7,765

Cooper Tire & Rubber Company—7,607

Ecolab Inc.—7,586

Tultex Corporation—7,513

Northern States Power Company—7,362

Lafarge Corporation—7,300
SouthTrust Corporation—7,243
First Tennessee National Corporation—7,074
UNUM Corporation—7,000
Meridian Bancorp, Inc.—6,917
Vulcan Materials Company—6,883
Nalco Chemical Company—6,802
Ferro Corporation—6,627
Safety-Kleen Corporation—6,600
Gibson Greetings, Inc.—6,500
Rich Products Corporation—6,500
Schwab (The Charles Schwab Corporation)—6,500
United States Fidelity and Guaranty Corporation—6,500
Union Electric—6,400
Kemper Corporation—6,335
Hanna (M. A. Hanna Company)—6,334
Burnett (Leo Burnett Company, Inc.)—6,300
Hon Industries—6,257
Chicago and North Western Transportation Co.—6,158
AMETEK Inc.—6,100 (worldwide)
Weirton Steel Corporation—6,026
Miller (Herman Miller Inc.)—6,005
Diamond Shamrock, Inc.—6,000+
Fuller (H. B. Fuller Company)—6,000
Maritz Inc.—6,000
Clark Equipment Company—5,948
Standard Register Company, The—5,769
Pet Incorporated—5,739
Shell Chemical Company—5,500
CUNA Mutual Insurance Group—5,500
Cabot Corporation—5,400
Oneida Ltd.—5,400
Sensormatic—5,000
Cray Research, Inc.—4,960
Alliant Techsystems Inc.—4,900
Clorox (The Clorox Company)—4,850
Pioneer Hi-Bred International, Inc.—4,807
Wisconsin Energy Corporation—4,750
Old Kent Financial Corporation—4,745
Applied Materials, Inc.—4,739

First Virginia Banks, Inc.—4,727

Washington Mutual Savings Bank—4,700

Illinois Power Company—4,540

Banta Corporation—4,204

Betz Laboratories, Inc.—4,115

Montana Power Company—4,089

Ply Gem Industries, Inc.—4,000

Universal Foods Corporation—4,000

Computervision Corporation—3,800

Atlanta Gas Light Company—3,764

Carpenter Technology Corporation—3,697

Wellman, Inc.—3,650

TCF Financial Corporation—3,625

Eastern Enterprises—3,600

Ace Hardware Corporation—3,405

LSI Logic Corporation—3,400

Northwestern Mutual Life—3,304

Stride Rite Corporation, The—3,300

WICOR, Inc.—3,222

SAS Institute Inc.—3,200 (worldwide)

First American Corporation—3,100

Winnebago Industries—3,100

Sanwa Bank—3,023 (full- and part-time)

Baldor Electric Company—3,000

Cenex Inc.—3,000

International Game Technology—3,000 (worldwide)

Owens & Minor—3,000

Mid-America Dairymen, Inc.—2,932

Donnelly Corporation—2,704

Texas Industries, Inc.—2,700

General American Life Insurance Company—2,691 (salaried)

Washington Gas—2,670 (utility and non-utility)

Deposit Guaranty Corp.—2,575

Butler Manufacturing Company—2,562

Wisconsin Public Service Corporation—2,562

Hibernia Corporation—2,522

New England Mutual Life Insurance Company (The New England)—2,500 (home office)

Coachmen Industries, Inc.—2,486

Turner (The Turner Corporation)—2,400

Duriron (The Duriron Company, Inc.)—2,350 (worldwide)
Kansas City Power & Light Company—2,340
Lyondell Petrochemical Company—2,283
Savannah Foods & Industries, Inc.—2,244
Landstar Systems, Inc.—2,230
Oklahoma Natural Gas Company—2,208
Mary Kay Cosmetics, Inc.—2,200
Varlen Corporation—2,030
Kansas City Life Insurance Company—2,000
Centura Banks, Inc.—1,870
Aristech Chemical Corporation—1,800
Dreyer's Grand Ice Cream, Inc.—1,800
Ethyl Corporation—1,800
Autodesk—1,788
Kaydon Corporation—1,661
Advest, Inc.—1,600
SkyWest Airlines, Inc.—1,600
Sta-Rite Industries—1,600 (worldwide)
Total System Services, Inc.—1,587
SpaceLabs Medical—1,575
Energen Corporation—1,568
Centerbank—1,500
Copperweld Corporation—1,350
State Auto Insurance Companies—1,325
First Financial Corporation—1,320
Tootsie Roll Industries, Inc.—1,300
Kaufman and Broad Home Corporation—1,241
Corporate Child Care Management Services—1,200
Geraghty & Miller, Inc.—1,200
Valassis Communications, Inc.—1,170
Commercial Federal Corporation—1,150
Georgia Gulf—1,124
Haemonetics Corporation—1,109
Protective Life Corporation—1,079
St. Paul Bancorp, Inc.—1,046 (full-time equivalent)
Perini Corporation—1,000+
American United Life Insurance Company—1,000
Wisconsin Dairies Cooperative—946
Ameritas Life Insurance Corp.—850

Maxus Energy Corporation—825
Kent Electronics Corporation—808
Shaklee U. S., Inc.—700 (at corporate office)
Comptek Research, Inc.—660
Ben & Jerry's Homemade, Inc.—600
San Francisco Federal Savings (SFFed Corp.)—577
International Dairy Queen, Inc.—538
Psicor, Inc.—537
Bay View Capital Corporation (Bay View Federal Bank)—476
Chemfab Corporation—427
UTILX Corporation—426
MBIA Inc.—350
Digi International Inc.—333
Keyport Life Insurance Company—308
Research Industries Corporation—200
Forest Oil Corporation—187 (salaried and hourly)
Adia Personnel Services—Not available
Anthony Industries, Inc.—Not available
ICN Pharmaceuticals, Inc.—Not available
Inland Container Corporation—Not available
Rainbow Technologies—Not available
Rollins Inc.—Not available
Rykoff-Sexton, Inc.—Not available
Stroh Brewery Company, The—Not available

Alabama

Bruno's, Inc.
Energen Corporation
Protective Life Corporation
SouthTrust Corporation
Vulcan Materials Company

Arkansas

Baldor Electric Company

California

Adia Personnel Services
American Protective Services, Inc.
Anthony Industries, Inc.
Applied Materials, Inc.
Autodesk
Bay View Capital Corporation (Bay View Federal Bank)
Chevron Corporation
Clorox (The Clorox Company)
Computer Sciences Corporation
Conner Peripherals, Inc.
Consolidated Freightways, Inc.
Dreyer's Grand Ice Cream, Inc.
First Interstate Bancorp
Hewlett-Packard Company
ICN Pharmaceuticals, Inc.
Kaufman and Broad Home Corporation
Levi Strauss & Co.
Lsi Logic Corporation
National Semiconductor
PSICOR, Inc.
Rainbow Technologies
Rockwell International Corporation
Rykoff-Sexton, Inc.
San Francisco Federal Savings (SFFed Corp.)
Sanwa Bank
Schwab (The Charles Schwab Corporation)
Shaklee U. S., Inc.

Southern California Edison Company
Southern Pacific Rail Corporation
Times Mirror Company
Unocal Corporation
Vons (The Vons Companies, Inc.)

Colorade
Forest Oil Corporation
Gates Rubber Company
Geraghty & Miller, Inc.

Connecticut
Advest, Inc.
Centerbank
General Electric Company
Landstar Systems, Inc.
Northeast Utilities
Olin Corporation
Union Carbide

District of Columbia
Marriott International, Inc.
MCI Communications Corporation
Washington Gas

Delaware
MBNA Corporation

Florida
Barnett Banks, Inc.
Blockbuster Entertainment Group
FPL Group, Inc.
Grace (W. R. Grace & Co.)
Kaydon Corporation
Knight-Ridder, Inc.
Ryder System, Inc.
Sensormatic
Wackenhut Corporation, The

Georgia
Atlanta Gas Light Company
Delta Air Lines, Inc.
First Financial Management Corporation
Georgia Gulf

Rollins Inc.
Savannah Foods & Industries, Inc.
Southern Company
Total System Services, Inc.
United Parcel Service

Iowa

HON Industries
Pioneer Hi-Bred International, Inc.
Principal Financial Group
Winnebago Industries

Idaho

Boise Cascade Corporation

Illinois

Ace Hardware Corporation
Ameritech
Baxter Healthcare Corporation
Borg-Warner Security Corporation
Burnett (Leo Burnett Company, Inc.)
Caterpillar Inc.
CBI Industries, Inc.
Chicago and North Western Transportation Co.
CNA Insurance Companies
Household International, Inc.
Illinois Power Company
Inland Steel Industries
Kemper Corporation
Nalco Chemical Company
Premark International, Inc.
Safety-Kleen Corporation
St. Paul Bancorp, Inc.
Sundstrand Corporation
Tootsie Roll Industries, Inc.
Tribune Company
Varlen Corporation
WMX Technologies, Inc.

Indiana

American United Life Insurance Company
Ball Corporation
Clark Equipment Company

Coachmen Industries, Inc.
Inland Container Corporation
Lincoln National Corporation

Kansas
Raytheon Aircraft Company

Louisiana
Entergy Corporation
Hibernia Corporation

Massachusetts
Cabot Corporation
Computervision Corporation
Eastern Enterprises
Gillette (The Gillette Company)
Haemonetics Corporation
Keyport Life Insurance Company
New England Mutual Life Insurance Company (The New England)
Perini Corporation
Stride Rite Corporation, The

Maryland
Martin Marietta Corporation
United States Fidelity and Guaranty Corporation

Maine
UNUM Corporation

Michigan
Chrysler Corporation
CMS Energy
Comerica Incorporated
Donnelly Corporation
Dow Chemical Company, The
Federal-Mogul Corporation
First of America Bank Corporation
General Motors Acceptance Corporation (GMAC)
General Motors Corporation
Kellogg's (Kellogg Company)
Miller (Herman Miller Inc.)
Old Kent Financial Corporation
SPX Corporation
Stroh Brewery Company, The

Valassis Communications, Inc.
Whirlpool Corporation

Minnesota
Alliant Techsystems Inc.
Cenex Inc.
Cray Research, Inc.
Deluxe Corporation
Digi International Inc.
Ecolab Inc.
First Bank System
Fuller (H. B. Fuller Company)
General Mills, Inc.
Hormel Foods Corporation
International Dairy Queen, Inc.
Jostens, Inc.
Medtronic, Inc.
Minnesota Mining and Manufacturing Company (3M)
Northern States Power Company
Pillsbury (The Pillsbury Company)
TCF Financial Corporation

Missouri
Anheuser-Busch Companies, Inc.
Butler Manufacturing Company
Edwards (A. G. Edwards & Sons, Inc.)
General American Life Insurance Company
Kansas City Life Insurance Company
Kansas City Power & Light Company
Kellwood Company
Maritz Inc.
Mid-America Dairymen, Inc.
Pet Incorporated
Union Electric

Mississippi
Deposit Guaranty Corp.

Montana
Montana Power Company

North Carolina
Centura Banks, Inc.

Duke Power Company
Lowe's Companies, Inc.
SAS Institute Inc.
United Dominion Industries

Nebraska
Ameritas Life Insurance Corp.
Commercial Federal Corporation

New Hampshire
Chemfab Corporation

New Jersey
Allied Signal Inc.
Bard (C. R. Bard, Inc.)
Becton Dickinson and Company
General Public Utilities Corporation
Hoechst Celanese Corporation
Merck & Co., Inc.
Public Service Enterprise Group Incorporated
Warner-Lambert Company
Wellman, Inc.

Nevada
International Game Technology

New York
AT&T Corp.
Avon Products, Inc.
Bausch & Lomb Incorporated
Chase Manhattan Corporation
Chemical Banking Corporation
Ciba-Geigy Corporation
Citicorp
Comptek Research, Inc.
Corning Incorporated
IBM (International Business Machines Corporation)
MBIA Inc.
Niagara Mohawk Power Corp.
Oneida Ltd.
PepsiCo, Inc.
Ply Gem Industries, Inc.
Rich Products Corporation
Turner (The Turner Corporation)

Ohio

Cooper Tire & Rubber Company
Dana Corporation
Duriron (The Duriron Company, Inc.)
Eaton Corporation
Federated Department Stores, Inc.
Ferro Corporation
GenCorp
Gibson Greetings, Inc.
Goodyear Tire & Rubber Company
Hanna (M. A. Hanna Company)
Huntington Bancshares Incorporated
Kroger (The Kroger Co.)
National City Corporation
Roadway Services, Inc.
Rubbermaid Incorporated
Scripps (The E. W. Scripps Company)
Standard Register Company, The
State Auto Insurance Companies
TRINOVA Corporation
TRW Inc.
United States Shoe Corporation, The
Wendy's International, Inc.

Oklahoma

Fleming Companies, Inc.
Oklahoma Natural Gas Company

Oregon

Meyer (Fred Meyer, Inc.)
Nike, Inc.
PacifiCorp

Pennsylvania

AMETEK, Inc.
AMP Incorporated
Aristech Chemical Corporation
Armstrong World Industries, Inc.
Betz Laboratories, Inc.
Carpenter Technology Corporation
Continental Medical Systems, Inc.
Copperweld Corporation
Harsco Corporporation

Hershey Foods Corporation
Meridian Bancorp, Inc.
Pennsylvania Power & Light Company
Rhône-Poulenc Rorer Inc.
Sun Company, Inc.
Unisys Corporation
VF Corporation
York International Corporation

South Carolina

Flagstar Companies, Inc.
Sonoco Products Company

Tennessee

Columbia/HCA Healthcare Corp.
Corporate Child Care Management Services
Federal Express Corporation
First American Corporation
First Tennessee National Corporation
Promus Companies Incorporated, The

Texas

AMR Corporation (American Airlines)
Burlington Northern Inc.
Continental Airlines
Diamond Shamrock, Inc.
Houston Industries Incorporated
Kent Electronics Corporation
Lyondell Petrochemical Company
Mary Kay Cosmetics, Inc.
Maxus Energy Corporation
Penney (J. C. Penney Company, Inc.)
Shell Chemical Company
Southwest Airlines Co.
Sysco Corporation
Texas Industries, Inc.

Utah

Research Industries Corporation
SkyWest Airlines, Inc.

Virginia

Best Products Co., Inc.

CSX Corporation
Ethyl Corporation
First Virginia Banks, Inc.
Gannett Company, Inc.
Lafarge Corporation
Mobil Corporation
Norfolk Southern Corporation
Owens & Minor
Reynolds Metals Company
Tultex Corporation

Vermont
Ben & Jerry's Homemade, Inc.

Washington
Airborne Express
Microsoft Corporation
SpaceLabs Medical, Inc.
UTILX Corporation
Washington Mutual Savings Bank
Westin Hotels & Resorts
Weyerhaeuser

Wisconsin
Banta Corporation
CUNA Mutual Insurance Group
First Financial Corporation
Firstar Corporation
Johnson Controls, Inc.
Johnson Wax (S. C. Johnson & Sons, Inc.)
Northwestern Mutual Life
Sta-Rite Industries
Universal Foods Corporation
WICOR, Inc.
Wisconsin Dairies Cooperative
Wisconsin Energy Corporation
Wisconsin Public Service Corporation

West Virginia
Weirton Steel Corporation

Advest, Inc.
Applied Materials, Inc.
AT&T Corp.
Atlanta Gas Light Company
Autodesk
Avon Products, Inc.
Ball Corporation
Bay View Capital Corporation (Bay View Federal Bank)
Boise Cascade Corporation
Butler Manufacturing Company
Chrysler Corporation
Comerica Incorporated
Comptek Research, Inc.
Computervision Corporation
Conner Peripherals, Inc.
Continental Airlines
Continental Medical Systems, Inc.
Cray Research, Inc.
Deluxe Corporation
Deposit Guaranty Corp.
Digi International Inc.
Dreyer's Grand Ice Cream
Eastern Enterprises
Eaton Corporation
Energen
Entergy Corporation
Federal Express Corporation
First Financial Management Corporation
First Tennessee National Corporation
Firstar Corporation
Forest Oil
FPL Group, Inc.
General Motors A.C.
General Public Utilities Corporation
Gibson Greetings, Inc.
Gillette (The Gillette Company)

Grace (W. R. Grace & Co.)
Hormel Foods Corporation
Illinois Power Company
Inland Steel Industries
Johnson Controls, Inc.
Kansas City Power & Light Company
Kaufman and Broad
Kellogg's (Kellogg Company)
Kent Electronics Corporation
Lafarge Corporation
Landstar Systems, Inc.
LSI Logic Corporation
Marriott International, Inc.
Maxus Energy Corporation
Merck & Co., Inc.
Microsoft Corporation
Mid-America Dairymen, Inc.
Niagara Mohawk Power Corp.
Nike, Inc.
Norfolk Southern Corp.
Northeast Utilities
Oklahoma Natural Gas
Old Kent Financial Corp.
Oneida Ltd.
Owens & Minor
Pet Incorporated
Pillsbury (The Pillsbury Company)
Principal Financial Group
Promus Companies Incorporated, The
Rainbow Technologies
Raytheon Aircraft Company
Research Industries Corporation
Ryder System, Inc.
Safety-Kleen Corporation
Savannah Foods & Industries, Inc.
SkyWest Airlines, Inc.
Southern Pacific Rail Corporation
Southwest Airlines Co.
SpaceLabs Medical, Inc.
Stroh Brewery Company, The

Times Mirror Company
Total System Services, Inc.
Tultex Corporation
Unisys Corporation
United Dominion Industries
Wackenhut Corporation, The
Washington Gas
Wendy's International, Inc.
Westin Hotels & Resorts
Wisconsin Dairies Cooperative
Wisconsin Energy Corporation
Wisconsin Public Service Corporation